# THE ORIGINS OF THE RUSSIAN CIVIL WAR

ORIGINS OF MODERN WARS
General editor: *Harry Hearder*

*Titles already published:*

**THE ORIGINS OF THE FRENCH REVOLUTIONARY WARS**
*T.C.W. Blanning*

**THE ORIGINS OF THE CRIMEAN WAR**
*David M. Goldfrank*

**THE ORIGINS OF THE ITALIAN WARS OF INDEPENDENCE**
*Frank J. Coppa*

**THE ORIGINS OF THE WARS OF GERMAN UNIFICATION**
*William Carr*

**THE ORIGINS OF THE SOUTH AFRICAN WAR, 1899–1902**
*Iain R. Smith*

**THE ORIGINS OF THE RUSSO-JAPANESE WAR**
*Ian Nish*

**THE ORIGINS OF THE FIRST WORLD WAR** (Second Edition)
*James Joll*

**THE ORIGINS OF THE RUSSIAN CIVIL WAR**
*Geoffrey Swain*

**THE ORIGINS OF THE SECOND WORLD WAR IN EUROPE**
*P.M.H. Bell*

**THE ORIGINS OF THE SECOND WORLD WAR IN ASIA AND THE PACIFIC**
*Akira Iriye*

**THE ORIGINS OF THE GREEK CIVIL WAR**
*David H. Close*

**THE ORIGINS OF THE KOREAN WAR**
*Peter Lowe*

**THE ORIGINS OF THE VIETNAM WAR**
*Anthony Short*

**THE ORIGINS OF THE ARAB-ISRAELI WARS**
(Second Edition)
*Ritchie Ovendale*

# THE ORIGINS OF THE RUSSIAN CIVIL WAR

*Geoffrey Swain*

## LONGMAN
London and New York

**Longman Group Limited,**
Longman House, Burnt Mill,
Harlow, Essex CM20 2JE, England
*and Associated Companies throughout the world*

*Published in the United States of America
by Longman Publishing, New York*

First published 1996

ISBN 0 582 05967 4 CSD
ISBN 0 582 05968 2 PPR

**British Library Cataloguing-in-Publication Data**
A catalogue record for this book is
available from the British Library

**Library of Congress Cataloging-in-Publication Data**

Swain, Geoff.
    The origins of the Russian Civil War / Geoffrey Swain.
      p.   cm. -- (Origins of modern wars)
    Includes bibliographical references and index.
    ISBN 0-582-05967-4 (csd). -- ISBN 0-582-05968-2 (ppr)
    1. Soviet Union--History--Revolution, 1917–1921.   I. Title.
  II. Series.
  DK265.S9  1996
  947.084'1--dc20                                              95–13287
                                                                   CIP

Set by 7A in Bembo
Produced by Longman Singapore Publishers (Pte) Ltd.
Printed in Singapore

To Di

# *Contents*

# Editor's Foreword

Dr Geoffrey Swain's account and interpretation of the complex and ill-fated developments that preceded the Russian Civil War is at once original and riveting. His book is the fourteenth in this series, and the second dealing with a civil war, following Dr David Close's *Origins of the Greek Civil War*. It is no coincidence that both wars occurred towards the conclusions of major international wars, and involved intervention by the great powers. International wars either stir up ideological rivalries, as in the Greek case, or give revolutionary movements a chance to assert themselves, as in the Russian case. Ideological rivalries lead to peculiarly bitter and tragic confrontations in the wake of the international war itself.

Dr Swain shows that in the initial crisis which was ultimately to lead to civil war, Kornilov, encouraged by Zavoiko, was the aggressor, but when the civil war eventually took shape it owed much to the ruthlessness and dishonesty of Lenin – all, of course, in the name of the high cause of world revolution. In *The Russian Revolution and the Civil War*, written on 8–9 September 1917, Lenin considered the alternatives of a peaceful coalition of Bolsheviks, Mensheviks and the Social Revolutionaries, on the one hand, and civil war, on the other. In Swain's words: 'there was no suggestion in Lenin's writing that the civil war option could harm the revolution or that the peaceful transfer of power was in any way more desirable'. A few days later Lenin assumed that civil war was inevitable, and his assumption was self-fulfilling. Lenin's argument, in greater detail, was that 'so long as the slogan "all power to the Constituent Assembly" masks the slogan "down with soviet power" civil war is inevitable, for we shall not for anything in the world surrender soviet power'.

The question of when, if ever, war becomes inevitable, so often considered in this series, is thus put in a new light by Swain's study. Lenin believed that, given certain conditions, war was inevitable. The argument is perhaps tautological. War can either be avoided or it cannot be avoided. To say that it is 'inevitable within certain conditions' is to say that it is not inevitable. But Lenin believed that so long as 'the enemies of proletarian power' continued to exist there must be a dictatorship of the proletariat, and it must be realised that such a dictatorship was a state of war. Here, then, was Clausewitz's war as a continuation of policy in a heightened sense.

Lenin was only too ready to accept war, a total war against 'the exploiters of the people', and he would have regarded the question of war guilt, another question often considered in this series, as being hardly worth asking. He fully accepted responsibility, but only because conditions made it inevitable that he should lead the proletariat in their ultimate struggle.

Swain's study suggests an interesting paradox. Civil war might have been avoided in the early spring of 1918 if a united socialist front had been formed against Germany. Such a front came close to formation, but it would have involved a continuation of the war, in alliance with France and Britain, against Germany. One kind of war (an international war) would have prevented another kind of war (the civil war). This kind of paradox seems unique in the series. There have been examples of preventive wars – wars apparently carried out to prevent other kinds of wars – but the idea of a civil war which would have as one of its aims the cessation of an international war is a novelty, though it is perhaps surprising that such wars have not occurred more frequently in history.

Dr Swain's book provokes such considerations, and is immensely valuable as a study of a moment in Russian history when vast vistas were opened – and sometimes closed – vistas of great importance for the future of the world.

Harry Hearder

# *Preface*

Three people associated with this study require individual mention. I owe a very special debt to Dr V.P. Butt of the Russian Academy of Sciences; his position as co-ordinator of the project on the history of the Russian Civil War meant he could give invaluable advice and support, as well as hospitality, at a time when the Academy itself was experiencing a period of traumatic change. As to my studies in England, they would not have been possible without the assistance of Mrs C. Menzies, Slavonic Reading Room librarian in the Bodleian Library, Oxford. Finally, Jane Goulden read the manuscript and made many helpful suggestions. A number of institutions also helped towards the production of this book; in particular the University of the West of England provided funding and study leave, while my visits to Moscow would not have been possible without the support of a generous grant from the Nuffield Foundation.

This book is a combination of primary research and a reworking of established material. Chapter One is based entirely on published work, but an attempt has been made to put the Kornilov conspiracy into the context of other anti-government plots and to escape from the rather arid debate about what Kornilov and Kerensky knew of each other's plans in the last week of August 1917. Chapter Two, on the other hand, is based substantially on the archives of the Russian Railway Workers' Union (Vikzhel), first made available to western scholars in 1990; a different version of this chapter was published as 'Before the fighting started' in *Revolutionary Russia*, December 1991. Chapter Three is again based largely on published work, but tries to pull together the available material on the dissolution of the Constituent Assembly, a topic remarkably under-studied by historians in both Russia and the west. Chapter Four is based largely on the personal papers of Lord Milner and Sir William Wiseman; a revised version, 'Maugham, Masaryk and the "Mensheviks" ', appeared in *Revolutionary Russia*, June 1994. Material first published in *Revolutionary Russia* is reproduced here with the kind agreement of the editor.

Although Chapter Five is largely based on published material, this is supplemented by more references to the Milner papers, supported by cabinet minutes, to reinforce how real the prospects were for a British–Soviet rapprochement in spring 1918; up to now historians have tended to dismiss the views of Sadoul and Lockhart as those of Bolshevik-sympathizing dreamers out of touch with their governments. Chapter Six is a similar mix: references from the British archives are used to show the extent of the 'great enterprise' planned in Russia; while long-ignored memoirs of Russian participants are used to reconstruct the importance of the Union for the Regeneration of Russia.

Chapters Seven and Eight can be considered together: both are based substantially on the Russian archives, opened fully to western scholars after December 1991. Use was made of three collections in particular: the Archangel government; the Committee of the Constituent Assembly (Komuch); and, to a lesser extent, the Socialist Revolutionary (SR) trial in 1922, the latter being used simply to fill in gaps. Material from the Archangel government archive makes clear that, while there was constant tension between the Allies and Chaikovskii's administration, the reason for the attempted coup in September 1918 had nothing to do with this; it was prompted by anger at the SR administration's attempt to exercise more control over the military. Material from the Komuch archive sheds new light on two aspects of its history: the intensity of Komuch's opposition to the Omsk government in July and August 1918, and the refusal of Komuch to resign in November 1918 in line with the Ufa accord; this latter incident enables a reinterpretation of the achievements of the so-called directory government to be made. Incorporating this Russian material into the British archival record reinforces the point made constantly by the British consul Francis Lindley, that if the Bolsheviks were to be defeated, democrats not monarchists needed to be supported.

It is remarkable how little has been written about the history of Russia over the summer of 1918; the temptation to dash from the excitement of the October Revolution to the blood and gore of the full blown civil war has been too much for most historians who have glossed over the early fighting on the Volga. In a very real sense, then, I can blame any errors in this book on no-one but myself.

# DATES

In general I have used the Russian calendar up until 1 February 1918 when this was brought into line with that of the west. The exception is Chapter Four, where events occurring in London are referred to by the western calendar, and events in Russia and the Ukraine by the Russian calendar; the reports sent back to England by Somerset Maugham and other agents were always dated according to the western calendar, and have been kept as such.

# *Introduction*

To the general public all that is known of the Russian Civil War is a dim memory of the film version of Boris Pasternak's *Doctor Zhivago*, of trains, of snow, and of bloodshed. To those with slightly more historical knowledge, the civil war was between Reds and Whites, between Bolsheviks and generals with strange names; and one of the generals actually an admiral, for some inexplicable reason leading an army in Siberia thousands of miles from the sea. To the more politically aware, the Russian Civil War showed the true nature of the imperialist stage of capitalist development, when a wide array of rival imperial powers – Britain, France, Japan, and the USA – sank their differences in a determined effort to destroy the first socialist state in the world by rallying to the White cause.

Yet even when approached through *Doctor Zhivago*, the civil war seems rather confusing, right and wrong are hard to determine, who exactly was fighting whom is not always clear; and for much of the novel Zhivago himself is fighting not with the Reds or the Whites, but with the Greens. Equally, when historians try to explain how the White generals could make such dramatic advances towards Moscow in 1919, followed by even more dramatic retreats, they have sought an explanation in the activities of Green commanders such as the peasant anarchist leader Nestor Makhno who was allied to the Bolsheviks, but remained independent of them. The civil war, it seems, was not fought between two sides, but three: the Whites are easy to identify, but their opponents were not all Bolsheviks, and those opposing the Bolsheviks from the democratic camp were far from always united. This ambivalence of the anti-White forces, so characteristic of developments throughout the civil war, is an echo of an earlier civil war, a war between Reds and Greens, between Bolsheviks and moderate socialists that is all too easily forgotten.

The Russian Civil War was not just the war between the Reds and the Whites, Bolsheviks and generals, which is etched in the popular memory; indeed, this war did relatively little to shape the subsequent Soviet regime – although it did much to create its propaganda image. The Russian Civil War was also a Red versus Green civil war, a war between the Bolsheviks and their socialist opponents led by the pro-peasant Party of Socialist Revolutionaries (SRs), which started in May 1918 and ended only in June 1922 when the leaders of that party were put on trial. It was this Red versus Green civil war which shaped the Soviet regime, by establishing at the heart of Bolshevik policy a deep-seated antagonism towards the peasantry, something epitomized within less than a decade by Stalin's policy of the forced collectivization of agriculture.

For the years 1919–20 this Red versus Green civil war became hopelessly entangled with the White versus Red civil war and subsumed within it. As a result, most studies of the Russian Civil War have concentrated on the White versus Red struggle, a complex enough topic in its own right, and skated over the Red versus Green civil war, describing the fighting of summer 1918 in terms of preliminary skirmishes before the fighting proper started, and treating all fighting after 1920 as essentially a policing operation by the victorious Bolsheviks, rather than a continuation of the events of 1918. This book takes a different approach: when the fighting which took place between 1918 and 1922 is seen as a whole, the origins of both the White versus Red and Red versus Green civil wars have to be traced. Indeed, any study of the origins of the Russian Civil War inevitably leads to a more detailed analysis of the Red versus Green war which both proceeded the Red versus White war and continued after it. A history of the origins of the Russian Civil War must be in essence the rediscovery of this forgotten civil war before the civil war.

The White versus Red civil war has been ably described many times and this book takes as read that the Russian Civil War, the well-remembered second civil war between Whites and Reds fought out between the autumn of 1918 and the autumn of 1920, was a war that the Whites were never going to win. In the conclusion to his definitive study, Evan Mawdsley was scathing about the Whites:

> The Whites had little chance of winning . . . The Bolsheviks had had a year to consolidate their position, they controlled most of the military resources of old Russia, they had more popular support, and their forces outnumbered those of the Whites by ten to one.[1]

As to the Allied powers that came to their aid he noted:

Contrary to what is often thought . . . the 'fourteen power'
anti-Bolshevik Allied alliance that was featured in Soviet propaganda was a
myth. The Americans were cool about intervention; the Japanese stayed
on the Pacific coast. The French gave up an active role after the spring of
1919; . . . few Allied troops were sent; none fought in the main battles.[2]

The White forces were so derisory, and attracted such half-hearted
support from the Allies, because their social foundation was the
property-owning minority, a small group of narrow conservative
nationalists, who disliked popular politics and the very idea of
motivating popular support for their regime by developing a
progressive social programme. The parties of the right in Russia never
commanded many followers, and the educated minority which
belonged to them found itself opposed to the revolution and more and
more isolated as time went on. 'The Whites feared the people',
Mawdsley concluded.[3]

The origins of the White versus Red civil war are not ignored in
this book. The continuity between the activities of Admiral Kolchak
in the early summer of 1917 and his overthrow in November 1918 of
the patriotic socialist government formed in opposition to the
Bolsheviks is something which is constantly stressed. But a recon-
sideration of these affairs only serves to reinforce Mawdsley's point that
the White generals represented no-one but themselves and a small
business and land-owning elite. The greater part of this book is
therefore devoted to the origins of the first forgotten civil war, the
Red versus Green civil war of Bolsheviks versus patriotic socialists.

For, after the defeat of the White generals in 1920, Russia's
forgotten civil war was sparked off again. Not in an organized way it
is true, but the Red versus Green tensions so characteristic of
Zhivago's experience and that of the battlefields of 1919 soon spilled
over into haphazard outbreaks of fighting. From the autumn of 1920
to the summer of 1921 civil war between the Bolsheviks and the
peasantry raged in Tambov Province, while nearer the centre of power
February 1921 saw strikes and demonstrations in Petrograd organized
by the Menshevik Party (moderate social democrats). The rebellion in
the Baltic naval base of Kronstadt in early March 1921 marked the
high point in this fighting, since it clearly revealed both the idealism of
the rebels – fighting for 'soviets without [Bolshevik] commissars' – and
the brutal determination of the Bolsheviks to concede nothing; the
Red Army marched across the ice and recaptured Kronstadt. Soviet
Russia's first 'show trial' in 1922 – that of the SRs, the party
committed to peasant socialism and the Bolsheviks' main rival for the
hearts and minds of the Russian population – was the logical

consequence of Bolshevik victory in the fighting in Kronstadt and Tambov.

The SR trial in 1922 marked the end of the first civil war in Russia, the forgotten Red versus Green civil war before the White versus Red civil war. The origins in the years 1917–18 of this forgotten civil war, and the way it became intertwined with the remembered White versus Red civil war, in November 1918, forms the subject matter of most of this book. As the reader will see, however, writing a history of that forgotten civil war involves rewriting history – for the concerns of the historian of the forgotten civil war are inevitably not always those of the historian of the Russian Revolution.

## WRITING A HISTORY OF RUSSIA'S FORGOTTEN CIVIL WAR

Rediscovering Russia's forgotten civil war requires that the history of the years 1917–18 be rewritten; the classic periodization of the Bolsheviks' rise to power and first year in office does not suffice. This is less of a problem where the origins of the White versus Red civil war are explored. The traditional concerns of the historian of the Russian Revolution are repeated here with only a small change of emphasis: the overthrow of the Tsarist monarchy in February 1917; the first crisis of the Provisional Government in April followed by the formation of the First Coalition Government in May, a government made up of liberals (mostly belonging to the Kadet Party) and moderate socialists (either Mensheviks or SRs) and supported by the First Congress of Soviets in June 1917; the disastrous disintegration of this coalition after the failure of the military offensive launched by the government against the Central Powers at the end of June 1917, which in turn sparked off the anti-government demonstrations known as the July Days organized by the Bolsheviks, and resulted in the formation of a shaky Second Coalition Government made up from the same political parties as the first; and finally the attempt by the Supreme Army Commander General Lavr Kornilov to overthrow the Prime Minister of the Second Coalition Government Alexander Kerensky and seize power on behalf of conservative politicians, generals and business leaders, the right in Russian politics. To this familiar story it is only necessary to add the web of intrigue surrounding the various anti-government plotters.

It is with the formation of Kerensky's Third Coalition Government in September 1917 that the history of the forgotten first Russian Civil War begins and the story of that war starts to diverge from the established history of the Russian Revolution. The Third Coalition Government was even weaker than the Second Coalition Government and to many contemporaries never established any authority in Russia beyond the immediate confines of the Winter Palace. Understandably, therefore, historians of the Russian Revolution have tended to concentrate on other things. Their concerns have been directed towards the Bolsheviks' preparations for an armed uprising to seize power from the government and the rising mood of popular anger against Kerensky as preparations began for the Second Congress of Soviets on 25 October 1917. They have not had time to explore what was taking place in the rather strangely named Preparliament established at this time by Kerensky in order to give some popular authority to his tottering regime.

For the historian of Russia's first civil war, however, the events of the Preparliament are of enormous importance. Boycotted by the Bolsheviks as they prepared for insurrection, the Preparliament became the arena in which the battle-lines for the future struggle between the patriotic socialists and their right-wing opponents were drawn. The same patriotic socialist politicians who ran the Preparliament in September and October 1917 went on in September 1918 to form the so-called directory, the anti-Bolshevik administration of patriotic socialists established in Siberia. The same tussle over co-operation between the patriotic socialists and left-leaning liberals was fought out in the autumn of 1917 as was fought out in the summer of 1918. These situations were not identical – in the summer of 1918 the patriotic socialists and the left-leaning liberals agreed to co-operate, while in the autumn of 1917 such agreement proved illusory – but for the historian of Russia's forgotten civil war the Preparliament cannot be ignored, especially since on 24 October 1917 the patriotic socialists passed a vote of no confidence in the Third Coalition Government, but were beaten in this constitutional attempt to overthrow Kerensky by the October Revolution, the Bolshevik insurrection which began that very same evening.

While to the historian of the Russian Revolution the Bolshevik insurrection on the night of 24–25 October 1917 and Lenin's announcement to the Second Congress of Soviets that his government would enact decrees on peace and land are of epoch-making importance, the very essence of the October Revolution, to the historian of Russia's forgotten first civil war these events can be mentioned, as it were, in passing. The Bolshevik insurrection is just one episode in a ten-day crisis which lasted from 24 October to 4 November 1917. It was during these ten days that the first shots in Russia's forgotten civil war were fired at the battle of Pulkovo Heights; but this was also a period when, more than once, it looked as if a compromise negotiated by representatives of the Railway Workers' Union would make civil war unnecessary. The October Revolution and its famous decrees were followed by talks aimed at persuading the Bolsheviks to surrender power and form a coalition administration with the patriotic socialists. Lenin's decision of 4 November 1917 that the Bolsheviks should remain in government alone put that civil war back on the agenda.

This divergence between the concerns of the historian of the Russian Revolution and those of the historian of Russia's forgotten civil war continues for the first three months of Bolshevik rule. The fate of the Constituent Assembly, the only freely elected parliament in Russia before the fall of communism, is just one of the many issues faced by Lenin's Bolshevik administration, and to the historian of the Russian Revolution it must be considered alongside such issues as the decree on workers' control; the nationalization of the banks; and the implementation of the land reform, something facilitated by the decision of left-wing members of the SR Party to form a new political party, the Left SRs, and join the Bolsheviks in government. To the historian of Russia's first civil war the fate of the Constituent Assembly is crucial: it was Lenin's willingness to allow the elections to the Constituent Assembly to go ahead in mid-November 1917 which stopped any further outbreak of fighting after Pulkovo Heights. Through the elections to the Constituent Assembly the moderate socialists, especially the SRs, hoped to supplant the Bolsheviks by constitutional means, thus obviating the necessity for civil war; the SRs' victory in those elections served notice on Lenin that the days of the Bolshevik government would be numbered when the Assembly convened. Lenin's decision to dissolve the Constituent Assembly after its single sitting on 5 January 1918 and base his rule on the soviets instead ensured that all subsequent moves by Russia's moderate socialists would be undertaken in the name of recalling the dissolved Constituent Assembly; the most significant of these was the Committee of the Constituent Assembly (referred to by its Russian acronym Komuch) established in Samara in June 1918.

When the interests of the historian of the Russian Revolution and the historian of Russia's forgotten civil war again coincide, as they do with the Treaty of Brest-Litovsk, the emphasis remains different.

When considering this treaty signed by the Bolsheviks with the Imperial German government on 3 March 1918, the historian of the Russian Revolution is concerned with the narrowness of Lenin's victory in the debate to ratify the peace; the formation as a consequence of the first significant opposition faction within the Bolshevik Party, the pro-war Left Communists; the decision of the Left SRs to leave Lenin's government in protest; and the opposition of both Left SRs and Left Communists to the new economic policy announced by Lenin in April 1918 which amounted to restoring one man management in the factories and confiscating grain from the peasantry by the establishment of fictitious 'committees of poor peasants'. For the historian of Russia's first civil war, it is not the peace brought about by the Brest-Litovsk Treaty that is important, but the war fever it provoked, the sense of outrage and a renewed sense of national unity in the struggle against a common enemy. The rebirth of the civil war between the Bolsheviks and the patriotic socialists, implied by the dissolution of the Constituent Assembly, was put on one side by the spirit of sacred unity against Imperial Germany. The SRs, the Allies, the army and many Bolsheviks, including such unlikely soul-mates as Trotsky and Stalin, came together between March and May 1918, working to annul what seemed to them the treaty of shame. It was Lenin's decision in mid-May 1918 not to annul the Treaty of Brest-Litovsk after a suitable breathing space but to make further economic concessions to Germany which ended this period of harmony.

After May 1918 the historian of the Russian Revolution and the historian of Russia's forgotten civil war must follow very different roads, for by then serious fighting had begun between moderate socialists and Bolsheviks. For the historian of the Russian Revolution action centres on Moscow and the story is one of the Bolsheviks clinging to power by the skin of their teeth as they became progressively more and more isolated. With the patriotic socialists making gains in soviet elections and announcing publicly that they would no longer be bound by the treaty with Germany, the Bolsheviks expelled the patriotic socialists from the soviets, allowing only the Left SRs to continue to participate. When the Left SRs staged a coup attempt on 6 July 1918 during proceedings at the Fifth Congress of Soviets, the Bolsheviks felt justified in removing them too from the soviets; in future they would rule alone with only the Bolshevik Party deputies in the soviets to serve as a constitutional check on their power. Thus isolated and surrounded by enemies, the Bolsheviks resorted to institutionalized terror in August 1918 until their military position in the forgotten civil war with the moderate socialists improved somewhat in September. From this Moscow perspective just who the Bolsheviks were fighting is less important than the ability of the Bolsheviks to survive.

For the historian of Russia's first forgotten civil war it is crucially important that the Bolsheviks' enemies in the summer of 1918 were the patriotic socialists who had first won the Constituent Assembly elections and then declined to take up arms against those who had dissolved it in the hope that the Treaty of Brest-Litovsk might be annulled. Far from having a Moscow focus, the historian of Russia's first civil war must roam far and wide: from Archangel in the north where the Allies tried but failed to give aid to the patriotic socialist leaders; down the railway network to Yaroslavl, where patriotic socialists unsuccessfully took up arms against the Bolsheviks; down the river Volga to Samara where the Allied Czechoslovak Legion joined with local SRs in overthrowing the Bolsheviks and establishing a rival socialist administration; and east to the Siberian towns of Ufa and Omsk where the socialist opponents of Bolshevism first sank their differences and then established the base for their government.

From a Moscow perspective it is understandable that little attention need be paid to the coup staged in Omsk by Admiral Kolchak on 18 November 1918; the Bolsheviks' enemy changed its leading cadres, but remained the enemy. Kolchak's coup, however, has monumental significance from the perspective of the historian of Russia's forgotten first civil war. Kolchak's coup meant this: Russia's first civil war had been brought to an end. It had been transformed overnight from a war between Bolsheviks and patriotic socialists to a war between Bolsheviks and right-wing generals. The first civil war had been brought to an end not by Bolshevik victory in that war but the armed action of White generals whose action changed the whole nature of the civil war. Kolchak's coup was the last act in Russia's first civil war and the first act of Russia's second civil war, the civil war of popular memory. Kolchak's action ended a war that the moderate socialists might have won and started a war the Whites would inevitably lose, putting the real civil war, the forgotten first civil war, on ice until 1920. By the time fighting resumed in Kronstadt and Tambov, the majority of Russians, after seven years of war, were no longer prepared to take up arms.

# THE LESSONS OF THE FORGOTTEN CIVIL WAR

What, then, does the rediscovery of Russia's forgotten civil war teach us? Ironically considering the short shrift given to the Whites, this study tells us something about the steadfastness of the counter-revolutionary right. The plans for armed action drawn up in the spring and summer of 1917, when men of property first moved to stem the revolutionary tide and restore order, were essentially similar to the plans of Kolchak's supporters in November 1918. The small group of property-owners referred to by Mawdsley did not distinguish between shades of red, between Red and Green, between Bolsheviks and SRs; to them all parties represented in the soviet were 'Reds', and all their actions were to weaken and destroy Great Russia. From April 1917 onwards this group was looking for a political saviour, turning first to General Kornilov, then to Admiral Kolchak, and then back to Kornilov, who obliged by staging an ill-judged and unsuccessful coup in late August 1917. Almost exactly a year would pass before such groups felt strong enough to act in a similar way again, but when they did it was the same people with essentially the same motivation.

As to the forgotten civil war itself, three main themes are subsequently developed. First, that this Red versus Green civil war, the civil war between the Bolsheviks and the SRs, Bolsheviks and democracy, was a quite unnecessary war. It was a war brought about by Lenin for purely doctrinaire reasons: the great social demands of the day – peace, land and a democratized economy – would have been implemented by Bolsheviks and SRs alike. In fact the most obvious solution to Russia's social crisis in the autumn of 1917 was the formation of a coalition socialist administration; Lenin was determined that only a government headed by himself, alone, could safely under-take the socialist experiment he envisaged. So he seized power to prevent the Second Congress of Soviets appointing a socialist coalition government, and refused to cede power even when the Railway Workers' Union succeeded in ending the SRs' attempt to remove his government by force and restored the idea of a socialist coalition government to the political agenda.

Lenin again faced the choice between coalition politics and dictatorial rule in January 1918 when the Constituent Assembly met. Lenin had prevented the Second Congress of Soviets appointing a socialist coalition government, but the Constituent Assembly might well do the same. The SRs, who won most seats in the Constituent Assembly elections, were alarmingly conciliatory. They endorsed the Bolshevik proposals on peace and land, and even seemed willing to accept the idea of a hybrid political institution known as the Revolutionary Convention, which would have brought together both the Constituent Assembly and the soviets. Confident that they would retain their following in both soviet and Constituent Assembly, the SRs threw down the gauntlet to Lenin, who responded by dissolving the Constituent Assembly.

Up until the Constituent Assembly crisis in January 1918, Lenin had looked to support for his socialist experiment from beyond Russia's borders, from socialist revolutions elsewhere in Europe. During the Constituent Assembly crisis he resolved for the first time to rely on a rather different source of support beyond Russia's borders, the Imperial German government. The enormity of this decision was not immediately apparent because, far from bringing immediate peace, the negotiations at Brest-Litovsk at first resulted in a brief war with Germany, and then the widespread belief that the 'breathing space' provided by the treaty would last no more than a few weeks. When the Germans overthrew the democratic government in the Ukraine at the end of April 1918, Lenin was forced to spell out clearly that this was not an appropriate moment to resume the struggle with Germany; his vision for Russia required the Bolsheviks to continue to rule alone, dissolving soviets as well as the Constituent Assembly, under a protective umbrella provided by the German Kaiser. But as this book shows, there was, even at this stage, an alternative. Democracy could have been restored in the soviets, the German protective umbrella could have been discarded; but that would have involved as in November 1917 and January 1918, a willingness to form a coalition government with the SRs. It would also have involved renewing the military alliance with the Allies.

The attitude of the Allies, and of the British in particular, to the nascent civil war in Russia is another theme of this book. Quite unlike the picture portrayed in Bolshevik propaganda, the Allies had no time for White politicians and devoted their energies to wooing the pro-war patriotic socialists. This was the avowed aim of the mission sent to Petrograd in autumn 1917 under the leadership of W. Somerset Maugham, a mission which laid the groundwork for developments in the summer of 1918 by linking the British closely both to the Allied Czechoslovak Legion and moderate socialist politicians like the veteran populist N.V. Chaikovskii, whose revolutionary pedigree went back to the 1870s. When the Bolsheviks themselves became pro-war socialists, as was the case between late February and early May 1918, the British did everything in their limited power to help, culminating by sending the mission of General Poole to Murmansk on 11 May, just two days before the Bolshevik Central Committee finally agreed to adopt Lenin's pro-German policy. Thereafter the Allies favoured action against the Bolsheviks, but action organized by Russian democrats like Chaikovskii, not the White generals.

With the Bolshevik decision in favour of Germany, and the related decision to expel the SRs and Mensheviks from the soviets, the civil war within democracy, the Red versus Green civil war, on hold since November 1917, began in earnest. The third theme of this book, therefore, is why the patriotic socialists in Russia failed to overthrow the Bolshevik dictatorship. Victims of hostile commentary on the part of both Bolsheviks and White generals, the history of the attempt by patriotic socialists to build an alternative democratic socialist state stretching from the Volga in the south to Archangel in the north and stretching eastward across the Urals has never been seriously addressed. Yet the failure of this experimental 'third way' was in no sense predetermined, and its People's Army's defeat at the hands of the Red Army by no means inevitable or final.

The very first fighting in this civil war took place in the Volga town of Samara in the first week of June 1918 and was linked to the mutiny a week earlier of the Czechoslovak Legion. That mutiny, while of tremendous importance on the lower Volga, actually set back the cause of Russian democracy by two crucial months, since it wrecked plans for co-ordinated Allied action, involving both the Czechoslovaks and the British in northern Russia; the first stage of this operation, the uprising in Yaroslavl, was completely mistimed as a consequence. The separate fighting on the Volga and in northern Russia was partly pure chance, but also in part a reflection of disagreements between the various wings of the SR Party as to how best to develop the anti-Bolshevik struggle.

Those commentators dismissive of the directory's socialist experiment, the Volga 'third way', have tended to seize on these divisions; this book, however, seeks to stress unity rather than disunity and the overall competence of those who established the directory administration in Ufa. By September 1918 there were two socialist states in Russia, that of Lenin and the Bolsheviks in Moscow and that of the SR-dominated directory formed at Ufa, which included the northern territory around Archangel. The social policies of the two were really very similar: in Ufa, just as in Moscow, land had been distributed to the peasantry; in Ufa, just as in Moscow, the economy was to be planned by the state; in Ufa, just as in Moscow, a degree of workers' control was to be exercised by the trades unions. The main difference between the two states was Ufa's more tolerant attitude to free trade and private enterprise, and the exercise of local democracy through regionally-based councils rather than workplace soviets.

It was precisely these similarities between the regimes established in Moscow and Ufa that breathed new life into that 'small class of property-owners', referred to by Mawdsley, who had been inactive since August 1917. First unsuccessfully in Archangel in September, and then successfully in Omsk in November 1918, the 'Kornilovite' generals and the class they represented moved against the democrats, those forerunners of the Greens, the people the generals still contemptuously dismissed as 'Reds'. Their action highlighted the weakest point of the directory's democratic regime. On both occasions, the generals acted when the democrats 'interfered' in military affairs. This interference was actually very timid, an attempt to clip the wings of ambitious monarchist officers; in reality the democrats should have interfered in military affairs more often, more consistently and more ruthlessly. Only a political commissar system similar to that of the Bolsheviks could have secured the loyalty of the old officer corps. In Archangel the British consul Francis Lindley could put the coup attempt into reverse; in Omsk the democrats' unpractical attitude to military affairs was their undoing.

Kolchak's coup against the directory on 18 November 1918 destroyed the Russian democrats as a fighting force and ended the first civil war. For the record, this happened before the democrats had been defeated in their war with the Bolsheviks. The German alliance enabled Lenin to transfer all his forces to the fighting on the Volga, and forced the democrats to cede ground, evacuating both Kazan and Samara; whether this was a definitive victory is an open question, for on the very eve of Kolchak's coup the front had steadied and the democrats were beginning an advance aimed at retaking Samara. But with Kolchak's coup the forgotten first civil war between the Bolsheviks and the democrats had become entwined with the second civil war between the White generals and the Bolsheviks. The Russian public was offered the depressing choice between dictatorships of the right and left, and, after some seven million deaths,[4] opted for the left; it at least would allow peasants to keep their land and offered the promise of a progressive social programme. When the struggle between the Bolsheviks and the democrats resumed in 1920, the population was on its knees; when the SR trial in 1922 put the final nail in the democrats' coffin, the population at large was too exhausted to protest and grudgingly accepted that between dictatorships of left and right there could be no 'third way' of democracy in Russia.

This book is in essence a history of the failure of that 'third way'. It is a sad, at times depressing story of lost opportunities and the triumph of brutality and naked political opportunism. It makes clear that Lenin's victory in October 1917 was insecure in the extreme, and that Russian politics remained fluid throughout the first year of Bolshevik rule. British official commentators were right: there seemed no way Lenin's regime could survive; its survival against all the odds was in large measure the responsibility of Kolchak and the White generals.

## NOTES

1. E. Mawdsley, *The Russian Civil War* (London 1987), p. 281.
2. Mawdsley, *Civil War*, p. 283.
3. Mawdsley, *Civil War*, p. 279.
4. Mawdsley, *Civil War*, p. 287.

# CHAPTER ONE

# The Failed White Counter-revolution

On 2 March 1917, in the face of mass popular demonstrations which had been endemic since mid-February, and near universal desertion by the elites of Old Russia, Tsar Nicholas II abdicated. After a bitter struggle, which had begun for some of the participants nearly fifty years earlier, democracy had triumphed. Liberal politicians from the Duma, the national assembly established by the Tsar after the 1905 Revolution, had established a Provisional Government even before the abdication and set themselves the task of administering the country until a Constituent Assembly could be summoned. The Constituent Assembly would then adopt a constitution for the new democratic Russia and elect a new government, an essential task since the Tsar's Duma was not a democratic body and gave little representation to the mass of Russia's workers and peasants. These, the vast majority of Russians, since they were denied fair access to the Duma, had formed their own alternative assemblies known as soviets; the Petrograd Soviet held its first formal session on 27 February. Yet despite these twin sources of political authority in post-Tsarist Russia – the dual power of which contemporaries spoke – March was a month of euphoria, and the soviet at first endorsed the Provisional Government, having little reason to doubt its commitment to democratic advance.

By April 1917, however, the honeymoon was over. The leaders of the great mass of Russians represented in the soviets and the members of the Provisional Government, the Duma politicians elected from the property-owners of Tsarist Russia, first realized that they could not necessarily trust each other since their visions of the future of democracy in Russia were essentially very different. The Duma politicians longed for an idealized vision of the British parliamentary system, but without a monarchy, a society which would welcome them retaining their wealth and privilege. The soviets wanted a new democracy, ill-defined but closer to the people, and a society where all privilege and wealth were a thing of the past. It was the realization that in a democratic Russia the soviet vision would ultimately be the one to triumph when all Russians were able to vote which prompted the first moves towards an anti-democratic counter-revolution, the opening gambit of the Whites in the future White versus Red civil war.

In April 1917, within two months of the Tsarist regime being over-thrown, counter-revolutionary groups within the Russian Army began to plot how best to overthrow the new democratic government. Six months later, they made their first serious attempt to stem the revolutionary tide when General Lavr Kornilov, Supreme Commander -in-Chief of the Russian Army, staged an abortive coup d'état. The plots which developed between April and August involved many of those generals who were to become key players later in the civil war, but that was not their true significance: the essence of these plots lay in their inability to attract any widespread support. Even politicians superficially sympathetic to the generals' aspirations soon began to question their methods, for those politicians in contact with the generals quickly learned that the military's programme had no place for democracy but was simply one of counter-revolutionary dictatorship.

## KORNILOV IN APRIL

Firm action by the military was first mooted at the end of April 1917, during the first major political crisis faced by the Provisional Government, a crisis which saw the leader of the liberal Kadet Party P.N. Milyukov forced to resign as Minister of Foreign Affairs, and the political complexion of the government transformed by the appoint-ment of new ministers from Russia's moderate socialist parties, the Mensheviks (Social Democrats) and Socialist Revolutionaries (SRs), Russia's peasant socialist party. At the height of this crisis, street fighting occurred in Petrograd, fighting which saw the future White General Kornilov keen to flex his political muscles for the first time.

The crisis related to the vexed question of war aims. The Russian Revolution made it possible to argue that the First World War was a war between the democracies of Russia, Britain and France (joined by the USA) against the imperial powers of Central Europe; but it also raised the question of how tied the new democratic Russia was to the secret imperial war aims of the Tsar agreed with Britain and France, namely expansion in the Balkans. In an infamous note to the Allied governments, the Foreign Minister in the Provisional Government, P.N. Milyukov promised 'fully to observe the obligations taken with respect to our Allies', a promise which contradicted the widespread view of the Russian people, reflected in numerous soviet resolutions, that the war Russia was then fighting was a war for a peace 'without indemnities and annexations'. Milyukov's concern for the 'obligations taken with respect to our Allies' meant honouring commitments to annex the Ukrainian population of Austria-Hungary and occupy Constantinople and the Dardanelles straits. This war aims crisis encapsulated the differing political visions of liberal and soviet politicians. Milyukov seemed to be arguing that the Tsar had gone but Russia would carry on much as before; soviet politicians wanted radical change, especially where war aims were concerned, for only idealism could inspire a war-weary army to remain in the trenches. The crisis created such popular excitement that the Bolsheviks were able to stage their first demonstrations against the government; it presented anti-democratic forces with their first opportunity to discuss counter-revolution.

Many of the soldiers who participated in the first anti-Milyukov demonstration of 20 April were so angry at his action, and so sure that the Petrograd Soviet would support them that they were unaware that the demonstration had been inspired by Bolshevik agitators and had not been endorsed by the soviet. Although armed, this demonstration by members of the Finland and Moscow regiments was accompanied by brass bands, and the rally outside the Mariinskii Palace, where the Provisional Government was then based, dispersed peacefully at 5 p.m. after being addressed by both the Petrograd Soviet leaders A.R. Gots (an SR) and M.I. Skobelev (a Menshevik), and by General Kornilov, then the Commander of the Petrograd Military District. The soviet leaders argued that the crisis could be resolved peaceably, while Kornilov explained:

> It is your legitimate right to voice your needs peacefully and in order; but that does not mean coming forward with weapons in hand, you must wait in your barracks for the legitimate resolutions to be made by your legitimate representatives.[1]

Trouble began the following day, 21 April, when workers rather than soldiers marched to both the Mariinskii Palace and the Tauride Palace, where the Petrograd Soviet was based, and vociferously repeated the demand for Milyukov's resignation. They were joined by some sailors from the naval base at Kronstadt and various armed Red Guards, and, unlike on the 20th, were met by a counter-demonstration organized by Milyukov's Kadet Party. It was a confusing day, with three separate groups of anti-government demonstrators taking to the streets, to be confronted by one group of pro-government demonstrators; the result was two outbreaks of street fighting. Subsequent police reports established that the first incident began around 3 p.m. when the first group of workers, protected by armed guards, crossed the River Neva from the working-class district of the Vyborg Side and marched towards the main shopping street of Nevskii Prospekt. As they approached the corner of Sadovaya Street and Nevskii Prospekt, a group of officers and critical bystanders tried to block their path and prevent them turning into Petrograd's main shopping street. When they tried to grab a banner with the legend 'Down with the Provisional Government' – a slogan never endorsed by the Petrograd Soviet – there was a scuffle, sabres were drawn, and revolvers pulled from their holsters; at that moment a shot rang out from somewhere down Sadovaya Street and the procession forced its way onto Nevskii Prospekt and on towards the Admiralty building.

Angered by the success of the workers at forcing their way on to Nevskii Prospekt, counter-demonstrating officers and officials assembled outside one of Nevskii Prospekt's premier shopping arcades, the Passage. A second workers' demonstration was spotted turning into Nevskii Prospekt from Sadovaya Street and the counter-demonstration went to confront it. The two groups met near the Kazan Cathedral, a banner was seized and as the workers began to retreat some of the armed guards moved off the street and onto the pavement, drew their guns and fell to the ground. Three or four shots rang out from the workers' side, though the counter-demonstrators had soon captured some of the workers' weapons, and a further exchange of fire took place before the counter-demonstrators let the demonstrators past.

The counter-demonstrators then held the day: they organized a pro-government rally at the Mariinskii Palace, they then marched to a house on the Moika River where the government was meeting in emergency session – the Defence Minister A.I. Guchkov was too ill to move from his bed, so the government met in his bedroom – and organized another pro-government rally outside the Kazan Cathedral. As this started to disperse at around 6 p.m. a third workers' demonstration arrived, this time entering the centre of town from the Vasilevskii Island district and starting to march up Nevskii Prospekt from the other, Admiralty end. This prompted a second armed clash.

All seemed to be going peacefully, until the demonstrators reached the junction with Sadovaya Street at about 10 p.m. Here counter-demonstrators tried to prevent the demonstrators turning into Sadovaya Street. After talks, in which the workers promised to disperse, they were let through, but the tail end of the demonstration became isolated from its armed guard. The temptation was too much for some pro-government counter-demonstrators who seized a banner from the outraged workers. In the confusion the workers' armed guards came running back up Sadovaya Street and turned into Nevskii Prospekt with their arms drawn, some firing as they came. These took up positions by the public library, diving to the ground, and shots were exchanged with counter-demonstrators by the Gostinyi Dvor shopping arcade. At least ten shots were fired over a period of some five minutes, before the workers began to disperse. The police later ruled out the theory that this second outbreak of firing had been started by a counter-demonstrating agent provocateur. Although the counter-demonstrators had acted in a provocative manner, it was the ill-disciplined Red Guards who had opened fire first during each incident, and General Kornilov was determined to take what he saw as appropriate action.[2]

Kornilov, however, did not get his way, and his climb-down was witnessed by another future White general, Admiral A.V. Kolchak. The April street fighting coincided with government moves to complete the work of the so-called Polivanov Military Commission, established after the Tsar's abdication to try and systematize the network of army committees which soldiers had been establishing throughout the Russian Army. In mid-April the government began to summon key commanders to the capital to discuss various drafts of the proposed Declaration of Soldiers' Rights, and among the officers summoned to Petrograd at this time was Admiral A.V. Kolchak, the man in charge of the Black Sea Fleet. He was very concerned at the effect sailors' committees were having on discipline in the navy and made his views clear not only to the Defence Minister Guchkov but to any prominent politician he met; on 21 April he was holding talks on this subject with the veteran Menshevik leader G.V. Plekhanov, the founder of Russian Marxism whose so-called Unity Group of Mensheviks was vociferously in favour of the war, when news of the street fighting reached him. Kolchak rushed from Plekhanov's house to Guchkov's house, where the Provisional Government was meeting, and arrived at the very same moment that General Kornilov asked for permission to use force against the armed demonstrators. Kolchak therefore witnessed the clash of wills between Kornilov and the

Provisional Government. Justice Minister A.F. Kerensky and Prime Minister Prince G.E. Lvov opposed the use of force and insisted on a negotiated settlement. When Kornilov nonetheless ordered troops to gather outside the Mariinskii Palace, the Petrograd Soviet banned all troops from leaving their barracks without its agreement; it was the soviet not Kornilov that the troops obeyed, a slight Kornilov never forgot.[3]

Kornilov, as Commander of the Petrograd Military District, had already made clear that he felt a firm line should be taken towards the Petrograd Soviet. Just prior to the April demonstrations he had twice intervened to clip its wings. He successfully prevented Kerensky appointing the Bolshevik A. Taras-Rodionov to the post of Commandant of the Peter-Paul Fortress, and he succeeded in securing military control over the soviet's radio station. The latter incident was resolved only after extensive negotiation, but once Kornilov had explained to a soviet delegation led by Skobelev that the demand for all radios to be put under military control stemmed from the security hazard implicit in the soviet's devil-may-care attitude to the use of military codes, it was agreed to compromise; the existing communications director, chosen by the soviet, would be reappointed by order of Kornilov. With this background of difficult relations between Kornilov and the Petrograd Soviet it was no wonder that on 21 April Kerensky and Kornilov should clash at Guchkov's house. And Kolchak saw at first hand how Kornilov was forced to abandon his firm line as the Provisional Government embarked on what both Kolchak and Kornilov saw as a climb-down. It was the soviet which resolved the crisis by negotiation, and in the process formed a new coalition government on 5 May 1917 in which the 'soviet parties', the Mensheviks and the SRs, joined the liberals in government.[4]

The negotiations leading up to the formation of the coalition government saw not only the resignation of Milyukov as Foreign Minister, but also of Guchkov as Defence Minister. Shortly before he resigned on 30 April, Guchkov asked the then Supreme Commander-in-Chief of the Russian Army, General M.V. Alekseev, to appoint Kornilov Commander-in-Chief of the Northern Front, so that he would be 'in the immediate vicinity of Petrograd in view of future political developments'. To Guchkov's fury Alekseev declined; he felt that this would mean passing over other experienced officers.[5] Guchkov was not alone among those who identified Kornilov as the man most likely to serve the cause of counter-revolution. From April onwards, a whole series of counter-revolutionary organizations were formed – the Military League by Guchkov himself – and all looked to Kornilov, or if not him Kolchak, as potential leaders.

The first group of counter-revolutionary plotters assembled on 5 April, a fortnight before the Milyukov crisis. The chief instigator was V.S. Zavoiko, the son of an admiral rewarded with a large landed estate for his services to the Tsar. Zavoiko had worked in the oil industry in Baku for the firm Nobel and in other mineral extraction industries in Turkestan and Western Siberia for firms supported by British capital; he also served on the board of the Russo-Asiatic Bank. To a meeting held in his flat Zavoiko invited B.A. Suvorin, owner of the mass circulation newspaper *Novoe vremya*; B.N. Troitskii-Senyutovich of the International Bank; and Colonel V.D. Pletnev, Kornilov's adjutant. They debated possible candidates for the post of strong man to save Russia and all agreed that Kornilov was the man for the job. Zavoiko contacted Kornilov four days later and dramatically resigned his lucrative business posts to join the army as Kornilov's orderly and *de facto* secretary. He did not, however, abandon his press interests; on 23 April he helped launch the patriotic pro-war weekly *Svoboda v borbe*, and the ability to manipulate the press would later serve Kornilov's cause well.[6]

Zavoiko's business contacts were extensive. He was a relative of A.F. Rafalovich of the Russian Foreign Trade Bank, who was a friend of Russia's premier industrialist A.I. Putilov. Zavoiko took care to inform Putilov and his fellow magnate A.I. Vyshnegradskii of the results of the 5 April meeting. Putilov and Vyshnegradskii were already in the process of establishing their own pressure group composed of representatives from the big banks and insurance companies which adopted the name the Society for the Economic Rehabilitation of Russia and comprised the dominant figures on the pre-revolutionary Council of Congresses of Representatives of Trade and Industry, whose members had all once looked to the Tsar for protection and now looked instinctively to the army. The primary purpose of the society was to raise funds to support candidates from the propertied classes in the Constituent Assembly election, then, wrongly, seen to be imminent; it also sought to combat the influence of socialists at the front and it was on this that the society concentrated once, after his resignation, Guchkov agreed to take over as its head.[7]

## KOLCHAK IN JULY

The members of the coalition government formed in May – liberals, Mensheviks and SRs – had little enough in common, but what kept them together was a determination to launch a summer offensive on the Eastern Front. Kerensky took over as Minister of War and set himself the twin tasks of preparing for the offensive and democratizing the army's command structure. It was this second ambition which led to conflict with the army and won new recruits to the cause of counter-revolution.

Officers began to organize themselves to defend what they saw as their own, and the country's, vital interests. The Supreme Army Command, GHQ, was based not in Moscow or Petrograd, but near the front in Mogilev. By the start of May the officer corps at GHQ had begun to draw up plans for an Officers' Union which would defend officers against the angry and frequently violent attacks of rank and file soldiers and their committees. The men most active in this campaign were Lieutenant-Colonel V.A. Lebedev – who in November 1918 became Admiral Kolchak's Chief of Staff – and Lieutenant-Colonel Pronin. The army command at GHQ was initially hostile to the idea; it was hard enough to cope with political organizations among the rank and file let alone among the officer corps. However, by the first week in May 1917 GHQ had changed its mind and the Officers' Union held its founding congress in Mogilev from 7–22 May; the main committee, elected by the delegates, was headed by the former Kadet deputy to the old Tsarist Duma, Colonel Novosiltsev. The high point of the congress was an emotive address by the Supreme Army Commander General M.V. Alekseev, in which he stated 'Russia is perishing'. In response Novosiltsev, Lebedev, Pronin and Colonel V.I. Sidorin organized a secret session of delegates at which Alekseev was cast in the role of Russia's saviour and future military dictator. In public the officers used the thirteen sessions to bemoan the insults heaped upon them by the rebellious soldiery, and decided 'putting all political aims to one side, to raise the military might of the army in the name of saving the Motherland'.[8]

Away from GHQ, officers' organizations were proliferating by early May, and the first attempt to co-ordinate their activities came from an organization established on 8 May and known as the Republican Centre. The Republican Centre established a military section which included in it representatives from all the variously named underground officers' groups: thus the Military League was represented by General I. Federov, the Officers' Union by Colonel Novosiltsev and Colonel Pronin, the Union of Cossack Troops by Colonel A.I. Dutov, and the Union of Military Duty by Colonel Finberg; the Union of Knights of St George was also represented. The Republican Centre itself was not a military organization, but an organization of industrialists. Unlike the Society for the Economic Rehabilitation of Russia formed by Putilov, it represented the interests of firms based on Russian capital, firms which had not held the Tsarist system in such high regard since they had never been favoured in the way foreign firms had. The first meeting of the Republican Centre was held in the home of F.A. Lipskii, on the board of the Siberian Bank, and all its leading members were officials in either the Siberian Bank or the Mayak Timber Company. Far from being associated with the leading politicians of the *ancien régime*, the dominant personality was K.V. Nikolaevskii, a member of one of the smaller moderate socialist parties, the Popular Socialists – they had broken away from the SRs after the 1905 Revolution and preferred constitutional struggle to revolutionary struggle.[9]

Casting around for a nationally known figure to head the Republican Centre's military section, Kolchak was immediately approached. He had resigned his post in command of the Black Sea Fleet after Kerensky had been appointed War Minister, because he could not accept the new discipline system being established. So, for six weeks, from early June to 20 July, he was based in Petrograd, waiting to finalize arrangements for a mission he had been asked to head in America as advisor for a planned attack by the United States Navy on Turkey through the Dardanelles. Shortly after his arrival in Petrograd he was almost besieged by counter-revolutionary groups wanting to adopt him as their leader. Not only did the Republican Centre make him the head of its military section, but Novosiltsev of the Officers' Union approached him to discuss his possible role as future dictator of Russia. The leader of Novosiltsev's party, the Kadet Party leader and former Foreign Minister Milyukov, also approached Kolchak at this time and had conversations on the same theme, as did another Kadet P.B. Struve and M.V. Rodzianko, President of the Tsar's Duma; and, forgetting its support for Kornilov in April, in late June the right-wing press launched a campaign calling for the resignation of Prince Lvov as Prime Minister and his replacement by Kolchak.[10]

This campaign reached its height during the political crisis of early July. The First Coalition Government, formed in May, duly launched its offensive on 18 June, but ten days later it had degenerated into a retreat, in parts a rout, with anti-war demonstrations breaking out both at the front and in the rear. The cement holding the coalition together had crumbled and on 2 July the liberal Kadet ministers withdrew from the government. The following 48 hours saw repeated Bolshevik demonstrations initially in protest at plans to transfer reserve army units to the front, but as the strength of working-class opinion became apparent, to capitalize on the resignation of the Kadets from the government. The First All-Russian Congress of Workers' and Soldiers' Soviets had met in Petrograd from 2–24 June and elected an executive for the whole of Russia; the Bolsheviks argued that their street demonstrations could force the Soviet Executive to establish a government comprising the socialist parties alone.

The government survived this so-called July Days crisis, and, its position strengthened, branded the Bolshevik leaders traitors and started criminal proceedings against them, forcing Lenin into hiding and putting Trotsky in prison. The crisis did indeed lead to Prince Lvov's resignation, but he was not replaced by Admiral Kolchak as the counter-revolutionary plotters had hoped but by the socialist Kerensky, who began the tortuous process of negotiating the formation of a Second Coalition Government. This took nearly three weeks to achieve, and during this interregnum Kolchak's conspirators were actively trying to broaden their enterprise. About the middle of July the two main anti-government organizations got in touch with one another for the first time. The Republican Centre was contacted by Putilov, the leader of the Society for the Economic Rehabilitation of Russia, and, as requested, sent a representative to the Crimea where Putilov was on holiday; after this initial contact the Republican Centre leader Nikolaevskii held talks with Putilov, and they agreed to co-operate. It was, in many ways, an unequal relationship: the 1,500,000 roubles raised by the Republican Centre was dwarfed by the funds at the disposal of the Society for the Economic Rehabilitation of Russia; the Siberian Bank could not compete with the Russo-Asiatic Bank; the poorer Republican Centre soon became the client of the richer Society for the Economic Rehabilitation of Russia.[11]

## KORNILOV'S PLOTTING BEGINS

As the time came for Kolchak's departure for the USA, the plotters' attention shifted back to Kornilov. When on 15 July Kerensky held talks with the Kadet Party, trying to woo them back into the government, they proposed that the new Minister of War should be Kornilov; as a partial concession to this demand Kornilov was appointed Supreme Commander-in-Chief on 18 July. This did not end the row about the personal composition of the Second Coalition Government. As a more overt concession to Kadet opinion Kerensky wanted to make S.N. Tretyakov Minister of Trade and Industry; Tretyakov was president of the Moscow stock exchange committee and a leading member of the council of the All-Russian Union of Trade and Industry. Unable to get agreement to this and other new appointments, Kerensky resigned on 21 July; this demagogic manoeuvre succeeded in 'banging heads together' and the Kadets, Mensheviks and SRs finally formed the Second Coalition Government on 24 July. Kerensky was nominally his own Minister of War, but in practice divided these functions between his Acting Minister of War B.V. Savinkov and his Navy Minister V.I. Lebedev; both would later play a significant role in the Red versus Green civil war of 1918. However, for the counter-revolutionaries it was Kornilov's appointment which transformed the situation; he again became their great hope.[12]

As soon as Kornilov's appointment was made public, the anti-government right-wing press began a campaign to popularize Kornilov and his demands, the most outspoken of these being the restoration of the death penalty for serving soldiers. In this press campaign the figure of Zavoiko re-emerged; he used his press contacts to publicize the daring exploits of Kornilov as an army commander, including a little hagiographical pamphlet about him. Unlike in April when no established politicians had associated themselves with Kornilov in this way, in July the council of the All-Russian Union of Trade and Industry issued a statement saying that 'only a radical break by the government with the dictatorship of the soviets' could save Russia, while a private session of the State Duma, chaired by Rodzianko, heard speeches from liberal as well as conservative politicians urging the Duma to act against the growing power of the soviet. At the end of July Rodzianko was contacted by General Alekseev, who reported that the view of all army commanders was that the government should cease its attack on officers, leave all military legislation to the Supreme Commander-in-Chief, end politics in the army by abolishing committees and commissars, and restore the death penalty throughout the army. The Officers' Union took up this campaign for the restoration of the death penalty when on 22 July it issued a special proclamation on the subject.[13]

While this public clamour in support of Kornilov was underway, further moves were being taken to try and weld together the disparate officers' organizations. On 31 July the Military League organized a meeting attended by its own representatives and representatives of the Union of Knights of St George, the Union of Military Duty, the Union for the Honour of the Motherland, the Union of Volunteers for Popular Defence, the Union for the Salvation of the Motherland, the 1914 Society, and the Republican Centre. The meeting decided to try and co-ordinate future activity and quickly agreed to send a telegram of support to Kornilov. However, although an umbrella organization called the Union of People's Defence was set up, on which all the groups were represented in proportion to their membership, nothing very tangible came from this initiative.[14]

At this stage Kornilov envisaged a fairly straightforward military coup and ruled out any collaboration with groups represented in the Provisional Government. Towards the end of July, or the very start of August, Kornilov held talks with another future White general, General A.I. Denikin. Kornilov told him of his plans: he had, he said, been approached by monarchist plotters, but would have nothing to do with restoring the Romanov dynasty of Nicholas II; on the other hand, he had made clear that he had turned down the suggestion that he join the Provisional Government, since it was too closely linked to the soviet. Kornilov went on:

> Give me the authority and then I will lead a decisive struggle. We need to see Russia through to the Constituent Assembly, and then let them do what they like; I would stand aside and be of no hindrance to them.

Denikin promised to support Kornilov in such an enterprise.[15]

Kornilov's first meeting with Kerensky since April reinforced his determination to act. The new Commander-in-Chief and the Prime Minister/Minister of War met on 10 August and although primarily to discuss military strategy, Kerensky spent much of the session warning Kornilov what might happen if he should be tempted to stage a coup. He raised the matter of anti-government plots and rumour-mongering against the government and blamed the Officers' Union. Kerensky then lectured Kornilov on how necessary a coalition government was for Russia's future and warned that if he were removed, Kornilov would be left in thin air since no-one would support him; the railways would stop and the telegraph would cease. Not surprisingly after a meeting held in such a spirit, Kerensky let it be known he might have to replace Kornilov with a left-wing general; after the meeting the left-wing press launched an attack on Kornilov, while the right-wing press rallied to his support.[16]

Kerensky was well-informed. A few days after Kornilov had arrived at GHQ, he was approached by Novosiltsev who put the Officers' Union's plans for a military coup to him; because of Novosiltsev's high public profile as chairman of the union, it was decided that his deputy Colonel Pronin rather than Novosiltsev himself should act as a go-between. At about the same time Kornilov had been approached by the Republican Centre and agreed to work with them and their military section, headed after Kolchak's departure by Colonel L.P. Desimeter. Immediately after the August meeting with Kerensky, Kornilov's plans began to be put into operation. The very same day he sent Zavoiko to hold talks with the cossack commander General A.M. Kaledin, and he held his first meeting with an emissary from Moscow A.F. Aladin, the leader of the Labour Group in the Duma back in 1906.[17] Aladin's arrival would highlight some of the political problems already inherent in Kornilov's scheme.

By the first week in August the clear outline of a conspiracy was beginning to emerge. On 6 August Kornilov divulged his plans to his Quartermaster General A.S. Lukomskii, and asked him to order General A.M. Krymov's Third Cavalry Corps to redeploy to the strategically important location of Velikiye Luki, thus putting them in striking distance of Petrograd. Kornilov revealed to Lukomskii that other moves were already underway, that Zavoiko and his adjutant Colonel Golitsyn were involved, and that Colonel Lebedev and Captain Rozhenko were handling the details, in particular the links with underground groups in Petrograd. At Rozhenko's suggestion, officers were being sent to Petrograd ostensibly 'on leave', but actually to take action at a given signal. Sidorin, vice-president of the main committee of the Officers' Union, was in charge of finance and had already contacted the Republican Centre.[18]

However, the involvement of the Republican Centre introduced the first element of confusion among the plotters as to what precisely they were trying to achieve; confusion that Kornilov did very little to clear up. When Nikolaevskii of the Republican Centre met Kornilov, it was understood that the establishment of a military dictatorship would not preclude the continued existence of the government; indeed, with certain minor changes, 'there would be no great shake up in the personnel of the provisional government' it was concluded. This clearly contradicted Kornilov's earlier assertion to Denikin that he wanted nothing to do with the Provisional Government, but reflected the fact that the Republican Centre had among its individual members V.L. Baranovskii, head of Kerensky's war cabinet, who back on 14 July had confided to Novosiltsev and Sidorin that, while it might take slightly longer than the Officers' Union wanted, Kerensky would soon limit the powers of soldiers' committees and government commissars. Since both the Chief Government Army Commissar N. Filonenko and Acting War Minister Savinkov supported Kornilov's key proposals for restoring discipline, the Republican Centre's proposal did not seem far-fetched.[19]

Aladin's arrival added to this confusion about aims. Liberal circles in Moscow were equally concerned at the fate of the government in the proposed military action. On 8–10 August the leading members of Russia's old social elite gathered in Moscow for what was to become known as the first Meeting of Public Figures, organized at the expense of the All-Russian Union of Trade and Industry and in preparation for the Moscow State Conference. This was to be an assembly of all Russia's public organizations summoned by Kerensky to mobilize support for his Second Coalition Government. Among those attending the Meeting of Public Figures were some of the most active anti-government plotters. There was Novosiltsev of the Officers' Union; V.A. Maklakov and Milyukov of the Kadets; Rodzianko of the Duma; P.P. Ryabushinskii and Tretyakov of the Moscow industrial elite; Putilov and Vyshnegradskii of the Petrograd-based Society for the Economic Rehabilitation of Russia; and V.N. Lvov, a right-wing liberal based in Moscow, dropped from the government in July during the negotiations to form the Second Coalition Government. The Meeting of Public Figures elected Rodzianko its president and S.N. Tretyakov its vice-president, with the Petrograd industrialist Vyshnegradskii and the Moscow industrialist Ryabushinskii both being made members of its permanent council.

During the meeting Novosiltsev was approached by Captain Rozhenko, who had been sent by Kornilov's advisors, and who asked for a secret session to be arranged so that he could outline Kornilov's intentions. Liberal politicians played a leading role in organizing this session – it took place in the house of the leading Kadet N.M. Kishkin and another leading Kadet A.I. Shingarev, Minister of Agriculture in the Provisional Government, was responsible for issuing at least some of the invitations – which was attended by Rodzianko, Maklakov, Milyukov and N.N. Lvov, V.N. Lvov's brother. However, the liberal politicians were not impressed with what they heard. Rozhenko explained that the plan so far was to wait for the Bolsheviks to try and prevent the planned Moscow State Conference from opening on 13 August, or for Kornilov to be sacked; a coup would then take place, Petrograd would be seized, the soviet dissolved and a dictatorship established. Not even Novosiltsev was impressed with the ideas of his fellow plotters: to him it was ill-thought out and smacked too much of the rather simplistic right-wing views of Zavoiko; they were trying to force events, and had skimped on such important planning considerations as what to do about radio stations or the telegraph network. His mood at the meeting was shared by all participants: while all sympathized with Kornilov's aims, this plan would not work. Milyukov was almost alone in responding openly. While most present kept their doubts to themselves and were non-committal, Milyukov dissociated himself from Rozhenko's proposals, while warmly endorsing the principle of dictatorship; this may have encouraged Rozhenko to think only minor changes were necessary.

Two or three days later a second meeting was held on the same theme to a slightly different audience which this time included Prince G.N. Trubetskoi, head of the GHQ Diplomatic Chancellery. At this meeting Milyukov was again ambivalent. He welcomed GHQ's decision to take action to end Russia's collapse and disperse the soviet, but pointed out that for this to succeed, the masses needed to be behind the action; since this could not be guaranteed at that moment the plotters could not rely on the Kadets. His warning was shared by his fellow Kadet leader Maklakov; a direct clash with Kerensky would not work, Maklakov warned Novosiltsev: 'no-one would support Kornilov, they would all run for cover'. Milyukov's private view was that more time was needed and a direct clash with the soviet would not be possible until October.[20]

The hostility of most Kadets to Kornilov's plans was a severe blow, but it reflected genuine concerns. The heart of Russian liberalism had always been in Moscow, where Russia's native capitalism was based. Before the abdication of the Tsar there had always been tension between the Petrograd industrialists, gathered in a golden circle around the Tsar and largely dependent on state-funded initiatives, and the home-grown textile magnates in Moscow. This tension had long been there, but had if anything been exacerbated during the war. Thus when the All-Russian Union of Trade and Industry was set up in March 1917 by the leading Moscow industrialists Ryabushinskii, Tretyakov and A.I. Konovalov, it was the result of an initiative dating back to 1916. The new union was seen as a counter-weight to the Council of Congresses of Trade and Industry, dominated by the Petrograd banking and monopoly interests of south Russia; it represented the banking and textile magnates of central Russia.

These tensions did not disappear with the abdication of the Emperor, they ran too deep for that. Although on 1–2 June 1917 a conference was held of Petrograd and Moscow magnates to establish a united voice for Russian capital, these proposals came to nothing. While Putilov and Vyshnegradskii had immediately turned to the military for support, the Union of Trade and Industry established a political department under N.N. Lvov which linked its campaign against 'anarchy' to a similar campaign being launched in August by the Duma which, never formally dissolved in March at the time of the abdication, continued to meet in private session under Rodzianko's chairmanship and was an important reference point for all those on the right. The dividing line was not absolute, for the Union of Trade and Industry donated 25,000 roubles to the Officers' Union after being approached by Novosiltsev, but it concentrated on political campaigning with sympathetic organizations like the All-Russian Congress of Land-Owners, at whose congress on 1–5 July N.N. Lvov was elected president of the new Union of Land-owners. A flavour of their campaigning style was seen in the speech N.N. Lvov made to a plenary meeting of the main council of the Union of Land-owners when it met on 29–31 July: he denounced the socialists and in particular the leader of the SR Party and opponent of the war V.M. Chernov, and called for anti-socialist co-operation in the Constituent Assembly elections; talks with bankers and industrialists had already started, he said, and would be strengthened by sending delegates to the All-Russian Congress of Trade and Industry on 3 August. At that congress, also held in Moscow, Ryabushinskii denounced the soviet in similar anti-socialist terms.[21]

## KORNILOV CHANGES TACK

When Kornilov came to Petrograd on 10 August for talks with Kerensky, he had other, perhaps more significant meetings with other politicians. Rodzianko both attended the meeting with Kerensky and had lunch with Kornilov; on his return to GHQ Kornilov's plans had changed significantly. He told General A.S. Lukomskii on 11 August that counter-intelligence reports showed that the Bolsheviks planned a new demonstration on 28–29 August to celebrate six months since the overthrow of the monarchy. As had happened during the demonstrations in April and July, they would demand a soviet government, and even if Kerensky's government survived these demonstrations, Kornilov went on, it would have to be broadened to 'include Chernov and the Bolshevik leaders'. It was 'time to put an end to this', he asserted and went on:

> I am not going to go against the provisional government. I hope that, at
> the last moment, I shall be able to come to an agreement with them . . .
> If I am unable to reach an agreement with Kerensky and Savinkov, then
> it is possible I shall have to strike the Bolsheviks without their support;

but afterwards they will thank me and it will be possible to create the firm authority which Russia needs . . .[22]

Kornilov's plans had significantly changed. He was showing more political acumen and aimed his hostility specifically at the Bolsheviks. Previously he had talked of acting at the Moscow State Conference or if he was dismissed by Kerensky. These were both occasions where his target was, or could easily be interpreted as being, the present government rather than the soviet. This was clearly the case if he acted in response to his own dismissal, but any action during the Moscow State Conference could easily be interpreted as an attack on Kerensky's government since it had proposed the conference. By choosing the demonstration of 29 August the Bolsheviks were being targeted much more carefully than before. The action was not to be one against 'reds in general' but the anti-war Bolsheviks. Even more significantly, in his statement to General Lukomskii, unlike his earlier statement to General Denikin, Kornilov said he would act together with the government rather than against it. Clearly, whatever Rodzianko had said to him over lunch, Kornilov had been listening to a more subtle politician than Zavoiko.

Kornilov's experience at the Moscow State Conference, held from 13–14 August, reinforced the necessity of acting in a politically more circumspect manner. His officers organized a secret session of those members of the Duma present at the conference; they were informed that plans were well advanced for the overthrow of Kerensky and, if the Duma agreed, the coup would be carried out in its name. The Duma members present were very cautious in their response: after detailed questioning of the officers, most concluded that the plan was simply not serious enough even to warrant talking to Kornilov on the subject; although Rodzianko was overheard promising that the Duma could be used as a parliamentary fig leaf for the new regime if the coup succeeded. As a few days earlier at the Meeting of Public Figures, only Milyukov was in any way committal. He was prepared to visit Kornilov, but told him face to face that there should be no break with Kerensky. In these circumstances Kornilov gave Milyukov no details of his plans, but asked only that the Kadets support his move by calling on their ministers to resign at the crucial moment, something Milyukov declined to do. Milyukov's views were essentially those the Kadet Central Committee adopted on 12 August: that a dictatorship, while desirable, was still premature. The message coming back to Kornilov was that liberal support could not be guaranteed even if he acted with, rather than against, the government.[23]

Enthusiastic backing for Kornilov's venture came only from the Petrograd industrialists. During the Moscow State Conference Colonel Desimeter asked Vyshnegradskii and Putilov to call on Kornilov, who told them of his plans:

> I only need order and a firm authority in the country and the army . . .
> In agreement with Kerensky I am dispatching a corps to Petrograd to disperse the Bolsheviks [who] must be arrested . . . A movement must be organized within Petrograd to help General Krymov; money is needed to accommodate and feed people before the action. Can you give the money?

Vyshnegradskii and Putilov agreed to put up the money; some 3,500,000 roubles were already held in accounts of the Russo–Asiatic, Azov–Don, International and Siberian Banks. Significantly, however, when the Moscow industrialist Tretyakov was approached by Putilov for a contribution to this fund, he refused to have anything to do with it. Tension between Petrograd and Moscow industrialists was indeed deep-seated.[24]

By the end of the Moscow State Conference Kornilov had come to a sort of compromise between his immediate advisors like Zavoiko and the liberal political establishment. To satisfy the first, he would act sooner rather than later, but to satisfy the latter the excuse would be a Bolshevik demonstration not the action of the government; just in case the Bolsheviks did not organize a demonstration Sidorin, Desimeter and Finisov were dispatched to Petrograd to organize one.[25] To secure as much support as possible from the liberals, he would try to act in conjunction with the government rather than in opposition to it. Yet this was not a stable compromise. Kornilov was almost besieged by advisors and, not a politician, constantly turned first one way and then the other. Although apparently persuaded of the need to co-operate with the government, as the date of the expected Bolshevik action approached he was gradually persuaded that a purely military dictatorship might, after all, be best. That crucial vacillation was made abundantly clear on 17 August when Kornilov organized a meeting at GHQ of all those involved in the plot. Among those invited was I.A. Dobrynskii. A political associate of the most liberal of the Tsar's former ministers, the former Minister of Agriculture A.V. Krivoshein, Dobrynskii was on the board of the League of the Knights of St George and rumoured to he capable of mobilizing some 40,000 Caucasian soldiers in the southern town of Vladikavkaz; he was also a close friend of the leading liberal brothers in Moscow N.N. Lvov and V.N. Lvov, and, on being summoned to GHQ, he held talks with the

Lvovs and agreed to put the moderate Moscow line at the 17 August meeting with Kornilov.

Dobrynskii's report back to V.N. Lvov in Moscow on 21 August was alarming. Although at the main session of Kornilov's meeting on the 17th the idea of a purely military dictatorship had been dropped in favour of action in co-operation with the government, at a secret *tête-à-tête* with Kornilov, Dobrynskii was informed that Kornilov simply intended to appoint himself military dictator. As V.N. Lvov and Dobrynskii were discussing the situation they were joined by Aladin, who announced that he had just been asked by Zavoiko to inform the Kadet ministers that, for their own good and in order to disrupt the government, they should find some pretext to resign from the Second Coalition Government before 27 August. Appalled at the way things were developing, V.N. Lvov decided to act. He offered to take this instruction to the Kadet Central Committee in Petrograd, and then go in person to Kerensky and try persuading him to 'reorganize the government in order to calm GHQ down'. With the agreement of Dobrynskii and Aladin he set off, arriving in Petrograd on the morning of 22 August. Having failed to track down Milyukov, he transmitted Zavoiko's message for the Kadet Central Committee to another member of the Central Committee V.D. Nabokov and then went to see Kerensky.[26]

## KERENSKY AND KORNILOV

At precisely the same moment that V.N. Lvov was waiting outside Kerensky's study to warn him that, whatever Kornilov might say he was up to, he was actually planning a purely military regime, Kerensky was inside his study with Savinkov, his Acting Minister of War, agreeing terms to be put to Kornilov which would strengthen the military's role in government and end the mutual hostility and recrimination. Savinkov had resigned his post on 10 August because Kerensky had excluded him from his talks that day with Kornilov. However, on 15 August, after the Moscow State Conference, Kerensky decided he would accept some of the major points in Kornilov's programme and on 17 August reappointed Savinkov to his post to act as intermediary. On 22 August Kerensky asked Savinkov to visit Kornilov and negotiate an understanding, stressing that the death penalty would be extended from the front to the whole army, thus meeting Kornilov's major concern on the question of discipline, and that the Petrograd Military District would be put under his direct control, except for the city of Petrograd which the government would rule directly. This was the proposal being hammered out for Savinkov to take to GHQ as Lvov sat waiting to see Kerensky.[27]

Kornilov received Savinkov on 23 August. As agreed with Kerensky, the meeting addressed a number of issues in dispute between the government and GHQ, and rapidly resolved almost all of them. One long saga had concerned the role of political commissars, government representatives charged with overseeing the actions of officers, and the plans for the establishment of a political department at GHQ: both seemed resolved when it was agreed that Chief Government Army Commissar Filonenko should head the political department. Since Filonenko was very concerned at the over-politicization of the army, his appointment, GHQ felt, would in practice substantially reduce the powers of the commissars. Another issue was the number of anti-government plots emanating from GHQ: Kornilov agreed that the Officers' Union should be moved to Moscow and that its funding from GHQ should be curtailed; but he refused to allow Colonel Pronin to be arrested for alleged involvement in such plots. As to the question of coping with possible Bolshevik demonstrations at the end of August, a broad level of agreement was reached. The only dispute was about the planned role for General Krymov. Savinkov felt that in any action against the Bolsheviks it would be inappropriate if General Krymov took part because of his known right-wing views and the popular suspicion of cossack troops; his place would have to be taken by another officer. Otherwise it was quickly agreed that when the Bolshevik demonstration started, Kornilov would tell Savinkov when he was ready, so that Savinkov could declare martial law in Petrograd and its immediate environs. The meeting then discussed the possible political changes resulting from a clash with the Bolsheviks. All agreed that if the soviet supported the Bolshevik demonstration, it too should be dispersed, and that a government reshuffle would be needed. Kornilov suggested that the new government should include the former Commander-in-Chief General Alekseev and pro-war socialists like the Menshevik Plekhanov and the Right SR A.A. Argunov. Savinkov insisted that Kerensky would have to stay, but perhaps in the new post of President.[28]

Understandably, when Kornilov reviewed events after Savinkov had left at 3 p.m. on 24 August, he felt that the government was already in his hands. There would be no need for an armed clash since negotiations seemed to be leading to the same result. The prospects for a negotiated settlement were strengthened when, after Savinkov's departure, Kornilov received a delegation from the other leading conspiratorial group, the Republican Centre. Its representatives announced that the Republican Centre believed that after the anti-Bolshevik action Kerensky had to stay in government, but should resume his post as Minister of Justice. They then proposed a cabinet which sought to balance all shades of opinion: former Tsarist ministers would sit alongside the former Prime Minister of the Provisional Government Prince G.E. Lvov, with both General Alekseev and Admiral Kolchak being included, alongside socialists like Plekhanov and Argunov. Kornilov raised only the most minor objection to this list, and reassured the Republican Centre that everything would be discussed with Kerensky, indeed everything had already been arranged with Savinkov.[29]

Kornilov's parting words to the Republican Centre delegation were that he was about to hold talks with V.N. Lvov, an emissary from Kerensky, on the subject of possible changes in the composition of the government. That was indeed the case. On the afternoon of 22 August Lvov had eventually managed to get to see Kerensky after Savinkov's departure. He explained that he represented certain groups, both military and other, who felt the time had come to broaden the government by bringing in those to the right of the Kadet Party and patriotic socialists not represented in the soviet. Kerensky was non-committal but agreed to explore the idea, even suggesting to Lvov that his position as Prime Minister was not sacrosanct. He then authorized Lvov to go to GHQ for further talks on the subject and to report back to him. Lvov returned to Moscow for more talks with Dobrynskii and Aladin, and all felt that Kerensky's apparent willingness to reshuffle the government meant bloodshed could be avoided. Then, on the evening of the 23rd Aladin received another message from GHQ, this time an order from Kornilov for transmission to the Don cossack leader General Kaledin to assemble cossack units for an advance on Moscow.

Lvov hurried to GHQ to try and establish what was really going on, arriving late on 24 August. Thus, immediately after the departure of the Republican Centre deputation, Lvov had two meetings with Kornilov, one at 11 p.m. on the 24th and the other at 10 a.m. on the 25th. What he was told was a version of what the Republican Centre had been told, but different in certain crucial respects. Kornilov was quite open with Lvov: he said that a dictatorship was the only way forward; however, Alekseev or Kaledin or himself could be dictator, in fact his own preference was for a Council of National Defence, chaired by himself, with Kerensky as his assistant and Savinkov,

Alekseev, Kolchak and Filonenko as members. Others to be involved in some capacity were the former Tsarist ministers mentioned by the Republican Centre, Aladin, Plekhanov, Prince G.E. Lvov and Zavoiko; he was also planning to summon Rodzianko and Maklakov to GHQ, he said. However, there was no mention in this list of the SR Argunov, and the Republican Centre had never imagined making Zavoiko a minister.[30]

When his talks with Kornilov resumed on the morning of the 25th, it seemed clear to Lvov that this subtle change in the composition of the planned new government was not pure chance, but the result of the growing influence of Zavoiko. That influence was clear: Kornilov repeated that the Supreme Commander-in-Chief needed to assume power, but that it did not have to be he who occupied that post. Then he added:

> I no longer trust Kerensky . . . I do not trust Savinkov either. I do not know whom he wants to stab in the back. It could be Kerensky, it could be me . . . However I could offer Savinkov the portfolio of Minister of War and Kerensky the portfolio of Minister of Justice.

At this point Zavoiko interrupted 'like a school teacher' and stressed Deputy Prime Minister, not Minister of Justice. As Lvov moved from talks with Kornilov to talks with Zavoiko himself he began to question whether what Kornilov had told him was the whole story.

Although Lvov gave the impression he was going along with the plot, readily agreeing to write a note to his brother N.N. Lvov asking him to encourage public figures to come to GHQ, Lvov was beginning to worry about the true aspirations of Zavoiko. Discussing further details of a future government, he became more and more alarmed. Zavoiko clearly planned to appoint himself Minister of Finance, but was quite cavalier about who should be offered other ministerial posts. He offered Lvov the post of Minister of the Interior, and when Lvov turned it down he cheerfully re-allocated it to Filonenko. Then, as they waited for the train to Petrograd, Zavoiko confided that the government they had been planning together would be a stop-gap, lasting for only three months at most; after that a real government would be established, dominated by representatives of the old financial elite; besides Zavoiko himself as Minister of Finance, there would be his colleague from the very first anti-government conspiracy of April Troitskii-Senyutovich as Minister of Production. Zavoiko also made clear that, whatever was said about guaranteeing Kerensky's safety, his death was 'necessary as an outlet for the pent up feelings of the officers'. In Zavoiko's own words, Kornilov had been ready to make so many concessions on the 24th simply because he

(Zavoiko) had been away from GHQ for much of the day; his resolve on dictatorship had been stiffened by his return.[31]

Lvov returned from GHQ convinced that Kornilov was interested in a bloody coup with any broadened cabinet serving simply as a temporary fig leaf for a military dictatorship. Zavoiko had urged Lvov to return to Kerensky and persuade him to come to GHQ to discuss the government changes. When Lvov reached Kerensky at midday on 26 August he had a difficult task to perform. He wanted to inform Kerensky that a coup was being prepared, but also to strengthen the position of the liberal politicians in the ensuing crisis. Thus he first fulfilled his promise to Zavoiko and sent a note to his brother N.N. Lvov explaining that Kornilov wanted leading public figures, and Rodzianko in particular, to leave at once for GHQ, then, at 7 p.m., he went to see Kerensky and informed him of the coup attempt.[32]

It was during this interview with Lvov that Kerensky hit upon a means of proving to the satisfaction of the other members of his cabinet that Kornilov was indeed planning a coup. He persuaded Lvov to accompany him to the War Ministry building and to ask Kornilov, in the presence of a witness, to confirm over the Hughes apparatus, a sort of teleprinter operating between the War Ministry and GHQ, that what Lvov had told him was true. Kornilov, in the light of his conversations with both Savinkov and Lvov about acting in co-operation with the government, was quite happy to confirm that Lvov had been fully authorized to talk to Kerensky on the subjects discussed at GHQ. By this vague wording Kornilov was referring to the plans to act in co-operation with the government, but Lvov's story of what was actually being discussed at GHQ meant that Kornilov had admitted to planning an assault on the government, thus putting his own head on the block. With this written evidence of a plot, Kerensky decided to act. He dismissed Kornilov on the spot before going to the cabinet to discuss the matter further. That night he received the resignation of all his ministers and cancelled the cabinet meeting planned for 27 August.

Kornilov at first interpreted the Hughes apparatus interview with Kerensky as proof that all had been going well. He promptly telegraphed Lvov, Rodzianko and Milyukov urging them to come to GHQ by the 29th, and telegraphed Savinkov instructing him to introduce martial law on the 29th. He was busy telling Lukomskii how the new government was to be formed and what he would say to Kerensky and Savinkov when he received the telegram informing him he had been dismissed. Kornilov assumed that Kerensky had succumbed to soviet pressure and resolved to take no notice. In deciding to ignore his dismissal and calling on General Krymov to advance, Kornilov was simply reverting to his original plan of a straightforward military coup, encouraged in this by Zavoiko, who dictated the angry response Kornilov sent Kerensky, accusing him of lying and making clear that the gauntlet had been thrown down.[33]

As Kerensky had predicted when he met Kornilov on 10 August, no-one supported Kornilov; the railways and the telegraph were indeed paralysed by the soviet. Kerensky threw himself on the soviet to resolve the crisis. The liberals, still tempted to make political capital from it, tried to persuade Kornilov to negotiate with Kerensky even after his dismissal. They tried to portray what had happened as a misunderstanding, which if Kornilov backed down promptly, could still result in a reshuffled cabinet. Maklakov told Kornilov on the 27th: 'Your proposal is understood here as the desire for a coup which would employ force. I am very happy that, apparently, this is a misunderstanding.'[34] Maklakov added that Kornilov had been inaccurately informed of the feelings 'of the popular masses'. As late as 28 August Kerensky was being urged by Kadet politicians to satisfy Kornilov by transferring power to the former Commander-in-Chief General Alekseev. Milyukov in particular backed this idea and persuaded Alekseev to put himself forward as a new head of state. But Kerensky stood firm. He did re-appoint Alekseev Commander-in-Chief, but this was a calculated move to produce calm in the army rather than a concession to the Kadets.[35]

Thus the Kornilov coup affair, rather than the coup itself, did much to discredit the liberals. Few knew of Milyukov's caution when approached in secret by Kornilov's agents, few knew that none of the public figures summoned to GHQ on 27 August ever agreed to go,[36] but all could see the way Kadet politicians politicked during the crisis. The distinction between calling for a military dictatorship at once and calling for a military dictatorship sometime in the future was a nice one. In the public mind liberal politicians were involved in a coup attempt, which, if it had not been so serious, would have seemed like a farce. Many of the officers smuggled into Petrograd on the pretext of going on leave or special training simply pocketed their 150 roubles per day and vanished into thin air. Putilov, asked by Sidorin and Desimeter to raise more money for the operation, refused to hand it over when he found them drunk in a restaurant. Indeed the plotters spent much of the crucial hours of the coup drinking to celebrate a victory they mistakenly believed they had already won; when they later tried to revive their planned Bolshevik 'uprising', General Krymov had already abandoned his advance on Petrograd.[37]

As a counter-revolution, Kornilov's coup was a shambles. However, it highlighted two important truths about the counter-revolutionary right in Russia. First its isolation: the plotters could win no mass support, and the Moscow liberals, well aware of this, tried as a consequence to keep their distance; the only group which did rally unhesitatingly to Kornilov's cause were the Petrograd industrialists. Kornilov was himself aware of this, for he told a fellow general on the eve of his coup that, while only the industrial elite supported him at that moment, his triumph would bring broader circles to his side.[38] Second, it proved a salutary warning to the Republican Centre: whatever might be said by the military in public about co-operating with a broad coalition government, the instinct of military men was for dictatorship pure and simple; the military were opposed not only to the Bolsheviks and the soviet, but to the coalition government as well. The military had been inspired to start its plotting in April 1917 by the entry of socialists into the government, and it was to the pre–April era that they wanted to return. The Tsar did not have to be restored, the precise constitutional arrangements could be left vague, but an authoritarian regime was their goal, decorated perhaps with some liberal public figures. This was what Kornilov had wanted and it would remain the aim of White generals until their defeat at the end of the White versus Red civil war in 1920.

## NOTES

1. A. Tarasov-Rodionov, *February 1917* (Westport CT 1973), p. 359.
2. 'Aprel'skie dni 1917 g. v Petrograde' *Krasnyi arkhiv* vol. 33 (1929).
3. K.A. Popov (ed.), *Dopros Kolchaka* (Leningrad 1923), p. 54 et seq.; F.I. Rodichev, *Vospominaniya i ocherki o russkoi liberalizme* (Newtonville 1982), p. 121; L. Schapiro, *1917: the Russian Revolution and the Origins of Present-Day Communism* (London 1984), p. 75.
4. Taras-Rodionov, *1917*, pp. 310, 333; Popov, *Dopros Kolchaka*, p. 61.
5. A.I. Denikin, *The Russian Turmoil* (London 1920), p. 300; E.I. Martynov, *Kornilov: popytka voennogo perevorota* (Moscow 1927), p. 19.
6. Martynov, *Kornilov*, p. 20; A.I. Denikin, *Ocherki russkoi smuty* (Paris 1921) vol. I, p. 195; F.I. Vidyasov, 'Kontrrevolyutsionnye zamysli inostrannykh imperialistov i Kornilovshchina' *Voprosy istorii* no. 5 (1965), p. 60, n. 60; V. Ya Laverychev, 'Russkie monopolisty i zagovor Kornilova' *Voprosy istorii* no. 4 (1964), p. 34; N. Ya Ivanov, *Kontrrevolyutsiya v Rossii v 1917 g. i ee razgrom* (Moscow 1977), p. 34; see also J.D. White, 'The Kornilov affair: a study in counter-revolution' *Soviet Studies* vol. 20 (1968).

7. Laverychev, 'Monopilisty', p. 34, n. 13; Ivanov, *Kontrrevolyutsiya*, p. 34; R.P. Browder and A.F. Kerensky, *The Russian Provisional Government 1917: Documents* (Stanford 1961), p. 1527 et seq.

8. N.G. Dumova, 'Maloizvestnye materialy po istorii Kornilovshchiny' *Voprosy istorii* no. 11 (1968), p. 70; Denikin, *Ocherki*, vol. 1, pp. 106–10; Denikin, *Turmoil*, pp. 229–31.

9. Ivanov, *Kontrrevolyutsiya*, p. 42; Dumova, 'Maloizvestnye', p. 75; Browder and Kerensky, *Documents*, p. 1534 et seq.

10. Popov, *Dopros*, p. 84; Dumova, 'Maloizvestnye', pp. 72, 76; V. Vladimirova, *Kontr-Revolyutsiya v 1917* (Moscow 1924), p. 46.

11. Browder and Kerensky, *Documents*, p. 1536; White, 'Kornilov', p. 188.

12. White, 'Kornilov', p. 196; Martynov, *Kornilov*, p. 41.

13. Martynov, *Kornilov*, p. 41; Browder and Kerensky, *Documents*, pp. 1013, 1016, 1400.

14. Vladimirova, *Kontr-Revolyutsiya*, p. 41.

15. Denikin, *Ocherki* vol. 1, p. 197. The monarchist plot seems to have been that of V.M. Purishkevich, see *Ocherki*, p. 156.

16. Martynov, *Kornilov*, p. 46.

17. Dumova, 'Maloizvestnye', p. 77; Vidyasov, 'Kontrrevolyutsionnye zamysli', p. 59; Vladimirova, *Kontr-Revolyutsiya*, p. 51. Aladin had been attending the Interparliamentary Conference in London in the summer of 1906 as the leader of the Labour Group of Deputies to the First State Duma when that assembly was dissolved by the Tsar. He then stayed in Britain and joined the army in 1914. The precise time of his arrival in Russia is not known, but it was some time in August.

18. A.S. Lukomskii, *Vospominaniya* vol. 1 (Berlin 1922), pp. 223, 232; Browder and Kerensky, *Documents*, p. 1536.

19. Dumova, 'Maloizvestnye', pp. 73, 77; Z.A. Vertsinskii, *God Revolyutsii* (Tallin 1929), p. 46.

20. P.N. Milyukov, *The Russian Revolution* (Gulf Breeze 1984), p. xv; Dumova, 'Maloizvestnye', p. 78; N.N. Golovin, *Rossiiskaya Kontrrevolyutsiya v 1917–18gg.* (Talinn 1937), Part 1 Book 2, p. 39.

21. 'Soyuz zemel'nykh sobstvennikov v 1917 godu' *Krasnyi arkhiv* (1927), p. 97 et seq.; V. Ya Laverychev, 'Vserossiiskii Soyuz Torgovli i Promyshlennosti' *Istoricheskii Zhurnal* no. 70 (1961), pp. 42–6; see also Laverychev, *Po tu storonu barrikad* (Moscow 1967).

22. R. Abraham, *Alexander Kerensky* (Columbia 1987), p. 253; Lukomskii, *Vospominaniya*, p. 228.

23. Dumova, 'Maloizvestnye', pp. 33, 79; Ivanov, *Kontrrevolyutsiya*, p. 99; S.I. Shidlovskii, *Vospominaniya* (Berlin 1923), p. 141.

24. Browder and Kerensky, *Documents*, p. 1529. Moscow industrialists had been quite happy to support general requests for financial support: Ryabushinskii had made a donation to the Officers' Union, for example – Dumova, 'Maloizvestnye', p. 72; it was the nature of Kornilov's plans that put them off on this occasion.

25. Dumova, 'Maloizvestnye', p. 89.

26. Browder and Kerensky, *Documents*, p. 1558 et seq.

27. Martynov, *Kornilov*, p. 75; G. Katkov, *The Kornilov Affair* (London 1980), pp. 55, 65.
28. Martynov, *Kornilov*, p. 80; Katkov, *Affair*, p. 70; Golovin, *Rossiiskaya*, p. 22.
29. Lukomskii, *Vospominaniya*, p. 235; Browder and Kerensky, *Documents*, p. 1537.
30. Browder and Kerensky, *Documents*, p. 1563; Martynov, *Kornilov*, p. 86 et seq.
31. Browder and Kerensky, *Documents*, pp. 1564–7; Laverychev, 'Monopolisty', p. 43. In talks with representatives of the Provisional Government, Kornilov continued to put across a more conciliatory line. On 25 and 26 August he held talks with Filonenko and discussed the possible formation of a Council of National Defence, presided over by himself and with Kerensky as his deputy. See Martynov, *Kornilov*, p. 90.
32. Martynov, *Kornilov*, p. 88; Katkov, *Kornilov*, p. 90.
33. Martynov, *Kornilov*, p. 111; H. Asher, 'The Kornilov affair; a reinterpretation' *Russian Review* vol. 29 (1970), p. 300.
34. Dumova, 'Maloizvestnye', p. 85.
35. Dumova, 'Maloizvestnye', p. 89; Ivanov, *Kontrrevolyutsiya*, p. 137.
36. Laverychev, 'Monopolisty', p. 44.
37. Details of these escapades can be found in Browder and Kerensky, *Documents*, p. 1532 et seq.
38. A.I. Verkhovskii, *Na trudnom perevale* (Moscow 1959), p. 323.

# CHAPTER TWO

# *Lenin Risks a Red–Green Civil War*

The Kornilov rebellion, the first act of the White versus Red civil war, failed because it had no popular base. It failed because telegraph operators immediately alerted soldiers' committees and soviets to what was going on; activists would then demand access to the telegraph network and if that access was refused, violent action would ensue. When the test came, Kornilov's supporters were reduced to a mere handful and soviets, commissars and soldiers, acting in unison, defended the revolution with an impressive display of power. Yet within two months the first shots in a different civil war would be fired. The impressive display of popular unity which defeated Kornilov would be torn asunder, and Bolshevik and SR forces would be spoiling to fight each other for control over the destiny of the Russian Revolution. At the same time, the majority of Russia's socialists would work to smother that fighting, to seek a compromise and prevent at all costs the outbreak of a Red versus Green civil war.

Although in retrospect the Kornilov rebellion was a thoroughly botched affair, it had a profound effect on the development of the Russian Revolution. Despite all the efforts of liberal politicians to distance themselves from the plotters, in the popular imagination the liberals had been as committed to counter-revolution as the generals. After the Kornilov rebellion, what was known at the time as 'democracy', i.e. all those who owned no property and had thus been effectively disenfranchized under the *ancien régime*, turned against the idea of continuing a coalition government with the liberals; property-owners should henceforth be excluded from government.

The most important group to be affected in this way were the soldiers. After the Kornilov rebellion, soldiers no longer trusted their officers and wanted an end to the war. After the Kornilov rebellion, there was constant pressure to re-elect soldiers' committees, to replace pro-war Mensheviks or SRs with anti-war Bolsheviks. This change in stance of the soldiers was of major importance, for it distinguished the political atmosphere of the autumn from the ill-fated Bolshevik demonstrations of July. In July, indeed even earlier, working-class members of the Petrograd Soviet had voted in favour of ending the coalition with the 'bourgeois parties' and forming a soviet government; it was the soldiers' representatives who prevented this resolution being passed. In September, however, in the immediate aftermath of Kornilov's rebellion, both the Petrograd and Moscow Soviets supported a Bolshevik resolution calling for a soviet government and the key change was that on this occasion the soldiers joined with the workers in making this demand. The Kornilov rebellion launched a second revolution in Russia, a revolution in which democracy demanded a soviet government.

In this context the chances of a civil war erupting, particularly a civil war between White counter-revolutionary generals like Kornilov and the parties represented in the soviet, were minimal. But a civil war 'within democracy', a civil war between extreme and moderate socialists, Bolsheviks and SRs, Reds and Greens, an unthinkable civil war of this sort was a possibility, since socialists disagreed about the best way forward for the Russian Revolution. Kerensky wanted to form a third coalition government; a majority of socialists, Bolsheviks, Mensheviks and SRs wanted to form a government from those parties represented in the soviet; and Lenin wanted to form a Bolshevik government. In this three cornered fight, there were those quite prepared to resort to arms.

## THE POLITICS OF COALITION

After the collapse of the Kornilov rebellion Russia was faced with two clear choices: counter-revolution was no longer on the agenda, but should the government be a coalition, between liberals and the socialists, or should it be a 'democratic coalition' composed only of those parties represented in the soviet. The impetus for a democratic coalition was almost irresistible in the atmosphere of a second revolution experienced in the aftermath of Kornilov's rebellion. Such was the popular anger against the liberals that the Menshevik and SR delegations to the soviet voted to reject any future collaboration with the liberal Kadet Party. Even Lenin was persuaded, momentarily, of the enormous prospects opened up by such a democratic coalition. When on 1 September Petrograd was swept by rumours that the SR leader V.M. Chernov was about to head a new government which would include Bolsheviks in charge of key ministries, Lenin wrote the essay *On Compromises* in which he supported the idea of the SRs and the Mensheviks forming a government responsible to the soviet. The Bolsheviks, he suggested, could not accept portfolios in such a government, but neither would they campaign against it until the Constituent Assembly elections were held.[1]

A similar proposal was simultaneously put to the Petrograd Soviet by the leader of the Bolshevik delegation L.B. Kamenev. As, during the crisis days of 31 August to 2 September, the soviet debated the future of the government, Kamenev called for an end to the present coalition and the formation of a government of workers and peasants; this would not be a soviet government as such, since not all sections of the working population were represented in the soviets, but a democratic government to include representatives of the trades unions and local councils as well. This Bolshevik call was endorsed by the Petrograd Soviet on 1 September, but such was the degree of agreement between the socialist parties at this moment that this resolution was not substantially different from the Menshevik policy of an all-socialist ministry responsible to the so-called Democratic Conference, an organization summoned by the soviet in response to the new political situation created by the Kornilov rebellion.[2]

The soviet had called the Democratic Conference as a counter-weight to the Moscow State Conference which had served as such a focal point for Kornilov's machinations. In the new political climate a forum was clearly needed for Russian democracy, but the Petrograd Soviet, while providing a potent forum for factory workers and soldiers, had no peasant representation nor any representation from the other soviets throughout Russia, and thus could not claim to represent fully the broad mass of non-property-owners. Summoning a Democratic Conference caused socialist politicians few problems; debate focused on what powers this institution should have. When it opened on 14 September, Kamenev spoke out for a policy clearly acceptable to many SRs and Mensheviks: 'the only way out is this,' he said, 'power must not be a coalition [with the Kadets]; power must pass into the hands of democracy, not to the Soviet of Workers' and Soldiers' Deputies, but into the hands of democracy which is quite fully represented here today; the government must be formed here'.[3] The degree of support for such a proposal was seen when the presidium of the Democratic Conference voted sixty for and fifty against the proposal for a socialist ministry, supported but not joined by the Bolsheviks, to govern until the Second Congress of Soviets met in October, when the situation could be reviewed.[4]

The intervening two weeks between the collapse of Kornilov's rebellion and the summoning of the Democratic Conference had given Kerensky time to manoeuvre and martial those forces which favoured a new coalition government. During the Democratic Conference backstage deals and contradictory votes enabled Kerensky to impose his own agenda on the proceedings. It was eventually decided that the government would remain a coalition, excluding only those liberals who had openly sided with Kornilov, and would not be responsible to the Democratic Conference; indeed, it would be responsible to no specific organization but would instead listen to the views of a new body to be called the Preparliament. Unlike the Democratic Conference summoned by the soviet, Kerensky's proposed Preparliament would represent both democracy and the property-owning bourgeois classes. While this would clearly make the Preparliament more fully representative of the Russian population than the Democratic Conference, it ignored the new popular mood of a second revolution: it seemed a device designed artificially to restore property-owners to a position of influence when their attitude during the Kornilov rebellion had deprived them of that privilege; the Preparliament seemed designed to stop the second revolution and restore the pre-Kornilov status quo.[5]

Understandably, Kerensky's triumph at the Democratic Conference and his success in winning support for a Preparliament breathed new life into the idea of a coalition and he was finally able to form his Third Coalition Government. This infuriated the proponents of a democratic coalition: the Bolsheviks were understandably very angry; but equally the Menshevik Central Committee was unhappy with these changes in which its original principle of a government responsible to the Democratic Conference had been surrendered. Even more dramatically unhappy was the SR leader Chernov who ceased to attend the SR Central Committee and announced his intention of boycotting the Preparliament in protest at his party's decision on 24 September to endorse continued SR participation in Kerensky's Third Coalition.[6]

The SRs had already suffered one split at the end of April 1917 at the time of the street demonstrations in Petrograd when the extreme right of the party had disassociated itself from the party daily *Delo naroda* and founded a rival paper *Volya naroda*. This venture was edited by the pro-war moderate Argunov, whose name had featured in some of Kornilov's fantasy governments, and was funded by the former populist and 'Grandmother of the Russian Revolution' E.K. Breshko-Breshkovskaya. Its editorial board included S.S. Maslov, P.A. Sorokin, and V.I. Lebedev, appointed Navy Minister in August 1917: all would become active participants in the Red versus Green civil war of 1918. This group remained in the party, but was increasingly willing to collaborate with the Popular Socialist Party. By the autumn of 1917 Chernov, who stood at the centre, was finding it increasingly difficult to keep control of a party, some of whose members were outspoken supporters of Kerensky – himself an SR – while others were bitterly hostile towards him. After Kornilov's rebellion, the left of the party was determined to form a democratic coalition government and break with Kerensky. By the time of the Democratic Conference politicians like L.A. Kalegaev, V.A. Karelin and P.P. Proshyan were no longer prepared to abide by Central Committee instructions concerning tactics. These Left SRs were well on the way to becoming a separate party, and it was to exacerbate the clear divisions within the SR Party, and indeed the Menshevik Party, between a stated policy of support for a democratic coalition and the presence of their leaders in a Third Coalition Government which persuaded Kamenev that the Bolsheviks should take an active part in the Preparliament; it could, he believed, be used to discredit Kerensky and eventually bring his government down.

Kerensky's Third Coalition Government was indeed built on very shaky foundations. The crucial role in frustrating those wanting to use the Democratic Conference to establish a democratic coalition had been played by right-wing SRs and Popular Socialists active in the co-operative movement. Since the defeat of the 1905 Revolution many Popular Socialists and some like-minded SRs, tired of revolutionary politics, had turned to co-operation as a means of bringing practical help to the peasants. By 1917 these co-operatives were well established and the biggest single vote at the Democratic Conference in favour of the principle of renewing the coalition came from the co-operative societies.[7] The co-operatives were, therefore, the key group in any attempt by Kerensky to build a political base within the Preparliament and their representatives were rewarded with several posts in the Third Coalition Government. However, those most active in support of Kerensky within the Preparliament were not the representatives of the co-operative societies, but the left-wing members of the Kadet Party. The Kornilov rebellion had forced many leading Kadets, like Milyukov, to flee Petrograd. Those who remained tended to be on the left of the party, and resolved to use the

Preparliament as a last redoubt from which to fight the Bolshevik menace.

Although the Kadets devoted considerable energy to trying to firm up a pro-coalition grouping within the Preparliament – a special party liaison group of Nabokov, Shingarev and M.S. Adzhemov met daily to co-ordinate strategy: Adzhemov was responsible for drafting most of the statutes governing the activities of the Preparliament – their strategy remained problematical. They needed to win the Popular Socialists, who were closely allied to the co-operative societies, away from the idea of a democratic coalition. However, at their congress on 26 September 1917 the Popular Socialists discussed their tactics for the forthcoming Constituent Assembly elections, and, far from building on an alliance with the Kadets, they voted against a proposal for improved links with the Kadets and insisted that alliances could only be formed with other socialist groups. More worryingly for the Kadets, at an emergency congress on 4 October the co-operative societies also rejected the idea of joint candidates with non-socialist groups.[8]

When Kerensky's Preparliament opened on 7 October under the chairmanship of the Right SR N.D. Avksentiev the pro-coalition grouping did begin to function, strengthened on 13–14 October when a second Meeting of Public Figures met in Moscow and resolved that it was 'not only permissable but desirable to associate with the Popular Socialist group'; the 10th Kadet Party Congress equally voted in favour of continuing to build the coalition. However, this unity did not survive the transition from abstract rhetoric to practical politics. On 10 October the Preparliament began to debate the fighting capacity of the army. With the aim of building a coalition, the Popular Socialist leader N.V. Chaikovskii, a peasant socialist since the 1870s and chief representative of the co-operative societies, drafted a programme for the coalition on 18 October which succeeded in uniting Popular Socialists, the co-operative societies, the Peasants' Union, Plekhanov's Unity group, with representatives of industry, the cossacks, the Public Figures and the Kadets in supporting the government; but this victory was transitory – although passed on a show of hands by five votes, a recount deprived the coalition of its first and only triumph.[9]

Indeed, this coalition was soon disintegrating. The key figure in this process was Kerensky's new Defence Minister General A.I. Verkhovskii, a man whose political views were close to those of the Popular Socialists. To the growing anger of the Kadets, and increasing alarm of Kerensky, he argued that the only way forward for Russia was to come to terms with democracy and recognize the key demands of the democratic coalition, or as he expressed it 'finding grounds for a compromise with the Bolsheviks'. He had been in conflict with Kerensky almost from the moment of his appointment. As early as 5 September he confided in his diary that Kerensky would have to go and that the government controlled little more than the Winter Palace. By 25 September he concluded that all the old political leaders had had their day. By 30 September he was convinced that the only way the masses, and by implication the Bolsheviks, could be persuaded to work for the defence of the country was for a peace proposal to be advanced by the Allies and for the Germans to reject it: 'only then would we create a volunteer army truly up to the task'. Verkhovskii succeeded in persuading the socialist members of the Third Coalition Government, including Kerensky, to agree that his proposal should be put to the Inter-Allied Conference due to be held in Paris at the end of October. However, the Foreign Minister M.I. Tereshchenko, who was to represent Russia at the conference, could not be persuaded, and neither could the Kadet Party with which he was associated. As a consequence, Verkhovskii resigned on 19 October, a resignation caused by disagreements within the coalition.[10]

The hopes of the coalition finally foundered on 24 October. Since 6 October the Commander of the Petrograd Military District had been under orders to prepare the troops of the Petrograd garrison for transfer to the front, since a German attack seemed imminent. The soldiers concerned reacted with fury, and to prevent this transfer happening the Petrograd Soviet, with a Bolshevik majority since the vote of 1 September, established a Military Revolutionary Committee (MRC) on 16 October. By 21 October the government and the MRC were at loggerheads and the MRC informed the Petrograd Military District that henceforth soldiers would only obey orders countersigned by the MRC; to ensure this happened the MRC would appoint its own commissars to military units. Then, when on 23 October its commissars were in place, the MRC announced that these commissars had the right to veto all military orders. Faced with what was tantamount to mutiny, the government announced on 24 October that criminal proceedings against the MRC would begin and moved to close down those Bolshevik newspapers supporting the MRC and its commissars. Against this background the Preparliament gathered later on 24 October to debate a motion of no confidence in the government's handling of the situation.[11] As in the Preparliament the Kadets gathered the forces of the coalition for a resolution in defence of the government, they were faced with the abstention of the co-operative leaders; if their abstentions had been added to the votes rallied by the Kadets, the vote of no confidence would have been defeated by five votes and the government might have survived. As it was, the Preparliament passed a vote of no confidence in Kerensky's government.[12]

Back in September, during the backstage intrigue which had surrounded proceedings at the Democratic Conference, a form of words had been adopted to describe the precise relationship between the Preparliament and the government. It was agreed that 'power must belong to a government which had the trust of the Preparliament': since Kerensky's government no longer had that trust, it had effectively been sacked by the vote of 24 October. In passing this vote of no confidence, the Preparliament also called for action on the most important issues of the day: land had to be transferred to the land committees, and peace talks had to begin at once in consultation with the Allies. Not surprisingly, the left wing of the Menshevik Party and the Left SRs began to revive talk of forming a government responsible to the Democratic Conference; a so-called 'Revolutionary Convention' would be formed by expelling the propertied classes from the Preparliament.[13]

Kerensky's Third Coalition Government collapsed on 24 October. There was no objective danger of this leading to civil war, since Kerensky had simply lost the authority to govern by rejecting the ever more vociferous calls for a democratic coalition government and insisting on the need to retain a liberal–socialist coalition. When even the Popular Socialists rejected such a coalition, Kerensky's fate was sealed. Just what would replace Kerensky's coalition was uncertain, but whatever government was formed, it would have to come to terms with the delegates to the Second Congress of Soviets, gathering in Petrograd at that very moment. The congress was due to open on 25 October, but before it did so Lenin and his supporters in the Bolshevik Party had seized power in a coup executed during the night of 24–25 October.

## LENIN AND THE BOLSHEVIK SEIZURE OF POWER

That the successful campaign to discredit the Third Coalition Government and overthrow it within the parliamentary atmosphere of the Preparliament did not result in the formation of a democratic coalition was the fault of the Bolshevik Party. Ever since Kerensky had taken the decision to call the Preparliament, the Bolshevik Party had been torn apart by an internal factional dispute on the issue of how best to achieve its aims. The soviet delegation, the parliamentary wing of the party as it were, led by Kamenev, was convinced that the government's hold over the Preparliament was so shaky that the Bolsheviks could easily lead the opposition to it; when it fell, as inevitably it would, the Bolsheviks would become the dominant group in a new democratic coalition government, which would prepare the way for the party emerging as the dominant force in the Constituent Assembly. Lenin's wing of the party took a very different view.

If Kamenev was a pragmatist, obsessed with the sort of day-to-day petty politicking and horse-trading which could bring the party possibly to absolute power, but certainly to the position of power broker, and that without a drop of blood being shed, Lenin was the dogmatic theoretician. Divorced from practical politics since July when a warrant had been issued for his arrest as a German agent who had instigated the July Days demonstrations, Lenin had immersed himself in political theory. His main work was *State and Revolution*, a volume in which he drew repeated parallels between his view of Russia in 1917 and the Paris Commune of 1871, and in which he stressed the lessons which needed to be drawn from such parallels if a new society were to be constructed. For Marx and Engels the Paris Commune had been 'the civil war in France' and the heroic attempt of workers' Paris to construct a new society in the teeth of opposition not only from the external enemy, Prussia, but also opposition from the rest of France. Lenin was convinced that a Petrograd Commune could succeed in the changed circumstances of 1917. Developments within capitalism since 1871 had created an interrelated economy of imperial states in which Russia served as the weak link in the chain: the Petrograd Commune would not be isolated as the Paris Commune had been, since the revolution in Russia would soon spread throughout Europe as imperialist economies collapsed one after another. For Lenin the opportunity to construct Marxian socialism was being presented to the Bolsheviks, if they would only broaden their horizons and stop looking no further forward than the next meeting of the Preparliament or how to ensure they emerged as the biggest single party after the Constituent Assembly elections.

The prospect of constructing the first Marxist state in history, of acting as the agent of history itself in opening up a whole new socialist epoch, justified for Lenin the most undemocratic of actions. With the right coalition visibly losing power by the minute, it was essential from his perspective that power did not get transferred to a democratic coalition, no matter how large the Bolshevik representation within it.

Such a government could only address the democratic issues of peace, land and worker participation in industry; it would not address the agenda of world socialism. Lenin therefore wanted power before such a government could be formed, and this meant seizing power before the unpopular Third Coalition Government actually collapsed, not after it had collapsed. From Lenin's point if view, it would be a disaster for the Second Congress of Soviets, planned for mid-October, to meet and endorse the idea of a democratic coalition government. Lenin needed to pretend he was seizing power from the unpopular 'bourgeois' right coalition, when in reality he would be depriving of power a democratic coalition of socialists not yet formed.

In private Lenin made no secret of his plans. On 30 August, in a *Letter to the Central Committee*, he urged Bolsheviks to be careful in their propaganda not to talk about seizing power too openly: 'we must speak about [taking power] as little as possible in agitation (remembering very well that even tomorrow events may put us in power and then we will not let it go)'.[14] Although at the same time, on 1 September, he wrote in *On Compromises* of the possibility of forming a democratic coalition in the aftermath of the Kornilov affair, he added as a postscript on 3 September that the moment for compromise might even have passed already, and within days he had changed his mind completely.[15] In *The Russian Revolution and the Civil War*, written on 8–9 September 1917, Lenin mapped out two possible scenarios for the Russian Revolution, one a continuation of the theme of coalition aired in *On Compromises*, and the other a bold call for civil war. Of the coalition tactic he wrote:

> if there is an absolutely undisputed lesson of the revolution, one fully proven by the facts, it is that only an alliance of the Bolsheviks with the Mensheviks and the SRs, only an immediate transfer of power to the soviets would make civil war in Russia impossible . . . A peaceful development of the revolution is possible and probable if all power is transferred to the soviets. The struggle of parties for power within the soviets may proceed peacefully, if the soviets are made fully democratic.

The other tactic of insurrection and 'a civil war in its highest and most decisive form' was equally possible, for 'we have learned much since the Paris Commune and would not repeat its fatal errors'.[16]

In Lenin's mind, which of the tactics to be pursued depended on the Mensheviks and the SRs. If the Mensheviks and the SRs remained stubbornly loyal to an alliance with the liberals, and the masses moved over to the Bolsheviks, the tactic of civil war should be followed. There was no suggestion in Lenin's writing that the civil war option could harm the revolution or that the peaceful transfer of power was in any way more desirable. By mid-September, with support for the Bolsheviks clearly growing and the Menshevik and SR leaderships beginning to waver in their opposition to a coalition as the Democratic Conference approached, Lenin dropped the idea of a transfer of power through soviet democracy and opted clearly for civil war. His letters to the Central Committee, *Bolsheviks Must Take Power* and *Marxism and Insurrection*, written on 12–14 September, argued that the Mensheviks and SRs had rejected a compromise: 'it would be a great mistake to think that our offer of a compromise had not yet been rejected and that the Democratic Conference may still accept it . . .'. Compromise had been rejected and the way forward for the Bolsheviks was insurrection, an insurrection which would start a civil war.[17]

The problem for Lenin was that his obsessive desire to implement an experiment in social engineering on an unprecedented scale was not shared by the whole of his party. Lenin's letters to the Central Committee of mid-September were ignored; only one copy was kept and activists were instructed to prevent any demonstrations in factories or barracks. As Lenin became increasingly angry at the way the Central Committee immersed itself in the parliamentary life of the Democratic Conference and ignored the appeal for direct action, he began to contact like-minded spirits, talking always of the prospects for worldwide revolution, and always stressing that power should be seized before the Second Congress of Soviets met. The party nevertheless continued to develop its parliamentary tactic. Ignoring Lenin's wish that the Preparliament be boycotted, the Central Committee decided that its own vote on the matter on 21 September had been so close (nine to eight), that the final decision should be left to a joint meeting of the Central Committee and the party's dele-gation to the Democratic Conference; this voted 77 to 50 to participate. As a result, two days later the Central Committee was discussing its attitude to the question of forming a 'ministry of similar parties', or a socialist coalition.

Under constant pressure from Lenin, the Central Committee began to reconsider its stance. On 24 September it decided to reduce the importance of parliamentary tactics by making activity in the Preparliament secondary to its other work; but that work was not defined as preparing for an insurrection before the Congress of Soviets met, as Lenin wished, but as the formation at the Second Congress of Soviets of a democratic coalition government. It took Lenin's threat of resignation on 29 September to make the Central Committee change its stance, and then only on the question of the Preparliament. On 3 October the Central Committee asked Lenin to move nearer to Petrograd, and on 5 October it was agreed to stage a demonstrative walk-out from the Preparliament. Yet even then Lenin had not got his way completely. On 10 October, as the Preparliament began its crucial debate on the state of the army, the Central Committee passed a resolution which talked of the revolution entering the era of insurrection, but no date for an insurrection was set, and certainly no date before the Second Congress of Soviets.

The Bolshevik Central Committee was split and had reached a form of stasis. Although Kamenev's papers in favour of parliamentary tactics were rejected, the Central Committee's support for insurrection remained rhetorical and Lenin's view that power had to be seized before the Second Congress of Soviets met was never endorsed. Thus on 16 October when an expanded session of the Central Committee sought to resolve the issue, the final resolution simply reaffirmed the imprecise decision of 10 October. Kamenev noted with ill-concealed glee that despite the opprobrium heaped upon him, the party was no longer talking, if it ever had been, of an insurrection before the Second Congress of Soviets. In fact, the general tenor of the 16 October discussion was that the mood of the masses was against an insurrection, and certainly would not support one led by the Bolshevik Party as Lenin wanted. The masses would, many delegates noted, only follow the lead of the Petrograd Soviet, or one of its sub-committees like the Military Revolutionary Committee, if it called on them to defend the gains of the revolution.[18]

Thus the Bolsheviks stumbled into insurrection. The garrison crisis prompted the Petrograd Soviet to establish its MRC on 16 October, a committee dominated by the Bolsheviks. It moved from open confrontation with the government towards a direct challenge to the government on 24 October, an event which prompted the Pre-parliament to deprive the Third Coalition Government of its moral authority to govern. The delegates gathering for the Second Congress of Soviets then began to prepare to announce the formation of a new democratic coalition, a government of the socialist parties represented in the soviets. At the very last minute Lenin could snatch victory from the jaws of defeat if he could persuade the Bolshevik Party that the MRC, which already effectively controlled the city's garrison, should seize power on behalf of the party – thus his frantic message of 24 October as he sought to convene the Bolshevik Central Committee.

> I am writing these lines on the evening of the 24th. In fact it is now absolutely clear that to delay the uprising would be fatal. With all my

might I urge comrades to realize that everything now hangs by a thread; that we are confronted by problems which are not to be solved by conferences or congresses . . . We must at all costs, this very evening, this very night, arrest the government . . . We must not wait! We may lose everything! . . . Under no circumstances should power be left in the hands of Kerensky and Co. until the 25th; the matter must be decided without fail this very evening . . .[19]

Sometime during the early hours of 25 October the Central Committee met and adopted Lenin's course. A full 24 hours after the MRC's confrontation with the government had begun, and less than twelve hours before the Second Congress of Soviets opened, Lenin finally persuaded his colleagues that they should make the most of the military advantage they had, and achieve his long-held objective of seizing power before the Second Congress of Soviets opened. Events had indeed 'put the Bolsheviks in power', and Lenin, true to his letter of 30 August, was determined not to let it go, even though the path he had adopted – of preventing power from being peacefully transferred from a right coalition to a democratic coalition – risked the danger of civil war within democracy. Lenin had succeeded in seizing power not from the bourgeoisie and the liberals, but from democracy, and its dominant voice, the SR Party.

## THE RAILWAY WORKERS' UNION TALKS

As Lenin directed operations from the Bolshevik Party headquarters at Smolny, and Kerensky made his escape from the Winter Palace under siege by Lenin's forces, the moderate socialists continued to work for the constitutional transfer of power from Kerensky to a new government. On the afternoon of 24 October the Menshevik delegation to the Second Congress of Soviets met to draw up tactics and resolved that a complete reconstruction of power was essential and that a democratic coalition government had to be formed. While condemning the Bolsheviks' mutinous activities within the MRC, they blamed Kerensky's Third Coalition Government for provoking it and, as rumours of fighting came in, ruled out any attempt to use force against the Bolshevik insurgents. The same day the SR-controlled Petrograd City Council called for the formation of a democratic coalition government. Then, when the Second Congress of Soviets opened on the afternoon of 25 October, the Menshevik proposal that a coalition socialist government be formed as the only way of peacefully resolving the crisis was passed unanimously.[20]

The next day the Mensheviks again tried to work for reconciliation. In protest at Lenin's action the SRs, led by M. Ya Gendelman and joined by some right-wing Mensheviks, decided to walk out of the Second Congress of Soviets and establish a rival body which they called the Committee for the Salvation of the Revolution and the Motherland (CSRM). On 26 October the Menshevik leader Yu O. Martov sought to open talks between those socialists who had walked out of the Second Congress of Soviets, and those who had stayed behind; the aim of the talks was to establish a democratic coalition government of Bolsheviks, Mensheviks and SRs. Within the Second Congress of Soviets a similar proposal was advanced by the left-wing members of the SR Party[21] who at this time formally resolved to establish themselves as a separate party: they, unlike the SR Party proper did not walk out of the Second Congress of Soviets, but recognized its legitimacy. The cause of reconciliation was then taken up dramatically by the leadership of the Railway Workers' Union. The Railway Workers' Union wanted to stop what appeared to be the nascent civil war between the Bolsheviks and the SRs, a Red versus Green civil war within the democratic camp. On arriving in the capital on 26 October, the Railway Workers' Union executive's delegation to the Second Congress of Soviets immediately adopted the stance the union would pursue throughout the following week: it told fellow delegates that, as it was then constituted, the congress was an unrepresentative body; the Bolsheviks had split the democratic front. The Railway Workers' Union therefore opposed the seizure of power by one party, called for a revolutionary government to be made responsible to revolutionary democracy, and announced that until that moment had come it would supervise all railway movements. After talks with both the Bolsheviks and the CSRM, it refined these demands into the neutrality statement issued on 28 October: this called for the formation of a government composed of all socialist parties from Bolsheviks to Popular Socialists, inclusive of both these, which would be responsible to a legislative body representing revolutionary democracy and would hold power until the Constituent Assembly met. A strike would be called if any force were used against members of the union seeking to implement this policy. Negotiations with the aim of establishing such a democratic socialist government were to begin at once.[22]

From the start those Bolsheviks not involved in the armed insurrection accepted the programme of the Railway Workers' Union.

On 28 October D.B. Ryazanov, who had opposed insurrection in the Bolshevik Central Committee, acted as an intermediary between the MRC and the Railway Workers' Union, and invited a delegation to talks later that evening; at these talks Kamenev stated that the Bolshevik Party endorsed the Railway Workers' Union programme. In its report to its Moscow headquarters the next day, the Railway Workers' Union could state: 'the Bolsheviks are making concessions and have accepted our programme. The Committee of Salvation [CSRM] is irreconcilable, but we will exert pressure on it . . .'. The Railway Workers' Union already believed it had the support not only of right-wing 'parliamentary' Bolsheviks, but all the other leftist groups, the Menshevik Internationalists, the Social Democrat Internationalists, the Left SRs, the Polish and Jewish socialist groups, plus some centrist SRs and the Council of Trade Unions.[23]

The chances of the Railway Workers' Union succeeding in its mission were greatly improved by the difficulties being experienced by those SRs and right-wing Mensheviks who had walked out of the Second Congress of Soviets to establish the CSRM; they now had to ask themselves if by so doing they wanted to re-establish a Kerensky-style coalition with the liberals. The liberals threw in their lot with the CSRM only to find no-one really wanted them. Although the CSRM had adopted the name 'motherland' at the insistence of the liberals, their influence ended there; those liberals who attended the CSRM did so as members of the city council and the Preparliament, not as members of the Kadet Party which was not represented on the CSRM executive. The divisions in the CSRM were noted by the British ambassador Sir George Buchanan who recorded that while some wanted a socialist government which would 'rely on the support of the Kadets', others were 'in favour of adopting the Bolshevik programme with regard to peace and the land'.[24]

These divisions within the CSRM camp were echoed in the question mark that hung over the future of Kerensky. Planning to overthrow the Bolsheviks by force and thus pour fuel on the simmering Red–Green civil war, he had fled Petrograd in search of loyal troops. He had little luck. Leaving at 11.00 a.m. on the morning of 25 October, he went to Pskov, the headquarters of the Northern Army, where he found few loyal troops. Only the Third Cavalry Regiment, a cossack regiment led by General Krasnov, was prepared to rally to his side; thus on 27 October Krasnov and Kerensky moved back towards Petrograd to base themselves at Gatchina. There they were joined by Chief Army Commissar V.B. Stankevich, who left Petrograd on the 26th with news that the CSRM had drawn up plans for an insurrection to be co-ordinated with Krasnov's advance. When Stankevich returned to Petrograd on 28 October he learned that little support for Kerensky remained. From the start the CSRM had been split over whether or not to insist on the restoration of Kerensky, and therefore a liberal–socialist coalition, or accept that Kerensky was a spent force and settle for a socialist administration, but preferably one excluding the Bolsheviks.

After talks with the Railway Workers' Union on 28 October, the CSRM came down in favour of abandoning Kerensky and supporting the idea of a socialist government. Although it wanted the Bolsheviks to be excluded from this government – something the Railway Workers' Union would not accept – this socialist government would give land to the peasants and establish peace without annexations, a stance also adopted by the SR Central Committee on the 28th.[25] In these talks the CSRM representatives, the Menshevik Skobelev and the SR V.M. Zenzinov rejected the idea of a liberal–socialist coalition and were scathing about Kerensky: Skobelev not only said Kerensky 'would not form part of any combination of ministers proposed by us', but added that if Kerensky refused to transfer power to a new socialist administration based on the CSRM, the CSRM would 'use all permissible methods to fight him, just as they were fighting the Bolsheviks'.[26]

However, the extent of the divisions within the CSRM can be seen from the fact that, despite what Skobelev and Zenzinov said, other Mensheviks and the co-operative leaders saw the main purpose of the CSRM as being to restore the Kerensky government; the SR Military Commission, put at the disposal of the CSRM, was already in touch with the officers' training corps, known as the Junkers, and even such Kornilovite officers as Colonel Finberg, leader of the Union of Military Duty. It was they who, unbeknown to many of the CSRM leaders, planned to stage an insurrection as Krasnov's troops reached the capital, and Stankevich's news on the 28th that these troops were at Gatchina led them to hasten their preparations. Unfortunately for them, in the early hours of 29 October, the Bolsheviks arrested a CSRM courier taking a message to the Junker officer school about how their proposed insurrection could be co-ordinated with that of the advancing cossacks; unnerved by this arrest, the Junkers began their insurrection prematurely as dawn broke on the 29th and by midday had been easily outgunned.[27]

This outbreak of fighting infuriated the Railway Workers' Union. It occurred the day after the Railway Workers' Union had been promised the CSRM would attend talks aimed at establishing a democratic socialist government. To prevent further double-dealing the Railway Workers' Union issued an ultimatum on 29 October. 'Democracy', the Railway Workers' Union argued, 'could not decide its internal disagreements by blood and iron', the only victor should this happen would be counter-revolution. The union would therefore organize a strike to:

> bring pressure to bear on the madmen who at this moment, out of personal interest, do not want to compromise. Instead of striving for a compromise, the right part of democracy [CSRM] . . . put to the Bolsheviks the impossible demand of total capitulation, quite unconcerned for the consequences.[28]

Meanwhile the Bolsheviks continued to be ready to compromise. On the afternoon of 29 October the Central Committee debated the issue of broadening the government as the Railway Workers' Union had asked, including the proposal that the Popular Socialists be included in the government and that Lenin and Trotsky be dropped as ministers. Neither of these points of detail was agreed, but the principle of broadening the government was approved by all present, and Kamenev and fellow Central Committee member G. Ya Sokolnikov were delegated to attend the talks.[29] In his opening statement to the Railway Workers' Union Conference on the evening of the 29th, Kamenev made clear that he favoured a government composed of all parties represented in the soviet. Sokolnikov, sent as a counter-weight to the 'soft' Kamenev, could also sound conciliatory; he reminded delegates that in mid-September the Bolsheviks had proposed an all-socialist government to the Democratic Conference, and would even now be quite willing to transfer power to the Constituent Assembly as soon as it met.

The divisions among members of the CSRM were as clear as ever on the 29th. Its official viewpoint was put to the Railway Workers' Union talks by one of its Menshevik members; but the most vociferous in opposing the position adopted by the Railway Workers' Union was Gendelman, the SR Central Committee member who had led the walk-out from the Second Congress of Soviets. His rejection of the inclusion of Bolsheviks in the government, and his refusal even to sit down together with them, included the declaration that 'even in the democratic camp there are moments when it is necessary to decide an argument with weapons'. This apparent call to arms caused a furore; he was not supported by the representative of the Union of Municipal Employees, a leading force in the CSRM, while F.I. Dan, for the Mensheviks, said he had no interest in using force against the

Bolsheviks. He suggested that the easiest way to struggle against the Bolsheviks was to include them in government: 'everyone would prefer it if the Bolsheviks were inside rather than outside the government', he said.

Most of the delegates to the talks favoured a solution on the lines adopted by the Railway Workers' Union, with the Left SRs and the Mensheviks putting forward positive proposals. Martov, for the Mensheviks, was the more articulate, stressing the importance of policies over personalities and reminding those present that in the last hour of its existence, the Preparliament had united around the basic programme of a future socialist government: the demand for talks about an immediate peace; the transfer of land to the land committees; and the calling of the Constituent Assembly. This programme was put forward 'by life itself': an interim government committed to this programme should be responsible not only to the soviets but to all organizations elected by universal suffrage, he concluded.[30]

Nevertheless the CSRM was still unwilling to back down on the question of Bolshevik membership of the government. A commission comprising one Menshevik, one SR, a representative of the city council, three Bolsheviks (Kamenev, Ryazanov and Sokolnikov), with a chairman from the Railway Workers' Union met all night but made no progress. By 7.30 a.m. on the 30th a second session of talks merely heard a repeat of the previous opening statements. Pressure for an agreement was increased, however, by the arrival of a delegation of workers from one of Petrograd's biggest industrial plants, the Obukhov factory. They demanded to know what was delaying an agreement among the socialist parties, and endorsed the Railway Workers' Union programme saying: 'we'll drop your Lenin, Trotsky and Kerensky into the same hole in the ice if workers' blood is spilt for your dirty business'.[31]

Thus, when on the evening of 30 October the talks returned to the question of a future government, the Mensheviks and SRs were far readier to be conciliatory. The SR V.N. Filipovskii was clearly embarrassed by the Junker rising, which he roundly condemned, insisting that as a member of the CSRM he had known nothing about it. Another SR representative announced that while the party could not join a government 'which originated from the Bolshevik coup', it would be prepared to support a government 'of individuals'. While Kamenev expressed some reservations about the principle of this, he stressed that he had no interest in quibbling about the number and status of various government posts. Like Martov, he argued that it was the programme and the representative body that were the most important issues.[32] The Mensheviks were even more conciliatory. Dan softened his attitude throughout the session: at first he made clear that while he favoured Bolshevik participation, he knew it would never be acceptable to the Popular Socialists whose participation in government he considered absolutely essential; later he made it clear that while he would never join a government which included the Bolsheviks, he and his party would be able to support such a government.[33]

With this degree of agreement among the various factions, they decided to set up a commission to establish the personnel of the new government and the nature of the democratic representative body to which it should be responsible until the Constituent Assembly could be summoned. The work of this commission continued the conciliatory tone. That evening, the 30th, a resolution condemning civil war and terror was drawn up and agreed, and it was established that the core of the new representative body would be the soviet with additional representatives from the trades unions and the city council.[34] This was endorsed by the SR Central Committee on 31 October when it dropped its demand for the recall of the Preparliament. The same day the Menshevik Central Committee formally endorsed the Railway Workers' Union call for a socialist government to include the Bolsheviks.[35] Even the tricky question of who was to be a minister in the new government caused few problems. The Menshevik, SR and Petrograd City Council representatives vetoed the participation of Lenin and Trotsky, while the Bolsheviks vetoed Kerensky and Avksentiev. The Bolshevik representatives, however, did not insist on Lenin's candidacy, and despite some concern that the Allies might have reservations, the SR leader Chernov was agreed as the most likely candidate for Prime Minister. The Menshevik Skobelev was rejected as Minister of Foreign Affairs in favour of the Bolshevik historian M.N. Pokrovskii, but Verkhovskii, Minister of Defence in the Third Coalition Government until his resignation, was to be given the same job in this all-socialist administration, with an SR as Minister of Agriculture, the Bolshevik L.B. Krasin as Minister of Industry and the Bolshevik A.I. Rykov as Minister of the Interior. By the end of 31 October the personnel of the government had been agreed.[36]

The conciliatory stance of the CSRM was not unconnected with events on Pulkovo Heights on 30–31 October where the first set-piece battle of the Red versus Green civil war had just taken place outside Petrograd. In order to reassess the situation after his visit to Petrograd on the 28th, the CSRM's contact person with Kerensky, Army Commissar Stankevich had returned to Gatchina, and with the help of Savinkov who was also present persuaded Kerensky that an effort should be made to fight; meanwhile time could be bought by feigning to agree to the call by the Railway Workers' Union for a cease-fire. Even so, the prospects for a successful attack were not good. General Krasnov had already been told by his cossacks that unless there was infantry support, they were unwilling to fight, and Savinkov's tour of surrounding units had yielded no volunteers to join the fray. Although Krasnov had a large quantity of arms – one armoured car, one armoured train and several airplanes – he had only 1,000 men. Thus as Krasnov's troops approached Pulkovo Heights on 30 October to be met by Bolshevik Red Guards led by the Left SR Lieutenant-Colonel M.A. Muraviev,[37] morale was already low. Muraviev had mustered between 8–10,000 men, haphazardly dug in and lightly armed – in fact many were unarmed – but with sufficient fire-power from their machine gun positions on the high ground to prevent the cossack advance. Krasnov hoped to induce panic by one devastating cavalry charge: when that failed, the battle degenerated into desultory exchanges of fire until, at the end of the day, the cossacks retreated to Gatchina.

The next day, 31 October, Red sailors led by the charismatic Bolshevik commander P.E. Dybenko approached Gatchina and began fraternizing with the cossacks, offering them free passage to their homes on the river Don. By midday on the 31st Krasnov had resolved that all was lost, and decided to encourage his troops to reach an accord with Dybenko. Later that day the French military attaché General Henri Niessel arrived; in a final bid to organize a last ditch stand Kerensky and Krasnov urged him to put foreign troops at their disposal, but Niessel ignored this request. In the growing confusion Kerensky donned a disguise and slipped away from Gatchina – to return to the life of an underground revolutionary. He did so just in time for at 1 a.m. on 1 November Dybenko and the cossack soldiers signed an armistice agreeing to Kerensky's arrest and allowing free passage to the Don not only for the cossack rank and file but for Krasnov as well; the battle was well and truly over. But this agreement was premised on the understanding that a coalition socialist government would be formed, based on the agreement being worked out by the Railway Workers' Union.[38]

Those in the CSRM on the right of the Menshevik and SR parties, who wanted to fight the Bolsheviks and were unhappy with the decision of their party leaderships to talk to the Bolsheviks, found they quite literally had nowhere to turn. A vociferous minority of right socialists rejected the decisions of their central committees to support the Railway Workers' Union and set off for GHQ hoping to find there forces more willing to fight; but the situation there was not as they anticipated. As they arrived, on 1 November, the All-Army Committee, the organization which stood at the apex of the nationwide hierarchy of soldiers' committees, announced that it too would participate in the talks organized by the Railway Workers' Union. This was a dramatic change of line, since the All-Army Committee had at first been cool towards the overtures of the Railway Workers' Union. Thus on 29 October the president of the All-Army Committee had contacted the War Ministry in Petrograd and made clear that it actively supported the CSRM and 'hoped it had enough real force at its disposal'; it would send additional troops when it could. Then on 30 October the All-Army Committee sought to get around the Railway Workers' Union ban on troop movements by asking that an exception be made, in return for which the Railway Workers' Union would be represented on any future government established, 'to combat anarchy and counter-revolution'.[39]

However, the army rank and file was steadily turning against the willingness of the All-Army Committee to sponsor a Red versus Green civil war. On 30 October the Railway Workers' Union negotiations received a telegram of support from the military organizations in the War Ministry; army representatives attended the session of talks held on the 30th; on 31 October a delegation from the Petrograd garrison arrived at the talks to declare support for the Railway Workers' Union programme; and on 1 November representatives from the army and fleet arrived to express support.[40] To hasten these changes a Railway Workers' Union delegation visited GHQ and soon succeeded in softening the bellicose line of the All-Army Committee. On 31 October the delegation rejected the idea that troops be sent to Kerensky 'to equalize the forces on both sides', and then asked to address a full meeting of the All-Army Committee. This meeting was also attended by the SRs Chernov, Verkhovskii and Gots, and at it Chernov made a speech in which he distanced himself from the programme of the CSRM; after much debate, the All-Army Committee adopted the Railway Workers' Union programme in the form of this resolution:

> in the name of immediately liquidating the crisis, the successful struggle against anarchy and the growing danger from the right, and also the preservation of calm and unity at the front, the All-Army Committee supports the formation of a democratic coalition government from the Popular Socialists to the Bolsheviks inclusive on the programme: 1. to call the Constituent Assembly on time, 2. an immediate peace agreement, and 3. the land fund to be given to the land committees.

On 2 November a Railway Workers' Union representative accompanied two members of the All-Army Committee to Petrograd to attend the talks aimed at finalizing the membership of the socialist coalition government.[41]

With the Railway Workers' Union talks on forming a socialist coalition government due to reconvene on 2 November, the prospects for agreement were remarkably good. The attempt by right-wing SRs and Mensheviks to respond to Lenin's coup by unleashing a Red versus Green civil war had petered out, and in the various commissions established by the Railway Workers' Union agreement had been reached on both the composition of a future government and the nature of the representative body to which it would be responsible until the Constituent Assembly met. A negotiated settlement really did appear to be underway, so long as the conciliatory Bolsheviks like Kamenev and Ryazanov remained in positions of authority. That, however, was precisely the problem. Once Krasnov's cossacks had melted away, Lenin could afford to resume what amounted to a civil war within the Bolshevik Party.


## LENIN WRECKS THE RAILWAY WORKERS' UNION TALKS

The Railway Workers' Union talks were aimed at preventing a Red versus Green civil war between Bolsheviks and SRs by forming a coalition socialist government. They failed not because agreement was not an objective possibility, but because conciliatory Bolsheviks like Ryazanov and Kamenev did not remain in positions of authority in the Bolshevik Party. At the very moment when agreement could have been reached, their authority was already clearly under question and what delayed final agreement on 2 November was the continued absence of these key figures from the Railway Workers' Union talks. On 31 October, as soon as the situation at Pulkovo Heights looked more stable, it became clear that Lenin and Trotsky, who had since the early hours of 25 October exercised their authority through the military power of the Petrograd Soviet's Military Revolutionary Committee (MRC), would reject the proposed agreement. Urgent talks were held that day between the Railway Workers' Union and the Bolshevik leaders. In a telegraph debate, held because the telephones were not working, the Railway Workers' Union quizzed both Trotsky and Ryazanov about what was going on. Trotsky was extremely forthright: the Bolsheviks had always supported the idea of a socialist coalition on the basis of a defined programme, and still did today, but 'we consider the process of talks cannot paralyse our struggle against the counter-revolutionary troops of Kerensky'. Talks with democratic organizations were one thing, he said, 'but we will allow no talks with the Kornilov brigade'.[42]

This outburst by Trotsky summed up the divisions between the Lenin–Trotsky wing of the Bolshevik Party and the conciliators like Kamenev. Lenin insisted on branding his enemies within the democratic camp as Kornilovites when, in reality, there was absolutely no evidence on which to base this assertion. No generals had rallied to Kerensky; the All-Army Committee supported the Railway Workers' Union; those involved in the Kornilov rebellion would soon be escaping to the Don, not to help Kerensky: Trotsky's remarks were simply guilt by association.[43] In turning the MRC into an insurrectionary body, Lenin and Trotsky had created an instrument of arbitrary power responsible to no representative organization. Under the catch-all justification of 'preventing counter-revolution', the MRC had developed a powerful momentum of its own and on 27–28 October at the very first session of the Soviet Executive elected at the Second Congress of Soviets, the soviet parliament as it were, the subject for debate was the excesses of the MRC, in this case the closure of newspapers and the threat by print workers to strike if more closures occurred. As early as 28 October the Railway Workers' Union had to send several delegations to intercede with the MRC to get its own members released from arrest.[44]

At the first session of the Railway Workers' Union talks, Dan had made much of the behaviour of the MRC: the Bolshevik revolution was not a revolution at all but a military coup carried out by a disorganized soldier mob, he said. It was a conspiracy against democracy, and as such its first victims were fellow democrats, for all the anti-bourgeois rhetoric. The bourgeoisie had not been touched, he went on, 'but there are few here who can say that terror will not be turned on them in the near future'. This use of terror surfaced as an issue once again on the 30th when the other Menshevik spokesman Martov opened the evening session by protesting at Lenin's plans to arrest the SR leaders Gots and Avksentiev, and Dan protested at the closure of his party's newspaper offices.[45]

Having opted for civil war and against soviet democracy by staging the October insurrection, Lenin and Trotsky were determined not to be dragged back down the democratic road. When the Railway Workers' Union summoned Ryazanov to the telegraph on 31

October to comment on Trotsky's outburst about 'Kornilovites', he explained that the Bolshevik Central Committee and the Soviet Executive were both about to meet and he hoped to be able to give them 'a final answer' on the Bolsheviks' attitude to the proposed agreement in two hours time.[46] Thus began the row within the Bolshevik leadership that was to culminate on 4 November in the resignation of all conciliatory Bolsheviks from the government and the Central Committee in protest at a coup staged by Lenin against his own party.

The Bolshevik Central Committee held few properly minuted sessions at this time. At its session on 31 October, for which no minutes have survived, the idea of a compromise political settlement was endorsed. Immediately afterwards, however, on 1 November Lenin passed a resolution suggesting that any attempt at further talks could only be made 'to expose the unviability of this attempt for the last time and to put a conclusive end to further negotiations'. Kamenev responded by 'an incredible effort' in organizing an expanded session of the Central Committee later on 1 November and getting this decision reversed. At this expanded session Kamenev outlined the proposed agreement, and, despite criticism from several members that he had exceeded his brief in even allowing discussion of a government not headed by Lenin – and angry outbursts from Lenin himself about the Railway Workers' Union being 'Kornilovite', how it had been wrong to talk to the Railway Workers' Union in the first place since it was not an organization represented on the soviet, and how talks should only serve as a cover for military operations – the majority of those present voted in favour of the talks continuing and an enlarged government being formed on the basis of the following ultimatum: that the decrees on peace and land should be endorsed, and that those appointed to the government should support the programme of workers' control, action to resolve the food situation, the struggle against counter-revolution, and the Soviet Executive as the basic source of governmental authority.[47]

Lenin responded at once. He summoned a further session of the Central Committee on 2 November, no longer with the additional members present, and passed a resolution which insisted that there 'could be no repudiation of the purely Bolshevik government without betraying the slogan Soviet power' and effectively demanding an end to the talks. This hard-line stance, however, was not to the liking of the more conciliatory Bolshevik group in the Soviet Executive, then debating a parliamentary question put by Ryazanov on the subject of arbitrary arrests; the tactics of arbitrary rule versus conciliation were thus neatly juxtaposed. Asked in the Soviet Executive by the Left SRs to drop their obstructionist stance in the Railway Workers' Union talks, the Bolshevik spokesman G.E. Zinoviev, an ally of Kamenev, made clear that the Bolshevik soviet delegation had not yet had a chance to discuss the Central Committee's statement drawn up by Lenin. After a lengthy delay in the proceedings, the Bolshevik delegation ignored Lenin's resolution and voted for a proposal which was endorsed by the Soviet Executive and then taken the next day to the final session of the Railway Workers' Union talks. Thus the Railway Workers' Union talks, due to reopen on the 2nd, were first postponed until the evening of the 2nd and then until the 3rd.[48]

Although the SR Central Committee pulled out of the talks on 2 November because it found the Soviet Executive proposal unacceptable,[49] the chances of compromise were still good since the proposal endorsed by the Soviet Executive was very close to that agreed by delegates to the Railway Workers' Union talks on the 1st (see Table 1).

Table 1   Proposed Composition of a Temporary Representative Body

|  | Union | Soviet Executive |
| --- | --- | --- |
| Soviet Executive | 100 (old and new) | 150 (new) |
| Peasant Soviet Executive | 25 | |
| Peasant provincial soviets | 75 | 75 |
| Petrograd and Moscow Dumas | 100 | |
| Socialists on Petrograd Duma | | 80 |
| Army committees | 80 | 80 |
| National trades unions | 20 | 25 |
| Railway Workers' Union | 15 | 10 |
| Telegraph Workers' Union | 5 | 5 |
| Total | 420 | 425 [50] |

The one major area of difference affected the seats allocated to the Soviet Executive. The Railway Workers' Union insisted that the Soviet Executive elected at the Second Congress of Soviets was unrepresentative because it had been elected after the walk-out by the SRs and some Mensheviks at the time the CSRM was established; therefore representation from the executive elected at the First Congress of Soviets had to be sought in compensation. Some Bolsheviks argued that this might reduce their representation to as little as 150, and therefore insisted that, rather than solving the problem by looking to the First Congress of Soviets, the SRs and Mensheviks should simply return to the Soviet Executive elected at the Second Congress of Soviets and seek representation through it. However, this Bolshevik estimate of 150 was based on a very pessimistic assessment, especially given the radicalization of the army committees and preparations then underway for a Peasant Soviet Congress where the Left SRs expected to do well. All the other issues, even the question of representation from the town councils, as Trotsky made clear,[51] were not of major importance. In fact any government which emerged from these proposals advanced by the Railway Workers' Union would be dominated by the Bolsheviks and would therefore agree to the Soviet Executive's proposal that the Bolsheviks should control the ministries of labour, internal affairs and foreign affairs. Even accepting the Bolsheviks' worst prognostications, there were sufficient similarities between the Soviet Executive and Railway Workers' Union proposals for serious negotiations to resume.

It was all the more likely that any composite version of the Soviet Executive and Railway Workers' Union proposals would have been closer to the soviet than the Railway Workers' Union version because of an incident which occurred at the opening of the 3 November session of the Railway Workers' Union talks. The negotiations were lobbied by workers from the Putilov and Aleksandrovskii factories, two of the biggest in Petrograd. After a general call for agreement between the parties, the formation of a coalition socialist government and an end to civil war, the detail of the resolution adopted at the Putilov plant meeting of 2 November was closer to the soviet than the Railway Workers' Union proposal. In particular it called for the Second Congress of Soviets, expanded by delegates from a future Peasant Soviet Congress, to be the sole source of government power, and wanted no representation at all for any organizations like the town councils not represented in the soviet. The Putilov resolution was scarcely any different from the proposals outlined by Kamenev and the more conciliatory Bolsheviks.[52]

What ruined the prospects for agreement between the soviet and the Railway Workers' Union were the continuing activities of the MRC and the determination of Lenin and Trotsky that the Bolsheviks should rule alone. When the Railway Workers' Union talks finally reopened on 3 November, instead of discussion centring on how to reconcile the soviet proposal read out by Ryazanov with the Railway Workers' Union proposal read out by the Left SR representative, the issue of arbitrary rule and arrests was again raised. By continuing to rule by arbitrary terror Lenin had succeeded in changing the agenda of the Railway Workers' Union talks. Compromise remained illusory so long as the conciliatory Bolsheviks were associated with the actions of Lenin and Trotsky. Thus the Menshevik R.R. Abramovich made clear that 'an agreement can be reached if there is an end to the terror', but the state of siege had to be lifted, political prisoners freed, and the limitations on press freedom removed. He detailed how throughout the Railway Workers' Union talks the MRC had continued to arrest people, and then put down five conditions for the Mensheviks' further participation in the talks. His stance was endorsed by Martov, and by the Left SRs. Abramovich concluded by asking whether the Bolshevik Central Committee and the Soviet Executive were prepared to accept that, as soon as agreement had been reached on reconciling the soviet and Railway Workers' Union resolutions, Lenin's government would issue a decree ending terror and lifting the state of siege.

By 3 November the Bolshevik Central Committee had removed Kamenev as its representative at the Railway Workers' Union talks and replaced him with Stalin; he was in no mood to compromise. He responded to Abramovich's request for an end to terror with the enigmatic rejection: 'nobody can guarantee that the troops standing at Gatchina will not advance on Petrograd', which ignored the fact that there were no longer any counter-revolutionary troops in Gatchina. It was Sokolnikov, however, who dropped the bombshell for the Railway Workers' Union negotiators. He made clear that, whatever impression Kamenev may have given on 2 November, the Bolshevik Central Committee still had to agree whether the Railway Workers' Union and soviet proposals were close enough to be reconciled and asked for an adjournment until the next day.[53] The Railway Workers' Union talks ended at 2 a.m. on the morning of 4th when it became clear the Bolsheviks were not going to agree to any compromise. The same day ten leading moderate Bolsheviks decided to resign en masse from Lenin's government, and one other associated himself with this move without resigning.

The essence of Kamenev's challenge to Lenin and the rest of the Central Committee was whether it was worth risking total isolation from other democratic groups for the sake of retaining a stranglehold on the Soviet Executive. Lenin clearly thought it was, for on the very day of the last session of the Railway Workers' Union talks, he personally interviewed every member of the Central Committee to get them to give their signed support to his 'ultimatum of the majority [of the Central Committee] to the minority'; this demanded total loyalty to Lenin's line and endorsement of the decision taken on 2 November even though it contradicted the decision of the expanded Central

Committee session on 1 November.[54] As a leading conciliatory Bolshevik A. Lozovsky told a meeting of the Bolshevik group in the Soviet Executive on 4 November:

> I cannot remain silent in the name of party discipline when I feel with every fibre of my being that the Central Committee's tactics are leading to the isolation of the proletariat, to civil war among working people, and to the defeat of the great revolution . . . I cannot suppress in the name of party discipline [my knowledge of] the sullen discontent of the working masses, who fought for soviet power [only to discover] by some incomprehensible manoeuvre that power is wholly Bolshevik.[55]

Yet what prompted the resignation of the conciliatory Bolsheviks from Lenin's government was not just the wrecking of the Railway Workers' Union talks, not just the manner in which this was accomplished, but Lenin and Trotsky's open defence of arbitrary rule. On 4 November Lenin and Trotsky appeared at the Soviet Executive not simply to justify one incident of arbitrary rule, in this case the closure of the 'bourgeois press', but to institutionalize arbitrary rule. They came to explain that the Soviet Executive, this soviet parliament, was not a 'bourgeois parliament' and therefore had only a very vague and general brief to oversee the government which could issue decrees in its own name as often as it liked. Lenin's final remark summed up his attitude: 'you call us extremists, but you are nothing other than apologists for parliamentary obstruction'. When, on Lenin's urging, the Soviet Executive agreed to accept that it, the soviet parliament, could not prevent the soviet government ruling by decree, the conciliatory Bolsheviks resigned; if the soviet parliament was to have no power, the debate as to who should be represented in any broadened soviet parliament had become simply irrelevant.[56]

The conciliatory Bolsheviks who resigned from Lenin's government justified their action by saying that all workers and soldiers wanted 'a speedy end to the bloodshed between the different sections of democracy' – in other words the nascent civil war between Bolsheviks and SRs, Reds and Greens. In their resignation statement they highlighted the question of arbitrary rule once again, in language the Menshevik Martov would have welcomed. They insisted that it was essential to form a government of all parties in the soviet: 'a purely Bolshevik government has no choice but to maintain itself by political terror'.[57] Arbitrary rule by decree, 'military' style discipline within the party, these hallmarks of a civil war mentality were essential parts of Bolshevik rule after 4 November, a date in many ways far more crucial than 25 October, the date of the October insurrection: it opened up the prospect of a civil war within democracy, something far more dramatic than the struggle between Russian democracy and Russian property previewed in Kornilov's rebellion. Lenin's only defence was that his was arbitrary rule with a mission, as one of his most lucid critics noted. Maxim Gorky wrote on 10 November 1917:

> Lenin . . . considers himself justified in performing with the Russian people a cruel experiment which is doomed to failure beforehand. The people, worn out and impoverished by war, have already paid for this experiment with thousands of lives and will be compelled to pay with tens of thousands, and this will deprive the nation of its leadership for a long time to come. This inevitable tragedy does not disturb Lenin, the slave of dogma.[58]

The collapse of Kornilov's rebellion had removed the danger of one civil war in Russia, a White versus Red civil war. As Lenin had himself noted, the transfer of power to a coalition socialist administration could have taken place quite peacefully. Such a coalition government would have addressed the great social issues of bread, peace and land, but it would not have engaged in an experiment predicated on one man's, Lenin's, interpretation of how the imperialist economy had evolved in the years since Marx's death. Every arbitrary act Lenin justified on the grounds that he was building socialism and that the new socialist epoch had begun. To this end Lenin launched his civil war within democracy, a Red versus Green civil war of Bolsheviks against SRs, at times even a civil war within the Bolshevik Party. Lenin acted on the understanding that the other imperial states of Europe were about to implode as Russia had done. Within weeks he was having to readjust his policies as international imperialism reacted in ways he had not expected.

## NOTES

1. For the rumours of a Chernov led government, see P.N. Milyukov, *The Russian Revolution* (Gulf Breeze 1984), p. 14; V.I. Lenin, *Collected Works* (Moscow 1960), vol. 25, p. 306.
2. A. Rabinowitch, *The Bolsheviks Come to Power* (New York 1978), p. 160.
3. R.P. Browder and A.F. Kerensky, *The Russian Provisional Government: Documents* (Stanford 1961), p. 1682.
4. Milyukov, *Russian Revolution*, p. 47.
5. D.V. Oznobishin, 'Burzhyaznaya diktatura v poiskakh parlamentskogo prikritiya' *Istoricheskie zapiski* 93, p. 132.
6. V.M. Chernov, *Pered burey* (New York 1953), p. 345.

7. Oznobishin, 'Burzhyaznaya', p. 116.
8. Oznobishin, 'Burzhyaznaya', p. 135; N.F. Slavin, 'Krizis vlasti v sentyabre 1917g. i obrazonvanie Vremennogo Soveta Republiki (Predparlament)' *Istoricheskie zapiski* 56, p. 54; Milyukov, *Russian Revolution*, pp. 73–6.
9. Browder and Kerensky, *Documents*, pp. 1752, 1759; Milyukov, *Russian Revolution*, p. 130.
10. A.I. Verkhovskii, *Rossiya na Golgofe* (Petrograd 1918), pp. 116–22, 125–34.
11. These events are fully covered in Rabinowitch, *Bolsheviks*.
12. A. Tyrkova-Williams, *From Liberty to Brest Litovsk* (London 1919), p. 245.
13. L.G. Murashev, ' "Odnorodno-sotsialisticheskoe" pravitel'stvo v anti-sovetskikh planakh men'shevikov v dni oktyabrskogo vooruzhennogo vosstaniya v Petrograde' *Uchennye zapiski kafedr obshchestvennykh nauk vuzov Leningrada: Istoriya KPSS* (Leningrad 1990), p. 54; Milyukov, *Russian Revolution*, p. 184. These talks are dismissed as legend by S.P. Melgunov in *The Bolshevik Seizure of Power* (Oxford 1972), p. 58.
14. Lenin, *Collected Works* vol. 25, p. 263.
15. Lenin, *Collected Works* vol. 25, p. 310.
16. Lenin, *Collected Works* vol. 26, pp. 36–9. Although this article was published on 29 September, it was written earlier, see Institute of Marxism-Leninism, *V.I. Lenin: Biograficheskaya khronika* (Moscow 1974) vol. 5, p. 11.
17. Lenin, *Collected Works* vol. 26, p. 24.
18. For the votes of the Bolshevik Central Committee concerning the Preparliament and the insurrection, see *The Bolsheviks and the October Revolution: Central Committee Minutes of the RSDLP(b)* (London 1974), p. 67 et seq. (hereafter *Minutes*). The crisis within the Bolshevik Central Committee at this time, and the absence of any party resolution to seize power before the Second Congress of Soviets, can be explored more fully in this author's computer assisted learning package *The Bolshevik Seizure of Power*, produced for the HiDES Project, University of Southampton.
19. Lenin, *Collected Works* vol. 26, p. 234.
20. Murashev, 'Odnorodnoe', p. 52; R.V. Daniels, *The Conscience of the Revolution* (Harvard 1960), p. 64.
21. Murashev, 'Odnorodnoe', p. 57.
22. P. Vompe, *Dni oktyabr'skoi revolyutsii i zheleznodorozhnikov* (Moscow 1924), pp. 16–18; A. Tanyaev, *Ocherki dvizheniya zheleznodorozhnikov v revolyutsii 1917g.* (Moscow 1925), p. 138.
23. The State Archive of the Russian Federation in Moscow (GARF) has the surviving records of the Railway Workers' Union talks in fond 5498 opis 1. These comprise stenographic records of the sessions held on 29 October, 30 October and 3 November (ed. khr. 58, 67 and 74), plus records of telegraph conversations between the Railway Workers' Union representatives in Petrograd and the headquarters in Moscow (ed. khr. 78). There is also a diary kept during the talks by an anonymous participant (ed. khr. 56). When consulted in 1990 only a poor quality

microfilm made in the 1950s was available. For the attitude of the Bolsheviks and the groups supporting the Railway Workers' Union, see 5498.1.78, the reports dated 28 October and 29 October.

24. N.G. Dumova, *Kadetskaya kontrrevolyutsiya i ee razgrom* (Moscow 1982), p. 25; V.D. Medlin and S.L. Parsons (eds), *V.D. Nabokov and the Russian Provisional Government* (Yale 1976), p. 165; G. Buchanan, *My Mission to Russia and Other Diplomatic Memories* (London 1923) vol. 2, p. 210.

25. A detailed insight into the activities of the CSRM can be found in the telegrams sent to the British Foreign Office by Sir George Buchanan, the ambassador in Petrograd. See the Public Record Office files FO 371.2999.247 and .278. For the attitude of the SRs, see V.V. Komin, *Istoriya pomeshchikh, burzhuaznykh i melko-burzhuaznykh partii v Rossii* (Kalinin 1970), p. 109.

26. GARF 5498.1.78, report dated 28 October; 5498.1.56, entry for 28 October.

27. L. Lande, 'The Mensheviks in 1917', in L. Haimson (ed.), *The Mensheviks: from the Revolution of 1917 to the Second World War* (Chicago 1974), p. 49; O.H. Radkey, *The Sickle under the Hammer* (Columbia 1963), pp. 19, 30, 37.

28. Tanyaev, *Ocherki*, p. 151.

29. *Minutes*, p. 127.

30. GARF 5498.1.58, protocols of session held on 29 October.

31. GARF 5498.1.58, protocols of morning session 30 October; 5498.1.56, diary entry for 30 October. There is some confusion as to quite when this workers' delegation arrived. The diary dates it as the 29th, but in his memoirs, the delegate to the talks from the Petrograd City Council dated the incident as 3.00 a.m. on 30 October. A diary written after a night's sleep from 29–30 October would consider events the previous day to have occurred on the 29th, even if strictly speaking the author was describing an event which took place in the early hours of the 30th, see J. Bunyan and H.H. Fisher, *The Bolshevik Revolution: Documents and Materials* (Stanford 1961), p. 167.

32. GARF 5498.1.67, protocols of the evening session 30 October; Radkey, *Sickle*, p. 66.

33. Vompe, *Dni*, pp. 34–7.

34. GARF 5498.1.78, report dated 30 October.

35. Radkey, *Sickle*, p. 67; V. Brovkin, *The Mensheviks After October* (Cornell 1987), p. 23.

36. Bunyan and Fisher, *Documents*, p. 192; GARF 5498.1.78, report dated 1 November.

37. Muraviev had a colourful career, as this book will show. According to the leading SR Central Committee member A.R. Gots, despite this enthusiasm for supporting the Bolsheviks, Muraviev had a day or two earlier asked the SR Central Committee if he could be empowered to use force against the Bolsheviks, in view of the MRC's challenge to the government's authority. See M. Jensen, *The SR Party After October 1917: Documents from the PSR Archives* (Amsterdam 1989), p. 128.

38. This account is taken from A.K. Wildman, *The End of the Russian Imperial Army* (Princeton 1980) vol. 2, p. 304 et seq. Lenin was furious about Dybenko's action and wanted to have him court-martialled.

39. Vompe, *Dni*, p. 44.

40. GARF 5498.1.74, protocols of evening session of 30 October; 5498.1.56, diary entry 31 October; Vompe, *Dni*, p. 34.

41. Vompe, *Dni*, pp. 44–7.

42. GARF 5498.1.78, report by Malitskii dated 30 October; 5498.1.78, transcript of conversation dated 31 October.

43. The suggestion that a 'second Kornilov campaign' was underway in October 1917 was an invention of Lenin and Trotsky which blighted the work of a generation of Soviet historians. It is rebutted in detail in this author's 'Before the fighting started' *Revolutionary Russia* vol. 4 (1991), p. 232.

44. J.L.H. Keep (ed.), *The Debate on Soviet Power: the Minutes of VTsIK, Second Convocation* (Oxford 1979), p. 42; GARF 5498.1.56, diary entry for 28 October.

45. GARF 5498.1.74, protocols of session 29 October; 5498.1.74, protocols of evening session 30 October. According to Martov, Trotsky had threatened to shoot five 'counter-revolutionaries' for every 'revolutionary' shot.

46. GARF 5498.1.78, transcript of conversation dated 31 October.

47. *Minutes*, p. 135. This resolution should be read in conjunction with those on p. 136 and p. 141. The suggestion on p. 135 that the ultimatum had to be accepted within two hours was not as threatening as it sounded, since the Soviet Executive was already in session and support for the Bolsheviks' programme, as opposed to support for Lenin's government, was widespread. These issues are explored more fully in this author's *Bolshevik Seizure of Power*.

48. *Minutes*, p. 139; Keep, *Debate*, pp. 59–63; GARF 5498.1.56, diary entry 3 November.

49. V. Vladimirova, *God sluzhby sotsialistov kapitalistam* (Moscow 1927), p. 48; Brovkin, *Mensheviks*, p. 27. The Menshevik conditions were the inclusion of all democratic groups in a representative body; the freeing of all political prisoners; and end to terror and the restoration of the freedoms of press, strike and assembly; a cease fire; and the transfer of army units to local government control to keep order and combat looting.

50. Tanyaev, *Ocherki*, p. 157. Keep (*Debate*, p. 62) gives fifty not eighty for the number of socialists on Petrograd City Council.

51. Trotsky, unlike Lenin, was quite happy to have representatives from city councils, so long as fresh elections were held, see *Minutes*, p. 129.

52. GARF 5498.1.74, protocols of session 3 November.

53. GARF 5498.1.67, protocols of session 3 November.

54. *Minutes*, p. 300.

55. Bunyan and Fisher, *Documents*, p. 206.

56. Keep, *Debate*, p. 85. This was not an isolated remark. In the same debate

Lenin said: 'in order to exercise control over the government's policy it is quite sufficient for the Soviet Executive to have the right to remove ministers. The new government could not have coped with all the obstacles which stood in its path if it had observed all formalities . . .'. In a similar vein Trotsky added: 'our Soviet parliament differs from others in that it does not contain representatives of antagonistic classes. Our government . . . has no place for conventional parliamentary machinery'.

57. *Minutes*, p. 142.
58. M. Gorky, *Untimely Thoughts* (New York 1968), p. 88.

# CHAPTER THREE

# *Peace for Renewed Civil War*

Despite the breakdown in the Railway Workers' Union talks, the Red versus Green civil war did not start up again at once. Although Lenin had refused to agree to the formation of a coalition socialist government – the proposal that the Railway Workers' Union and a majority of socialists felt was the essential basis for peace between the Bolsheviks and SRs – Lenin had agreed that the Constituent Assembly elections should go ahead; this they did within a week of the conciliatory Bolsheviks storming out of Lenin's government.

For the SRs, the elections to the Constituent Assembly obviated the necessity for civil war. The SRs argued that they would win the elections and the Bolsheviks would then transfer power to them. On the first point the SRs were right: they won the Constituent Assembly elections; but on the second point they were completely wrong: Lenin had no intention of transferring power to the SRs. Like a rugby football player under pressure from all sides Lenin treated the Constituent Assembly elections as a desperate kick for touch; it would buy time and relieve his struggling government until external forces came to his aid. For in the weeks immediately after the seizure of power, Lenin believed that world revolution was imminent.

Lenin's theory of Russia being the weak link in a chain of interlocking imperialist countries presupposed that a socialist revolution in Russia would quickly spread to other countries, and Germany in particular, as workers throughout Europe turned against their governments, transforming the First World War into a Europe-wide civil war. Despite the revolutionary unrest in Finland in December 1917, nothing went according to plan in the six weeks between the Constituent Assembly elections and the moment deputies began to assemble in Petrograd. By January 1918 Lenin had concluded that world revolution would not happen in the foreseeable future and certainly not before the Constituent Assembly opened, that German imperialism was still in the field, and that if his regime were to survive he would have to look for a different source of external support. Thus his decision to sign a separate peace with the German imperialists. However, this epoch-making decision was not made after any detailed analysis of the condition of the international labour movement – the revolutionary general strikes in Berlin, Vienna and Budapest of late January 1918 had still not taken place – the decision was forced on Lenin by the domestic political agenda, how should the Bolshevik Party react to the SRs' victory in the Constituent Assembly elections. Rather than come to terms with the SR-dominated Constituent Assembly, Lenin preferred betraying the international labour movement by signing the Brest-Litovsk peace with Imperial Germany, thus keeping open the danger of a Red versus Green civil war within Russia.

## THE ELECTIONS TO THE CONSTITUENT ASSEMBLY

Between Lenin's announcement on 4 November 1917 that the Bolsheviks would rule alone and their decision to dissolve the Constituent Assembly on 5 January 1918, Russia was in a curious state of limbo. The Bolsheviks, and the Bolsheviks alone, headed the government, but that government was universally seen as an interim administration until the Constituent Assembly met. In the debates within the Bolshevik Central Committee about the fate of the Railway Workers' Union compromise and the possibility of sharing power in a coalition government 'from Popular Socialists to Bolsheviks', Lenin had got his way by securing the crucial support of centrists like Sokolnikov and Stalin; but Sokolnikov expected power to be ceded to the Constituent Assembly. He had stated publicly 'power will not remain in our hands for long: we are not planning to delay the Constituent Assembly; we will assemble it immediately after the elections and transfer power to it'. And the official position of Lenin's government was that it had established a 'provisional workers' and peasants' government' pending the Constituent Assembly. That the Soviet Executive still expected this arrangement to hold was evident from the fact that on 8 November it agreed to set up a Finance Commission to control the expenditure of funds requested by the Council of People's Commissars 'until the Constituent Assembly meets'.[1]

There were other clear signs that, whatever Lenin may have felt in his heart of hearts, whatever hopes he might have had of world revolution breaking out before the Constituent Assembly could convene, the majority on the Bolshevik Central Committee still assumed its administration to be purely temporary and would soon cede power to a socialist coalition administration, since this was seen as the most likely outcome of the Constituent Assembly elections. Indeed Bolshevik propaganda posters for the Constituent Assembly election campaign made clear that by voting Bolshevik, people would be voting for a party prepared to take the lead in forming a socialist coalition government.[2] This reflected the continuing influence of Kamenev, who despite his resignation from the government and Bolshevik Central Committee on 4 November, was on 6 November nominated by the Soviet Executive as both a member of its presidium and the person heading the department overseeing the Constituent Assembly elections; he also served on the editorial team running the soviet newspaper *Izvestiya*. No doubt because of this continuing conciliatory activity Kamenev was ordered by the Bolshevik Central Committee to leave all his official posts in the Soviet Executive on 8 November.[3]

For Bolsheviks like Kamenev, who took the Constituent Assembly elections seriously and wanted the Bolsheviks to work with the assembly, it was important that it should adequately reflect the divisions which had emerged within the SR Party since the Kornilov rebellion. The issue was this: the SR electoral lists had been drawn up before the Kornilov rebellion, before the consequent 'second revolution' had radically changed many party members' attitude to the continued existence of a coalition government. The lists favoured the more conservative SR establishment, rather than dissidents, and, of course, predated the decision of the Left SRs to form a separate party. Thus, when discussing the Constituent Assembly elections on 6 November the Soviet Executive raised the possibility of delaying the poll so that a separate electoral list could be drawn up for the newly formed Left SR Party. Its leaders, however, decided against such action, since they confidently expected to win over a hundred seats.[4] Thus on 8 November the Soviet Executive resolved that the elections should go ahead as planned on 12 November.

The results of the Constituent Assembly elections, in which the turnout was approximately 55 per cent, gave the Bolsheviks 23.7 per cent of the vote and the SR Party 37.3 per cent, although if the votes of allied parties like the Ukrainian SRs were added to these the SRs had won approximately 50 per cent of the votes. In terms of the numbers of deputies elected, the combined total for the SR Party and its allies was 54 per cent and the Bolsheviks 24 per cent. Thus, as the details began to come in after 15 November, the picture emerged of a spectacular SR triumph. The SRs had clearly won and had scored particularly well in the Volga provinces. The Bolsheviks, on the other hand, had done far worse than the 30 per cent or so that Kamenev had hoped for; but they had retained their solid working-class support in Petrograd and the central industrial region. As to the Kadets, their overall vote at 7 per cent and a mere seventeen deputies was derisory, but in Moscow and in Petrograd their vote had increased since the local elections in August and September to 35 per cent and 26 per cent respectively.

For conciliatory Bolsheviks like Kamenev the only good news in these results was the fact that the SRs did not have an absolute majority; they needed the support of the Ukrainian SRs, well to the left of the mainstream of the party. There were other signs that the SR majority might be whittled away in time. A large number of unofficial peasant lists put up in opposition to the official SR candidates had been successful, and potentially more significant still, in nine areas – Petrograd City, Petrograd Province, Kaluga, Kazan, Ufa, Poltava, Kharkov, Kherson and the Baltic Fleet – those elected as SRs had been nominated by party organizations which were after October 1917 in the hands of the Left SRs.[5] Things would have been easier if the Left SRs had won the hundred seats they had hoped for and the Bolsheviks the one-third of the vote they had anticipated – then the Bolsheviks and Left SRs could have formed a coalition socialist government which commanded a majority in the Constituent Assembly – but it was still possible that some sort of arrangement might be reached between the Bolsheviks, Left SRs and dissident peasant deputies. The chances of this happening were reinforced by the results of elections to the Extraordinary Congress of Peasant Soviets which assembled in Petrograd on 10 November and gave a small but significant victory to the Left SRs.

The Left SR victory at the Extraordinary Congress of Peasant Soviets did not resolve the question of how to form a government responsible to the Constituent Assembly, but it did help point to a possible way forward. First, it meant that until the Constituent Assembly convened, the Soviet Executive, elected at the Second Congress of Soviets, and the Peasant Soviet Executive, elected at the Extraordinary Congress of Peasant Soviets, could form a joint executive to which Lenin's government could be held responsible, a joint executive representing the vast majority of Russia's population. Thus the Extraordinary Congress of Peasant Soviets endorsed a resolution which demanded that the two central soviet executives should merge on the basis of parity; a new government should then be formed comprising representatives of all the socialist parties 'from Popular Socialists to Bolsheviks', but bound by the programme endorsed at the Second Congress of Soviets. As the only two parties to endorse the programme of the Second Congress of Soviets were the Bolsheviks and the Left SRs, this resolution opened the way for the formation of a Bolshevik–Left SR coalition government.

Negotiations then began which resulted in the membership of the Soviet Executive being dramatically expanded along lines not dissimilar to those proposed in the Railway Workers' Union talks. The agreed compromise was reached on 14 November and on 15 November the new structure of the Soviet Executive was announced: there would be 108 representatives from the workers' and soldiers' soviets; 108 representatives from the peasants' soviets; 100 representatives from the army and navy committees; 35 representatives from the trades unions; 10 representatives from the Railway Workers' Union; and 5 representatives from the Post and Telegraph Workers' Union. The agreement was welcomed by conciliatory Bolsheviks, by the Left SRs, and by the Railway Workers' Union. The constitutional principles underlying the relationship between this new Soviet Executive and Lenin's government were agreed on 17 November when it was established that the government was responsible to the Soviet Executive acting as a kind of interim parliament; all legislation and ordinances had to be confirmed by the Soviet Executive; counter-revolutionary measures were the concern of the government, but actions related to such measures had to be accounted for to the Soviet Executive; government ministers had to give weekly reports to the Soviet Executive; and 'parliamentary' questions from the Soviet Executive, supported by fifteen signatures, had to be answered by the government at once. These arrangements were finally endorsed when the Second Congress of Peasant Soviets took place on 27 November; thereafter the Bolshevik–Left SR coalition could be formally established on 8 December with the Left SRs taking up four government posts.[6]

However, forming a Bolshevik–Left SR coalition was only the first part of the problem faced by those wanting to construct a government which might have a majority in the Constituent Assembly. There was no weakening of the Left SRs', and indeed the Railway Workers' Union's resolve to convene the Constituent Assembly, and the Second

Congress of Peasant Soviets insisted that it should assemble on time,[7] but the dogged fact which would not go away was this: unless the Left SRs found some way to increase their representation at the expense of the victorious SRs, the Bolsheviks and Left SRs together would never command a majority. But, in nine parts of the country the Left SRs had captured control of party organizations represented in the Constituent Assembly by SRs. Could this not be 'put right', as it were, by the local soviets in these regions demanding the recall of their Constituent Assembly deputies?

## THE CONSTITUENT ASSEMBLY AND THE SOVIETS

The idea of some sort of continuing relationship between the Constituent Assembly and the soviets was not new. It had been raised by Kamenev in the paper he and Zinoviev wrote after the Bolshevik Central Committee had agreed on 10 October that an insurrection was 'inevitable'; in this paper they noted 'the Constituent Assembly and the soviets – here is the mixed type of state institution we are going towards'.[8] Precisely what Kamenev and Zinoviev envisaged was left vague at the time, but after the Constituent Assembly elections, the suggestion that the soviet might bring popular pressure to bear on the Constituent Assembly was formalized into the right to recall deputies. The soviets had always had the right to recall deputies; if workers felt their deputies were not performing properly they could be recalled at any time. Instituting the same procedure for Constituent Assembly deputies would accelerate the process already seen during the elections themselves of unofficial radical peasant lists being elected in opposition to the SR Party establishment.

On 21 November, once the results of the Constituent Assembly elections were known in outline, Lenin went to the Soviet Executive to propose that the right of recall be extended to Constituent Assembly deputies: the electoral rules would have to be revised to allow this 'exercise of the people's revolutionary will', it might be difficult to do, given the system of proportional representation which had been used in the elections, but such technicalities would have to be overcome. The problem was, he went on, that the SRs were 'a party which no longer exists' and therefore the results did not fairly reflect the voters' sentiments, 'but there is no need to be afraid of the results if the right of re-election is introduced . . . the right of recall should be given to the soviets [and] in this way power can pass from one party to another bloodlessly, by means of re-elections'. A Left SR spokesman endorsed the idea wholeheartedly, although he felt a constituency-based referendum on recall might be a better way of organizing things than giving the power to the soviets. The Soviet Executive then endorsed the principle of recall, leaving the details of how it was to be implemented to a commission. [9]

If the right of recall were to be exercised in a planned way, and to effect the political outlook of the Constituent Assembly, the assembly itself could not gather as planned on 28 November. Equally, if the hope was to organize the recall of certain deputies under soviet pressure, the affairs of the Constituent Assembly could not be left in the hands of the commission established by the Provisional Government. So on 23 November the members of the Electoral Commission were arrested, and on the 27th it was announced that the assembly could not open until a quorum of 50 per cent, or 400 deputies, had arrived in Petrograd. It was one thing to delay the Constituent Assembly, quite another to envisage how to implement the policy of the Constituent Assembly and soviets. When the Bolshevik Central Committee addressed the question, only one proposal was put forward. N.I. Bukharin suggested that the liberal Kadets should be expelled from the assembly, thus transforming it into a 'Revolutionary Convention'; but while this was supported by Trotsky, it was opposed by Stalin and no decision was taken.[10] The Left SRs seemed similarly uncertain. At the Soviet Executive session on 1 December they denounced the 'arbitrary and repressive' action taken in arresting the members of the Constituent Assembly Electoral Commission, but then went on to welcome Bukharin's suggestion. They wanted the people to decide how best to merge the Constituent Assembly and the soviets, and agreed that 'we should seek to turn the Constituent Assembly into a Revolutionary Convention'. Supporting this same line the Soviet Executive passed a resolution declining to guarantee that 'both the socialist and bourgeois' sections of the assembly would be summoned.[11]

However, as the Bolshevik deputies to the Constituent Assembly began to gather in Petrograd, it was clear that many of them, while happy to go along with the recall of deputies, were unimpressed with the idea of excluding any deputies at all, including the Kadets, from any new Revolutionary Convention formed by the Constituent Assembly and the soviets. The Bolshevik deputies, like all parliamentary party groups, elected a bureau to run their affairs; those elected to that bureau were all the key Bolshevik conciliators who had resigned on 4 November. By 11 December the Central Committee was seriously concerned that the deputies were getting out of control: it debated the worrying development that they had adopted 'right-wing' attitudes and Lenin proposed that the way forward was to 'remove the bureau', to issue some theses on the situation and 'remind them of party rules that all representative bodies come under Central Committee authority'; a Central Committee representative should also be appointed to guide the group. Lenin's proposal was accepted, and in a move reminiscent of the 4 November resignation crisis, all Bolshevik deputies to the Constituent Assembly were instructed to sign an undertaking to resign if the Central Committee so requested. When the parliamentary group assembled on 12 December with Sokolnikov and Bukharin as the Central Committee's representatives they were told for the first time that the Constituent Assembly might have to be dissolved.[12]

In public the Bolshevik Party was still talking about an arrangement whereby the Constituent Assembly and the soviets could be transformed into a Revolutionary Convention, but by mid-December 1917 two views had developed concerning timing. To those around Kamenev there was no hurry, the Constituent Assembly needed to be convened and then 'tested'; if it failed to respond to the needs of the time, radical deputies could then walk out and form a Revolutionary Convention. But this idea was attacked in *Pravda* on 20 December which criticized the 'constitutional illusions' of those who defended it. The other view, put in the Soviet Executive two days later, was that the Constituent Assembly should not be allowed this 'test' proposed by Kamenev and that moves to form a Revolutionary Convention between it and the soviets should begin at once. Thus when the government announced on 20 December that the Constituent Assembly would convene on 5 January 1918, the Bolshevik spokesman informed delegates at the same time that the Third Congress of Soviets and Third Congress of Peasant Soviets would be brought forward by two weeks 'so that when the Constituent Assembly meets the opinion of the oppressed classes on the most important questions of the day may be represented'. What the Bolsheviks proposed after 20 December was that a Revolutionary Convention could be formed by a simultaneous session of the Constituent Assembly and the two congresses of soviets.[13]

The attitude of the Left SRs was more or less the same. On 21 December they held talks with their former comrades in the SR Party. If they had hoped to win them over to the sort of Constituent Assembly–soviet arrangement envisaged by the government coalition they were mistaken. A week later the Left SR paper *Znamya truda* described the Revolutionary Convention in terms of the Constituent Assembly continuing in being as a rump parliament surrounded by the soviets. When they and the Bolsheviks began working out details of just how precisely a joint session of the Constituent Assembly and the soviets might operate, Lenin insisted that the only way forward was to take a hard line. On 3 January the Soviet Executive debated the question of a Revolutionary Convention and decided to offer the assembly an ultimatum. The Constituent Assembly had the chance of joining with the Third Congress of Soviets to form a Revolutionary Convention only if it accepted the Declaration of the Rights of Labouring and Exploited People, adopted by the Soviet Executive the same day; this committed the assembly to accepting the principle of the right of soviets to recall Constituent Assembly deputies. The same Soviet Executive meeting adopted an ordinance which stated that since the declaration made clear that all power rested with the soviets 'any attempt by any individual or institution to appropriate any function of state authority will be regarded as a counter-revolutionary act and suppressed'; powers were taken to dissolve the assembly in the event of non-compliance.[14]

When the Constituent Assembly held its only session on 5 January 1918 it quickly endorsed a land reform programme submitted by the SR Party and endorsed the peace negotiations that had begun with the Germans; it was not these social issues that the SRs refused to support in the government's programme, but the Declaration of the Rights of Labouring and Exploited People. When the Bolshevik I.M. Sverdlov asked on behalf of the Soviet Executive that the deputies accept the declaration 'as the basis on which you can enter the coming convention with the Third Soviet Congress', his tone was offensive:

> you have spent months in betraying the revolution to the Kadets. Therefore the only authority that can have the confidence of the proletariat and the peasantry is that of the soviets, and the Constituent Assembly can only serve the revolution if it recognizes the proletarian dictatorship and the removal of the propertied classes from political rights.[15]

When the assembly still would not accept the declaration, it was dissolved. Sverdlov's denunciation of the bourgeoisie was picked up by Lenin in a special session of the Soviet Executive to debate the dissolution. Riding roughshod over the conciliatory Bolsheviks who argued that the assembly should not have been dissolved before it could have been tested by 'confronting it with the Third Congress of Soviets', Lenin said:

so long as Kaledin exists, so long as the slogan 'all power to the Constituent Assembly' masks the slogan 'down with soviet power' civil war is inevitable, for we shall not for anything in the world surrender soviet power.[16]

## THE MISSING WHITE COUNTER-REVOLUTION

If Lenin were to be taken at face value, the greatest threat to his government came from General Kaledin, one of the key figures in the Kornilov affair, and the 'bourgeois' counter-revolution being organized on the river Don by other White generals. However, while it is true that the 'bourgeoisie' caused Lenin's regime some momentary discomfiture, the counter-revolutionary forces gathering in the cossack heartland of the Don were never a serious force until the autumn of 1918. The White counter-revolution was a mirage, but a useful one since it provided Lenin with a ready justification for his attack on the Constituent Assembly.

It was only in the very first days after Lenin's seizure of power that the liberals posed anything like a 'counter-revolutionary' threat. After the arrest of the Provisional Government, the so-called Minor Council of Ministers, comprising various junior ministers, continued to meet clandestinely as an 'underground' Provisional Government, assembling almost daily until 16 November. The key figure in this was Countess Sophia Panina, the Assistant Minister of Education, in whose house the clandestine counter-government usually met. Although they hoped in the long run to reinstate Kerensky's government, their main activities were to frustrate the Bolsheviks by exercising continued control over the civil service and instituting a policy of non-co-operation, thus depriving the Bolshevik government of funds. The Assistant Minister of Finance, the Kadet A.G. Khrushchev, diverted 42 million roubles belonging to Kerensky's government into foreign bank accounts or the account of the Petrograd City Council, acting on the express orders of the former Industry Minister A.I. Konovalov, whom Kerensky had nominated 'Acting Prime Minister' as he left Petrograd, and this money was used to fund the civil servant strike which lasted nearly two months. These actions undoubtedly troubled Lenin's government, especially since these clandestine moves against the Bolsheviks were accompanied by a very vociferous Kadet campaign from the city council: A.I. Shingarev in particular used his position there to lambast the government on every conceivable occasion and cheerfully proposed expelling the Bolshevik delegates from the council. As a former minister in Prince Lvov's government, and the leading Kadet in Petrograd at the time, he was the *de facto* leader of the party and his speeches turned the council into a continual anti-Bolshevik rally. His efforts were rewarded by an increase in the Kadet vote to 26.2 per cent in the Constituent Assembly's Petrograd constituencies elections.

Lenin's first move against this Kadet enterprise came on 16 November. When the city council announced plans to organize a welcome for the Constituent Assembly, the government decided to close it down. Then, when on 23 November the Bolsheviks instructed the Constituent Assembly Electoral Commission to wind up its affairs, the Kadet-dominated commission refused and its deputy chairman V.D. Nabokov and others were promptly arrested, although they were released five days later. On 27 November, when the government announced that the Constituent Assembly, instead of opening as promised on 28 November, could not meet until a quorum of 50 per cent had been achieved, the Kadet Central Committee met under Shingarev's leadership at Panina's flat: they decided to turn up as if nothing had happened and try to establish a temporary presidium until the assembly was quorate, but they were arrested on the morning of 28th. Other members of the electoral commission gathered on 28 October at the Tauride Palace, where the Constituent Assembly was due to meet, and established a commission to welcome the delegates, but hearing of the arrest of the Kadet Central Committee and fearing for their own safety, they abandoned the attempt. This marked the end of any serious Kadet opposition to the government. On 1 December the Minor Council of Ministers issued a farewell statement which not only denounced the Bolsheviks but was highly critical of the behaviour of the SRs and Mensheviks in doing nothing to help bring back Kerensky's legitimate government but instead supporting the creation of a socialist coalition.[17]

The reality was that, whatever its success in November, the Kadets' opposition to the government had been abandoned by the start of December. They could still embarrass the government – between 10–19 December Petrograd was entertained by the trial of Countess Panina, who cheerfully admitted she had been in possession of 93,000 roubles from the Ministry of Education, but pointed out that she had merely prevented these public funds of the Third Coalition Government from being handed over to a non-governmental political organization, the Bolshevik 'government'; sentenced to be detained until the sum was repaid, by 19 December the Women's University in Petrograd had organized a collection and obtained her release.[18] Systematic, organized opposition by the Kadets, however, was over.

And yet it was the Kadets who bore the brunt of the government's criticism. After the attempt to open the Constituent Assembly on 28 November, it was the Kadet Party which was declared to be the 'enemy of the people'. For the government, what the Kadets were trying to do was clear: by their campaign in Petrograd and their constant focus on the Constituent Assembly they were trying to get legality for what was happening on the Don, where General Kaledin was gathering his White forces for an armed counter-revolution. On 29 November Lenin's government proclaimed: 'there must be no place in the Constituent Assembly for enemies of the people, for land-owners and capitalists'. For Lenin the links between the Kadets and Kaledin's activity on the Don were self-evident. Addressing the Soviet Executive on 1 December he pointed out:

> we have introduced the right to recall, so that the Constituent Assembly will not be the sort of gathering which the bourgeoisie dreamed of . . . The Kadets scream 'all power to the Constituent Assembly' but in fact this means 'all power to Kaledin' . . .[19]

Links between the Kadet Party and the Don region did indeed go back a long way. Before the February Revolution the leading Kadet M.S. Adzhemov had represented the cossack territory of the Don in the Tsar's Duma. In 1917 further links had begun to be forged as early as May when V.A. Kharlamov, president of the Don-Kuban Committee of the All-Russian Land Union, was elected to the Kadet Central Committee. Their interest in the region increased when the Provisional Government introduced a measure of regional autonomy to the cossack lands by recognizing as the local authority for the Don area the so-called Don Krug, with powers to elect a regional authority known as a Voisko government headed by an elected leader or ataman; General Kaledin was elected the first Don ataman towards the end of June. Kadet politicians were keen to exploit the traditional conservatism and patriotism of the Don cossacks to electoral advantage, and during May and June 1917 the leading Kadets Shingarev and Adzhemov toured the Don country to campaign for the establishment of a joint cossack-Kadet list in the Constituent Assembly elections. In June 1917 Milyukov and Nabokov, both members of the Kadet Central Committee, took care to address the Second All-Russian Cossack Congress when it met in Petrograd. By August it looked as if an electoral pact between the Kadets and the cossacks had been agreed and a joint list of candidates drawn up; however, these negotiations eventually foundered on the question of land rights for non-cossack inhabitants of the Don region, and the pact collapsed even before the Constituent Assembly elections had been held.[20]

In August 1917 the Don featured prominently in Kornilov's military plans. Kaledin was to have been a key player in the conspiracy, particularly when it came to moving troops up towards Moscow. Kaledin had vigorously denounced Kerensky's government at a session of the Moscow State Conference, and had made little attempt to hide his support for Kornilov. On 29 August, as the crisis developed, Kaledin announced that he intended to support Kornilov and threatened to cut communications between Moscow and the south. The same day he persuaded the Don Voisko government to order all cossack forces to obey only their ataman, Kaledin himself, and not Kerensky's government. To Kerensky this was rebellion and Kaledin was dismissed as ataman.

After the Kornilov crisis was over, Kerensky had to decide what to do about Kaledin, who, unlike the other plotters, had not been arrested. Kaledin relied on the support of his Don government. On 3 September not only the government but the entire elected assembly, the Krug, met in the regional capital Novocherkassk and remained in session for an entire week to debate the future of Kaledin. Faced with this display of popular support, Kerensky began to back down. On 4 September he informed Novocherkassk that Kaledin would not be arrested, but should come to GHQ to report to the Investigating Commission. Then, at the end of the week, a delegation from the government and soviet arrived to request the surrender of Kaledin; the Krug assembly refused. By 8 September Kerensky had cut his losses and announced that there was insufficient evidence to implicate Kaledin; he added that in some respects he had even been misinformed of Kaledin's activities. During the confrontation Kaledin denied he had ever participated in Kornilov's plot, or that he favoured autonomy for the Don; he conceded only that if Kornilov had taken power, those cossack military units formed on the Don would have stayed on the Don.[21]

This concern for Don regionalism or Don autonomy was crucial to Kaledin retaining his power base and avoiding arrest, but a constant weakness for those liberal politicians hoping to put the cossacks to their own purposes, as seen by their complete misreading of the cossacks' attitude to the land rights of the non-cossack population. As the authority of Kerensky's government disappeared after the failure to bring Kaledin to book, moves towards autonomy gathered pace. On 20 September representatives of the Don, Kuban, Terek, Astrakhan, Kalmyk, Ural and Dagestan cossacks met in the southern town of Vladikavkaz and formed the South East Union; its twin aims were the establishment of a Russian Democratic Federal Republic and the fight against Bolshevism. The South East Union chose as its capital Ekaterinodar and the Kadet Kharlamov was to be its head. However, a question mark was soon put over the future of the union when on 30 October, after the Bolshevik seizure of power, a separate Don Republic was proclaimed.[22]

Thus although the Don seemed the natural focus for liberal counter-revolutionaries, the regionalism of the local population meant that they were uncertain of the welcome they would receive. Counter-revolutionary forces began to concentrate on the Don after 2 November, the day former Commander-in-Chief General Alekseev arrived there; he immediately appealed for the formation of a Volunteer Army which would continue the war with Germany, but his appeal met little response among the local population since many younger cossacks were opposed to the war. Only fellow officers in flight rallied to him, and although from the Bolsheviks' point of view the activities of leading Kadets like A. Tyrkova-Williams showed a clear Kadet–Don conspiracy – her Petrograd flat became a staging post for officers fleeing to the Don – it was easy to overestimate this danger. The reality was that tension was high between the cossack population, on whom Kaledin's authority rested, and the incoming liberal volunteer officers.

By the end of November many important Kadet politicians had gathered on the Don. Milyukov had moved there from Moscow; Khrushchev had arrived with some of the funds he had appropriated from the State Bank; and Novosiltsev, leader of the Officers' Union, had also made the hazardous journey. They were joined by Kornilov himself on 3 December, who had escaped from detention with his fellow conspirators on 19 November and spent an eventful two weeks dodging Bolshevik patrols. The problem for the new arrivals was that the Kadets had failed to foresee the indifference of the local population. At one point Kaledin even asked Alekseev and the Kadet officer volunteers to leave his capital town Novocherkassk, but the Bolshevik attack on nearby Rostov on Don at the end of November 1917 brought the two groups together again.

The Bolshevik commander V.A. Antonov-Ovseenko had been given the task of martialling Red Guard units from Petrograd, Moscow, Kharkov, the Donbass and Odessa to take action against the Don counter-revolution. On 25 November local Bolsheviks succeeded in seizing power in Rostov and Antonov-Ovseenko sent his units in to support them. Kaledin's forces counter-attacked, but after three days fierce fighting the Bolsheviks were still in control. Thus at that time when the Kadet Party in Petrograd was anathematized as the 'enemies of the people', its forces on the Don were more or less on the run.[23] Only on 2 December, when supported by Alekseev's Volunteer Army, did Kaledin succeed in retaking the city and driving the Bolsheviks from Rostov. After this joint action Kaledin allowed the Volunteer Army to carry arms in public, something he had refused to agree to until then.

The situation would scarcely improve in the following two months. During December all the old tensions among the Kornilov plotters began to resurface. Kornilov saw no need for a political apparatus, but Alekseev and his Kadet advisors' did. The issue was resolved on 18 December when the politicians and generals held a large and at times vitriolic conference, during which it was agreed to establish a sort of triumvirate on the Don: Alekseev would be in charge of politics, Kornilov in charge of the military campaign, and Kaledin in charge of Don affairs. Alekseev's role was perhaps the most important for the long term. His Special Council, dominated by Kadet politicians like Struve, Milyukov and Prince G.N. Trubetskoi, came out against the Constituent Assembly even before it had had a chance to assemble. The Constituent Assembly, it was argued, had not fairly represented the views of the people: it would therefore be the job of the Volunteer Army to stand guard over the country's civil liberties until the country could express its will by electing a new Constituent Assembly; this was an open call for the establishment of a military dictatorship.[24]

By 10 January 1918 Bolshevik forces were ready to start a co-ordinated anti-Kaledin campaign, again led by Antonov-Ovseenko. On 17 January, in an effort to distance itself from wavering cossack support and rely on the bourgeois citizenry of a Russian town, the Volunteer Army moved its base from Novocherkassk to Rostov. But, despite the arrival of such prominent liberal figures as Rodzianko and N.N. Lvov, the local population raised little money to support them, and financial support promised from Moscow never arrived. By the end of January Kaledin's military situation appeared to be so tenuous that the Volunteer Army decided to retreat to the Kuban, leaving Novocherkassk to soviet occupation; by 24 February Rostov had been recaptured by the Bolsheviks. As the volunteers' retreat continued, Ekaterinodar, the nominal capital of the once proclaimed South East Union, fell to the Red Army in mid-March. Its recapture on 12 April 1918 did little to help the morale of the volunteers, since Kornilov was killed in the fighting. The Volunteer Army was at rock bottom and after its retreat beyond the Don, the cossack government collapsed in crisis. Kaledin committed suicide and the Don cossacks elected as their new ataman General Krasnov, who established a stable regime only by agreeing to co-operate with the Germans.[25]

Thus, at the time of the dissolution of the Constituent Assembly on 5 January 1918, the counter-revolutionary threat from the Kadets had virtually disappeared. Their forces on the Don were already in check, and the party itself had dropped all interest in the Constituent Assembly as the salvation of Russia, preferring instead to pin its hopes on a military dictatorship – to be led by generals who were about to be sent into an ignominious rout. The Bolsheviks had won this skirmish in the White versus Red civil war, the war against the generals, as easily as the soviet had prevented Kornilov seizing power in his rebellion: any counter-revolution Lenin would have to face in January 1918 would not come from the Whites but the Greens, the SRs, the victors in the Constituent Assembly elections.

## THE SRs AND THE CONSTITUENT ASSEMBLY

When the Kadet politicians turned up on 28 November 1917 to try to open the Constituent Assembly on the planned date, an act for which they were declared 'enemies of the people', they found themselves outnumbered by SRs and their supporters, with the SR mayor of Petrograd G.I. Shreider in the chair and Chernov making a speech promising that the Constituent Assembly would give peace, land and freedom. The SRs' dominant position reflected the fact that a week earlier, on 22 November, they had set up the Committee to Defend the Constituent Assembly under the leadership of the veteran Popular Socialist Chaikovskii; from that time on the Constituent Assembly was very much an SR concern. They dominated the proposed welcoming committee on 28 November, which included both Chernov and Chaikovskii. Of the 46 deputies who attended this first attempt to open the assembly, 37 were SRs, including Zenzinov, Sorokin, Ya T. Dedusenko, and N.P. Oganskii – all fey figures in the summer of 1918. Sorokin took an especially high profile.[26]

The attempt to open the Constituent Assembly on 28 November coincided with the Fourth Congress of the SR Party, which took place from 26 November to 5 December. This was a triumph for the cautious policies of the Central Committee led by Chernov. By an overwhelming majority (126–7) it voted to adopt a 'businesslike' approach to the Constituent Assembly. As Chernov himself recalled, the party should:

counter-pose the Bolshevik method of giving out unobtainable promises with the tactic of serious and well-thought-out legislation, divorced from any opportunist compromise. In the first rank that meant addressing the questions of peace, land, control of production, and the restructuring of the Russian Republic on federal principles; equally all issues of social policy should be linked to the task of demobilizing the army and industry.

The party would put these issues to the masses and eschew any thoughts of plotting terrorist activity. Those on the right of the party who had been so quick to take up arms against the Bolsheviks in October were to be kept in check.[27]

SR deputies to the assembly gathered in Petrograd throughout December – by the end of December some 250 had arrived – and met almost daily under the leadership of an elected bureau whose membership included Argunov, Gendelman, S.S. Maslov, K.S. Burevoi, Gots, Dedusenko and Zenzinov. For a time this bureau became even more influential than the SR Central Committee. Some fourteen commissions were established, to which the Mensheviks and Popular Socialists were invited to send representatives; that with the most difficult task was the commission for the opening day, whose membership included Gots, S.S. Maslov and M.A. Likhach, head of the party's military commission – more key figures in the summer of 1918.[28] Ironically, given the triumph of Chernov at the Fourth Party Congress, the majority of these leading deputies were on the right of the party. This was not a problem at this stage since there was a community of interest between the Central Committee's deter-mination to use the Constituent Assembly for businesslike work, and the traditional passivism and political caution of the right. Thus the veto powers over the deputies, which the Party Central Committee had insisted on instituting at the Fourth Congress – making SR deputies to the Constituent Assembly either accept Central Committee instructions or resign – were never a serious issue.[29] (The question of the veto powers of the SR Central Committee would only cause controversy in autumn 1918.)

The SR Party was not planning any spectacular developments. It made no response when on 16 December 24 leading members of the Committee to Defend the Constituent Assembly, including Avksentiev, were arrested. It agreed *de facto* to go along with the government decision that a quorum of 400 was needed before the assembly could open and that the opening should take place on 5 January. The opening ceremony would be accompanied by nothing more than a peaceful demonstration. The majority of party leaders clearly felt that, on its first day, by issuing manifestos on peace, land

and workers' control, the Constituent Assembly would win sufficient popular support to win the hearts and minds of the people. The SRs simply found it hard to believe that an assembly which had introduced such legislation could be dispersed without a popular outcry.[30]

When the details of the Declaration of the Rights of Labouring and Exploited People became clear on 3 January, along with the open statement by the Soviet Executive that any organization which refused to accept it would be 'counter-revolutionary' and subject to arrest, the SRs took no serious measures. They simply set up a special commission including Likhach, Dedusenko and B.N. Moiseenko to draft a manifesto. Indeed, while the party's military commission had been asked to draw up plans for possible military action, and S.S. Maslov, a strongly pro-war right-winger, had been busy assembling a force of 11,000 men, the Central Committee saw this simply as a policy option to be used or rejected according to the circumstances. The day after this military commission held its final meeting with its military staff on 3 January at Chaikovskii's flat, the Central Committee simply informed them on the night of 4–5 January that there would be no armed action; it should act only if the assembly were dissolved and a spontaneous insurrection developed from below. Likhach had to inform members of the Semenovskii regiment that their services would not be required.[31]

What was also clear by the eve of the Constituent Assembly was that the SRs were quite happy to play the Revolutionary Convention game, and hoped to win. When the SR Central Committee met on 26–27 December to finalize its plans, it agreed to take part in the Third Congress of Soviets, but at the same time to rally a parallel Congress of Soviets which supported the Constituent Assembly. This was not empty rhetoric: SR successes in recalling Bolshevik delegates from the soviets had forced the Bolsheviks increasingly to delay by-elections, prompting in turn the SRs to organize counter 'workers' conferences'. Thus it was extremely likely that if the Revolutionary Convention went ahead it would have to operate against a backdrop of rival congresses of soviets supporting rival groups of peasant deputies in the Constituent Assembly. This was not the sort of risk Lenin was prepared to take, hence the decision to impose the Declaration of the Rights of Labouring and Exploited People.[32]

## PEACE AND THE UKRAINE

At their Central Committee meeting on 26–27 December the SRs raised another issue that caused Lenin discomfort. In planning their future activities within the Constituent Assembly they agreed to use their contacts with the Ukrainian SRs to reopen talks with the Ukrainian government (the Rada, which was SR in outlook) about the constitutional position of the Ukraine in a reformed Russian federal state. They did so at the precise moment when Lenin's relations with the Rada had deteriorated to the point where military operations against the Ukrainian government had begun.

Shortly after Lenin's seizure of power, the Rada had claimed full power in a newly declared People's Republic of the Ukraine on 7 November 1917, making clear that, henceforth, the Ukraine would have a federal relationship with Russia. At first this caused few problems: on 17 November, Stalin, as Lenin's Commissar of Nationalities, had talks with the Secretary of Labour in the Rada and asked simply that a Congress of Soviets be held in the Ukraine with the aim of establishing soviet power there; the Secretary of Labour readily agreed, and the Rada duly summoned a Congress of Soviets for 4 December 1917.[33] It was only the following month, when peace negotiations began between the Bolsheviks and the Central Powers that the attitude of the Ukraine began to cause problems.

Moves towards peace began on 8 November when Lenin called on the last Supreme Commander-in-Chief of the Russian Army General N.N. Dukhonin to begin armistice talks with the aim of establishing a general armistice on all fronts of the First World War. General Dukhonin consulted the All-Army Committee and the Allied representatives of Britain, France and Italy then at GHQ. The All-Army Committee responded by proposing the formation of a socialist coalition government led by Chernov and backed by the SRs Gots and Zenzinov and the Menshevik Skobelev, all of whom were at GHQ; the Allies suggested playing for time. Dukhonin followed the Allies' advice and on 9 November replied that he needed further talks with the Allies before agreeing to an armistice. When Lenin questioned the necessity of this, Dukhonin conceded that he did not recognize the legitimacy of Lenin's government; for the Bolsheviks it was then a simple matter to portray GHQ as 'counter-revolutionary', since it had refused to take the first steps towards peace, and Dukhonin was dismissed.

Dismissing Dukhonin was one thing, enforcing his dismissal quite another. In a classic instance of Lenin using the 'creativity of the masses', he appealed on 9 November for the troops to take matters into their own hands and organize local armistices. Although motivated by a desire to circumvent GHQ, the armistice ferment Lenin unleashed involved the population at large in the struggle for peace and greatly strengthened the position of the Bolsheviks in the army; the idea of a GHQ supported government headed by Chernov was promptly vetoed by the SR and Menshevik central committees at meetings held on 10 November. Popular enthusiasm for peace was such that Lenin's nominee as new Supreme Commander-in-Chief, N.V. Krylenko, had little difficulty taking over GHQ on 20 November with a force of 3,000 sailors and garrison troops. Indeed the wrath directed at Dukhonin for trying to resist the armistice was such that he was brutally murdered by Krylenko's forces on the 21st.[34] Armistice talks with Germany began at Brest-Litovsk two days earlier, on 19 November 1917.

The Ukraine, however, was not bound by this decision. Since the Rada's declaration of 7 November, control of GHQ did not give Lenin control over Ukrainian troops; the Ukrainian army might conceivably carry on fighting on the Allied side. At first nothing of the sort happened. The Rada issued a separate call for a general peace on 10 November, and separately proposed an armistice on 26 November. Relations between Lenin and the Rada began to deteriorate when, at the time of the Bolsheviks' attack on Rostov on Don, on 24 November, the Rada refused Krylenko's request to allow Bolshevik troops to cross Ukrainian territory to reach the Don; the refusal contrasted sharply with the blind eye it had turned to White officers trying to join Alekseev's Volunteer Army. A few days later, on 29–30 November, in what was seen by the Bolsheviks as a further hostile act, but for the Rada was simply a stage in the Ukrainianization of the old Imperial Army, the Rada dissolved pro-Bolshevik units in Kiev.[35]

But these issues were symptomatic of a more fundamental antagonism. This worsening of relations between the Russian and Ukrainian governments coincided with Lenin's decision to change his policy towards peace with Germany; he moved from linking his request for an armistice to German acceptance of a general armistice on all fronts, to simply requesting a separate armistice with Germany in order to struggle towards a general peace. The armistice talks had begun in Brest-Litovsk with opening statements concerning the need for a general peace, and then adjourned for a week. On 24 November Kamenev, who had been a member of the delegation to this first round of talks, told the Soviet Executive:

> We can only accept an armistice that is the prelude to a general peace
> which will render impossible any resumption of hostilities . . . My
> impression is that Germany is willing to make very great concessions to
> get a separate peace, but that is not what we have been negotiating for
> . . . Our representatives proposed not some secret treaty but peace
> without annexations or indemnities on the basis of self-determination.[36]

Yet within days, Lenin had decided to authorize the delegation on its
return to explore the concessions available in a separate armistice, and
the Soviet Executive suitably amended its instructions. By 27
November the mandate of the Soviet Executive's representatives was
to 'undertake all steps necessary to achieve an armistice as rapidly as
possible in order to struggle for a general peace, on a democratic
foundation, between the peoples'. The escape clause 'to struggle for a
general peace' opened the way for a separate armistice to be
negotiated, and an armistice was rapidly agreed on 2 December.[37]

Until the beginning of December, Lenin's government could
justifiably hope that its nascent disagreement with the Rada would be
put right when the Ukrainian Congress of Soviets met and established
a more sympathetic government than the Rada. However, the
Ukrainian Congress of Soviets, far from endorsing soviet power when
it gathered in Kiev on 4 December, turned out to be dominated by
the Ukrainian SRs who endorsed the Rada as the legitimate
government. Lenin was furious. The same day he issued an ultimatum
to the Rada demanding that within 48 hours it should stop allowing
White officers to join Alekseev's Volunteer Army on the Don, join
the struggle against Kaledin, and stop disarming pro-soviet regiments.
Lenin's ultimatum prompted the Bolsheviks at the Ukrainian Congress
of Soviets in Kiev to walk out and move to Kharkov where the
Regional Congress of Soviets of the Donets Basin and Krivoi Rog was
then in session. The Bolsheviks transformed this congress into a rival
Ukrainian Congress of Soviets. On 11–12 December this rival Congress
of Soviets declared itself the legitimate First All-Ukrainian Congress of
Soviets with power over the whole of the Ukraine and on 13
December the Ukrainian Soviet Republic was declared in Kharkov.[38]
Lenin had thus engineered a potential Red versus Green, Bolshevik
versus SR civil war in the Ukraine, but one in which the Ukrainian
Bolsheviks would have the support of Russian Red Guard troops.

In Kiev the Rada rejected Lenin's ultimatum on 7 December and
the following day the Soviet Executive in Petrograd debated the
situation. After noting that 'self-determination for the Ukrainian
people is not, of course, self-determination for counter-revolution',
the executive called for talks; Ukrainian representatives duly came to

Moscow and invasion plans were shelved. Lenin's problem was that he had to take the views of the Left SRs into account. They were deeply sceptical about the idea of encouraging Red versus Green civil war in the Ukraine, since they had much support in the Ukraine. On 12 December they told the Soviet Executive that the struggle against the Ukrainian bourgeoisie could only be waged from inside the Ukraine and pointed out 'we should not rely on the military forces present in the Ukraine or on the chance of a military victory'. In contrast, two days later Stalin was justifying the government's actions before the Soviet Executive in the following words:

> It may seem strange that the Council of People's Commissars, which has always resolutely defended the principle of self-determination, should have come into conflict with the Rada, which likewise proceeds from the principle . . . [But] if the Rada prevents us moving against Kaledin and shields him, then our blows against Kaledin will fall upon its forces.[39]

However, in the same speech Stalin hinted at the government's true concerns, since the danger on the Don was quite ephemeral. Stalin noted that Lenin's government had intercepted a coded telegram making clear that the Rada was in touch with the French military mission and was considering ways of delaying the conclusion of the peace talks until the spring. The danger presented by a separate Ukrainian delegation at the Brest-Litovsk peace talks, a delegation that might follow a pro-Allied policy, this was Lenin's true concern regarding the Ukraine. On 11–12 December a Ukrainian representative in Moscow told the *Guardian* journalist Philips-Price that this really was the crux of the matter: the Ukraine wanted special representation at the peace conference and although from 9–15 December they had simply been prepared to observe the Russian delegation, on 11 December the Rada formally demanded that their delegation be separate; ominously for Lenin after 12 December the German side in the Brest-Litovsk talks began to ask pointed questions about the exact status of the Ukraine. A welcome recess allowed the Bolshevik government some time to consider its position before the talks were due to resume on 28 December. But when on 24 December news came that a Rada delegation had reached Brest-Litovsk before the Russian delegation and was already talking to the Germans, something had to be done.[40]

## A SEPARATE PEACE FOR CIVIL WAR

The Ukraine, peace, the Constituent Assembly: issues were crowding in on Lenin, and all were interrelated. If the Constituent Assembly gathered, if the SRs succeeded in turning the Revolutionary Convention to their advantage, if they made common cause with the Ukrainian SRs at the Brest–Litovsk talks, if those talks then broke down and the war recommenced, if any of these things happened the days of the Bolshevik revolution were numbered. As Lenin had done throughout his career at times of crisis, he took a short break and settled down to think things through from first principles. Thus Christmas 1917 found Lenin in Finland sketching out the future in two short works *Fear of Collapse of the Old and Fight for the New* and *From a Publicists Diary; Notes for Elaboration.*[41]

Getting back to first principles for Lenin meant getting back to Marx and Engels and what they had had to say about the transition from capitalism to socialism. Thus he wrote in *Fear of Collapse of the Old and Fight for the New*:

> We have always said that a long period of 'birth–pangs' lies between capitalism and socialism; that violence is always the midwife of the old society; that a special state (that is a special system of organized coercion of a definite class) corresponds to the transitional period between the bourgeois and the socialist society, namely the dictatorship of the proletariat. What dictatorship implies and means is a state of simmering war, a state of military measures of struggle against the enemies of proletarian power. The Commune was a dictatorship of the proletariat, and Marx and Engels reproached it for what they considered to be one of the causes of its downfall, namely, that the Commune had not used its armed force with *sufficient* vigour to suppress the resistance of the exploiters.[42]

Clearly Lenin had resolved on the use of force, and in this essay in which he was essentially musing to himself, there was no mention of Kaledin or the Don; neither was there any mention of the peasantry or even poor peasantry. Lenin was talking about 'the enemies of proletarian power', and they were the SRs.

Lenin's concerns were expressed even more clearly in *From a Publicist's Diary: Notes for Elaboration*. The points to be elaborated at a later date included 'how to "win over" to the side of the Russian Socialist Republic of Soviets other nations, in general, and the nations formerly oppressed by the Great Russians in particular', the Ukraine was the most prominent of these; 'the Constituent Assembly', a justification for its dispersal; and 'a separate peace', how it was not a compromise with the imperialists. As the list of points neared its end, the direction of Lenin's thought became clear: 'first defeat the bourgeoisie in Russia, then fight the foreign, alien bourgeoisie', 'gain time through a separate peace'.[43] Lenin was not entirely abandoning the notion that Russia was the weak link in the chain of imperial powers, but he was abandoning the vision of a transnational civil war against imperialism with simultaneous insurrections throughout Europe; the struggle would have to be waged country by country and his revolution would have to be defended first, to ensure the survival of the revolutionary ideal.

Lenin's idea on how to 'win over' the Ukrainians, so long victims of Great Russian chauvinism, was immediately put into effect. It was clear to all Bolsheviks that the presence of an antagonistic Ukrainian delegation at Brest-Litovsk would make the work of the Bolshevik delegation doubly difficult. When the talks resumed on 28 December Trotsky was at first willing to recognize the Ukrainian delegation after it had agreed to consult the Russians on all matters. However, on 1 January 1918 the Ukrainian delegation broke this undertaking and met the Germans alone for the first time. So in the last days of December 1917 the Bolsheviks launched an all-out invasion of the Ukraine from their base of the Ukrainian Soviet Republic in Kharkov. From there Red Guard units from Petrograd, Moscow and other industrial centres advanced into the Ukraine extending soviet power to Ekaterinoslav, Odessa, Poltava, Aleksandrovsk, Mariupol, Kherson and Zhmernik.[44]

Antonov-Ovseenko was the nominal head of this army, but he was also engaged in driving the Volunteer Army from the Don. The main army in the Ukraine was headed by Muraviev, the victor of the battle of Pulkovo Heights, who took the task of social revolution seriously: as his troops advanced the local soviets were ignored and revolutionary committees of Bolsheviks and Left SRs established in the towns he conquered; in Poltava he threatened to arrest the entire local soviet executive and physically destroy the city unless it obeyed. Militarily, however, Muraviev's campaign was a triumph. Although his advance towards Kiev was too slow to coincide with the Bolshevik uprising there on 29 January – 2 February 1918, which was suppressed by the Rada, by 7 February he had captured the Ukrainian capital and by the 11th the Bolshevik Ukrainian Government, the People's Secretariat, had arrived from Kharkov. But Muraviev's campaign came too late to prevent the Germans playing the Ukrainian card. On 5 January 1918 the Germans presented their demands to Trotsky and called an adjournment for ten days; during those ten days, on 9 January, the

Ukraine declared itself a fully independent state and was recognized as such by Germany on the 19th.

The Germans' skilful handling of the Ukrainian issue reinforced Lenin's growing conviction that the only way forward was a peace treaty with Germany. Trotsky returned to Petrograd to find Lenin openly arguing for his policy of accepting the German terms for a separate peace.[45] The ensuing clash between Lenin and Trotsky was reminiscent of an earlier disagreement between the two men when, before returning to Russia, they had fallen out over the policy of 'revolutionary defeatism'. Lenin, unlike any other leading anti-war socialist, had argued that the logic of an anti-war stance required a commitment to take measures which might result in the defeat of your own country; for Trotsky this was impossible, since the consequent strengthening of German imperialism implied in such a stance meant imperialism would be strengthened rather than weakened. In 1916 this dispute had been carried out on the pages of obscure émigré journals; now it was being carried out for real.[46]

On 8 December Trotsky had told the Soviet Executive the following:

> If Europe continues to be silent as the grave, and if this silence gives
> Wilhelm the chance to attack us and to dictate his terms to us, terms that
> would insult the revolutionary dignity of our country, then I am not sure
> whether, given our shattered economy and the general chaos (the result of
> war and internal strife), we could fight. I think, however, we could do so.
> For our lives, for our revolutionary honour, we would fight to the last
> drop of blood . . . we would sound the call and would raise an army of
> soldiers and Red Guardsmen, strong in its revolutionary enthusiasm,
> which would fight for as long as it could. We have not yet played our last
> card . . . If they offer us conditions that are unacceptable . . . we shall
> present them to the Constituent Assembly and say: decide. If the
> Constituent Assembly accepts them, the Bolshevik Party will relinquish
> power . . .[47]

In the last weeks before the Bolshevik seizure of power Lenin had frequently spoken in similar terms about the need for revolutionary war – on 13 September he had said of the Bolsheviks after seizing power 'we will become the defencists, we will head the war party'[48] – but in January 1918 a clash with Trotsky seemed inevitable.

When the issue was first discussed at an expanded Central Committee session on 8 January, a clear majority favoured war rather than succumbing to a dictated peace. However, in the less public atmosphere of an ordinary Central Committee session on 11 January, with echoes of the sequence of expanded and ordinary sessions seen on 1 and 2 November 1917 when discussing the issue of a coalition socialist government, Lenin secured a compromise: the meeting adopted the formula advanced by Trotsky of 'no peace, no war'; this would be put to the Germans when the talks resumed after the recess and if there was no adequate response, Trotsky promised Lenin, he would support peace. In public, however, as his speech to the Third Congress of Soviets on 13 January showed, Trotsky spoke of 'No peace with German militarists! Revolutionary war against world imperialism!', and the congress itself resolved that Russia 'would never willingly sign an unfortunate and imperialistic peace and would prepare to defend itself against the exploiters of all lands'.[49]

When Trotsky returned to Brest-Litovsk four days later, he hoped against hope that the industrial unrest then sweeping through Berlin and Vienna might result in the overthrow of the imperial regimes in Germany and Austria. On 17 January the third phase of the talks began and, as Lenin had feared, was dominated by the Ukraine. After some ten days of negotiations, with the strikes in Berlin and Vienna visibly on the wane and Muraviev's army still not in control of Kiev, the Germans signed a treaty with the Ukrainians on 28 January and prepared to issue an ultimatum to Trotsky, who issued the declaration 'no war, no peace' later that same day. Trotsky returned to Petrograd on the 30th and three days later, on 16 February – the western calendar was adopted on 1 February 1918 – the Germans announced they would resume the war on the 18th, and did so. The policy of 'no war, no peace' had led directly to war and the German occupation of the Ukraine. The Bolshevik Ukrainian government moved to Poltava on 28 February, and then retreated with some degree of order to Ekaterinoslav on 15 March, but within a month further the German advances had put an end to its brief existence.[50] Lenin had wanted peace with Germany so that he could dissolve the Constituent Assembly in relative safety and resume the Red versus Green civil war against the SRs, but Trotsky had let him down. Russia and Germany were again at war, and that put the nascent Red–Green civil war on ice for a further three months.

## NOTES

1. State Archive of the Russian Federation (GARF) 5498.1.74, protocols of session 3 November; J.L.H. Keep (ed.), *The Debate on Soviet Power, the Minutes of VTsIK, Second Convocation* (Oxford 1979), pp. 107, 307.
2. In September 1993 the Lenin Museum in Moscow had a poster display

on the Constituent Assembly elections, and the Bolshevik posters clearly implied that the Bolsheviks would be taking part in a coalition socialist administration.

3. *The Bolsheviks and the October Revolution: Central Committee Minutes of the RSDLP(b)* (London 1974), p. 151; Keep, *Debate*, p. 90.
4. O.H. Radkey, *The Sickle under the Hammer* (Columbia 1963), p. 359.
5. O.H. Radkey, *Russia Goes to the Polls* (Cornell 1990). Mostly these figures are taken from chapter 2.
6. Keep, *Debate*, pp. 135–41, 374; T.A. Sivokhina, *Krakh melkoburzhuaznoi oppozitsii* (Moscow 1973), p. 72 et seq.
7. V.M. Chernov, *Pered burey* (New York 1953), p. 347.
8. *Minutes*, p. 90.
9. Keep, *Debate*, p. 144 et seq.
10. *Minutes*, p. 153.
11. Keep, *Debate*, p. 180.
12. *Minutes*, p. 167; Keep, *Debate*, p. 403.
13. Keep, *Debate*, pp. 243, 403.
14. Keep, *Debate*, pp. 257, 414.
15. M. Philips-Price, *My Reminiscences of the Russian Revolution* (London 1921), p. 219.
16. Keep, *Debate*, p. 264.
17. These events are described in W.G. Rosenburg, *Liberals in the Russian Revolution* (Princeton 1974), p. 264 et seq.; A. Tyrkova-Williams, *From Liberty to Brest Litovsk* (London 1919), p. 275 et seq., V.D. Medlin and S.L. Parsons (eds), *V.D. Nabokov and the Russian Provisional Government* (Yale 1976), p. 165 et seq.; N.G. Dumova, *Kadetskaya kontrrevolyutsiya i ee razgrom* (Moscow 1982), p. 30 et seq.
18. Rosenberg, *Liberals*, p. 279.
19. Keep, *Debate*, p. 177.
20. Dumova, *Kadetskaya*, p. 41 et seq.; G.A. Brinkley, *The Volunteer Army and Allied Intervention in Southern Russia* (Notre Dame 1966), p. 12 et seq., F.I. Rodichev *Vospominanii i ocherki o russkoi liberalizme* (Newtownville 1982), p. 133 et seq.
21. P.N. Milyukov, *The Russian Revolution* (Gulf Breeze 1984), p. 219; N. Ya Ivanov, *Kontrrevolyutsiya v Rossii v 1917g. i ee razgrom* (Moscow 1977), p. 204 et seq.
22. Brinkley, *Volunteer*, p. 13; A.K. Wildman, *The End of the Russian Imperial Army* (Princeton 1980) vol. 2, p. 395.
23. This summary is taken from: Rosenberg, *Liberals*, p. 309 et seq.; Brinkley, *Volunteer*, p. 15 et seq.; Dumova, *Kadetskaya*, p. 43 et seq.; A. Suvorin, *Pokhod Kornilova* (Rostov on Don 1918), pp. 2–9.
24. Brinkley, *Volunteer*, p. 19.
25. For the funds from Moscow, see Suvorin, *Pokhod*, p. 8; otherwise Brinkley, *Volunteer*, p. 20 et seq.
26. O.N. Znamenskii, *Vserossiiskoe uchreditel'noe sobranie* (Moscow 1976), p. 309.
27. Chernov, *Pered burey*, pp. 347–51.

28. Znamenskii, *Uchreditel'noe*, p. 322.
29. Radkey, *Sickle*, p. 355.
30. For the arrests on 16 December, see Keep, *Debate*, p. 403; otherwise Znamenskii, *Uchreditel'noe*, p. 325.
31. Znamenskii, *Uchreditel'noe*, p. 337; Radkey, *Sickle*, p. 421.
32. Znamenskii, *Uchreditel'noe*, p. 331; Chernov, *Pered burey*, p. 351.
33. Keep, *Debate*, pp. 365–7.
34. For events at GHQ, see Wildman, *Imperial Army*, p. 353 et seq.
35. Keep, *Debate*, pp. 193, 366–70.
36. Keep, *Debate*, p. 154.
37. Keep, *Debate*, p. 169; for the details of the peace negotiations, see R. Debo, *Revolution and Survival* (Liverpool 1979).
38. J. Reshetar, 'The Communist Party of the Ukraine and its role in the Ukranian Revolution', in T. Hunczak (ed.), *The Ukraine, 1917–21: a Study in Revolution* (Harvard 1977), p. 169; O. Fedyshyn, *Germany's Drive to the East and the Ukrainian Revolution* (New Brunswick 1971), p. 63.
39. Keep, *Debate*, pp. 194, 198, 217.
40. Keep, *Debate*, p. 370; Philips-Price, *Reminiscences*, p. 197; Debo, *Revolution*, p. 55.
41. For Lenin's ideas at this time, see Debo, *Revolution*, p. 62 et seq., on whom part of this section is based.
42. V.I. Lenin, *Collected Works* (Moscow 1960) vol. 26, p. 401.
43. Lenin, *Collected Works* vol. 36, p. 460.
44. Debo, *Revolution*, p. 66; Fedyshyn, *Drive to the East*, p. 66.
45. Reshetar, 'Communist Party of the Ukraine', p. 173; Debo, *Revolution*, p. 70.
46. B. Pearce, 'Lenin versus Trotsky', *Sbornik* 13 (1987).
47. Keep, *Debate*, p. 187.
48. *Minutes*, p. 63.
49. Debo, *Revolution*, p. 79; Philips-Price, *Reminiscences*, p. 226.
50. Debo, *Revolution*, p. 124; Reshetar, 'Communist Party of the Ukraine', p. 174.

# CHAPTER FOUR
# The British and the Patriotic Socialists

The renewal of hostilities on the Eastern Front on 18 February 1918 was most welcome news for Russia's Allies. That Russia might sign a separate peace with Germany had been the Allies' nightmare since the failure of the offensive in June 1917. Over the summer British policy in Russia had been to prevent this by working for co-operation between Kerensky and Kornilov. Alexis Aladin, who had returned to Russia in the summer of 1917 and became actively involved in the work of those liberal politicians seeking to prevent Kornilov taking hasty dictatorial action and hoping to engineer the formation of a Kerensky–Kornilov alliance, acted in accordance with British policy. During the First World War Aladin had worked for the British government on other occasions, putting his experience of revolutionary politics to particular use on a visit to Ireland in the aftermath of the Easter Rising of 1916. The British did not back Kornilov. When it became clear Kornilov was moving against Kerensky's government and not seeking simply to transform its composition, the British were not impressed: the ambassador Sir George Buchanan was asked by Kornilov's most loyal industrialist supporter Putilov if British armoured cars could be put at Kornilov's disposal; Buchanan politely refused, pointing out that such an enterprise was bound to fail and could only strengthen the Bolsheviks.[1]

Although Britain's military representative General Alfred Knox was more proactive in support of Kornilov, his actions never strayed beyond Buchanan's clear guidelines. Knox did pay for the production of the pamphlet *Kornilov, the National Hero* distributed during the Moscow State Conference, and did not object to the frequent visits to the British military mission of Zavoiko and the Kadet officers like Colonel Golitsyn. But, while just before the coup attempt he urged

Kerensky's War Cabinet to let Kornilov have a free hand in restoring the army, during the coup he went along with the official British line asking Kerensky to seek an accommodation with Kornilov. British officers in Russia were aware of Kornilov's plans, indeed Commander Oliver Locker-Lampson and Major-General Sir Charles St Leger Barter, the British Military Representative at GHQ, were active participants in its early preparations, but their reports to London of an imminent coup prompted the firm rebuke; they should keep out of politics. The British line was clearly for reconciliation between Kornilov and Kerensky.

During the Kornilov affair Sir George Buchanan became increasingly disenchanted with the liberal politicians who constantly sought his support. At the time of the Moscow State Conference he recorded in his diary his growing doubts as to whether 'a purely Kadet and Octobrist government could do any better than the present one'. Kerensky was far from ideal, but who could replace him, he concluded rhetorically.[2] He was thus receptive to a change in policy which began to emerge in the autumn of 1917. Increasingly policymakers began to talk about the need to make links with patriotic socialist groups prepared to continue the war effort, referred to indiscriminately in British parlance as 'Mensheviks'. This unlikely alliance between the world's greatest empire and Russian patriotic socialists began with the mission to Russia of W. Somerset Maugham in autumn 1917.

In his later life Maugham always made light of his mission. There was indeed something faintly surreal about a British gentleman spy sitting in the European Hotel in Petrograd supping drinking chocolate with Professor Thomas Masaryk, the future President of Czechoslovakia, and holding secret planning meetings with his agents in the hotel bedroom of the patriotic feminist Mrs Emmeline Pankhurst. There was even an element of farce to the mission, when Maugham dashed from Petrograd to London with an urgent message from Kerensky to Lloyd George, arriving just after the Bolsheviks had seized power.[3] Nevertheless, the mission set in train a strategy that was to dominate British thinking until November 1918.

## THE MAUGHAM MISSION

The idea of intervening in Russia by cultivating patriotic socialist groups had been around in embryo since the late spring of 1917 but was first clearly formulated by Maugham. All versions of this idea, Maugham's and all subsequent permutations, had two key elements: one was to involve all patriotic socialist groups, the key ones being Plekhanov's 'Unity' Mensheviks, the Popular Socialists, and the right-wing SRs; and the other was to involve the Czechoslovak Legion and any other national armies which could form the core of a revived Russian army. Even before the abdication of the Tsar, the Russian Army had been recruiting from Czechoslovak and other slav national groups detained as prisoners of war after the capture of Austrian Army units; the largest such grouping by the summer of 1917 was the so-called Czechoslovak Legion.

One of the first to make this link was Bernard Pares, later Sir Bernard Pares, the founder of Russian Studies in British universities. In May 1917 he began working in Petrograd for the British ambassador Sir George Buchanan and in the course of his engagements to promote the war effort, got in touch with a follower of Plekhanov with whom he went on a 'Unity' speaking tour of the front accompanied by the former Bolshevik deputy to the Tsar's Duma of 1907 G. Aleksinskii; this tour included a visit to the headquarters of the Czechoslovak forces in the Ukraine. En route Czechoslovaks and Serbs were called on to help drum up support for the war effort, and Pares was willing to tell anyone who would listen of the fighting capacity of the Czechoslovaks he had met.[4]

So, over the summer of 1917 reports began to come back from Russia of the need to strengthen contacts with both patriotic socialists and the oppressed slav nations. Maugham's involvement in such matters was more or less accidental. He had worked as an agent in Switzerland from the autumn of 1915 to the summer of 1916, but had then given up the service, visited New York and toured the South Seas, before settling in America in the spring of 1917. There, towards the middle of June, he was contacted by an old family friend Sir William Wiseman, head of British Intelligence operations in the United States, who proposed the idea of a mission to support moderate socialists and 'keep Russia in the war'. This was to be a private mission. He was not, at first, expected to contact any British Intelligence officers in Petrograd and his activities 'could be disavowed if necessary'. Maugham agreed although, unlike for his work in Switzerland, he did ask to be paid.[5]

On 20 June Maugham had his first meeting with E. Voska, who headed the Intelligence Department of the Czechoslovak National Council which had helped British Intelligence penetrate the murky world of New York émigré groups. Maugham was to head a group of four Czechoslovak activists, Voska, Reverend A. Koukol, J. Martinek and V. Svarc, who would establish a 'Slav Press Bureau', to be the centrepiece of the operation. They left for Petrograd via Tokyo and the Trans-Siberian Railway shortly before Maugham, and arrived on 2 September.[6] Within a week the Press Bureau had been established, as a channel not merely for Czechoslovak propaganda, but Yugoslav and Polish as well; Voska had held talks with the Polish nationalist leader Paderewski in New York not three hours before his departure for Petrograd. Its work can be seen in the content of the patriotic socialist press in September and October; *Unity*, the newspaper of Plekhanov's group, produced a steady stream of reports on the national liberation struggle in Poland, Yugoslavia and Czechoslovakia, with Plekhanov himself endorsing the line they took.[7]

Maugham's own preparations proper began in July, when William Wiseman organized for him a series of contacts in Russia, which highlighted the role to be played in the venture by non-Russian nationalities. Thus it was the London-based Polish nationalist Jan Horodyski who furnished him with letters of introduction for use in Petrograd and Moscow. Among other contacts made in the first days of July were Commandant Stefanik of the Czechoslovak armed forces, a close associate of Voska, and a Professor Shatsky, a close friend of the British ambassador in Petrograd. On 18 July Maugham signed for $21,000 and under the codename 'Somerville' set off for Russia via Tokyo, leaving the Japanese capital on 27 August.[8]

On arriving in Petrograd Maugham was immediately put in touch with the main protagonists of the patriotic socialist movement. Despite his various letters of introduction, his main contact was one of his own making, Sasha Kropotkin, daughter of the anarchist leader Prince Peter Kropotkin. She was married to Boris Lebedev, who had taught with Pares at Liverpool University, and she and Maugham had had a brief affair in England before the war. Now she could introduce Maugham not only to Kropotkin, but through him to Chaikovskii and Plekhanov; the same path would lead him to Kerensky – he dined once a week with him or a member of his cabinet while Sasha acted as interpreter – and Savinkov, the man who impressed him most.[9]

In his first report home, Maugham was clearly impressed with the scale of the Czechoslovaks' organization and the potential it offered, over 1,200 outlets and 70,000 men all recorded on card indexes. The only problem, one that he left to a colleague to report, was that the Czechoslovak National Council had responded to the German capture of Riga by deciding to evacuate their offices to Moscow, something which hampered the smooth running of the operation.[10] His initial contact had been with Masaryk, to whom he was introduced by the Czechoslovak members of his mission. Masaryk had a very negative opinion of the state of affairs in Russia: he believed that there was no longer an audience for patriotic speeches, and, presumably, was unenthusiastic about the idea of a press bureau; the situation in Russia was far worse than appeared on the surface and Japanese intervention, talked about frequently at this time, seemed the only way forward. Maugham, however, was less down-hearted and warned London that Masaryk could well have fallen under Milyukov's spell. Indeed, Maugham at once formed a very negative impression of the Kadets; his first report home was dominated by a denunciation of the apparent presidential ambitions of liberal politician N.V. Nekrasov, who in August 1917 had been both Finance Minister and Deputy Prime Minister but was sidelined by Kerensky in September as Governor General of Finland – allegedly Nekrasov had ingratiated himself with the British ambassador and courted popularity by suggesting that he alone could persuade the Allies to propose a negotiated peace. Maugham added that he had been out on the streets during the Kornilov rebellion and found the crowds 'good-natured'. They were unlikely to commit excesses and the likelihood was that, while 'severe riots may be expected during the winter', there would not be a separate peace.[11]

Maugham's suspicions of the Kadets showed that he had grasped at once the need to distance the Allied cause from 'Kadets and counter-revolutionaries'. He reported:

> I have seen complaints that the foreign correspondents give news coloured exclusively by Kadet and counter-revolutionary opinions. I would suggest that it would be well worth while if the radical views were put as sympathetically as possible. The idea that the ambassadors and the press are entirely supporting one side is very galling to many Russians, and this partiality may very well defeat its own aim. At any rate to this is due much of the unpopularity from which the Allies are now suffering.[12]

Increasingly his views became paraphrases of those of the Popular Socialist and right-wing SR circles in which he mixed: if the Bolsheviks won a majority in the Democratic Conference they would seize power, with the connivance of reactionary forces, and Kerensky would go to GHQ; after a week-long reign of terror the Bolsheviks would be driven from power, but the power of the reactionary right would be strengthened. Despite this chaos theory, Maugham remained optimistic: 'Petrograd is heartily sick of agitations and next outbreak of Maximalists (as he termed the Bolsheviks) may be anticipated to be their last. Situation looks more hopeful for the future', he stated in a report dated 21 September.[13] (All his reports were dated according to the western calendar.) Kerensky's success at the Democratic Conference clearly impressed Maugham still further. While the report of 19 September stressed Kerensky's loss of popularity, that of 29 September noted Kerensky's chances of retaining power were much greater, since his enemies had no-one with whom to replace him. Partly this was put down to the success of Kerensky's War Minister Verkhovskii who 'has grown much less socialistic since his appointment', and seemed to be ready to reorganize the army.[14]

Verkhovskii did indeed become an enthusiastic supporter of the sort of army reform envisaged by Maugham and his slav team. Under Verkhovskii not only were the last objections to the formation of a Czechoslovak Legion dropped, but he began a veritable campaign to 'nationalize' the army in order to reinvigorate it – for only volunteers joined these 'foreign' army units and there were no soldiers' committees to sap morale. Working closely with the French military attaché General Niessel, Verkhovskii, despite opposition from some fellow ministers, began to encourage the formation of Ukrainian, Polish, South Slav and Czechoslovak units. The gist of the scheme was put to the autonomous government in the Ukraine, where the Czechoslovak Legion was based, just before Kerensky's overthrow: General Tabouis and Major Fitzwilliams, the French and British military representatives in Kiev respectively, told A. Shulgin, the putative Ukrainian Foreign Minister, that Ukrainian forces should be attached to the Army of Romania, while the Polish Corps and the Czechoslovak Legion should join any cossack forces concentrating on the Don; these would be the core of a new army.[15] In the week before the Bolshevik seizure of power Masaryk, presumably with Verkhovskii's support, had talks in Kiev with Polish and cossack leaders on the subject of military co-operation.[16]

As the Democratic Conference gave way to the Preparliament, Maugham continued to exude confidence. He was dismissive of rumours: Voska had been in Kiev when there were supposed to have been riots, and there were no riots; the food supply in Petrograd, now that the city council had taken over responsibility for it, was looking up.[17] This assessment then changed dramatically when his report of 10 October stated that although a Third Coalition Government had been formed, it was not expected to last more than three weeks; trouble would come when the Congress of Soviets assembled, which was now 'completely under the control of the extreme left'. This sudden change of heart was brought about by a report from Voska which described the total collapse in morale of the Russian Army.[18]

Even so, Maugham and his team were not despairing, and their reports were soon more up-beat. Early in October Maugham met Savinkov, someone who made an extraordinary impression on him. As he recalled many years later:

> The deliberation of his speech, the impressive restraint of his manner, suggested a determined will which made his ruthlessness comprehensible. I had come across no one who filled me with so great a sense of confidence.[19]

His report to Wiseman on 19 October stated:

> In the course of long conversation with me Savinkov, lately Minister for War, said as follows:
> a) He is trying to form strong centre party, consisting of co-operative societies, populists, moderate policy socialists and cossacks in Preparliament. Kadets will form right and Bolsheviks the left. Programme of the new party is abolition of soviet committees on the front, reorganization of the army and continuation of the war. Important newspapers will be issued to support policy.
> b) He thinks this party will be strong enough to force above mentioned abolition peacefully, but if there is no time to organize it civil war inevitable.
> c) Notwithstanding contrary announcement there is no intention to convoke national assembly before the end of the war.[20]

The degree to which Savinkov's ideas were taken on board by Maugham's team can be seen from a report sent by Voska on the very eve of the Bolshevik seizure of power, after he had left Petrograd. The current government was weak and could be brought down by the soviet at any moment.

> It is necessary for the Allies to be prepared for such an eventuality. They should not, however, rely upon the bourgeois parties, but upon the popular leaders of democratic socialism who will surely finally defeat the anarchistic socialism which is doomed to failure.

In another proposal submitted the same day he took up the theme of Savinkov's proposed centre party as 'the only way out of the present anarchy'.[21]

In his report of 16 October Maugham finally forwarded to Wiseman the plan he had drawn up in consultation with Masaryk. These were to maintain the Slav Press Bureau as a cover for more covert operations, at the cost of $25,000 per annum. Some of the details of its operation were spelt out in a subsequent report by one of the members of Maugham's mission, Koukol:

Besides our own workers, we planned to have an advisory committee composed of some of the most prominent Russian journalists and political leaders. I had already secured the co-operation of the following men: Professor Yastrebov of Petrograd University; Nikolai Sokolov, a close friend of Prof. Milyukov and co-editor of *Rech* (the Kadet daily); Pitirin Sorokin, a prominent Social Revolutionist and a member of the editorial staff of *Volya naroda*; Vladimir Burtsev; and Professor Adrianov . . . to act as the Russian Director of the Bureau [and former] assistant editor of the official Petrograd Telegraph Agency.

The bureau would establish three departments under men drawing salaries of 500 francs per month each: department 1 would distribute well-illustrated literature in all the languages of Russia, as well as regular Allied propaganda (cost, $25,000 per annum); department 2 would send speakers to all public meetings, as well as organizing meetings (cost, $50,000 per annum); and department 3 would 'support moderate socialist party known as Menshevik', and launch a new anti-Bolshevik paper at the front, as well as subsidizing other newspapers (cost, $150,000 per annum). Maugham warned that Masaryk was insistent that any lesser sum would be a waste of money, and would only participate if these terms were met.

In a subsequent report Maugham made clear that the Slav Press Bureau would involve others than the Czechoslovaks. Polish and Yugoslav representatives had also been sent to Russia in the summer of 1917, and 'a second branch of the organization would concern Poles in Russia, and be run entirely by them, but supervised by our chief agent [Maugham] and partly financed by us'.[22] A probable part of Maugham's operation was discussed in a US intelligence report, dated January 1918, which described how:

early in October we organized a Polish deputation which called on Kerensky to endeavour to persuade him to agree to the formation of an absolutely independent state under the guarantee of the Allies, with the capital at Minsk to be defended by Polish troops. Kerensky favoured the plan, but was too weak to put it into operation although the Poles themselves began to concentrate their forces at Minsk from that time on.[23]

Finally, Maugham reported, in addition to these two branches, there would be 'a special sector organization', working separately and 'recruited from Poles, Czechoslovaks and cossacks'. This organization would have the chief object of unmasking German plots and propaganda in Russia and would be headed by Voska. Presumably it would also be responsible for covert operations. Maugham sought and got authorization to lift the earlier ban on contacts with British agents so he could co-operate with the British Intelligence officer operating in Petrograd; he also tried to get an agent placed within the 'secret meetings' of the Bolshevik Party. By November American Intelligence did claim to have established such an (un-named) agent within the Bolshevik Party.[24]

The response of Wiseman to the project was enthusiastic – there clearly was potential in the tactic of supporting both patriotic socialists and oppressed slav nationalities – but also cautious; Maugham's proposals were expensive. Wiseman had already suggested to Maugham on 17 October that they should meet in London some time between the middle of November and the middle of December to discuss the mission: on 21 October, having digested Maugham's report of the 16th more fully, he asked whether too much of the scheme did not depend on Masaryk and the slavs; Maugham should definitely meet him in London 'about 10 November' for consultations.[25] Aware that Maugham was planning to visit London, Kerensky contacted him precisely one week before the Bolshevik seizure of power with a request that he take a message to Lloyd George. Maugham set off just five days before the Bolshevik insurrection and arrived in London on 18 November.

The fate of this message did much to introduce an element of cloak and dagger farce into Maugham's mission. Kerensky's biographer Richard Abraham described the incident as follows:

> To keep this message safe (from the Germans or from Tereshchenko?) Maugham was instructed to write nothing down, an instruction broken only after his arrival in London. The British took every precaution to ensure that the message arrived in total secrecy, sending a destroyer to Christiana to pick Maugham up, but it did not reach Lloyd George until November 18.[26]

In reality, Maugham was planning to return home at this time on Wiseman's orders, and Kerensky's message itself was fairly routine. Although it did contradict Kerensky's public stance on some matters, it only confirmed what was well known to be the policy of the Kerensky government in diplomatic circles – that they were unhappy with the level of British military supplies, unhappy with Allied press coverage, and keen for the Allies to offer the Germans 'peace without annexations or compensations', in other words a peace 'the Germans would refuse'; only if the Germans rejected such peace terms could Russian soldiers be persuaded to go on fighting. Ironically, Kerensky also criticized Buchanan and asked for his replacement, unaware that Buchanan had been urging the Allies to make the self-same peace offer.[27]

# MASARYK ACTIVATES THE MAUGHAM PLAN

When Maugham arrived in London on 18 November he found a willing audience in the British Cabinet. The day after his arrival he, Wiseman and their Polish Nationalist contact Jan Horodyski had urgent talks, and on 20 November the British cabinet minister Sir Edward Carson and the Director of Military Intelligence General Macdonagh were brought into the discussions. As a consequence, Carson told the British Cabinet on 21 November that 'he believed that the formation of a nucleus of Poles, Cossacks, Romanians and Armenians [Carson inexplicably omitted the Czechoslovaks from this list although they clearly featured in Maugham's plan] was a practical proposition, which might be realized, should we be able to get at General Kaledin through the Romanians'.[28]

Further evidence of the viability of a link between the Czechoslovaks and the cossacks appeared to come in a telegram sent by Buchanan on 23 November in which he explained how he had been contacted by a group of bankers acting on behalf of Kaledin. This telegram was discussed by the cabinet on 26 November, and the idea was enthusiastically taken up. The same day Sir Edward Carson contacted Buchanan asking for more details. Buchanan sent back a very sceptical reply,[29] but the cossack myth had seized the cabinet. When full discussion began in the cabinet on 29 November, Buchanan's suggestion that the Russians be freed from their obligation to continue fighting was severely criticized by Acting Foreign Secretary Lord Robert Cecil, who spoke enthusiastically about the support gathering around Kaledin. When the cabinet next discussed the matter on 3 December it was decided to inform Buchanan that the War Cabinet considered the only thing to do was to 'strengthen by every means in our power those elements who are genuinely friendly to the Entente of whom the chief are Kaledin, Alekseev and their group'. Therefore any funds needed to support the cossacks would be authorized, 'no regard should be made to expense'.[30]

However, Kaledin's operation was more myth than reality. Some three weeks after the October seizure of power General Alfred Knox, initially a supporter of Kaledin, informed the Director of Military Intelligence in London that Kaledin would never be able to undertake offensive operations. A few days after this Knox was to complain about the 'talkers' from the Don who continually 'pestered the embassy', while Buchanan stated clearly that: 'the forces at Kaledin's and Alekseev's disposal are not sufficient to engage in any serious enterprise, and it is useless to found exaggerated expectations on overtures made to us by their emissaries'.[31]

As Allied representatives made contact with these groups, these doubts were confirmed. More and more negative reports arrived; thus in a report dated 7 December London was informed that 'the cossacks [are] absolutely useless and disorganized', while Lieutenant-Colonel Jacks's report on 31 December stated that Kaledin's forces were insignificant and fit only to defend their existing territory. General de Candolle reported on 6 January that the so-called South East Union, based in Ekaterinodar, 'constituted the merest embryo of political authority', and 'passive resistance' was the most that could be expected from Novocherkassk. By the end of February, detailed reports from Novocherkassk showed that recruitment to the Volunteer Army was proceeding at half the estimated rate and that a total of only 3,000 men had been assembled. The Allies were not surprised when the Don country fell to the Red Army.[32]

The weakness of Maugham's strategy was the link he made between the Czechoslovaks and the cossacks. This had long been a source of tension between him and the Czechoslovak leader Masaryk, for if the Czechoslovaks were to co-ordinate their actions with the cossacks, they would have to be moved from their base near Kiev to the extreme south and west, linking in one direction to the Don cossacks and in the other to Romania. Despite their close contacts during September and October, relations between Maugham and Masaryk were not free from tension. One of the characters in Maugham's *Ashenden* novels noted that it was occasionally necessary to get around 'the professor's' scruples by keeping him in the dark, and in the real life drama, Maugham's agent Voska, the head of the Slav Press Bureau, bypassed Masaryk to pay two visits to the Czechoslovak headquarters in Kiev. Masaryk's scruples were to be the one weak spot in the patriotic socialist strategy: he, apparently unlike Maugham, had no confidence in Romania, could see no point in keeping Romania in the war, and certainly did not want his forces transferred to the south west front. When at the end of October the Allies proposed just this, Masaryk visited the Romanian headquarters at Jassy and the Romanian front, but prevaricated; Kerensky's fall gave him the perfect opportunity to refuse the request.[33]

Masaryk was no more co-operative at the end of November 1917 when the logic of the Maugham strategy being adopted in London called on him once again to sandwich his troops between the Romanians and the cossacks. The King of Romania had told the British and French governments that he was prepared to try and keep his resistance to the Germans going by forcing a passage through to link up with the Don cossacks, if he could rely on Allied support. When the Czechoslovak forces were asked if they would move to occupy the territory between Bessarabia and the Don, however, Masaryk refused, ignoring the apparent support for the scheme from General Alekseev.[34] Masaryk was determined to pursue a 'Ukrainian' strategy. His legion was based there, and the Ukrainian government was made up of the sort of moderate socialists and nationalists to whom Masaryk could relate. He favoured the formation of Ukrainian, Polish and Czechoslovak armies within the Ukraine which would co-operate with Romania but not get sucked into joint action with a country which was doomed and cossacks whose strength was imagined rather than real. For Masaryk's own contacts with the Don had been as negative as those of Britain; he sent a close confidant to contact Alekseev and he returned with a negative report which served only to reinforce Masaryk's lack of faith in Alekseev, despite the fact that some Czechoslovaks were members of Kornilov's regiment and had followed him to the Don. Masaryk ignored Alekseev's request to send troops to the Don at the end of November, and a second request was intercepted by the Bolsheviks in late January. Only in mid-February did he allow a sapper battalion to join those Czechoslovaks already on the Don.[35]

Masaryk was convinced that the Czechoslovaks were strategically better placed in the Ukraine than on the Don, and explained to Alekseev that this would be even more the case when a Polish army had been formed. With the active support of the French, who were prepared to drop the order sending the Czechoslovaks to the Romanian front, the Ukrainian government and Masaryk developed a version of the Maugham strategy which recognized the collapse of Romania. By the end of December there were detailed plans for two Czechoslovak legions, supported by a Polish corps and a Serb corps, which would stay in the Ukraine and become the nucleus of a new army for Russia. Masaryk would build in the Ukraine the force he and Maugham had tried to construct in Russia as a whole, and on 5 January 1918 a key step forward was taken when he and the Poles signed an operational agreement for their two armed forces. Niessel, the French military attaché, showed his full support for Masaryk when he bypassed official channels to try and get all Polish forces concentrated in the Ukraine.[36]

The British attitude to this Ukrainian version of the Maugham plan was perhaps best summed up on 3 January 1918 by the Chief of the Imperial General Staff in a memorandum to the War Cabinet:

I do not see at present that more can be done than that of which the War Cabinet is aware, namely, to make the best use of the forces in South Russia which are more or less willing to co-operate with the Entente. There is the Romanian Army of fifteen divisions which merely requires supplies and perhaps these may be obtained, given the goodwill of the Ukrainian government. The latter is collecting Little Russian (Ukrainian) troops from different parts of the front and has the support of two Czechoslovak divisions now about Kiev. Its special need is money and organization and these will be furnished by the French. In the Polish Army a force of over 32,000 rifles which may perhaps be increased seven or eight times that number and which is now being supplied with money through Gen Niessel.

Such forces, based in the Ukraine, could form a bridge to Alekseev on the Don.[37]

Politically, however, the attitude of the British to Masaryk's Ukrainian policy was a little ambivalent. British representation in Kiev was strengthened in the first week of January by sending to the Ukrainian capital Mr Picton-Bagge as official 'representative' and Lady Muriel Paget, of the British Hospital in Petrograd; she had experience of Kiev having been there in the summer of 1916. However, the British were clear there was to be no recognition of the Ukraine and the cabinet's Russian Committee was only lukewarm about following what it described as this 'French' policy. Indeed, so as to avoid Bolshevik accusations of arming the Ukrainians, the British moved their detachment of armoured cars from Kiev to Kursk, where they were promptly requisitioned by the Bolsheviks. Yet as the Russian Committee noted 'in spite of doubts as to the real power of the Rada, we must be ready to back the French' and, because of a French cash shortage, it was the British who provided Masaryk with his money in Kiev. The British military advisor on the spot, General de Candolle, supported Masaryk's contention that the Czechoslovak Legion was better placed where it was near the Poles than on the Don.[38]

From the very start Masaryk's scheme was confronted with two problems. First, he talked about using the Ukraine as a base to reform the Russian Army and was convinced that the Constituent Assembly elections would result in the formation of an SR government ready to resume the war, alongside the similar government already established by the Rada in Kiev. Perhaps he had heard an over-optimistic report from his friend Sorokin, closely involved in the Maugham operation, who was a member of the committee which tried to open the Constituent Assembly on 28 November and an active member of the SR commission preparing for the opening on 5 January 1918; perhaps he knew too of the SR plans agreed on 26–27 December 1917 to approach the Rada about forming a new federal Russian state. By the first week in January it was clear that this was a pipe dream. Second, even before their participation in the Brest-Litovsk negotiations, Masaryk found problems when confronting the nationalism of the Ukrainian authorities. Although he was allowed to hold an 'Oppressed Nations Rally' in Kiev on 12 December, which brought together Poles, Czechs, Slovenes, Slovaks and Serbs, when it came to the Polish forces, he found himself trying to mediate between the rival Ukrainian and Polish claims to Galicia.[39]

When Masaryk finally signed an accord with the Ukrainian government on 16 January 1918 it was an ambivalent one. If the Ukraine declared war on the Central Powers at the end of the armistice, then the Czechoslovaks would rally to the Ukrainian Army; if they did not the Czechoslovaks would leave the country. As Ukrainian nationalists gained the upper hand over the socialists in the Rada and agreed to send a delegation to Brest-Litovsk, the Ukrainian option seemed doomed. The head of the French military mission General Niessel had been convinced since early January that the tactic had run into the sand, although officially the French support continued. By the end of January Masaryk had lost patience with the Ukrainian government: when they asked if he would allow his Czechoslovak Legion to be used to police Kiev, he said this would only be possible if war was declared on the Central Powers.[40]

What finally ended Masaryk's dream of a Ukrainian version of the Maugham mission was the demise of the Polish Corps. It was Kornilov who in the summer of 1917 had given permission for the various Polish forces in Russia to be formed into a corps, led by Lieutenant-General Dowbor Musnicki; like the Czechoslovak Legion, there were to be no soldiers' committees in the Polish Corps. Dowbor Musnicki was impatient with politicians. Despite Verkhovskii's sympathy to the cause of national brigades, Dowbor Musnicki convinced himself that the government was against the idea and at the end of October instructed his supporters to expand the size of the corps without waiting for government permission. He was even more intolerant of the Bolsheviks, moving his cavalry to Minsk, which Kerensky had been considering using as the embryo of a future Polish state, and using his forces there to protect the local Polish gentry from the land-hungry Byelorussian peasants. To enforce their land distribution policy the Bolsheviks made several attempts to disarm individual Polish units.

Things came to a head on 11 January 1918 when Dowbor Musnicki declared that if any attempts at disarmament occurred after

12 a.m. on 12 January, the Polish Corps would resist. Thus the Poles and the Bolsheviks found themselves in a state of war over an essentially trivial and private matter, at a time when Masaryk was desperately trying to co-ordinate the activity of the Poles with that of his Czechoslovak Legion. Dowbor Musnicki acted on the assumption that the Bolsheviks would be unable to crush him because of the slow progress of Muraviev's advance into the Ukraine, which would enable the Poles, if necessary, to retreat to the Ukraine where the Second Polish Uhlan Regiment was being formed. Both assumptions proved wrong: his emissaries sent to the Ukraine never arrived and so could not negotiate his retreat there, and Muraviev succeeded in seizing Kiev far more quickly than he anticipated. By 21 January the Polish Corps was surrounded by the Bolsheviks in the fortress at Bobruisk and quite unable to help Masaryk form the core of a pro-Allied army in Kiev.[41] Indeed, they ended up playing a pro-German role. When the Brest-Litovsk negotiations broke down and the Germans renewed their advance on 18 February, Dowbor Musnicki's forces were trapped between the advancing Germans and the Red Army. Dowbor Musnicki felt he had no choice but to sign an agreement with the advancing Germans and seize Minsk on their behalf on 19–20 February 1918.[42]

## NOT MAUGHAM, NOR MASARYK BUT MURAVIEV

In the Ukraine, however, the German advance breathed new life into the Masaryk scheme, with reinforcements arriving in the most unexpected of guises. As Muraviev's forces took Kiev in the first week of February 1918, overturning the government of patriotic socialists and nationalists on whom Masaryk placed so much hope and imposing the Ukrainian Soviet Government first formed in Kharkov, Allied representatives were astounded to find Muraviev quite willing to ally himself with the Czechoslovak Legion in a joint struggle against Germany and Austria. The possibility of an alliance with the Bolsheviks, of turning them into patriotic socialists fighting alongside the Czechoslovaks against the Germans was suddenly opened up. Muraviev, despite his reputation for being the most ruthless of Red commanders, was a patriotic socialist of the first calling; when Muraviev arrived in Kiev the astonished British representative Mr Picton-Bagge recognized his former partner in the men's doubles at the previous years' Odessa tennis tournament.[43] Muraviev first came to the attention of British policy-makers in July 1917 when, encouraged by Bernard Pares, he became the chairman of the League of Personal Example, a socialist group in the army committed to the formation of volunteer brigades. In carrying out this work he clashed with the reactionary officers of the General Staff, and called upon Pares to try and smooth things over. Described by Pares even then as 'an extreme SR', he rapidly became disillusioned with Kerensky; after the Kornilov rebellion he joined the Left SRs.[44]

Muraviev's bitterness against the officer corps of the old army led him to rally to the support of Lenin's coup. He volunteered to lead the Bolshevik forces at the battle of Pulkovo Heights, when General Krasnov and his cossacks tried to march on Petrograd, and his subsequent attempt to put Petrograd under martial law led to an outcry in the Soviet Executive. His fiery temperament was displayed again when he organized the Bolshevik Commander-in-Chief Krylenko's advance on GHQ, which led to General Dukhonin's assassination; it was Muraviev who pulled Dukhonin's epaulettes from his uniform. He then joined Antonov-Ovseenko in the mid-December campaign in the Eastern Ukraine. There, at meetings of the Supreme War Council in Odessa, he met the British agent George Hill and shortly afterwards the French agent Captain Bordes. Despite his temperament, he made a good impression on all the military men who met him; a British government Eastern Report for 21 February 1918, produced in London for the cabinet, spoke in awesome tones of the Bolshevik commander Muraviev 'whose orders are obeyed and who enforces discipline'; this was the first time this had happened since the abdication of the Emperor, the report concluded.[45]

It was as Chief Commander of the Ukrainian campaign that Muraviev arrived in Kiev on 10 February 1918 and held talks with the Allied military attachés General Tabouis and Major Fitzwilliams, two Serbian colonels, and Masaryk, who acted as interpreter. Muraviev explained that the soviet campaign against the Ukrainian Rada had been necessary because of the reactionary nature of that regime. However, somewhat to their surprise, Muraviev then presented the Allies with the following plan: he agreed with Masaryk that the Czechoslovak Legion should be concentrated in order to attain a greater mobility, but then, he said, it should be deployed together with the Polish Corps on the northern flank of the Romanian front to be ready when Austria struck; this was precisely what the British General de Candolle had been suggesting in his reports to London.

Muraviev stressed that this plan was his personal initiative and Petrograd still had to be consulted. However, the caution of Petrograd was not the only problem the plan faced. The very mention of the Romanian front was enough to turn Masaryk against the idea. He was adamant that his troops were not going to the Romanian front and insisted that the time had now come for the Czechoslovak Legion to leave for France. Muraviev acquiesced and, far from turning aggressive at the rejection of his proposal, promised to take over responsibility for supplying the legion until their departure could be arranged.[46] On 18 February 1918 the French liaison officer with the Czechoslovak Legion, A. Verge, informed Masaryk that the funds had arrived to begin the journey to Vladivostok.

The very same day, however, the Germans began their advance and Muraviev again turned to the Czechoslovak Legion commanders to ask for help. Talks took place on 19 February 1918 between Masaryk's closest associates and the Czechoslovak Legion's Russian commander General Diteriks on the one hand, and the army commanders of the new Ukrainian Soviet Government on the other. The agreement which was reached greatly benefitted the Czechoslovaks, for under it they were not to be isolated near Romania, but stationed close to the border with Russia: the Red Army was to bear the brunt of the German advance, but, if their front held, the Czechoslovak Legion would launch a counter-offensive; if, on the other hand, the front did not hold, the Czechoslovaks would be well placed to retreat into Russian territory and resume their journey to France via Siberia.[47]

General Tabouis who endorsed the scheme on 21 February 1918 was greatly impressed by Muraviev's 'enthusiasm to resist Berlin'. However, it was all to no avail. Patriotic socialists and Czechoslovak legionaries fought side by side as Maugham and Masaryk had dreamed they would, but the front against the Germans rapidly disintegrated and on 22 February 1918 Muraviev put Masaryk, Fitzwilliams and Tabouis on a train to Moscow. Masaryk left Russia for good on 7 March 1918.[48] Back in the Ukraine Muraviev's Red Army and the Czechoslovak Legion were left to fight their way out of the Ukraine. As they did so they met the British agent George Hill who, once it had become clear that a military stand was hopeless, began organizing detachments of guerrilla partisans who would stay and work behind the lines.[49] On 8 March 1918 more talks were held between the Ukrainian Soviet and Czechoslovak forces, and, despite some mutual hostility, an agreement was reached which resulted in the two armies again fighting side by side at the Battle of Bakhmach on 15 March 1918, where the German forces were temporarily held in check.

Indeed, at the time of this battle it looked momentarily as if the Russian Red Army was determined to confront German operations in the Ukraine and would support this alliance of patriotic socialists. On 12 March 1918 the British learned that Trotsky was pledged to war in the Ukraine. In a newspaper interview of 16 March 1918 Trotsky stressed 'we are still continuing the war with Germany in the Ukraine'. Niessel recalled in his memoirs that he had been reliably informed that both Trotsky and Lenin judged German operations in the Ukraine to be inadmissible and were determined to defend a Soviet Ukraine; and the minutes of the Bolshevik Central Committee confirmed that a decision was taken on 15 March 1918 to establish a 'united defence front', although the linked decision to flood the Donbas mines suggested that there was little optimism about military success. This turned out to be the case and shortly afterwards Muraviev was recalled from the Ukraine; apparently in his enthusiasm for opposing the Central Powers he had been willing to consider joint resistance with the remnants of the Rada's army which he had so recently defeated.[50]


## BALFOUR REVISES BRITISH POLICY

With the recall of Muraviev and the return of Masaryk, the Maugham mission had run its course. The British government's response to the Bolshevik seizure of power had been confused and ambiguous since the crucial decision of 3 December 1917 to intervene in support of Kaledin was taken in the absence of the Foreign Secretary A.J. Balfour, who was attending the Inter-Allied Conference in Paris, and in the teeth of the diplomatic reports being sent by the British ambassador Sir George Buchanan. These messages were clear, if in many ways unpalatable: Buchanan rejected all contact with counter-revolutionary groups and favoured the formation of a coalition socialist government; when that failed to materialize, he called for *de facto* recognition of a Bolshevik dominated government; but above all Buchanan favoured peace talks.

Thus, while the British military attaché Alfred Knox doubted whether the moderate socialists still had a chance and initially preferred to look to Kaledin as the agent to remove the Bolsheviks,[51] Buchanan was always sceptical about Kaledin and the counter-revolution. Reporting to London two days after the Bolshevik coup that he had been contacted secretly by Rodzianko who had asked for help, Buchanan had 'begged he would only act in conjunction with the CSRM as any attempt at a counter-revolution with which his name was so closely connected might under the present circumstances cause moderate socialists to join the Bolsheviks'. Buchanan's report on the opening of the Railway Workers' Union talks, on the other hand, was optimistic, commenting that 'it would appear that the proposal is favourably regarded by the majority'.[52]

A week after the coup Buchanan had talks with Kerensky's War Minister Verkhovskii, who was nominated to the same position in the socialist coalition government planned by the Railway Workers' Union, and there was a hint of embarrassment in Buchanan's response to Verkhovskii's request for the Allies to present peace terms to Germany; he replied 'they [the British government] were unlikely to go as far as he wished them to'. He informed London that 'as far as peace terms were concerned there was little difference between the programme of the Bolsheviks and the moderate socialists' and 'unless the unexpected happens and the cossacks succeed in winning the day, we must be prepared to face the new situation. Whether the Bolsheviks are admitted into the new government or not, the real power will be in their hands.' This was still his attitude when the Railway Workers' Union talks stalled, and he argued for *de facto* recognition of the new regime by the British until the Constituent Assembly met.[53]

In further contacts with the moderate socialists after the collapse of the Railway Workers' Union talks, Buchanan urged the Menshevik Skobelev to drop plans to form a coalition government 'supported by the Kadets' and pressed London to make the peace offer requested by the moderate socialists:

> though socialist government does not inspire me with much confidence, as regards the conduct of the war it is everything for us to gain time, while the Kadets, though not represented in the new government may well be able to make their influence felt. It is to my mind of such supreme importance to keep Russia in the war as long as possible in order that Germany may not obtain supplies from her during the war or secure a predominant position here after the war that I earnestly hope the Allied Governments will consent to give the assurances asked for. Discussion of peace terms commits us to nothing, while the defection of Russia may have such serious consequences for us that we ought to stave it off as long as possible.[54]

Two days after his talks with Skobelev, Buchanan was visited by the Popular Socialist leader Chaikovskii and the issue of a socialist government excluding both the Bolsheviks and Chernov was discussed; a few days later he was informed that the sticking point for any agreement between the socialists and the liberals was the formers' insistence on accepting the decrees on peace and land.[55] On the eve of the cabinet's decision on intervention, Buchanan again telegraphed the Foreign Office to express the Verkhovskii view that the Russians should be allowed a free choice as to whether or not they continued to fight:

> if anything could tempt Russia to make one more effort, it would be the knowledge that she was perfectly free to act as she pleased, without any pressure from the Allies . . . I am not advocating any transaction with the Bolshevik government. On the contrary, I believe that the adoption of the course I have suggested will take the wind out of their sails . . .

This view was supported ten days later by Knox, who agreed it was 'useless to try to hold any Russian government to the strict fulfilment of obligations which nine out of ten of the people repudiate'.[56]

In Balfour's absence the cabinet was unsympathetic to such an approach. In the telegram of 3 December endorsing the policy of intervention and support for Kaledin, Buchanan was told that the government 'do not believe that the constitution of a coalition between Bolsheviks, SRs and even Mensheviks would be any real improvement. Such a combination would be under Bolshevik influence and would besides consist of talkers and theorists.' The only thing to do was to contact friends like Kaledin.[57] However, on his return from the Inter-Allied Conference in Paris, Balfour forced through a dramatic change in policy. In a detailed memorandum written on 9 December and presented to cabinet on the 10th, Balfour attacked his cabinet colleagues and called for the decision they had taken to be changed. The view that the Bolsheviks could only be considered as avowed enemies was 'founded on a misconception'. Any break with 'this crazy system' and the 'dangerous dreamers' who ran it had to be delayed as long as possible. 'It is certain, I take it,' he wrote, 'that, for the remainder of this war, the Bolsheviks are going to fight neither Germany nor anyone else. But, if we can prevent their aiding Germany we do a great deal, and to this we should devote our efforts'.

He went on:

> If we drive Russia into the hands of Germany, we shall hasten the organization of the country by German officials on German lines. Nothing could be more fatal, it seems to me, both to the immediate conduct of the war and to our post-war relations. Russia, however incapable of fighting, is not easily overrun. Except with the active goodwill of the Russians themselves, German troops (even if there were German troops to spare) are not going to penetrate many hundreds of

miles into that vast country. A mere armistice between Russia and Germany may not for very many months promote in any important fashion the supply of German needs from Russian sources. It must be our business to make that period as long as possible by every means in our power, and no policy would be more fatal than to give the Russians a motive for welcoming into their midst German officials and German soldiers as friends and deliverers.[58]

While events were gathering momentum in the Ukraine, the British government began to follow a conciliatory strategy towards the Bolsheviks in Russia. Whatever might or might not come of the Ukraine or the ephemeral South East Union, *de facto* recognition of Bolshevik rule in Russia seemed essential. Meeting with the French in Paris on 23 December 1917 it was decided to keep all options open. Liaison with the Ukrainians would be left to the French and liaison with the South East Federation to the British, but more important than both these was the decision to establish relations with the Bolsheviks in Russia as soon as each country saw fit by sending out unofficial agents. The British acted at once: immediately after this meeting R.H. Bruce Lockhart, the former Consul-General in Moscow, began a series of meetings with the Prime Minister, senior cabinet ministers and senior civil servants and on 4 January 1918 was formally asked to go to Petrograd at once as the British diplomatic agent; he left on 14 January 1918 hoping to get there before the Brest-Litovsk negotiations were completed and had arrived by the end of the month.[59]

Thus Lockhart arrived in Petrograd at a crucial turning point for the Bolshevik regime. Lenin had wanted peace with Imperial Germany to confront the SR victors in the Constituent Assembly elections – what he termed 'defeating the bourgeoisie in Russia', but what actually meant provoking a Red versus Green civil war. But Trotsky had not delivered the goods; his prevarication at the Brest-Litovsk talks in the hope of encouraging the workers of Berlin and Vienna to seize power had failed. Instead of peace Lenin was faced with war, and in this war Muraviev was not alone in responding to the German advance by calling for an all-out war in alliance with any patriotic socialist groups, and slav national organizations like the Czechoslovak Legion.

## NOTES

1.  R.F. Christian, 'Alexis Aladin: Trudovik leader in the first Russian Duma: materials for a biography' *Oxford Slavonic Papers* vol. 21 (1988),

p. 148; G. Buchanan, *My Mission to Russia and Other Diplomatic Memories* (London 1923) vol. 2, p. 175; J.D. White, 'The Kornilov affair: a study in counter-revolution' *Soviet Studies* vol. 20 (1968), p. 190.

2. White, 'Kornilov', p. 190; Buchanan, *Mission to Russia*, vol. 2, p. 173; M. Kettle, *The Allies and the Russian Collapse* (London 1989), p. 50 et seq.

3. These incidental details concerning the Maugham mission are mostly taken from E. Voska, *Spy and Counter-Spy* (London 1941).

4. B. Pares, *My Russian Memoirs* (London 1931), pp. 424–63.

5. Maugham's mission is briefly described in T. Morgan, *Somerset Maugham* (London 1986), pp. 226–9 and W.B. Fowler, *British–American Relations 1917–18: the Role of Sir William Wiseman* (Princeton 1969), pp. 114–15, who makes the point about the mission being deniable. Both these authors cite the papers of Sir William Wiseman. The William Wiseman papers are held in Yale University Library, and for this study I have consulted Boxes 9 and 10. The question of a salary is raised in a letter of Maugham to Wiseman dated 7 July 1917. All subsequent references will be given as 'Wiseman Papers' followed by the date of the document.

6. There is some confusion about when the mission arrived in Petrograd. Voska states it was early August in his memoirs published long after the event; in his report to the Bohemian National Alliance in March 1918, however, one of the participants in the mission, Alois Koukol, stated that they arrived early in September, two weeks before Kornilov's attempted coup (Wiseman Papers, document dated 20 March 1918). Voska's memoirs describe his early work in the New York émigré community.

7. *Edinstvo* carried articles on the Czechs, Poles or South Slavs on 12 and 13 September, 4, 6, 11, 15 and 17 October; Plekhanov's endorsement of Masaryk was published on 20 October. For the Slav Press Bureau and the meeting with Padarewski, see Voska, *Spy*, p. 181 et seq. and p. 193.

8. Wiseman Papers, documents dated 3, 7, 14 and 18 July 1917.

9. For Maugham's contacts, see Morgan, *Somerset Maugham*, pp. 226–9. Information about Kropotkin can be found in S.P. Turin, 'Ot"ezd P.A. Kropotkina iz Anglii v Rossii' *Na chuzhoi storone* no. 4 (Berlin/Prague 1924), p. 223 et seq.

10. Wiseman Papers, documents dated 11 September 1917 and 20 March 1918.

11. Wiseman Papers, documents dated 11 and 16 September 1917.

12. Wiseman Papers, document dated 16 September 1917.

13. Wiseman Papers, document dated 21 September 1917. The dates for all Maugham's reports back to London are according to the Western calender.

14. Wiseman Papers, document dated 29 September 1917.

15. For Verkhovskii's relations with General Niessel, see General H. Niessel, *Le Triomphe des Bolcheviques et la Paix de Brest Litovsk* (Paris 1940), p. 9. For the Ukraine, see A. Choulgine, *L'Ukraine contra Moscou* (Paris 1935), p. 159.

16. J.F.N. Bradley, 'T.G. Masaryk et la revolution russe' *Etudes Slaves et Est-Europeenes* vol. IX (1964), p. 14.
17. Wiseman Papers, document dated 6 October 1917.
18. Wiseman Papers, document dated 19 October 1917.
19. W. Somerset Maugham, *A Writer's Notebook* (London 1949), p. 177.
20. Wiseman Papers, document dated 16 October 1917.
21. Wiseman Papers, document dated 6 November 1917.
22. Wiseman Papers, documents dated 16 and 21 October 1917 and 20 March 1918.
23. Wiseman Papers, document dated 19 January 1918.
24. Wiseman Papers, documents dated 19 September and 21 October 1917, and 19 January 1918.
25. Wiseman Papers, documents dated 17 and 21 October 1917.
26. R. Abraham, *Alexander Kerensky* (Columbia 1987), p. 298. Abraham appears inadvertently to misdate the occasion when Kerensky and Maugham met to discuss the message. He states it occurred on 1 October, when all other sources state 18 October.
27. The attitude of the British ambassador at this time is discussed in my 'Before the fighting started', *Revolutionary Russia* vol. 4 (1991). The full text of the message is in the Lloyd George papers held in the House of Lords Record Office, F 60/2/36. While Kerensky liked Buchanan and understood his 'social patriot' stance, his association with the Tsarist regime and monocled appearance made him an easy target for Bolshevik propaganda. He is also ridiculed unfairly in one of Maugham's *Ashenden* stories.
28. Fowler, *British–American Relations*, p. 117; War Cabinet Minutes, CAB 23, 21 November 1917, item 16.
29. Public Records Office FO371.3018.109, 371.3018.114, 371.3018.136. Although this bankers' telegram does not appear in CAB 24 GT series, the memoranda discussed at Cabinet, it is clear from the Carson telegram described above and a note dated 25 November attached to Buchanan's telegram which reads 'presumably the cabinet will consider it tomorrow' that the bankers' telegram was discussed in Cabinet.
30. See the copy of a telegram to Sir George Buchanan dated 3 December 1917 (western calendar) in the Lord Milner papers held at the Bodleian Library, Oxford, dep 366, f. 40.
31. Milner Papers, 366, ff. 32, 34, 36–7, 45, 47, 50, 51.
32. Milner Papers, 369, ff. 35, 44–5; 366, ff. 58, 73, 92–3, 100.
33. For the need to 'dupe' Masaryk, note Voska's visits described in *Spy* pp. 201–5. For Masaryk's trip to Jassy, see V.M. Fic, *Revolutionary War for Independence and the Russian Question* (Delhi 1977), p. 189 and Bradley, 'Masaryk' p. 86. Masaryk's other scruples revolved around his publicly declared stance that he would not intervene in Russian politics, and a latent desire to do so. Although he opposed Kornilov's adventure, he did have talks with him about what might happen to his corps in the event of Kornilov's success (see J.F.N. Bradley, *La Légion Tchécoslovaque en Russie 1914–20* Paris 1965, p. 56); he also told Verkhovskii that the

Czechoslovak corps would fight the internal Bolshevik enemy, see J. Kalvoda, *The Genesis of Czechoslovakia* (Columbia 1986), p. 208.

34. Kalvoda, *Genesis*, pp. 220–1; Fowler, *British–American Relations*, pp. 117–18.

35. Bradley, 'Masaryk', pp. 83–90; Bradley, *Légion Tchécoslovaque*, p. 65; Fic, *Revolutionary War*, pp. 175–9; and T.G. Masaryk, *The Making of a State* (New York 1969), pp. 181–3.

36. Fic, *Revolutionary War*, pp. 160–6; and Niessel *Triomphe*, pp. 130–1.

37. Milner Papers, 357 f. 251.

38. Choulgine, *L'Ukraine*, pp. 160–1, 175–6 (Lady Muriel Paget's earlier visit to Kiev is recalled by Sir Bernard Pares in *Memoirs*, p. 399); Milner Papers 364 ff. 5–6 and 366 f. 90; Niessel, *Triomphe*, p. 153; Masaryk *Making of a State*, p. 188.

39. Fic, *Revolutionary War*, pp. 161, 189; Bradley, 'Masaryk', p. 84; and Niessel *Triomphe*, pp. 130–1.

40. Fic, *Revolutionary War*, pp. 169–72; Niessel, *Triomphe*, p. 238.

41. V.P. Agapeev, 'Korpus generala Dovbor-Musnitskogo' *Beloe Delo* no. 4 (Berlin 1928), pp. 184–8.

42. Agapeev, 'Korpus', p. 189; Niessel, *Triomphe*, pp. 266–7; and J. Noulens, *Mon Ambassade en Russie Soviétique, 1917–19* I (Paris 1933), p. 246.

43. W. Blunt, *Lady Muriel* (London 1962), p. 124.

44. Pares, *Memoirs*, pp. 473–6.

45. For Muraviev's early career see D.L. Golinkov, *Krakh vrazheskogo podpolya* (Moscow 1971), p. 95; Niessel, *Triomphe*, p. 89; J.L.H. Keep (ed.) *The Debate on Soviet Power, the Minutes of VTsIK, Second Convocation* (Oxford 1979), p. 140 et seq; G. Hill, *Go Spy the Land* (London 1932), p. 167. The Eastern Report is in D. Jones, 'Documents on British relations with Russia, 1917–18' *Canadian-American Slavic Studies* vol. 7, no. 2 (1973), p. 237.

46. Fic, *Revolutionary War*, pp. 200–1; Milner Papers, 366 f. 90.

47. Fic, *Revolutionary War*, pp. 202–9.

48. Masaryk, *Making of a State*, pp. 187–9; Kalvoda, *Genesis*, pp. 244–8.

49. Hill, *Go Spy*, pp. 177–8.

50. For Trotsky's attitude, see Milner Papers, 364 ff. 95–6. For Trotsky's press interview, see Milner Papers, 364 f. 121. For Niessel, see *Triomphe*, p. 284. For the government, see E. Bosh, *God borby: borba za vlast' na Ukraine s aprelya 1917g. do nemetskoi okkupatsii* (Moscow 1928), p. 191; and *Izvestiya TsK KPSS* (1989) no. 3, p. 102. Bosh, who was a leading member of the Ukrainian Soviet administration, goes into considerable detail about how Muraviev ignored the civilian government and acted with brutality and political insensitivity. The same reports were picked up by the *Guardian*'s Philips-Price, see *My Reminiscences of the Russian Revolution* (London 1921), pp. 242–3, and are repeated as hearsay by Noulens in his memoirs. However, there must be a question mark over the reliability of these reports. A real personal animosity seems to have developed between Bosh and Muraviev, and the circumstances of his dismissal remain rather obscure. The worst allegations of brutality were

always levelled against Muraviev's aide rather than Muraviev himself and it is hard to reconcile the brute depicted in some accounts with the tennis player from Odessa.

51. A. Knox, *With the Russian Army, 1914–17* (London 1921), p. 719; War Cabinet Memoranda, Public Records Office CAB 24 GT series, 2683 and 2761.

52. Public Records Office FO371.2999.249, 371.2999.310.

53. Public Records Office FO371.2999.323, 371.2999.347.

54. Public Records Office FO371.2999.398.

55. Public Records Office FO371.2999.407, 371.2999.433.

56. Buchanan, *Mission to Russia*, vol. 2, pp. 220–6; Public Records Office CAB 24 GT series, 2812.

57. See note 30 above.

58. Public Records Office CAB 23, Minutes of War Cabinet 295.

59. K. Young (ed.), *The Diaries of Sir Robert Bruce Lockhart* vol. 1 (London 1973), p. 31; R.H. Bruce Lockhart, *Memoirs of a British Agent* (London 1946) p. 213.

# CHAPTER FIVE
# *Defending the Socialist Fatherland*

Lenin had not wanted war with Germany in February 1918. Since his Christmas retreat in Finland his eyes had been focused on a renewed Red versus Green civil war, a civil war against the SR victors in the Constituent Assembly elections. The revival of hostilities completely changed the political agenda: for three months, from mid-February 1918 until mid-May 1918, civil war was shelved and a patriotic war in defence of the socialist fatherland began. Although within ten days of the resumption of hostilities, talks with the Imperial German government had resumed and a peace of sorts agreed, this did little to change the climate of war fever. The peace imposed at Brest-Litovsk on 3 March 1918 was so outrageous in its terms, and the Germans so unwilling even to limit their ambitions in Russia to its terms, that few people, other than Lenin, saw the treaty as offering anything other than the briefest of breathing spaces. The Russian Army were at once preparing to reopen the Eastern Front, and in that endeavour they were to be offered military support by the Allies.

This mood only changed in the first week of May 1918, when the Germans overthrew the democratic government in the Ukraine, installing in its place an aristocratic dictatorship, and advanced well beyond the originally agreed demarcation line with Russia. To many in Lenin's government this presented the Bolshevik Party with the *casus belli* on which to end the breathing space peace achieved at Brest-Litovsk. For Lenin, who again got his way after a series of Central Committee meetings, it was the occasion to end talk of a patriotic war to defend the socialist fatherland and resume the Red versus Green civil war, reverting to the strategy of an assault on the SRs and the peasantry which he had been advocating since his Christmas retreat.

## THE ANTI-GERMAN MOOD

Several factors showed the strength of anti-German feeling after 18 February 1918 and the possibility of shelving the nascent civil war in the democratic front. After appealing to the people to defend the socialist fatherland – in the last days of February 10,000 volunteers joined the Red Army – the Bolsheviks released many of their political prisoners, including the editorial board of the right-wing SR daily *Volya naroda*, the spiritual home of the likes of Sorokin and the Navy Minister in the Second Coalition Government V.I. Lebedev. There was even renewed talk of political reconciliation; the military commission of the SR Party, dominated by right-wing SRs and for so long the focal point for those socialists keen to overthrow the Bolsheviks by force, even drew up plans to join the Red Guard in its defence of Petrograd. Chernov was even optimistic that joint action against Germany, backed by the Allies, might lead to the restoration of the Constituent Assembly. In local soviets throughout the country the Mensheviks and SRs made clear their willingness to co-operate with any Bolsheviks willing to continue the war.[1]

Even more important than the reaction of the SRs was the reaction of the Bolshevik Party itself. In the country at large, before the German advance started, a majority of local party organizations opposed the idea of a separate peace. The Petrograd Committee of the Bolshevik Party was no exception to this mood: on 18 January it endorsed a resolution opposing the idea of a separate peace; it was only the renewal of the German offensive on 18 February that persuaded the Bolshevik group in the Petrograd Soviet to come out in favour of peace, although many of the district soviets and the factory committees were still even then in favour of a revolutionary war. On 26 February 1918 the Soviet Executive began a survey of 200 local soviets; by 10 March 1918 a majority (105–95) had come out in favour of a revolutionary war, although the soviets in the two capitals voted (Moscow on 3–5 March 1918 and Petrograd on 5 March 1918) to accept a separate peace. In the debates in the Moscow Soviet, the Mensheviks and Left SRs co-operated with pro-war Bolsheviks in trying to reject the peace.[2]

Little of this pro-war feeling was seen in public after Lenin's government's decision on 23 February 1918 to accept German peace terms and the signing of the Brest-Litovsk Treaty on 3 March 1918. At the Seventh Congress of the Bolshevik Party on 6–7 March 1918, the pro-war communists found themselves in a minority of the hurriedly assembled 70 delegates, only 46 of whom had voting rights.

Nor was it in evidence at the Fourth Extraordinary Congress of Soviets called to ratify the treaty: when the communist group met prior to the Fourth Congress of Soviets, it voted 453–38 against a revolutionary war and in favour of a separate peace; at the Congress of Soviets itself, which met on 14–16 March 1918 and was attended by 1,232 delegates – 795 Bolsheviks, 283 Left SRs, 25 SRs, 21 Mensheviks and various other groups – the crucial peace vote saw 784 voting for, 261 against with 115 abstentions and 84 delegates not taking part.[3] However, both assemblies witnessed extensive gerry-mandering. Delegates' reports in fact revealed strong pockets of resistance to Lenin's peace policy from within his own party: on the Volga – in Saratov, Simbirsk and Samara – there were strong pro-war communist groups both in the party and soviet organization; the same was true in the Urals, where support for revolutionary war was particularly strong in Perm; and in the Ukraine and on the Don, where a German advance would spell the end of all the social achievements of the revolution. In all these regions, support for continuing partisan resistance was considerable.[4]

Even after the ratification of the treaty, pro-war communists continued to control important party organizations. Most significantly they retained control of the Moscow regional party committee until mid-May 1918, with other late pockets of support in Ivanovo-Voznesensk, where the city party conference voted to support them on 28 April 1918, and in Yaroslavl where on 13 May 1918 the city conference did the same. The Urals, however, was the heartland of the pro-war communists. The Urals regional bureau and the Ekaterin-burg party organization remained in their hands, endorsing calls for a revolutionary war well into April 1918, while a conference in Perm endorsed the idea of a revolutionary war as late as 12 May 1918. Significantly here they found themselves co-operating in opposing the treaty with any pro-war groups, including the SR and Menshevik contingents in the soviets. Such alliances were formed in Ufa, Perm and Vyatka, where the soviets firmly rejected the treaty; in Zlatoust, co-operation with the Mensheviks and SRs was particularly marked.[5]

The anti-German mood was also fostered by developments in the Ukraine. As Muraviev's action had made clear, there at first seemed at least a chance that the Ukrainian Soviet Government might be able to retain control of some Ukrainian territory. The retreating government of the Ukrainian Soviet Republic was solidly pro-war in outlook and on the day Lenin sued for peace, 23 February 1918, resolved to adopt a scorched earth policy of partisan-based revolutionary war. Nearly two weeks later, on 6 March 1918, after the treaty had been signed, the official Ukrainian Soviet Government newspaper reaffirmed the opposition of both government and soviet to the peace and bitterly condemned as spurious all Lenin's arguments in its favour; the same day the government of the self-proclaimed Donets Soviet Republic called for a continuing revolutionary war. Although on 8 March 1918, from its temporary base in Poltava, the Ukrainian Soviet Government was persuaded to recognize the peace signed between the Rada and the Central Powers on 9 February 1918, it did so only with the proviso that the Germans should not intervene in internal Ukrainian affairs by trying to overthrow the soviet government; since this was already happening, the recognition of the peace treaty was meaningless.

The remnants of the Ukrainian Red Army, still led by Antonov-Ovseenko, implemented the decision on partisan warfare. The army was broken up into small detachments which could operate behind the lines, and although this opened the way to German advance, it was an advance constantly harried by partisan units supported by the local population. As the Germans marched forward, so what remained of soviet power in the area went over to partisan warfare. On 28 March 1918 the Donets Soviet endorsed the strategy of revolutionary war; on 30 March 1918 the Bolsheviks in Sebastopol formed armed partisan detachments; and on 10 April 1918 the military revolutionary committee of the so-called Taurida Republic declared for revolutionary war. As the Bolsheviks fled before the German advance, their organization remained in pro-war hands. The Ukrainian Communist Party, at its foundation congress in Taganrog on 19–20 April 1918 was dominated by the pro-war group, and even after its leadership's flight to Moscow on 21 April 1918 calls for revolutionary war continued to be heard.[6]

Unlike the Bolshevik Party, which was split on the issue of the Brest-Litovsk Treaty, the Left SRs were totally behind the policy of revolutionary war. After the vote for peace at the Fourth Congress of Soviets, the Left SRs left Lenin's government and established an Uprising Committee to run party operations in occupied areas. Their opposition to the peace was endorsed by the Second Left SR Party Congress held in Moscow on 17–25 March 1918. Well into May 1918 the *Guardian* correspondent Philips-Price noted how the Left SR delegates he had met at the Third Congress of Soviets in January 1918 would disappear 'for weeks at a time' on raiding parties into the Ukraine, where they would attack German troop positions at the head of bands of Ukrainian peasants. These raids had the tacit support of the Russian soldiers who guarded the demarcation line between Russia and the Ukraine, helping the participants slip across the line under cover of darkness.[7]

A key person in the reorganization of the Ukrainian armed forces for guerrilla warfare was the British military representative George Hill. It was in mid-February 1918 that he persuaded the Red Army commander in the Ukraine, Antonov-Ovseenko, to transfer to his command a cavalry division to be used as the core of a guerrilla unit. Thereafter the army took guerrilla operations against the Germans very seriously indeed, despite the formal existence of the peace treaty between the two states. On 18 March 1918 the Moscow Military District published a long report on how to organize and operate partisan brigades against the Germans. Long into April 1918, once Hill had retreated to Moscow, the authorities did nothing to prevent him continuing to organize groups of partisans fighting in the Ukraine. This 'splendid band of irregular troops composed of ex-Russian officers' would slip into the Ukraine, dress up in peasant clothes, spray German encampments with machine-gun fire and melt into the night; they would also deliver arms to those Ukrainian peasants prepared to resist German grain requisitioning brigades. It was only at the end of April 1918 that the Ukrainian communists were prevented from operating across the border from safe havens in Russia.[8]

Opposition to the Treaty of Brest-Litovsk was tempered by the near universal belief that the treaty would not last long, and that very soon action against the German imperialists could resume. This was the clear tenor of a circular letter which the Bolshevik Central Committee sent to all party organizations on 22 March 1918. It urged them to take the initiative in forming the new Red Army, since 'the peace that has been signed gives in fact only a breathing space after which we must prepare for the most bitter war with the imperialists of the whole world; the Germans are already showing their true colours, restoring the landowners in the regions they occupy'.[9] Indeed, Lenin had been careful in the keen debates about whether or not to accept the peace treaty to sow the idea of an early resumption of military activity. At the crucial Central Committee meeting on 23 February 1918, when the decision to sign a separate peace was finally taken, Lenin got his way by the twin strategy of threatening to resign and proposing a resolution calling for the party to begin immediate preparations for a revolutionary war.[10] By so doing he was encouraging the formation of the Red Army and the notion that the breathing space won by the treaty need not be a long one. This ambiguity enabled many unhappy with the decision, Trotsky in particular, to busy themselves with military preparations for the moment the breathing space was over.

This notion was reinforced by events at the Seventh Party Congress and the Fourth Congress of Soviets. As well as endorsing the Brest-Litovsk Treaty, the Seventh Party Congress empowered the Central Committee to break any treaty and declare war on any imperialist power whenever the Central Committee thought a suitable moment had come. Then, at the Fourth Congress of Soviets, the Bolshevik Foreign Affairs Commissar G.V. Chicherin made clear that the army was to be demobilized, not disbanded, and that the Germans had implicitly recognized that, for the Bolsheviks to retain order and enforce the treaty effectively, a large army would be needed. And, according to George Hill, who attended the congress, as Lenin told delegates 'we have signed this treaty and we will keep it', he winked; Hill may have imagined this, but he left the hall, as many other delegates apparently did, convinced that all was not lost and the anti-German campaign would resume once the army had been restored.[11]

## THE ALLIES AND THE RED ARMY

From the moment of the armistice with Germany in December 1917, Jacques Sadoul, a Bolshevik sympathiser on the French military mission, had reported that Trotsky and Lenin were interested in seeking Allied support in reorganizing the Russian Army, just in case the peace talks led nowhere. Nothing came of this original suggestion, although Sadoul repeated the idea when the announcement was made early in January 1918 establishing the Red Army. In the days immediately prior to the German resumption of hostilities, the French ambassador Joseph Noulens, the British consul Francis Lindley and the US ambassador David Francis repeatedly informed Trotsky that they would support Russia should the need arise, and in an interview for the newspaper *Novaya zhizn'* Noulens looked forward to the prospect of improved relations with the government. It was, of course, precisely with this sort of development in mind that the British government had sent its diplomatic agent to Russia, Bruce Lockhart.[12] On 18 February 1918, as the German advance began, Trotsky was full of bravado and told Lockhart that 'even if Russia cannot resist she will indulge in partisan warfare to the best of her ability'. At that stage he clearly believed the Central Committee would decide to fight. As things turned out the Central Committee met twice on the 18th and on the second occasion Trotsky sided with Lenin in asking the Germans to resume negotiations. However, although this was communicated to the Germans on the morning of 19 February 1918, the Germans did not respond, and so Sadoul was eagerly received by Lenin and Trotsky on the 19th. He urged upon them a partisan war to the bitter end, retreating if necessary from Petrograd and Moscow; Trotsky appeared to have been convinced, but not Lenin.[13]

As it became clear that the Germans would continue to advance until they had occupied all the territory they claimed, the government resolved to resist. On 20 February 1918 a meeting took place in the War Ministry attended by the War Commissar N.I. Podvoiskii, the Navy Commissar P.E. Dybenko, the Commander-in-Chief Krylenko, and representatives of the General Staff. Krylenko reported on the catastrophic position at the front and the difficulties being experienced in mobilizing the population for the defence of Pskov; he bitterly noted the betrayal of the Polish Corps and the consequent fall of Minsk. Podvoiskii then raised the issue of tactics: should they, he asked, fight a partisan or positional war. Dybenko supported the idea of a partisan war enthusiastically, but the military advisors present pointed out that there was little evidence that this was developing spontaneously, and even if it were to develop it could never stop a modern army in full advance; the only thing to do was to retreat to a defensible line, and behind that try to build up reserves. The meeting decided to adopt a conventional positional war and as part of this defensive strategy GHQ was pulled back to Orel.[14]

Given this bleak scenario, it was hardly surprising that Trotsky turned to the Allies. Sadoul was much more up-beat than the Russian generals had been, and when he met Trotsky on 20 February 1918 immediately offered Allied help in the form of 40 staff officers, 40 field officers and 300 men, plus the Allied mission to Romania headed by General Berthelot which was in the process of being evacuated from that country after its surrender to the Germans. Trotsky asked for this proposal to be put in writing by ambassador Noulens, who duly obliged on the 21st. When Trotsky asked on 22 February 1918 for a detailed written explanation of what the Allies could do to help stem the German advance, this was rushed to him the same day.[15] But the proposal for co-operation with the Allies caused dissension within Lenin's government. When the proposal was discussed on 21 February 1918, the Left SR commissars objected to the principle of a socialist government receiving aid from the imperialist Allies; the issue was referred to the central committees of both parties. The Left SRs rejected the proposal, but the Bolsheviks were less dogmatic. On 22 February 1918 Trotsky put the idea to the Bolshevik Central Committee; it led to a bitter debate, with Bukharin leading the opposition and Trotsky finding support from Sokolnikov, and after the meeting, from Lenin. By just six votes to five Trotsky got his way; the Central Committee would accept Allied aid. With some justification Lockhart could report to London that the Bolsheviks were preparing to fight 'the most bitter partisan war', retreating if necessary to the Urals.[16]

On 23 February 1918 Trotsky and General Niessel, the French military attaché, duly drew up plans for a harrying retreat; but on the same day the Germans presented new terms to the Bolshevik government. As well as further territorial concessions, the Russians were called upon to demobilize the Russian Army and Red Guard, disarm all warships, restore the 1904 trade treaty and pay an indemnity. Lenin, Trotsky, Krylenko and the leading generals immediately held an emergency meeting: the generals argued that Petrograd would fall if the German advance continued, and the Petrograd–Moscow railway would soon be cut. After some recrimination about the deployment of artillery in the fighting so far – Krylenko said not enough was available, while the generals argued that it had been poorly used – Lenin concluded that further resistance was impossible. The Central Committee voted to accept what amounted to a German ultimatum; the proposal was put to the Soviet Executive on the night of 23 February 1918 and endorsed at 5 a.m. on the 24th. Sokolnikov then set off for Brest-Litovsk to finalize the Russian surrender.[17]

However, the Germans were determined to keep up their offensive until Sokolnikov actually arrived in Brest-Litovsk and signed the revised treaty. Thus, even after the decision had been taken in principle to accept the German ultimatum, there was a danger that the Germans would reject the Russian acceptance. Indeed, for a moment the military situation improved, with the Red Army retaking Pskov on 25 February 1918 and holding it for a couple of days. There was a certain irony about the reconquest of Pskov, given the hostility of GHQ to partisan operations. This was the area where the First Partisan Brigade had been formed; indeed on 26 February 1918 soviets were called upon to form partisan brigades and on 27 February 1918 successful partisan operations were being reported from behind enemy lines not only in Pskov but particularly in Minsk, operations which reached their peak on 2 March 1918. The downing by a partisan group of a German airplane caused particular excitement.[18]

During these continuing hostilities, while the peace treaty was far from secure, Lenin's government remained in constant contact with the Allies. Lockhart visited Lenin on 29 February 1918, while

Sokolnikov was still *en route* to Brest-Litovsk having been trapped by the bitter fighting in Pskov. Lenin made it clear the Bolsheviks could only co-operate with the Allies if they were not treated as a 'cat's paw'. He went on:

> So long, therefore, as the German danger exists, I am prepared to risk a co-operation with the Allies, which should be temporarily advantageous to both of us . . . As a result of this robber peace Germany will have to maintain larger not fewer forces on the East. As to her being able to obtain supplies in large quantities from Russia, you may set your fears at rest. Passive resistance – and the expression comes from your country – is a more potent weapon than an army that cannot fight.[19]

On 1 March 1918, during the final days before the signing of the treaty on 3 March 1918, the Bolshevik government suddenly received a message requesting a train to bring its negotiators back to Petrograd. Fearing the collapse of talks and a renewed invasion Lenin issued a call for general resistance; as part of this he authorized the soviet in Murmansk, where the Allies had large quantities of stores, to co-ordinate its operations with the Allied military mission there. The same day he had further talks with Lockhart, who reported back: 'there are still considerable possibilities of organizing resistance to Germany'. On 2 March 1918 Lockhart told London that, whatever happened, peace would only hold for 'a few weeks'.[20]

No sooner had the peace been signed, than the Bolshevik government began constructing a new army. On 4 March 1918 the Petrograd Defence Staff was converted into the Supreme Military Council, chaired by Trotsky, whose membership was expanded on 30 March 1918 to include a representative of the Left SRs. It approved a campaign plan for 1918 which envisaged a fighting retreat behind the Volkhov river, should there be a new German advance, and the establishment of 'screens' to protect the two capitals. The plan envisaged a conventional army of 1,500,000 men, formed by conscription with no elected officers and military specialists brought in from the old army. Many in the Bolshevik government were unhappy with such a conventional approach, and were more in favour of a militia army; in the end the generals had to settle for a conventional army of 1,000,000 men, with the question of military specialists from the old army left open. Trotsky's support for a conventional army put him at loggerheads with his natural allies in the anti-German camp, since most pro-war communists favoured partisan brigades and militia units, and were consistently hostile to the idea of a traditional conscripted army. For all the hostility to military specialists, they were used extensively; on 31 March 1918 Admiral D.V. Verderevskii, the

Navy Minister in the Third Coalition Government, was appointed to the Supreme Military Council.[21]

The Allies continued to offer help in this process. Talks between Lockhart and Trotsky continued throughout March 1918. On the 7th the British suggested that Commander Locker-Lampson, who in August 1917 had tried to put his armoured car detachments at Kornilov's disposal, should be asked to return to Russia; on the 13th Lockhart attached Captain Hicks, a member of his mission, to the Supreme Military Council;[22] on the 16th Trotsky and Lockhart travelled to Moscow together, and thereafter these ad hoc decisions began to be systematized. Lockhart held daily meetings with General J.G. Lavergne of the French military mission and representatives of the Italian and American military; at these sessions Allied aid to the Red Army constantly topped the agenda. Trotsky was only too willing to respond. On 20 March 1918 Sadoul persuaded Trotsky to ask Lavergne formally to collaborate in organizing the Red Army and request that 40 Allied officers be attached to it; by 26 March 1918 these officers had been selected.[23]

One of these was George Hill who found himself appointed to the post of Inspector of Aviation, Trotsky's personal advisor on aviation matters. This was a wide-ranging brief: because of the need to evacuate air planes and spare parts, Hill served on the army's evacuation committee, charged with moving crucial military equipment well to the rear of enemy lines. But he also helped the army establish an Intelligence Section, charged with identifying German units on the Russian front and keeping all German troop movements under observation; this invaluable information was reported straight back to the War Office in London, as was the other success of the Intelligence Section, breaking German codes and establishing a counter-espionage system to spy on German secret service operations in Petrograd and Moscow.[24]

The first success of these Allied efforts was to persuade Trotsky to turn Lockhart's informal liaison group into a proper committee of Allied military personnel to advise him. At the first meeting of this advisory committee, Trotsky duly made a formal request for help, Lavergne accepted the request, and it was agreed that General Berthelot's former Romanian mission should remain in Moscow.[25] This was a period of almost unbounded optimism for the small team of military advisors surrounding Lockhart. On 21 March 1918 he reported to London that war with Germany was 'unavoidable'. On 25 March 1918 the Bolshevik Foreign Affairs Commissar Chicherin told Lockhart that when war with Germany resumed, the Bolsheviks would even welcome Allied support from Japan, something Lockhart confirmed to London on 28 March 1918 with the news that Trotsky himself had stated he had no objection to Japanese troops being part of an Allied force supporting the Red Army in a renewed conflict with Germany.[26] The attachment of Berthelot's mission to Trotsky was part of an ever more grandiose scheme, drawn up at Trotsky's request, which would have involved 500 French officers being used to re-establish order in the army, and 300 British officers performing the same function in the navy.[27]

Lockhart, as the diplomatic agent of the British government, was fully empowered to engage in such politically sensitive matters. The others involved in the Berthelot scheme were military men, and the involvement of so many French officers in such an unusual venture needed the endorsement of French diplomats and politicians. The French ambassador Noulens had left Petrograd for Finland at the end of February 1918 and only got to know about the activities of Lavergne when stories circulating among the French community in Moscow began to be reported to Paris and then forwarded to him in Finland. He was determined to reassert his political authority over the military mission as soon as he returned to Russia on 29 March 1918, basing himself with the majority of the diplomatic corps in Vologda, a town whose strategic position was ideal – with railway connections to both Archangel in the North and Vladivostok in the East – should a German advance lead to the fall of Moscow.

Noulens put an immediate freeze on the talks with Trotsky. He felt Lavergne had acted without awaiting proper authorization, particularly in assigning three French officers to Trotsky as technical advisors. These officers were withdrawn, the Berthelot scheme stopped, and Berthelot instructed to return to France; but Noulens did not want a complete break in this potentially fruitful relationship with Trotsky. He called a high level meeting with the military representatives in Vologda on 3 April 1918 to discuss under what conditions military aid to Trotsky might continue. Some of these, like the willingness to accept Japanese help, the Bolsheviks had already accepted; the real stumbling block was the question of discipline in the restored army. Noulens wanted to link aid to discipline, in particular he wanted to see the end of the commissar system and the reimposition of officers' insignia. The *Guardian*'s Philips-Price soon got wind of the fact that discipline was the stumbling block in these talks.[28]

Noulens held further talks in Vologda on 9 April 1918. Those present accepted that Trotsky was prepared to envisage Japanese intervention, and that he could hardly be expected to make a public statement in favour of the Allies until the very moment the Brest-Litovsk Treaty was repudiated; however, Trotsky's assurances about discipline were still considered too vague. Noulens wanted to stop the talks with Trotsky at this point and called for the closure of the French military mission, but he was persuaded to back down. Clarifications were sought from Trotsky and discussed further on 11 April 1918, but Trotsky's views were still not acceptable to Noulens and the French military mission was disbanded on 16 April 1918.[29] For Noulens it was all very simple: the Germans were themselves violating the Brest-Litovsk Treaty by advancing well beyond the originally agreed demarcation line in the region of Kursk and Voronezh; this gave the Russians a *casus belli* and they should respond by forming a disciplined army which would fight. He said almost as much at a rather undiplomatic press conference in Vologda on 18 April 1918 when he talked publicly of the sort of joint anti-German action with the Allies which he and his military advisors had been discussing with Trotsky in private for several weeks.

Noulens did not see his press conference as breaking off relations with the Bolsheviks, but simply as raising the stakes. Indeed, the statement caused little stir in Moscow until after the arrival of the German ambassador Count Wilhelm Mirbach on 26 April 1918; it was Mirbach who insisted that the Bolshevik Foreign Affairs Commissar Chicherin request Noulens recall on the 29th. The press conference was given chiefly to opposition papers, and the SRs probably understood the message correctly when they concluded that it was a message to them, to warn them that their suspicions were correct and that the Allies were preparing to do a deal with the Bolsheviks.[30] For, from mid-April 1918 onwards relations between Trotsky and Lockhart became particularly close. Despite the intense debate about the future of the French military mission, on 13 April 1918 Trotsky asked Lockhart if another member of his staff, Colonel Boyle, could be assigned to administer the railway system; he had already distinguished himself by sorting out the Moscow railway network in the days before the armistice in December 1917. Then, on 22 April 1918, the British Foreign Minister Balfour instructed Lockhart to make one last effort to win Trotsky round.[31]

## THE ALLIED MISSION TO THE BOLSHEVIKS

Both at the time, and in his memoirs, Lockhart was concerned that the British government was not taking the prospect of collaboration with the Bolsheviks seriously. This was not in fact the case, but communications between Moscow and London were at times so haphazard that telegrams could often take five days or more to arrive. The British government had at first been deeply divided about the status of Lockhart's mission: the cabinet was at loggerheads from 21 January 1918 to 7 February 1918 over whether to allow Lockhart to make serious contact with the Bolsheviks, or whether he should concentrate his efforts on the cossacks in the Don. After strong intervention from the Prime Minister David Lloyd George, Balfour was victorious and thereafter the cabinet backed Lockhart.[32] British policy was clear: it was working towards a Bolshevik invitation to land an Allied force in Russia to resuscitate the Eastern Front.

At first the British Cabinet was obsessed with the idea of Japanese intervention, something that had been mooted even before the Bolshevik seizure of power. This was at once put to Lockhart, who expressed his reservations on 4 March 1918, and continued to be seen as an essential element in any mission for a further fortnight until on 21 March 1918 the cabinet recognized that the real question was not so much the Japanese as 'whether there was any prospect of the Bolsheviks really making good their intentions of renewing the contest'; and Lockhart's telegrams on this seemed encouraging.[33] From early April 1918, the British government worked on the assumption that some sort of deal with Trotsky could be done. The ambassador in Peking was told firmly on 7 April 1918 to do nothing to encourage the anti-Bolshevik movement of the cossack commander G.M. Semenov, then operating in Siberia. Semenov's force, the ambassador was told, was only small and could easily cause unnecessary complications since 'at the present moment we are endeavouring, with some appearance of success, to induce the Bolshevik government at Moscow not only to renew fighting against the Germans but even to accept Allied, including Japanese co-operation and assistance'.[34] On 9 April 1918 the message to the ambassador in Tokyo was the same, there was 'real hope' that Trotsky would co-operate. Thus on 10 April 1918 Lockhart was told 'we are quite ready to discuss Allied intervention on the basis agreed between the military representatives and Trotsky'.[35] At the cabinet meeting of 12 April 1918 it was agreed that the only thing to do was to seek agreement with Trotsky via Lockhart, and on 15 April 1918 Lockhart was told that Trotsky had until the end of the month to show himself to be serious.[36]

Trotsky was indeed serious. In response to the message of 10 April 1918, Lockhart forwarded to London on 13 April 1918 an invitation to the Allies from Trotsky asking them to put in writing what military help and what guarantees the British could give.[37] On 14 April Captain Garstin, the senior British officer in Moscow, assembled the Allied military representatives and proposed the following terms:

1. renewal of the alliance with Russia;
2. guarantee not to interfere with Russian internal affairs;
3. loyal collaboration with government of soviets;
4. guarantee of integrity of Russian territory;
5. allies shall declare that operating forces will cross Siberia solely in order to reach war zone;
6. troops shall be Allied and not only Japanese;
7. Russia shall be helped on Murman and Archangel railways;
8. co-operation shall be given to Armenia against Turks if desirable.

This proposal was forwarded by Lockhart on 15 April 1918, received in London on 20 April 1918 and discussed in cabinet on 22 April 1918. After some debate that paragraph four might tie Britain to the impossible task of recovering all the territory Russia had lost, it was agreed to send Lockhart the following reply:

> I think suggestions of military representatives may well serve as a basis for discussion. As far as HMG are concerned, two, four, and six can be accepted as they stand. We have always considered Russia as our ally, and word 're-affirmation' should therefore be substituted for 'renewal' in one. As three stands at present, it might in certain conceivable circumstances conflict with two. I therefore prefer 'loyal co-operation with Russian authorities against common enemy'. In order to give requisite military latitude, five should be amended as follows: 'Allies should declare that operating forces will cross Siberia solely for the purpose of carrying out military operations against the enemy.' If by help on Murman and Archangel railways aid given by ships and by marines landed from them is meant, seven can remain unchanged; but employment of troops must necessarily be subject to military exigencies, as must also acceptance of eight. We are, however, most anxious to help in both cases.[38]

While this exchange of telegrams was underway, Trotsky was keen to get the talks going and clarify their parameters. In a conversation with Lockhart, summarized to London on 19 April 1918, Trotsky wanted to know if he would be talking to the British alone or the Allies as a whole, and where they would be held. He felt Noulens' attitude was unhelpful, and therefore suggested that the talks should not be held in Vologda; since Mirbach was about to arrive in Moscow, time was pressing and he needed to know when the Allies could act.[39]

Lockhart was not starry-eyed about the chances of the talks

resulting in the Allies being formally invited to send a force to Russia. On 21 April 1918 he telegraphed that there was a 'fair chance' of such an invitation from Trotsky being received, 'although I am not so optimistic as the French or Italian generals on this point'. The enthusiasm of the French military representative Lavergne was tempered by the continuing caution of Noulens, who felt that the sending of a mission should not be dependent on a formal invitation from the Bolsheviks; the Allies should force the issue by landing anyway. A visit by Lavergne to Vologda did nothing to soften Noulens' position, but when Lockhart, Lavergne and the Italian and American representatives met on 29 April 1918, they re-affirmed their support for the pro-Trotsky policy despite Noulens' views. Lockhart had reassured London the previous day that Foreign Affairs Commissar Chicherin was 'as anxious as ever' to reach an agreement, despite the arrival in Moscow on 26 April 1918 of the German ambassador Mirbach.[40]

British enthusiasm for the enterprise soon brought Noulens into line. On 5 May 1918 Lockhart reported 'much improved' relations with Vologda; Lavergne had told him that Noulens had come round to support the views of the Allied military representatives. Ironically this happened just when Balfour himself was having last minute doubts about the enterprise: he asked Lockhart on 6 May 1918 if he was sure of Trotsky's attitude; could not more have been done to organize guerrilla warfare, destroy railways and the like, if the Bolsheviks really were in earnest. But the British decision had been made. Thus the British cabinet minister Lord Milner could write to the ambassador in Paris on 9 May 1918: 'it is desirable to work as well as we can with the Bolshevik government now in power'. A week later, on 15 May 1918, he informed the ambassador in Washington:

> The whole recent progress of events tends to show that the Bolshevik government are prepared to accept our intervention, though they cannot give a formal invitation, while if the Allies hesitate much longer the position of Germany will be so strong that not only will intervention be useless but will be opposed.[41]

## THE CZECHOSLOVAK LEGION

The problem for the British was this: what practical support could the British give the Bolsheviks, given the situation on the Western Front. It was the shortage of available troops that had prompted Allied planners to premise all schemes for a strengthened Eastern Front on the idea that Japanese troops could be used. Although Japan was an ally of Russia, Britain and France, the experience of the Russo–Japanese war of 1904–5 was not easily forgotten, and the Allies' new ally in the First World War, the United States, was very wary of involving their Pacific rivals in any Russian venture. All the talk of using Japanese troops as the basis for an intervention force foundered on the rocks of the US President's refusal to countenance the idea; Japanese imperial ambitions in the region were all too clear. In the absence, then, of a Japanese intervention force, where were sufficient troops to be found to send to Russia? On 17 April 1918 the outline of a plan began to emerge in London. Balfour pointed out in cabinet that it might be possible to persuade Trotsky to allow the Czechoslovak Legion to be moved from Kursk, where it had retreated after the fall of the Ukraine, to a new deployment in the Archangel and Murmansk regions: the idea was favourably received, partly because such approval on Trotsky's part would go some way to persuade those cabinet members who still doubted his 'honesty of purpose with regard to the Allies'. The same cabinet meeting welcomed a report that the British naval attaché had been asked by Trotsky to secure British help with the Black Sea Fleet. Thus on 20 April 1918 Lockhart was informed that the Czechoslovak Legion was to be used in Archangel, Murmansk and the 'railways leading to those parts', and Trotsky's agreement to this should be sought.[42]

Balfour's proposal concerning the Czechoslovak Legion did not come out of the blue, and Trotsky's acceptance of it was almost certain; the fate of the Czechoslovak Legion had been on the agenda in London, Paris and Moscow for over a month. Back on 15 March 1918 the Czechoslovak National Council in Moscow informed the Bolshevik Commissar of Nationalities responsible for such matters, Stalin, that they planned to recruit a second legion from prisoners of war in Siberia; Stalin endorsed the idea and pointed out that it was important to strengthen Red Army forces behind the Urals since conflict with the Central Powers was inevitable. Stalin's sympathy for the Czechoslovaks was shared by Trotsky. On 19 March 1918 he informed the Russian Supreme Military Council that he was disappointed to hear the news that the Czechoslovak Legion had decided to leave Russia – after the Brest-Litovsk Treaty. Leaving Russia seemed the only way to fight the Central Powers, and the Czechoslovak Legion was resolved to depart via the same route taken in March 1918 by Masaryk, across the Trans-Siberian railway to Vladivostok. On 20 March 1918 Trotsky informed Sadoul that he hoped the Czechoslovaks would change their minds and not only stay in Russia but become the nucleus of a reorganized Red Army; on this issue he clashed with Lenin who wanted the Czechoslovaks to leave since the presence of this Allied force on Russian soil might put the peace treaty with Germany in jeopardy. In this clash with Lenin, Trotsky emerged victorious: on 20 March 1918 he stopped all Czechoslovak train movements in a move designed to keep the legion in Russia to serve alongside the Red Army and prevent a precipitate departure for France.[43]

At the same time in Britain and in France pressure was put on the Czechoslovaks to stay put. On 21 March 1918 Marshall F. Foch, the Supreme Commander of Allied Forces, suggested the Czechoslovak Legion should stay in Russia if they so wished, and the same day the British Foreign Office prepared a memorandum for the War Office on the role and usefulness of the Czechoslovak Legion. The problem was not the attitude of the Allies but the unwillingness of the Czecho-slovaks themselves to stay in Russia. When on 22 March 1918 General Lavergne had talks with the Czechoslovak National Council, its leaders made clear their refusal to allow the Legion to stay and insisted on returning to France as soon as possible. Rebuffed in Moscow, the Allies turned to the Moscow Czechoslovaks' superiors in Paris. On 1 April 1918 the British and the French asked the Paris-based Edward Benes, Masaryk's deputy within the Czechoslovak nationalist move-ment, if he would agree to the Czechoslovak Legion staying in Russia to help Trotsky; but the following day he too refused, conceding only that those Czechoslovak soldiers stationed to the west of the Urals could be evacuated to France via Archangel if this proved more convenient.[44]

Thus when the cabinet took its decision on 17 April 1918 to make the Czechoslovak Legion the core of any intervention force sent to support Trotsky – a decision communicated to Lockhart on 20 April 1918 – it had only secured an agreement for some Czechoslovak soldiers to leave the country via Archangel, not an agreement that they would secure those railway lines against the Germans in renewed fighting. Pressure on the Czechoslovaks therefore continued and the editor of the *Times*, Henry Wickham Steed, a long-time supporter of the Czechoslovak cause, was sent to Paris for private talks with Benes; as a result on 22 April 1918, the same day the cabinet endorsed formal contacts with Trotsky, it was agreed that orders would be sent to those Czechoslovaks west of the Urals, some 45,000 men, instructing them to move to Archangel in order to resist any attempts by the Germans to advance into Russia. This order was immediately sent to Lavergne, who the following day informed the French liaison officer with the Czechoslovak Legion, Arsene Verge, that the British and the Bolsheviks wanted the legion moved north.[45]

However, the Czechoslovak soldiers in Russia were still unwilling to co-operate. On 30 April 1918 the cabinet was informed that both divisions of the Czechoslovak Legion were refusing to move to the northern ports; the following day it was told that while one Czechoslovak division was determined to leave Russia via Siberia, the other could still be persuaded to move to the locations originally planned for them on the Murmansk and Archangel railways. The reality, however, was slightly different. When on 6 May 1918 the cabinet asked Balfour to approach Trotsky via Lockhart with a view to concentrating one of the Czechoslovak divisions in Archangel and Murmansk, it was unaware that agreement with the Czechoslovak soldiers on the ground had still not been reached. It was only on 7 May 1918 that Noulens held talks in Vologda with the leaders of the Czechoslovak National Council and informed them of the plan, mentioning only the 'possibility' that they would be stationed to defend Archangel.[46]

Believing the support of the Czechoslovak Legion to be secured, the cabinet finally felt able on 11 May 1918 to endorse the proposal that Trotsky should be supported by sending a British military mission to Archangel to be led by General F.C. Poole.[47] Poole had only just returned from Russia where he had served as head of the British military equipment section in Petrograd. He was keen to return to Russia to take charge of the many stores still in northern ports and on 1 May 1918 wrote to the Chief of the Imperial General Staff asking to be sent on the next sailing to Archangel. Within the week he had been appointed head of a mission to Russia, to return with Francis Lindley, the former British consul in Petrograd; the two men were soon discussing the demarcation line between political and military authority while lesser officials planned the details. The services of Hill and Garstin, both well connected with the Bolsheviks, were allocated to Poole, as was Boyle with whom Poole was on good terms and who had established excellent relations with the Bolsheviks. In essence the plan was this: Poole would take command of the 20,000 Czechoslovaks and 3,000 Serbs believed to be making their way to Archangel and Murmansk. The precise deployment of these troops would depend on Poole's own judgement after he had had talks in Moscow with Lockhart; however, the cabinet had a very clear outline of what was wanted. On 13 May 1918 it suggested that, having secured Archangel, Poole should 'consider how far he could work up from Archangel towards Vologda with the forces at his disposal'.[48]

The Czechoslovaks were absolutely central to the operation. After Poole had set sail on 17 May 1918, his final instructions dated 18 May 1918 stressed this. They made clear he would:

> carry out the organization, training and operations of all fighting men of whatever nationality in Russia who are allotted to Great Britain or who volunteer for this purpose . . . [but his immediate duty was] the organization and operations of the Czechoslovaks and other contingents now en route to Archangel for the defence of the northern ports.[49]

And yet, even as he weighed anchor, the cabinet was suddenly made aware of the uncertainty as to whether it really had persuaded the Czechoslovaks to deploy to the north. On 17 May 1918 Lord Milner told the cabinet that he doubted whether the scheme would work because of the Czechoslovaks' unwillingness to co-operate; the French Prime Minister Georges Clemenceau, no doubt informed by Noulens of his talks with the Czechoslovak National Council which had started on 7 May 1918, had contacted Lord Milner before the cabinet meeting to warn him. Another cabinet minister, Lord Cecil, was deputed to hold further talks with Benes, and a week later, on 23 May 1918, the cabinet was reassured to learn that Clemenceau would publicly endorse the agreement that Czechoslovak troops would be used at Murmansk and Archangel. By then, however, the situation in Russia had totally changed.[50]


## A GOVERNMENT OF DEMOCRATIC CONCENTRATION

The endorsement of the Brest–Litovsk Treaty at the Fourth Congress of Soviets in mid-March 1918 had left the Bolsheviks in government alone. During the next six weeks their isolation began to be increasingly felt. This was seen most obviously in the reaction of the Left SRs, for although the Left SRs left the government, they did not leave the Soviet Executive and its constituent bodies. In particular they still controlled the peasant section of the soviet; from this power base the Left SRs were soon mounting an electoral challenge to the Bolsheviks, for the Fourth Congress of Soviets had agreed to hold fresh soviet elections during the spring and early summer in preparation for the next ordinary Congress of Soviets due to be held in July. Immediately after the Fourth Congress an election campaign began for all provincial, district and town soviets; but the Left SRs were not the only beneficiaries of this. The fluidity of the political situation convinced both the Mensheviks and the SRs that the time had come when political activity in the soviets could force Lenin from power; with the Left SRs and even pro-war communists as potential allies, nothing seemed impossible. So in March 1918 both the Menshevik and SR parties resolved to work within the soviets to defeat the Bolsheviks and recall the Constituent Assembly. A period of what might be termed semi-pluralism began in Russia's political life.[51]

As soviet elections were held in April and May 1918 throughout provincial Russia, the Bolsheviks triumphed only in Moscow. Elsewhere they suffered electoral reverse after electoral reverse, making their grasp on power shaky in the extreme. In the central industrial region – such towns as Kaluga, Orekhovo Zuevo, Kostroma, Tver, Tula, and Yaroslavl – the Bolsheviks were defeated by the Mensheviks; and in the Volga, Urals and North – such towns as Vologda, Archangel, Saratov, Nyzhnyi-Novgorod, Samara, Izhevsk, Syzran, and Ufa – the Mensheviks and SRs acted in coalition and won the elections. Singly or in alliance they were victorious in all recorded provincial and town elections.[52] This weakening of popular support for the Bolshevik Party in the provinces was bad enough, but their popular support was also ebbing away in Petrograd, the cradle of the revolution. There, as the factories closed in spring 1918, all the Bolshevik administration could offer was six weeks severance pay and soup kitchens; labour exchanges simply gave out rail passes to enable workers to leave Petrograd. Between January and April 1918 nearly 60 per cent of Petrograd's once swollen workforce found themselves on the streets, and in the key war industries of metallurgy and chemicals the figure was as high as 75 per cent. Even for those in work life was hard since supplies of basic foods had sunk dramatically. In such conditions workers' factory councils were practically powerless and the Bolsheviks, in the face of repeated demands for the re-election of soviet deputies, could hardly be confident of victory.[53]

During the spring of 1918 the Mensheviks and SRs were able to construct a powerful workers' organization of their own in Petrograd, to both rival the Petrograd Soviet and pressurize it into calling early elections. Their Assembly of Petrograd Factory Delegates was first formed during the chaotic attempts to evacuate Petrograd's key industries as the German advance on the city began on 18 February 1918; by 13 March 1918 the assembly had held its first conference, followed by five more meetings and a second conference on 3 April 1918. Founded by metal workers, it was always dominated by representatives from the 26 big metal-working plants of the capital, formerly engaged in defence work which by spring 1918 were under the greatest threat of redundancy since the number employed in these plants was only half the January 1917 level. Throughout March and April 1918 the assembly built up a power base in the Putilov plant, the Obukhov factory, the Old Lessner factory, in short the factories famed in 1917 for their revolutionary activism. The Bolsheviks, uncertain how to respond, allowed the assembly and the Petrograd Soviet to coexist; by the end of April, the Petrograd Mensheviks could be satisfied with the results of their efforts for, together with the SRs, they had the potential to challenge the Bolsheviks for the leadership of the working class. By mid–May 1918 the assembly comprised 200 delegates representing 100,000 workers or two-thirds of employed workers. One of its leaders was Likhach, an SR who had played a leading role in the various committees preparing for the opening of the Constituent Assembly.[54]

If workers' support for the Bolsheviks was evaporating by the spring of 1918, the same was true of the Baltic sailors, so long a source of radicalism in 1917. Since the Brest-Litovsk peace treaty put a huge question mark over the future of the Baltic Fleet, it was not long before the sailors began to renew contacts with the Mensheviks, SRs and their assembly. In Kronstadt the Bolshevik share of the seats in the newly elected soviet shrank from 131 to 53; in mid-April 1918, at a Congress of Sailors in Moscow, speeches critical of the Bolsheviks were heard; and at a conference of sailors in Petrograd held at the same time the denunciations of Lenin and Trotsky were even more vociferous. Simultaneously the SRs were developing close links between their members in the Obukhov factory and the sailors stationed at the nearby mining unit of the Baltic Fleet; these became the base for an effective SR armed militia run by the party's military commission. On 9 May 1918 the Baltic Fleet's mining unit made a public call for the abolition of the Petrograd Soviet, the resignation of the Bolshevik government, and the reconvening of the Constituent Assembly; this call was the main agenda item when the Baltic Fleet held its conference in Petrograd on 11 May 1918 and invited a delegation from the assembly to attend. When the Red Army held a conference in Petrograd at precisely the same time, the Bolsheviks suffered further embarrassment. A Left SR was elected chairman, and the conference voted that its decisions would be binding on the soviet authorities. Angry soldiers demanded: 'why is there so much hubbub against reconvening of the Constituent Assembly?'. It was not the Constituent Assembly people should be afraid of, they added, but the threat of a German sponsored counter-revolution.[55] The very social classes that had supported the Bolsheviks in October 1917 were turning against them in May 1918.

The steady erosion of the Bolshevik power base clearly put a question mark over how much longer the Bolshevik Party could remain in power. But civil war was not on the agenda in the first week of May, far from it. The Mensheviks, SRs and Left SRs, separately but sometimes together, were not engaging the Bolsheviks in armed struggle but destroying them through democratic struggle in the soviets. Nor was their purpose necessarily to supplant the Bolsheviks; what the opposition parties all had in common was a rejection of the Brest-Litovsk peace. The most likely outcome of the growing opposition strength was the overthrow of Lenin and the formation of a coalition socialist government committed to war. That certainly was what Allied representatives were working for.

Far from encouraging opposition parties to take up arms against the Bolsheviks during April and May 1918, Lockhart and his team were trying to ensure that the opposition would support a Bolshevik government committed to the war, and should the logic be followed through, join a coalition administration. It was at the end of March 1918, on the 28th and 30th, that Lockhart first reported he had made contact with opposition groups to see how they would respond to Allied support for the Bolsheviks. He felt he had persuaded them to co-operate since their main worry about the proposal seemed to be not the Bolsheviks but the possible involvement of too many Japanese troops in any Allied force. Lockhart continued his talks with all opposition parties between 7 and 21 April 1918,[56] while from London ambassadors were contacted with the same message. The British had least luck with Semenov in Siberia. When asked to co-operate with the Bolsheviks in resisting Germany, Semenov point blank refused. On 13 April 1918 the Foreign Office was informed by the local British consul that Semenov had made clear 'that in no case will he or his organization co-operate with any Bolshevik-controlled military movement whatever its ostensible purpose'. They had more luck with Kornilov. On 15 April 1918 Lockhart was approached by an officer in 'General K's Army in South Russia' who explained that his sole aim was to fight the Germans and he therefore was willing to operate jointly with the Bolsheviks, providing that they did not try to take over the Volunteer Army.

The first hint of possible rapprochement between the Bolsheviks and the other socialist parties was reported on 11 April 1918 by Major Fitzwilliams, who, after leaving the Ukraine in February 1918, had just returned from a tour of Siberia. He warned against any precipitate intervention in Siberia via counter-revolutionaries such as Semenov arguing that this would 'tend to upset the highly desirable and probable rapprochement of moderate Bolsheviks and Socialist Revolutionaries'.[57] The idea of just such a coalition socialist government was taken up with even greater enthusiasm by Sadoul, the Bolshevik sympathizer on the French military mission. On 17 April 1918 he met the Bolshevik Commissar for Social Welfare and former Menshevik Alexandra Kollontai and told her that he hoped that the Bolsheviks' current course would end in the formation of a coalition socialist government, to include the Mensheviks and the SRs. Ten days later he wrote of the talks he had had with the SR and Menshevik leaders in recent days and how hopeful he was that if the Allies supported 'the Bolsheviks for the sake of Russia' the Mensheviks and the SRs would call a truce and come to an understanding with the Bolsheviks; this would result in the formation of what he called a 'government of democratic concentration', a development he saw not so much as a dream but as a reality. On 8 May 1918 he was surer than ever that democratic reconciliation was the order of the day. With some exaggeration but more than an element of truth, a German embassy report published somewhat later characterized Trotsky as 'almost an SR working for the Allies' and complained of the willingness of the Bolsheviks to co-operate with the SRs.[58]

## PEACE FOR CIVIL WAR

The emerging political crisis in Russia was brought to a head by the military coup staged by the Germans in the Ukraine on 29 April 1918; this overthrew the democratic Rada government and brought to power the right-wing dictator General P. Skoropadskii, whose clear mandate from the land-owners who greeted his action with enthusiasm was to deal firmly with agrarian disturbances and secure the grain deliveries demanded by the Germans by annulling the 1917 land reform. Since the German ambassador Mirbach had arrived in Moscow on 26 April 1918, he had at once begun to throw his weight around, and speculation was rife that Mirbach intended to treat Russia in the same way as his compatriots had treated the government in the Ukraine and stage a coup against the Bolsheviks. Many Bolsheviks argued that if their government wanted to avoid this, a break with Germany was essential and should be carried out at once; Skoropadskii's coup showed the true face of German imperialism and indicated that the time for a breathing space was over. It was with this eventuality in mind that on 4 May 1918 Russian border troops were told to resist any further incursions by German forces. Lockhart was quite right when he reported on 7 May 1918 that the government was in crisis over the news from the Ukraine and 'a rupture with Germany was possible at any moment'.[59]

It was to debate the implications of the German action in the Ukraine that the Bolshevik Central Committee began a series of crisis meetings which lasted from 6 May until 13 May 1918. The international situation was first discussed at a late night session on 6 May: that meeting adopted a resolution proposed by Lenin which spoke of 'rejecting the English ultimatum' and accepting the German one, even though he recognized that this would mean agreeing to peace treaties with Finland and the Ukraine which would involve accepting further territorial losses for Russia. However, that was not the end of the matter. The Central Committee met again on 10 May 1918 and debated a resolution proposed by Sokolnikov, which stated that, in view of the coup in the Ukraine, war with Germany was inevitable and the 'breathing space given by the Brest-Litovsk Treaty was over'; war preparations should begin at once and an agreement signed with the Allies. This resolution was again defeated, but not even that ended the crisis: the Central Committee met once more on 13 May 1918 and this time fully supported Lenin's *Theses on the Present Situation* and rejected once and for all a military alliance with the Allies after having heard a report from A.A. Ioffe, the recently arrived Russian ambassador in Berlin, which stated that the threat of German intervention had passed; only Sokolnikov and Stalin did not support Lenin on this occasion.[60]

The defection of Sokolnikov and Stalin, two politicians who had stood by Lenin in the previous crises concerning the Railway Workers' Union talks and the signing of the Brest-Litovsk peace, showed just how severe the situation was, and rumours of a split in the Central Committee and the emergence of a 'Sokolnikov group' were soon strong enough to be picked up by the *Guardian*'s Philips-Price. As debate raged, Allied observers were convinced that it would be resolved in their favour: thus on 7 May 1918 Sadoul wrote that the Bolsheviks' willingness to collaborate with the Allies could no longer be denied, and the same day Lockhart reported that Foreign Affairs Commissar Chicherin had told him that a break with Germany was possible at any moment because of developments in the Ukraine; even as late as 15 May 1918 Trotsky told Lockhart war with Germany was inevitable.[61]

Of course, Allied observers could be accused of naivety, but the enormity of what Lenin was proposing went beyond ordinary logic. Lenin planned to buy off the threat of a German coup by offering a trade deal to the voracious German imperialists. On 15 May 1918 the German ambassador was presented with Lenin's 'bribe': he proposed the resumption of economic relations with Germany, a large loan from German banks to the Soviet government, the payment of interest on this loan with Russian raw materials, large soviet purchases in Germany, concessions to German companies for the exploitation of Russian natural resources and German assistance in constructing railways and modernizing agriculture. In return Germany would have to refrain from interfering in Russia's internal economic affairs and its economic relations with the former states of the Russian Empire, recognize the nationalization of the banks and foreign trade, guarantee the delivery to Russia of half the total iron ore production of the Krivoi Rog region of the Ukraine, and agree a border with the Ukraine which ceded the Donets Basin to Russia.[62]

When the Germans took the bait, Lenin was free to build what he termed socialism in the rump state of Soviet Russia. Lenin had first drafted his ideas on socialist construction at the end of April 1918 and, with the agreement of the Bolshevik Central Committee, presented them to the Soviet Executive on 29 April. The *Theses on the Tasks of the Soviet Government at the Present Moment* introduced into Russia's economic policy many ideas associated with capitalism: out went workers' control and in came one-man management and the employment of bourgeois specialists. The programme met sustained criticism while being debated in the Soviet Executive, from both left and right: to the Left SRs and many of the pro-war communists it was capitulation to the capitalists, to the right it was proof that Russia was not ready for socialism. Although the scheme was endorsed by the Bolshevik Central Committee on 3 May 1918 as *Six Theses on the Current Tasks of Soviet Power* and issued to all local soviets on 4 May 1918, there was little practical chance of the programme being implemented. The proposals were denounced in the opposition press and the Bolsheviks' poor position in the provincial soviets meant that in many parts of the country they would simply be ignored.[63]

Negotiating a German economic treaty meant German protection could be used to 'build socialism' according to this programme. But what Lenin termed 'building socialism' in May 1918 in fact meant the same thing which in December 1917 he had termed 'first defeating the bourgeoisie at home'; the reality behind this rhetoric was the launching of a Red versus Green civil war against the SR victors in the Constituent Assembly elections. The German alliance meant the Mensheviks and SRs could be expelled from the soviets and the Assembly of Factory Delegates dissolved. It made possible a complete break with the Left SRs, for it created the possibility of breaking the influence the party still had on the peasantry. When the Left SRs tried to use their control over peasant soviets to resist the Bolsheviks' new economic policy, Lenin launched a policy of 'class war' in the countryside and established committees of poor peasants to replace the 'kulak [rich peasant] dominated' peasant soviets. In short, accepting the economic treaty with Imperial Germany meant ending the brief spell of semi-pluralism in political life, when the Mensheviks and SRs had felt able to use democratic methods to dislodge the Bolsheviks, and restarting the civil war within democracy.

## NOTES

1. For Chernov, see H. Niessel, *Le Triomphe des Bolcheviques et la Paix a Brest Litovsk* (Paris 1940), p. 221; for the SR military commission, see M.S. Bernshtam (ed.), *Nezavisimoe rabochee dvizhenie v 1918 godu* (Paris 1981), p. 43; otherwise R.I. Kowalski, *The Bolshevik Party in Conflict* (Basingstoke 1991), pp. 13, 152, 159.
2. Kowalski, *Bolshevik Party,* pp. 12, 15.
3. Kowalski, *Bolshevik Party,* p. 17; T.A. Sivokhina, *Krakh melkoburzhuaznoi oppozitsii* (Moscow 1973), p. 136.
4. Kowalski, *Bolshevik Party*, p. 145 et seq.
5. Kowalski, *Bolshevik Party*, pp. 157, 167.
6. Kowalski, *Bolshevik Party*, pp. 171–6.
7. Sivokhina, *Krakh*, p. 138; K. Gusev, *Krakh partii levykh eserov* (Leningrad 1963), p. 156; M. Philips-Price, *My Reminiscences of the Russian Revolution* (London 1921), p. 277.
8. G. Hill, *Go Spy the Land* (London 1932), pp. 177, 203; G.D. Kostomarov and R.I. Golubeva (eds) *Organizatsiya Krasnoi Armii: Sbornik dokumentov i materialov* (Moscow 1943), pp. 134–6.
9. 'Deyatel'nost' TsK partii v dokumentakh' *Izvestiya TsK KPSS* (1989) no 3, p. 105.
10. R. Debo, *Revolution and Survival* (Liverpool 1979), p. 144.
11. Debo, *Revolution*, p. 190; Hill, *Go Spy*, p. 183.
12. J. Sadoul, *Notes sur la Révolution Bolchevique* (Paris 1920), pp. 153–5, 210; J. Noulens, *Mon Ambassade en Russie Soviétique, 1917–1919* (Paris 1933) vol. 1, p. 218.
13. K. Young (ed.), *The Diaries of Sir Robert Bruce Lockhart* (London 1973), vol 1, p. 33; Sadoul, *Notes*, p. 240.
14. Z.A. Vertsinskii, *God revolyutsii* (Tallin 1929), pp. 50–5.

15. Sadoul, *Notes*, pp. 241–4.

16. *Bolsheviks and the October Revolution: Central Committee Minutes of the RSDLP(b)* (London 1974), pp. 213–15; Milner Papers, 364.53.

17. For the meeting with the generals, see Vertsinskii, *God revolyutsii*, p. 57; otherwise, Debo, *Revolution*, pp. 142–6.

18. S. Naida, 'Pochemu den' sovetskoi armii prazdnuetsya 23 fevralya' *Voenno-istoricheskii zhurnal* no. 5 (1964), p. 115; Kostomarov and Golubeva, *Organizatsiya*, pp. 46, 111, 118, 123, 128.

19. R.H.B. Lockhart, *Memoirs of a British Agent* (London 1946), pp. 235–40.

20. Debo, *Revolution*, pp. 154, 232; Milner Papers, 364.67.

21. 'Deyatel'nost' TsK', p. 107; J. Erikson, 'The origins of the Red Army', in R. Pipes (ed.), *Revolutionary Russia* (Harvard 1968), p. 241; Kowalski, *Bolshevik Party*, p. 138.

22. Milner Papers, 364.83, 364.103.

23. Lockhart, *Memoirs*, pp. 242, 274.

24. Hill, *Go Spy*, p. 190 et seq.

25. Lockhart, *Memoirs*, p. 150.

26. For Chicherin, see Debo, *Revolution*, p. 245; for Lockhart's reports to London, see Milner Papers, 364.149, 364.156.

27. Noulens, *Ambassade* vol. 2, pp. 28, 53–6.

28. Lockhart, *Memoirs*, p. 250; Noulens, *Ambassade* vol. 2, pp. 28, 53–6; Philips-Price, *Reminiscences*, p. 252.

29. Noulens, *Ambassade* vol. 2, pp. 51, 55, 66; see also M.J. Carley, *Revolution and Intervention: the French Government and the Russian Civil War* (Montreal 1983), p. 426.

30. Noulens, *Ambassade*, pp. 69–71.

31. For Boyle, see Hill, *Go Spy*, p. 107 and Milner Papers 141, copy of telegram date 15 May 1918; for Balfour, see Debo, *Revolution*, p. 254.

32. Minutes of War Cabinets, 327, 330, 340 and 341.

33. Minutes of War Cabinets, 358, 359 and 369.

34. When Semenov refused to co-operate with this plan, London was furious, see Milner Papers, 367.158, 367.175 and 367.188–190.

35. Milner Papers, 364.196.

36. Minutes of War Cabinet, 390; Milner Papers, 364.221.

37. Milner Papers, 364.208.

38. Minutes of War Cabinet, 396.

39. Milner Papers, 364.225.

40. For the meeting of 29 April, see Lockhart, *Memoirs*, p. 271; otherwise Milner Papers, 364.230 and 141, report of 28 April 1918.

41. For Noulens, see Milner Papers, 364.268; for Balfour's hesitation, see Milner Papers, 364.272; otherwise Milner Papers, 141, reports of 9 and 15 May 1918.

42. Minutes of War Cabinet, 393; Milner Papers, 364.228.

43. V.M. Fic, *The Bolsheviks and the Czechoslovak Legion* (New Delhi 1978), pp. 8–14.

44. For Foch and the British Foreign Office, see J. Kalvoda, *The Genesis of Czechoslovakia*, (Columbia 1986), p. 273 and J.F.N. Bradley, *Allied*

*Intervention in Russia* (London 1968), p. 72; for the refusal of the Czechoslovak National Council and the talks with Benes, see Fic, *Bolsheviks*, p. 14; Kalvoda, *Genesis*, p. 279.

45. For the message to Lockhart, see Milner Papers, 364.228; for Wickham Steed, see Milner Papers, 357.45; for Lavergne, see Noulens, *Ambassade* vol. 2, p. 82; for Verge, see A. Vergé, *Avec les Tchécoslovaques* (Paris 1926), p. 107.

46. Minutes of War Cabinets, 401, 402, 405; Noulens, *Ambassade* vol. 2, p. 82.

47. B.M. Unterberger, *The United States, Revolutionary Russia and the Rise of Czechoslovakia* (University of North Carolina Press 1989), p. 165.

48. For the military details, see Public Records Office, WO 32.5643.4a, 5643.4c and 5643.5a; Minutes of War Cabinet, 410.

49. Public Records Office, WO32.5643.19a.

50. Minutes of War Cabinets, 413 and 415.

51. Sivokhina, *Krakh*, p. 141.

52. V. Brovkin, *The Mensheviks After October* (Cornell 1987), p. 159.

53. M. McAuley, *Bread and Justice: State and Society in Petrograd 1917–22* (Oxford 1992), p. 89; see also W.G. Rosenberg, 'Russian labour and Bolshevik power after October' *Slavic Review* (1985).

54. Rosenberg, 'Russian Labour'; Brovkin, *Mensheviks*, p. 162 et seq.

55. Brovkin, *Mensheviks*, pp. 181–4; G. Semenov, *Voennaya i boevaya rabota Partii Sotsialistov-Revolyutsionerov za 1917–18* (Moscow 1922), p. 22.

56. Milner Papers, 364.157, 364.233.

57. Milner Papers, 367.173–5, 364.222.

58. Sadoul, *Notes*, pp. 316, 323, 344; V.L. Israelyan, 'Neopravdivshiisya prognoz Grafa Mirbacha' *Novaya i noveishaya istoriya* no. 6 (1967), p. 63.

59. For the Russian border troops, see V.K. Koblyakov, 'Bor'ba sovetskogo gosudarstva za sokhranenie mira s Germaniei v period deistviya Brestskogo dogovora' *Istoriya SSSR* no. 4 (1958), p. 9; for Lockhart, see Milner Papers, 264.276.

60. 'Iz arkhivov partii' *Izvestiya TsK KPSS* no. 4 (1989), p. 141 et seq.

61. Philips-Price, *Reminiscences*, p. 276; Sadoul, *Notes*, p. 338; Milner Papers, 364.276; Young, *Lockhart*, p. 36.

62. Debo, *Revolution*, pp. 218–22.

63. Sivokhina, *Krakh*, pp. 150–2.

# CHAPTER SIX
# The Start of the Red–Green Civil War

The Red versus Green, Bolshevik versus SR civil war, that had been latent since Lenin's seizure of power in October 1917, but delayed by the Railway Workers' Union talks, the elections to the Constituent Assembly, and the patriotic mood after Germany's resumption of hostilities in February 1918, finally began on 13 May 1918 when the Bolshevik Central Committee decided to reject the proposal for an alliance with the Allies. This civil war was unnecessary: negotiated settlements of all Russia's social conflicts had been available in November 1917 and May 1918, but on both these occasions Lenin would have had to agree to the formation of a coalition socialist administration. To this he preferred risking civil war, and by the end of May a quite unnecessary war had begun between the Bolsheviks and the SRs.

As the fighting began, some of the weaknesses of the Green side were immediately apparent. The members of the Allies 'great enterprise' in Russia, as General Poole's mission was termed, found themselves not as they had anticipated being welcomed by Trotsky, but as the shock troops of the Red versus Green civil war. They were put at the disposal not of Trotsky but of the Green patriotic socialists once wooed by Somerset Maugham; for the Allies these patriotic socialists offered the only hope of re-establishing a new Eastern Front. Yet Poole's mission itself was still plagued by uncertainty as to the role planned in it for the Czechoslovak Legion. They still refused to link up with the Allies in Archangel, severely weakening both the mission and the military arm of the Green force favoured by the Allies, the so-called Union for the Regeneration of Russia.

When the Czechoslovaks did begin to fight, it was not in the vicinity of Archangel as planned, but far to the south on the river

Volga, and in the company of SR forces unaware that their party leaders had made any commitment to the Allies and the Union for the Regeneration of Russia. To make matters worse, communication problems meant that a planned joint Allied–Union for the Regeneration of Russia action in Archangel and Yaroslavl, a town providing the key to access from the north to the Volga, was a failure. As the Red versus Green civil war started, all the actors were in the wrong place at the wrong time, and everything went off at half cock. Yet by early August 1918 these problems were in the process of being resolved. The Allies did land in Archangel, the Czechoslovaks did secure a base on the Volga, and supported by the SR-inspired People's Army these units were seeking to march north and perform a vast pincer movement with General Poole's forces descending from Archangel, to rendezvous at a strategic point on the Trans-Siberian railway.

## THE MUTINY OF THE CZECHOSLOVAK LEGION

Lenin's rejection of an alliance with the Allies on 13 May 1918 meant that London had to revise General Poole's mission even before he had arrived in Murmansk. If the Allied force was not to be welcomed by the Bolsheviks but likely to meet opposition from the Red Army, control of Vologda was essential; every blueprint for military operations against the Bolsheviks revolved around the basic premise that control of the town of Vologda, and preferably Vyatka as well, would secure the essential north–south and east–west arteries of Russia (see map, p. 278).[1] On 22 May 1918 the British Cabinet discussed a paper, 'Future military strategy', which assumed for the first time that the government established in Russia to stop the German advance would be anti-Bolshevik; in the accompanying War Office memorandum it was made clear that this change of circumstance meant that it was more important than ever, indeed Poole's 'first and foremost duty', to 'organize' the Czechoslovaks. A rough plan was discussed in a paper for the Director of Military Intelligence of 24 May 1918 which argued that the arrival of Poole's mission would be 'the signal for those elements among the Russians who are ready to throw in their lot with the Allies rather than the Germans to rally to the Allied cause'; General Lavergne, the French military representative in Moscow, and his staff would help organize these forces and prolong the fighting line to link up the Allied effort based on Archangel with

Siberia via the Viatka–Perm railway.[2] A map produced at this time envisaged deploying the Czechoslovaks along the length of the railway system from Penza in the south via Vologda to Archangel in the north, with the main concentration of Czechoslovak forces guarding the Vologda–Archangel line.[3]

These changed priorities were made even clearer by Poole's deputy, General R.G. Finlayson as he sailed with the second part of the mission, due to rendezvous with Poole in Murmansk approximately a month after Poole's departure. He spelt out four aims: the seizure of Archangel to prevent the formation of German submarine bases in the area; the seizure of Vologda and its railway connections, a town 'of greatest strategical importance to us' whose 'possession is vital to ensure great success . . . our main jumping off point'; to reach Vyatka via Kotlas, and thus control the vital Siberian trade; and to rally 'influential Russians'. He admitted that while the first of these priorities could be achieved by the British forces alone, the others all depended on fruitful co-operation with 'friendlies' like the Czechoslovaks. As he developed his scheme for what would happen after the seizure of Vologda, the references to the Czechoslovaks in his memorandum became more and more frequent.[4]

But just as the Czechoslovaks featured more and more prominently in British plans, they mutinied. As part of the same *volte face* which saw the Bolsheviks abandon plans for an Allied alliance, they were compelled to regularize the position of the Czechoslovak Legion. On 15 May 1918, to satisfy German objections to the existence of an Allied military force in neutral Russia, Stalin drew up plans to dissolve the Czechoslovak National Council and transfer its activities to his Commissariat of the Nationalities; at the same time Trotsky began moves he hoped would culminate in the disbanding of the Czechoslovak Legion, for after the Central Committee decision of 13 May 1918 Trotsky performed an about-turn, and instead of wanting to work with the Czechoslovak Legion, was thereafter only interested in seizing its arms and equipment. However, disbanding the legion meant disarming it, something that would not be easy given the poor fighting capacity of the Red Army. Trotsky's task was made immeasurably easier by the behaviour of the Czechoslovak Legion itself.[5]

In the final Allied plan for the future of the Czechoslovak Legion, its second division, then stationed in trains to the east of Omsk, was to continue its eastward journey to Vladivostok and France; but the first division, the bulk of which was scattered along the railway system from Penza to Chelyabinsk, was to proceed to Omsk, and thence, performing a U-turn, west to Vologda and north to Archangel. On 15

May 1918, having concluded talks with the French ambassador Noulens which began on 7 May 1918, the Czechoslovak National Council instructed its army command to divide the legion as agreed with the Allies; the legion did not obey. The idea of splitting the legion was far from popular among the rank and file and on 18 May 1918 delegates from the seventy trains spread the length of the railway lines from Penza to Vladivostok began to assemble in Chelyabinsk to hold a long planned congress of the legion; the main topic to be discussed was the move to Archangel. The first division was determined not to go; its delegates arrived in Chelyabinsk earlier than the others and voted on 15 May 1918 not to obey the new order. On the 18th a leading member of the Czechoslovak National Council, Bogdan Pavlu, warned the French liaison officer Verge of the growing unrest, but despite appeals from Verge, the first division persuaded an informal delegate session held the same day to endorse its stance. Ignoring this pent-up emotion, Verge was informed by Noulens later on the 18th that the move to Archangel had to begin at once, so on 21 May 1918 train commanders were instructed to issue orders for the trains to start moving on the following day. When the legion congress opened its formal sessions on 21–23 May 1918 it mutinied and resolved not to go to Archangel, but to leave Russia via Vladivostok as originally planned, forcing its passage there if necessary. By mutinying, the congress also rejected the right of the Moscow-based Czechoslovak National Council to control its affairs. Despite more pleas from Verge, the rank and file congress delegates refused to believe that the Allies had sponsored what to them appeared the suicidal plan of dividing the legion and sending the entire first division into a trap.[6]

This rebellion against the Czechoslovak National Council was perfectly understandable, since Stalin's announcement of 15 May 1918 outlining plans to incorporate the council within the Commissariat of Nationalities was followed up by a further broadside from Trotsky. On 21 May 1918 he made skilful use of an incident which had taken place in Chelyabinsk between 14–17 May 1918, but about which he had only been informed on 20 May 1918. After a fight between some Czechoslovak legionaries and a Hungarian prisoner of war, the Chelyabinsk soviet had imprisoned a number of the Czechoslovaks involved in the fracas; the Czechoslovaks had then forced the soviet to set their men free. This high-handed action gave Trotsky the excuse to demand the disarming of the legion, and when the Czechoslovak National Council refused he promptly arrested the council leadership in Moscow and forced them to order the legion's disarmament. When two days later the legion congress decided to ignore all orders from the Czechoslovak National Council, they did so on the grounds that, since the threat to incorporate it in the Commissariat of Nationalities, it was no longer the independent voice of the Czechoslovaks. The order to move to Archangel and the order to disarm both seemed part and parcel of the same attempt to emasculate the legion, a policy being forced on the leadership after its arrest. The legion's refusal to disarm gave Trotsky the excuse to demand that the legion be disarmed by force, which he did on 23 May 1918.

This mutiny against the Allies prompted a strange coalition of interests between Trotsky, who wanted to see the Czechoslovaks disarmed before they could be disbanded, and the Allies, who wanted them in Archangel at any cost, for in Archangel they could always be re-armed even if they were disarmed *en route*; both Trotsky and the Allies wanted the Czechoslovak mutiny ended. The Allies, desperate to get the Czechoslovaks to Archangel, were more than willing to help Trotsky reach a peaceful solution. On 23 May 1918 a French liaison officer Major Guinet arrived in Omsk where the legion's military command was based. In talks held on 24 May 1918 he stressed that it was Marshal Foch himself who had endorsed the move to Archangel, and orders were sent to Chelyabinsk condemning the mutiny and calling on the legion to co-operate with the Bolsheviks in their transfer to Archangel; the congress was told to halt all further discussion until Guinet arrived. But the damage had already been done. Czechoslovak trains were already starting their journey eastward from Chelyabinsk to Omsk, and on the same day, 25 May 1918, as a Czechoslovak National Council delegation set off from Omsk to Chelyabinsk to try and reassert its authority over the legion, the first trains from Chelyabinsk were approaching Omsk. Implementing Trotsky's order that they be forcibly disarmed, the Red Army attempted to intercept those trains at Marianovka halt; this incident led to a bloody clash in which the Czechoslovaks gained the upper hand over the Bolsheviks.

Over the next three days large sections of the Trans-Siberian Railway east of Omsk were seized by the Czechoslovaks, with only Irkutsk responding to Verge's pleas for talks; almost overnight Soviet control over much of Siberia was lost. In Omsk itself Guinet and the Bolsheviks tried to persuade the Czechoslovaks that the fighting at Marianovka had been a misunderstanding, but with little success. To the west of Omsk the Czechoslovak action was less dramatic, since the soviets of Penza, Syzran and Chelyabinsk at first continued to co-operate with the Czechoslovaks, but when that co-operation wavered they too were overthrown; thus on 27 May 1918 Chelyabinsk was seized by the Czechoslovaks and on 29 May 1918 the tail-end of the Czechoslovak convoy seized control of Penza before heading further east. By the end of May 1918 it seemed increasingly unlikely that any Czechoslovak forces would rendezvous with Poole in Archangel. As he sailed into Murmansk on 24 May 1918 the strategic assumptions on which his mission had been based had both disappeared: there was no sympathetic Bolshevik government, and no Czechoslovak Legion.[7]

## THE ANTI-BOLSHEVIK UNDERGROUND

When General Finlayson sailed to join Poole in Murmansk, his reassessment of the mission's purpose included the hope that the arrival of their mission would be 'the signal for those elements among the Russians who are ready to throw in their lot with the Allies rather than the Germans to rally to the Allied cause'.[8] From the end of May and throughout June and July 1918 Allied representatives intensified their contacts with the anti-Bolshevik underground; not surprisingly given the experience of the Somerset Maugham mission, these contacts centred on the patriotic socialists. When at the end of May 1918 Lockhart performed an about-turn, dropped his Bolshevik contacts and began working with anti-Bolshevik forces, it was to Maugham's Russians that he turned, to Chaikovskii and the politicians who had sought to overcome the Bolshevik threat in autumn 1917, and at the turn of the year to guarantee that the Constituent Assembly opened on time; but above all he turned to Savinkov, the politician in whom Maugham had placed so much faith.

Purely military contacts had long been established between the Allies and Savinkov. He was the most frenetic opponent of the Bolsheviks: as they stormed the Winter Palace on 25 October 1917, he was holding despairing talks with former Commander-in-Chief General Alekseev and desperately trying to rally cossack regiments to retake the palace. In the following week, although spurned by Kerensky, he tried to rally every conceivable opponent of Bolshevism, dashing towards Pskov in an unsuccessful effort to persuade the Polish Corps of Dowbor Musnicki to join General Krasnov's cossacks at Pulkovo Heights. Once it was clear that the Bolshevik regime had consolidated its hold on power, Savinkov went to the Don in December 1917 and persuaded General Alekseev to include him on his Don Citizens Council; but the atmosphere on the Don was not conducive to close co-operation between Green patriotic socialists and White generals. After a failed assassination attempt on his life, Alekseev agreed that Savinkov would do better as the council's representative within Soviet Russia; he duly returned to Petrograd in mid-January 1918, but failed to establish contact as hoped with other patriotic socialists like Plekhanov and Chaikovskii. Then, in the early spring, he was left stranded in Moscow as General Alekseev's Volunteer Army retreated from the Don. Disillusioned with his experience in the south, Savinkov determined to build an underground organization inside Soviet Russia and held talks in Moscow on 2 and 5 March 1918 with the Czechoslovak leader Masaryk, who donated 200,000 roubles to Savinkov's cause; Masaryk had just left Kiev after its fall to the Germans and was on his way to Vladivostok, America, and ultimately an independent Czechoslovakia.[9]

Between March and May 1918 Savinkov's organization was essentially military rather than political, and during the period of Allied co-operation with the Bolsheviks was used by the Allies for intelligence gathering, both behind enemy lines in the Ukraine and among the former War Minister's numerous sympathizers within the General Staff and the Supreme Military Council; one of those involved in this operation was the British military agent George Hill, at the very same time an honoured associate of Trotsky.[10] The Allies were impressed with Savinkov's use of partisan detachments, but wanted them to operate well behind the German line, not as at first happened, in its immediate vicinity. Savinkov's ability to pass both this test and supply crucial intelligence information brought immediate rewards. By the end of April 1918 he was receiving regular support from the French totalling 500,000 roubles – enough to pay the salaries of key personnel – and he had at least four meetings with the French consul in Moscow and General Lavergne; his aide A. Dikgof Derental, a former French officer, met them more frequently.[11]

It was only after the about-turn in Bolshevik–Allied relations in mid-May 1918 that Savinkov was drawn back into the political arena, and as he did so he felt closest to a group called the National Centre. Despite his cool reception among the White generals on the Don, Savinkov saw it as essential to keep contacts with liberal politicians open, and the National Centre, founded in May 1918 by leading former Kadets like N.I. Astrov seemed closest to Savinkov's political stance. However, these liberal politicians were deeply split in their attitude to the Allies; many liberals, most notably the Kadet Party leader Milyukov, had abandoned all thought of contact with the Allies after the collapse of the White Volunteer Army on the Don and looked instead to the Germans to help overthrow the Bolsheviks. The most active of these pro-German liberals were grouped around the former Tsarist minister A.V. Krivoshein and included the Moscow industrialist S.N. Tretyakov. Their pro-German stance was shared by many monarchists with whom they began to co-operate.[12]

This split within the liberal camp between pro and anti-German groups meant that by far the most important underground political organization as far as the Allies were concerned was the Union for the Regeneration of Russia (URR), which sought to resuscitate the political alliance which had struggled to keep alive the Third Coalition Government during the days of the Preparliament, the same politicians on whom Somerset Maugham had placed such hope when the British had first considered intervention in Russia, the same politicians that Savinkov had once talked of welding into a 'Centre Party', between the Bolsheviks and the Kadets. In early March 1918 a so-called 'inter-group council of Constituent Assembly deputies' met in Moscow in a private flat. The sixty to seventy deputies who attended discussed the question of how the assembly could be reconvened and agreed that attempts should be made to re-establish a quorate session so that the assembly could resume its work; but many present felt that bickering among the party leaders had made the meeting quite futile. A coalition socialist government, the accepted goal of the socialist opponents of the Bolsheviks since October 1917, only made sense in the context of the two dominant socialist parties, the SRs and the Bolsheviks, coming to some sort of accommodation; the Bolsheviks' determination to dissolve the Constituent Assembly and the SRs' determination to reconvene it put a socialist coalition off the agenda: but what should be put in its place, a government formed by the SRs alone? The March 1918 meeting of Constituent Assembly deputies served to bring together the Popular Socialist deputies, the Kadet deputies and the SR deputies, who had always been to the right of the Central Committee, and these three groups began to discuss how a new political alliance could be forged.[13]

In the following weeks it was Chaikovskii's Popular Socialists who took the initiative in holding talks with the central committees of the other opposition parties, and when no progress was made it was they who proposed bypassing the central committees in the search for wider unity by forming a new organization based on what they called the 'personal principle'. Individual members of the opposition parties would form a union and bind themselves to work within their separate parties for the common goal; the parallel with the Union of

Liberation set up prior to the Revolution of 1905 was frequently drawn. Thus the URR was founded in April 1918. Among those most actively involved were, for the Kadets, Astrov, of the National Centre, and L.A. Krol, a member of the Kadet Central Committee; for the SRs, Avksentiev, one time president of the Preparliament, Argunov, a patriotic SR whose name had featured in some of Kornilov's fantasy governments, and Moiseenko, of the SR military commission; and for the Popular Socialists, their leader Chaikovskii. Its aim, also agreed in April, was twofold: to win back the territory ceded to Germany by forming an alliance with the Allies; and to establish a democratic state based initially around the restoration of local town and rural councils but, on liberation, around elections to a new Constituent Assembly. In the interim, central power would belong to a body they named 'the directory'. The agreement to call a new Constituent Assembly, rather than reconvene the existing one, was hard for many SRs to accept, but for the sake of unity they did so. The most important member of the organization was Chaikovskii, who was able to raise considerable sums of money from the co-operative movement with which he had long been associated. The other central figure was General V.G. Boldyrev, one of its instigators and the only prominent military figure associated with it, other than the former Navy Minister in the Second Coalition Government in 1917, V.I. Lebedev.[14]

Although the URR established a military commission under General Boldyrev, its lack of a really effective military organization meant there was little choice but to co-ordinate activity with other groups, particularly the military organization of the SRs, which, like the party's Constituent Assembly deputies, was on the right-wing of the party; it was headed by the URR member Moiseenko. He was keen to broaden this co-operation to include not only Boldyrev and the URR but Savinkov's organization as well; but despite talks nothing came of the move, largely as a result of a personality clash between Savinkov and Boldyrev.[15] But although Savinkov retained his link with the liberal National Centre, differences between it and the URR should not be overplayed. Both sides informed each other of their activities and joint meetings were held; indeed an agreement was made according to which the results of all talks with Allied representatives would be shared by both organizations. When Sorokin, formerly of the right-wing SR paper *Volya naroda* and a leading player in the moves to prepare for the Constituent Assembly, arrived in Moscow on 4 May 1918 as an enthusiastic recruit to the URR, he noted how the URR and Savinkov's organization were ready to 'work zealously together' with all socialists willing to sink doctrinaire differences for the greater good. This greater good found its first public expression in mid-May 1918 when Sorokin published the first and only legal edition of the paper *Regeneration*. Immediately banned by the Bolsheviks, several illegal editions appeared before the end of May 1918 when Sorokin and most of the URR leaders fled from Moscow.[16]

When on 13 May 1918 the Bolshevik government came down firmly in favour of a pro-German policy, the URR began to operate in earnest. During the last fortnight in May 1918 the Mensheviks, SRs and Kadets all held party conferences which rejected the Brest-Litovsk Treaty, and which in the case of the SRs called for the overthrow of the Bolsheviks; on 14 May 1918 the SRs and Mensheviks made similar statements at a joint session of the Soviet Executive and Moscow Soviet.[17] Then on 18 May 1918 the URR called a second 'inter-group conference of Constituent Assembly deputies', attended by over 400 people, which voted in favour of a resolution declining to recognize the validity of the Brest-Litovsk Treaty and insisting that a state of war with the Central Powers continued to be in force; to make this declaration real, the resolution also called for Allied intervention.[18] Avksentiev, a leading member of the URR and former president of the Preparliament, sought an immediate meeting with the French ambassador Noulens, who deputed the rendezvous to his French consul while assuring the URR of Allied support. At the same time Kerensky, closely involved in all these discussions despite several months living 'underground' in Moscow, contacted Lockhart to arrange an escape route via Archangel for talks with Lloyd George and the French Prime Minister Clemenceau. Kerensky's message when he arrived in London was that he represented an alliance of Mensheviks, SRs, Popular Socialists and liberals – in other words the URR – who wanted immediate Allied intervention to create a rallying point for the masses who were deeply hostile to both Germany and, as the success of the Petrograd Assembly of Factory Delegates and provincial soviet elections showed, increasingly hostile to the Bolsheviks. The URR called for Allied intervention to establish a new anti-German front on the Volga.[19]

## THE ALLIES AND THE UNDERGROUND

Avksentiev's initiative led to the first formal contact between the Allies and the anti-Bolshevik underground early in June 1918, at a meeting held in the Moscow flat of Prince E.N. Trubetskoi, who had in March 1918 introduced Masaryk to Savinkov. The meeting was the occasion for the final split between the pro-Allied and the pro-German elements among liberal members of the National Centre. All shades of opinion were present, from rightists like Krivoshein, to centrists like Struve and Astrov, and, of course, the URR. The French consul outlined a proposal, allegedly sent from V.A. Maklakov the Russian ambassador in Paris, calling for the formation of a new Eastern Front to be formed from the joint forces of the Russian opposition, the Czechoslovaks and the Japanese. It was mention of the Japanese which caused the biggest problem. As Kerensky was to inform Lloyd George on 24 June 1918, the URR consented to Japanese involvement so long as they formed part of a broader Allied force;[20] the pro-German liberals, however, were still opposed. Their military advisor insisted that it would take six to eight months for the Japanese to arrive, so the whole scheme for a renewed Eastern Front was pointless; for the URR General Boldyrev argued that Japanese troops could arrive on the Volga very quickly indeed.[21]

Of course, as things turned out, no Japanese ever were involved in this stage of the intervention, but it provided the pro-German liberals with a patriotic reason to leave the meeting. Henceforth they adopted the title 'Right Centre' and most of them, like their leader Milyukov, left at once for the more comfortable pro-German atmosphere of the Ukraine. The URR and the pro-Allied section of the liberal National Centre immediately began to lay their plans, encouraged by the French consul's confident statement that Allied intervention would begin before the end of June. The URR's efforts were to be concentrated on the Volga; although National Centre liberals were encouraged to make contact with Alekseev's forces in the distant south, this was a secondary thrust of the operation and funded accordingly.[22] By the end of May 1918 the URR's top military figures, the former Navy Minister Lebedev, the head of the SRs' military organization Moiseenko and General Boldyrev, had drafted plans identical to those being developed by the Allies: there would be insurrections in the Volga region accompanied by Allied landings in Archangel to link up with Vologda, where control of the Trans-Siberian railway could bring further long-term support. Optimistically the URR talked of 25,000 Allied troops landing in support.[23]

True to its programme, the URR planned to establish a new interim administration in the form of a three-member directory comprising Astrov, Boldyrev, and Chaikovskii, and all three men were instructed to head towards the Volga. On his way there, however, Chaikovskii passed through Vologda and there re-established contact with two long-term associates on the right-wing of the SR Party, S.S. Maslov and Dedusenko. Maslov was the SR Constituent Assembly member for Vologda and Dedusenko the same for Archangel, and both had been active together with Chaikovskii in preparations for the opening of the Constituent Assembly in 1918; Maslov had been involved in plans for its military protection. By June 1918 both were leading figures in the Vologda branch of the URR and soon became key figures in the attempt by the Allies to co-ordinate a planned Allied landing in Archangel with the activities of the URR. Maslov in particular, with his extensive contacts with the local co-operatives and peasants' organizations, was at the centre of the Archangel operation, and it was he who persuaded Chaikovskii that, rather than continue his journey eastward to the Volga, he should instead put himself at the head of the Archangel operation. After talks with E.K. Breshko-Breshkovskaya, the Grandmother of the Russian Revolution, and by then also a leading figure in the URR, Chaikovskii agreed; after all, as the Allies marched south from Archangel, seized Vologda and liberated the Volga, he would be at the head of a movement which would establish a new all-Russian government.[24]

Since the URR had no developed military organization of its own in the north, it was encouraged by the Allies to make use of the services of G.E. Chaplin, a naval captain who spoke fluent English, having served on a British submarine during the first year of the war and who had come to the attention of the naval attaché and intelligence officer in the British embassy Captain F.N.A. Cromie. Early in May 1918 Cromie commissioned Chaplin to travel to Murmansk where he would be attached to General Poole, but before he had completed this mission, Poole had arrived in Murmansk and sent an emissary, Colonel McGrath, to Petrograd for talks with Cromie and Lockhart, talks which were held at the beginning of June 1918. Cromie, 'the spirit behind the whole undertaking', put forward Chaplin as the man who could organize a URR insurrection in Archangel, and at once Chaplin was on his way to Vologda, operating under the name of Thomson with a British passport and posing as a member of the British military mission. After two weeks in Vologda he set off for Archangel in mid-June.[25]

Chaikovskii left Vologda for Archangel slightly later than Chaplin, on the night of 30 June. He was to travel by steamer and rendezvous en route with Sorokin. Sorokin, also an SR Constituent Assembly deputy for Vologda, was a native of Velikii Ustyug, and had been sent by the URR from Vologda to the Ustyug-Kotlas region. This was an area of immense strategic importance. If the attack on Vologda failed, it offered a second route to the Trans-Siberian, up the Dvina to Kotlas by boat and thence by train to Vyatka and the Trans-Siberian. Sorokin's task was to plan action timed to coincide with the Allies' disembarkation at Archangel and subsequent advance up the Dvina. By the middle of June everything was in place, and Sorokin was instructed to join Chaikovskii at Kotlas as his steamer sailed down the Dvina towards Archangel. The two travelled on together, but there was a breakdown in the URR's communication network and, as they neared Archangel, the necessary papers were only provided for ·Chaikovskii. Sorokin was forced to await further instructions.[26]

When these came the news was bad indeed. Sorokin was informed that the Allied landing in Archangel had been delayed and he should return to Ustyug. The news of the delay came with the British consul Francis Lindley. He had left England a month after Poole and with diplomatic immunity wasted no time in travelling on from Poole's base in Murmansk to Archangel, where he arrived on 28 June 1918 accompanied by Poole's associate Admiral Kemp. It was Kemp who broke the news to Chaplin of the delay, adding that even when Poole did land Chaplin could expect no military support from Poole, other than his arrival at the moment of liberation; with the few forces at his disposal, Poole insisted the town would have to be taken by Russian patriots before he arrived. News of the delay was communicated to Maslov and Dedusenko in Vologda on 5 July 1918 when they were contacted by the British agent Lieutenant Maclaren who headed what remained of Maugham's network in Russia.[27]

## THE FALL OF SAMARA

Poole decided to postpone his landing because he had finally become convinced that there was absolutely no chance of support from the Czechoslovak Legion. Ironically he took this decision precisely at the moment when French military representatives had succeeded in reasserting some authority over their mutinous Czechoslovak allies, persuading them if not to move towards Archangel then at least to stay on the Volga rather than hurrying east across Siberia.

The French ambassador Noulens had long considered it worth exploring the possibilities offered by using the Czechoslovaks on the Volga rather than transferring them to Archangel. On 1 May 1918 he had met some anti-Bolsheviks from the Volga town of Saratov who had suggested to him that the Czechoslovaks could offer decisive help in an anti-Bolshevik rising. Noulens noted in his next report to Paris that this was worth considering if the Archangel venture failed to materialize; he repeated the point on 9 May 1918. When the Bolsheviks turned against the Allies and the Czechoslovak Legion rebelled, Noulens was quick to try to link their rebellion to the anti-Bolshevik movement, rather than simply allowing them to fight their way to Vladivostok; if they would not go to Archangel, at least they should be put to some use. Thus for a while Noulens and the French military were following different policies: until the end of May 1918 Lavergne was still working with Trotsky trying to persuade a disarmed Czechoslovak Legion to regroup in Archangel; but Noulens' representatives were already trying to give the Czechoslovak revolt a clearer political direction.[28]

What persuaded the Czechoslovak Legion to become involved in Russia's Red versus Green civil war was not the impact of Marshall Foch's orders, but the activities of a small group of SRs who persuaded Colonel Stanislaus Cecek of the Czechoslovak Legion to help them liberate the Volga town of Samara. P.D. Klimushkin, I.M. Brushvit and B.K. Fortunatov, all of them SR deputies to the Constituent Assembly for Samara, had been active in the Samara region since the spring of 1918, busy organizing a peasant congress as a focal point for anti-Bolshevik activity and focusing their attention on fostering growing peasant unrest into an insurrection, anticipated for the autumn. Then, in the middle of May 1918, came the news of the Bolsheviks' economic alliance with Germany and the SR Party Conference with its call for the immediate resumption of the war with Germany and the overthrow of the illegitimate Bolshevik regime; coincidentally news came from another SR N.A. Galkin, a Central Committee representative who had recently travelled from Moscow to Samara past the stationary Czechoslovak trains, that in Penza the Czechoslovaks were in angry mood.[29]

On approximately 1 June 1918 Brushvit went to Penza to contact the Czechoslovak commander, while Fortunatov set about mobilizing the SR's own militia. Klimushkin meanwhile took on the task of planning the new administration to be established in Samara when the Bolsheviks had gone; it would be based on the deputies to the Constituent Assembly and local government councils. Klimushkin also planned a General Staff for the insurrectionary army which would include Fortunatov himself and Galkin. The depressing thing for Klimushkin was the refusal of the Mensheviks and Kadets in Samara to associate themselves with the proposed insurrection, but undeterred, Klimushkin planned everything to the smallest detail, making contact with local government representatives, local military units and even the local treasury.[30]

Brushvit reached Colonel Cecek as his train was moving from Penza towards Samara. He was not at first made welcome: a delegation from a group of local liberal politicians had already approached Cecek and offered first two million roubles and then three million roubles if the Czechoslovaks would stay behind in Penza; Cecek had refused to be 'bought' in this way, and would have dismissed Brushvit's approach out of hand if Brushvit had not been a Latvian, and therefore of use in talks if, as was quite likely, the Bolsheviks sent Latvian troops to intercept the Czechoslovaks. Although Brushvit explained the SR view that the Czechoslovaks would never be able to leave the country peacefully and should therefore co-operate with anti-Bolshevik forces like the SRs, Cecek was not convinced. Not easily put off, Brushvit promised to help the Czechoslovaks get through Samara, and sent word to his associates to start preparations for the uprising; but it was only when Brushvit and the Czechoslovaks had already reached Syzran – where the railway crossed the Volga about fifty miles short of Samara itself – and SR emissaries had presented Cecek with detailed plans of the city's defences and Galkin's views on how the city could best be taken, that Cecek's attitude began to soften. Yet only after a 600-strong SR peasant militia, led by Fortunatov, had staged an insurrection in the workers' suburb of Ivashchenkovo, stormed the Timashevskii factory and won control of the bridge over the river Samara, did Cecek agree that the Czechoslovaks would help the SRs take Samara.[31]

As Brushvit pleaded with the reluctant Colonel Cecek and the other preparations continued, the French agent Captain Bordes became actively involved in the plot to take Samara. In his railway carriage he organized a meeting between a leading SR Bogolyubov, the French consul in Samara Jannot, and one of the leading officials of the Czechoslovak National Council Dr Fischer; he urged them to co-operate in overthrowing the Bolsheviks in Samara. At a subsequent meeting Galkin and Jannot met two Czechoslovak officers who acknowledged that, although they planned only to pass through Samara, if the Bolsheviks tried to stop them there would be a fight and this would inevitably create a suitable climate for anti-Bolshevik action. On the eve of the insurrection Bogolyubov joined Galkin's insurrectionary military staff. In this way the French did not instigate the Czechoslovak action, but they did help facilitate it. Samara fell to the SRs and Czechoslovaks on 8 June 1918; the insurgents were greatly strengthened when two of the Red Army commanders who had been responsible for defending the town were persuaded to change sides; thus General Kappel and General Notbek became two of the most active commanders of the SRs' newly established People's Army.[32]

The key commander of the People's Army was the former Navy Minister in the Second Coalition Government V.I. Lebedev. A leading figure in the URR and close collaborator of Sorokin, he had been sent by the URR to the Volga area at the end of May 1918 to try and win the Ural cossacks to its cause. His journey took him to Samara, where he arrived on 14 June 1918 and, caught up in the town's liberation, he immediately changed his plans. At once he was put in charge of leading the People's Army in taking Syzran, through which the Czechoslovaks had passed a week or so earlier without overthrowing the Bolshevik administration; control of the town's bridge over the Volga was essential if the SR's insurrection was to succeed. Lebedev arrived on 22 June 1918 and soon took the town, but heavy fighting forced him to evacuate it temporarily on 7 July 1918, before reoccupying it on the 10th. Here he was informed by the French officer Major Guinet that the Allies were soon to land in Archangel, and he should move north as quickly as possible to take Simbirsk and Kazan. Guinet's order reflected the fact that the French were at last beginning to exert some sort of control over the Czechoslovaks.[33]

Colonel Cecek had initially agreed with Brushvit and the SRs that he would help them establish themselves in Samara for a fortnight or so and then move on. This was in line with the instructions still being sent by the Czechoslovak leaders in Vladivostok that the Czechoslovak Legion should keep out of politics and concentrate on travelling east. However, not all Czechoslovak commanders took that view. Making a virtue out of a necessity given the events in Samara, the commander of Czechoslovak forces west of Novonikolaevsk instructed his subordinates after 15 June 1918 that 'involvement in politics' was no longer excluded. This change of heart was largely due to the pleadings of the French liaison officer Arsene Verge, who believed that fate had offered the Czechoslovaks a unique opportunity to re-open the Eastern Front by turning round, leaving Siberia and returning to the Volga. On 23 June 1918 he was given permission by the chief French military representative in Russia, General Lavergne, to make the hazardous journey east to Vladivostok – partly by boat because the Trans-Siberian railway would not be fully under Czechoslovak control until 31 August 1918 – to convince the Czechoslovak leadership there that help was needed to restore the Eastern Front.[34]

Thus when the time came for Colonel Cecek to leave Samara, he was told by the French consul on 22 June 1918 that the Czechoslovak forces should abandon all thoughts of leaving Russia and prepare to open an Eastern Front on the Volga by fortifying all the positions currently held; Major Guinet had told the Czechoslovaks in Chelyabinsk a day earlier that while their uprising had been premature, it coincided with Allied policy. These orders were gradually confirmed. When, at the end of June 1918, Colonel Cecek did start to move east – as he approached Ufa the local Red Army commander but clandestine SR Party member Colonel Makhin opened the town to him – he found himself confronted on 6 July 1918 by Czechoslovak forces coming towards him down the railway line to stabilize the new Eastern Front; on 7 July 1918 he received the first official order from the Czechoslovak Chief of Staff that the Czechoslovaks were to defend the Volga front 'until the arrival of the Allies'. On 28 June 1918 Lockhart had been sent the same message by London: he should now 'take every possible step to encourage the Czechoslovaks'; they should not surrender their arms nor abandon their positions on the Volga 'the key of the Russian position'.[35]

But few of these encouraging developments concerning the Czechoslovaks were known to Poole in distant Murmansk. Although it soon became known that the Czechoslovak Legion had rebelled against the Bolsheviks, their future plans remained obscure; what if anything would come of their dealings with the French and the SRs was even less certain. Poole faced endless contradictory reports. On 29 May 1918 he 'definitely heard from Moscow that there was no hope of getting the Czechoslovaks as they were fighting the Bolsheviks at Penza'; it was part of Colonel McGrath's mission to Petrograd to find out exactly where the Czechoslovaks were. Lockhart tried to give McGrath the latest picture and his subsequent report to London on 5 June 1918 was to the effect that the Czechoslovaks, in their current mood, would hear nothing of going to Archangel and simply wanted to leave Russia as soon as possible.[36]

However, the situation was constantly changing and poor communications between Moscow and Murmansk made things even worse. The possible arrival of at least some Czechoslovaks was still being discussed by Poole for another fortnight, and as late as 14 June 1918 both Lockhart and Noulens were still getting requests from him to facilitate the transfer of the Czechoslovaks to Archangel. It was only on 20 June 1918 that Poole was finally informed by Lockhart, via London, that the chances of the Czechoslovaks arriving in Archangel were 'slender to a degree'.[37] Thus it was only a month after his arrival in Murmansk that Poole finally had to face up to the absence of the Czechoslovaks. This realization coincided with the arrival in Murmansk of the bulk of Poole's mission led by Finlayson and accompanied by the consul Francis Lindley. On 24 June 1918 Lindley spelt out to London the strategic implications of the new situation brought about by the 'deplorable failure' of the Czechoslovaks to come north;[38] instead of the Czechoslovaks being organized by the British to secure the Archangel railway, the British would now have to secure the railway as far as Vologda in order to give support to the Czechoslovaks on the Volga. This merely echoed what Lockhart had reported on 12 June 1918: the Poole plan would not work without the Czechoslovaks and its resuscitation required a massive landing of Allied troops.[39]

The absence of the Czechoslovaks convinced Poole there was no choice but to wait for reinforcements and he informed London of his decision on 27 June 1918. On 29 June 1918 Lord Geddes, the First Lord of the Admiralty visiting Poole on a private mission, sent a memorandum to Lloyd George outlining his perceptions of the situation. He suggested that if Poole were sent 5,000 additional men he could descend to Vologda, attracting anything up to a 100,000 irregulars, and once Vologda had been taken, the 20–25,000 Czechoslovaks in Siberia could be contacted; it was a gamble, he said, but Poole believed 'if you are going to gamble at all, you should stake boldly'. Unconvinced that he would get his 5,000 men, he quietly resolved on 11 July 1918 that he could go when French reinforcements arrived 'early in August with about fifteen hundred men; with five hundred of which I could hold the town and district and push on a thousand to Vologda'. But unfortunately for the Allies' 'great enterprise' word of the postponed landings had not reached Savinkov.[40]

## INSURRECTION IN YAROSLAVL AND MOSCOW

Control of Yaroslavl and the nearby towns of Rybinsk, Murom and Kostroma was essential to the Allies' plan. It would establish a direct rail link from Archangel via Vologda to the freely navigable Volga. Success there was absolutely essential to the whole mission, and no doubt for that reason the insurrection in Yaroslavl was entrusted to

Savinkov, the man in whom the Allies had most trust.

Although Savinkov's organization had been weakened by arrests at the end of May, it had survived intact and by June 1918 detailed planning had begun. In principle the decision for an insurrection was taken on 20 June 1918, and its chief planner A.P. Perkhurov arrived in the area at the end of the month, with Savinkov arriving at the beginning of July. Savinkov won working–class support for the action after talks with the local Mensheviks; a complex formula was agreed whereby 150 workers would arrive after ninety minutes fighting, a further 300 after four hours fighting and a final 300 if fighting continued until the evening. However, things were already beginning to go wrong. The insurgents learnt that the Bolsheviks were aware of their plans, and that reinforcements had arrived: some wanted to call everything off, but this was overruled, and the insurrection went ahead, despite the fact that only about 100 of the anticipated 300 volunteers assembled to launch the attack.

Initially things went roughly according to plan. Not as many workers' groups supported the insurgents as had been anticipated, but the population at large was enthusiastic, with a flood of volunteers in the early days. By the fifth day of fighting, however, it was clear the adventure was doomed; by day six only 700 fighters were still in the field; on 20 July 1918 they were forced to ask for a cease-fire and then they surrendered on the 21st.[41] The planned insurrections elsewhere also failed; only in Rybinsk was there substantial fighting, but Savinkov's men there had expected the operation in Yaroslavl to begin a day later, and, forced to delay their action until the planned starting date, lost the element of surprise. As a result they failed to capture any of the large artillery depots in the town, control of which would have given the insurgents enormously increased fire power.[42]

Savinkov's decision to act when he did later caused great controversy, since he acted after the Archangel landing had already been called off. Antagonism between his forces and the URR was one possible explanation: tension certainly existed between Savinkov's organization and the URR; in his memoirs the URR's military leader General Boldyrev felt that relations between the URR and the liberal National Centre steadily worsened during June, and he held Savinkov partly responsible for this since he had fallen too much under the influence of the National Centre. Certainly Savinkov was very keen to get the full endorsement of the National Centre for his action, and there was more than mere symbolism in his decision to call his Yaroslavl army the Volunteer Northern Army, echoing the Volunteer Army of General Alekseev on the Don rather than the People's Army formed by URR activists on the Volga. Yet, once Savinkov had escaped to the Volga in August 1918, he cheerfully merged his forces with the People's Army, and before the Yaroslavl insurrection began he sent a steady stream of his supporters to Kazan and the Volga to be put at the disposal of the URR. Savinkov's decision to launch a 'premature' insurrection was not a result of any self-willed refusal to co-ordinate plans with the URR, but the simple fact that Poole's decision to postpone the Archangel landings reached him too late.[43]

When the French ambassador Noulens had arranged for his consul to inform the opposition groups early in June that the Allies would intervene by the end of the month, he was simply reflecting Poole's original plan. This was that as soon as Poole's mission was fully assembled, it would leave Murmansk and disembark in Archangel, link up with the Czechoslovaks, and move south towards Vologda. The full mission was duly assembled on time by 23 June 1918: by then, however, the true state of affairs concerning the Czechoslovaks had become clear and Poole decided to await French reinforcements to take the place of the missing Czechoslovaks; but news of this only reached Vologda via the British consul Lindley, his escort Admiral Kemp and the secret agent Maclaren on 5 July 1918. Savinkov began his action on the 4th. Perhaps if he had acted on the 5th, as the Rybinsk insurgents had anticipated, he would have received a message cancelling the operation, but, with the Bolsheviks aware that something was afoot, his decision to act one day early, on the 4th, was dictated by military necessity. Although Savinkov was in regular communication with Lockhart, Lockhart's links with Poole were always poor: the two never established direct communications and messages had to go via London; at one point Lockhart received no messages from London for a fortnight. Thus a message sent on 27 June 1918 from Poole via London to Lockhart for Savinkov would hardly have reached its destination before 4 July 1918, especially once Savinkov had left Moscow for Yaroslavl.[44]

Savinkov's plans had been drawn up in close consultation with both Noulens and Lockhart. When the idea of an insurrection had first been mooted, Savinkov had proposed a putsch in Moscow carried out by 5,000 of his supporters. It had been the French who proposed abandoning this scheme: Lavergne explained to Savinkov how Noulens anticipated the formation of a new Eastern Front on the Volga, linked to an Allied landing at Archangel; if the insurgents could seize the towns on the upper Volga, a secure base could be made for supplying the Volga from the north. As one of Savinkov's close advisors noted, the whole planning of the Yaroslavl uprising was made on assumptions derived from the French. Savinkov always maintained that he had been told by the French that the landings at Archangel would take place in the first week of July, and Perkhurov later recalled being told by Savinkov that he would only have to hold the town for four days before the Allied landings began.[45] The British too inadvertently helped supply misleading information. Thus on 26 May 1918 Lockhart asked London for confirmation of rumours that the French had agreed intervention would start on 25 June 1918, the approximate date of Finlayson's rendezvous with Poole in Murmansk; thereafter he acted as if confirmation had been received. If on 2 June 1918 he was still uncertain about the date of the landing and could urge London to commence operations within the next ten days, after his meeting on 5 or 6 June 1918 with Poole's agent McGrath in Petrograd he must have been informed that the mission would reach its full complement within three weeks, again confirming the rumour of a landing on or around 25 June 1918.[46]

Once Lindley had reached Vologda and the Murmansk and Moscow wings of the operation were brought together, the British consul immediately realized the full import of Savinkov's doomed venture. He urged immediate action in the following telegram to London sent on 7 July 1918:

> General Poole does not expect to occupy Archangel until first week of August. This delay is too long [since] civil war is breaking out in Russia . . . Profoundly convinced of this necessity heads of Allied missions at Vologda desire their respective governments to expedite all steps calculated to hasten despatch of Allied forces to Archangel . . . When decision was taken by Poole to postpone military operations until arrival of larger force I entirely agreed. Since then events have precipitated themselves and I now think that if the General can scrape together one thousand men and can expect reinforcements at an early date he should occupy Archangel at once . . . now that the attention of Bolshevists is concentrated at Moscow and Yaroslavl . . .[47]

Poole, however, made no move, even though Lockhart believed as late as 18 July 1918 that a landing was imminent, late, of course, but still in time to prevent Savinkov's surrender.[48]

Tragically for the 'great enterprise' of bringing Allied support to the patriotic socialist or Green cause, the Allies were unable to benefit from Savinkov's insurrection in Yaroslavl; but they were able to benefit considerably from events in Moscow. On 6 July 1918 the German ambassador Mirbach was assassinated by the Left SRs as part of a co-ordinated effort to restart the war with Germany; the assassination prompted a mutiny on the Volga by the Left SR General

Muraviev. Muraviev, after falling out of favour with the Bolshevik leadership since his campaign in the Ukraine, had recently been appointed to head the Red Army's offensive against the Czechoslovaks. For Lenin his reputation as a military commander counted for more than his support for the Left SRs.

Up until the very last minute the Left SRs had been confident that as the voice of Russia's peasant masses, they would achieve a majority when the Fifth Congress of Soviets assembled in Moscow on 6 July 1918, a majority which would enable them to deprive Lenin of power and launch a revolutionary war against Germany. Between April and the end of June 1918 membership of their party had almost doubled, from 60,000 to 100,000, and to prevent them securing a majority at the congress Lenin was forced to rely on dubious procedures; he allowed so-called committees of poor peasants to be represented at the congress. Thus as late as 3 July 1918 returns suggested a majority for the Left SRs, but a Congress of Committees of Poor Peasants held in Petrograd the same day 'redressed the balance in favour of the Bolsheviks', to quote the *Guardian*'s Philips-Price, by deciding it had the right to represent all those districts where local soviets had not been 'cleansed of kulak elements and had not delivered the amount of food laid down in the requisitioning lists of the Committees of Poor Peasants'. This blatant gerrymandering ensured a Bolshevik majority at the Fifth Congress of Soviets.[49]

Deprived of their democratic majority, the Left SRs resorted to terror and assassinated the German ambassador Mirbach, hoping this would force a renewal of the war. At the same time Left SR military units seized the telegraph building to proclaim to the country that they had secured a majority at the congress and that the war was being resumed. It was with some difficulty that the Bolsheviks were able to restore order in the capital, and those who had seized the telegraph building clearly thought that their broadcast would prompt sympathetic action in the country at large, and in particular from General Muraviev.[50] Sympathetic action by the Left SRs on the Volga could indeed be expected. During the fighting to take Syrzan, the People's Army commander Lebedev had noted that the Left SR press was sympathetic to the Czechoslovaks and very critical of Trotsky's actions towards them. Similarly in Simbirsk relations between the Bolsheviks and the Left SRs in the local soviet were near breaking-point; the Left SRs had a majority on the local soviet and no doubt made use of this when assembling in the town after 8 July 1918 several units of the party's armed militia, ready in case an insurrection broke out; in response the Bolsheviks had arrested the Left SR leader

Klim Ivanov. Sympathetic action by General Muraviev was more difficult to predict, however, since in the aftermath of Mirbach's assassination he had announced he was leaving the party.[51]

Muraviev had been arrested by the Bolshevik government in April 1918 for refusing to take up an appointment offered him and after allegations that he had misused his power. However, pressure from the military had resulted in his release, and on 13 June 1918 he was appointed to overall command of the Czechoslovak Front. The appointment was controversial, but supported by Lenin who himself later overruled any suggestion that he should be dismissed in the light of the Left SRs' assassination of Mirbach; but it was an odd decision to place at the head of the army fighting the Czechoslovaks the man who in February 1918 had proposed joining them in a joint struggle against Germany. On 10 July 1918 Muraviev abandoned the Red Army command in Kazan and sailed with 1,000 men to Simbirsk where he informed the local Left SRs that the party should seize power and establish a 'Volga Soviet Republic'. The new government would immediately negotiate with the Czechoslovaks and declare war on Germany, and to this end Muraviev sent a telegram from Simbirsk to the German embassy announcing the war was being renewed. At the same time he telegraphed the Czechoslovaks, urging them not to leave Russia but to resume the struggle against the Germans.[52] Conceivably he acted with the knowledge of the French, since the French agent Bordes arrived in Kazan on 8 July 1918 and certainly witnessed events. Bordes's role was possibly greater than this, since both Bordes and Muraviev had served with Antonov-Ovseenko in the Ukraine, both had long-standing associations with the Czechoslovaks, and, while in Odessa, Muraviev had already been in contact with the French military agent Colonel Arquier.[53]

Muraviev's rebellion lasted no more than a day: the Bolsheviks in Simbirsk persuaded him to attend a special meeting of the soviet to explain his actions and gunned him down as he entered the building; however, the impact of the rebellion on the Czechoslovak front was dramatic. The Red Army was soon in disarray and the People's Army, supported by the Czechoslovaks, could accelerate their progress up the Volga towards Kazan. A new rendezvous with the Allies in the Vologda-Vyatka area did not seem so impossible after all. The twin disasters of the Czechoslovak mutiny and the Yaroslavl insurrection could perhaps still be overcome and the Allies' 'great enterprise' in support of Russia's Green patriotic socialists put back on course.

## TO VOLOGDA AND VYATKA?

The People's Army took Simbirsk on 22 July 1918. Bordes was there at once, arriving with clear orders from Lavergne concerning the future of the Allied enterprise. Kazan should be captured at once, since the Allies were about to land at Archangel and seize both Vologda and Vyatka. Lebedev's forces were to move north, take Kazan, and then divide, with one branch moving up the Volga to Nizhnyi Novgorod, Yaroslavl and Vologda, and the other heading across country to Vyatka. Despite these clear instructions, Lebedev experienced momentary doubts when on the eve of his advance to Kazan he met the leader of Savinkov's insurrection in Murom who told him how the Allies had let them down; but this time the Allies did not fail them.[54]

Despite the delay to the Archangel landing, planning for this URR-linked operation continued. Lockhart held two meetings with URR leaders designed primarily to strengthen contacts with General Alekseev in the south. At the first of these on 16 July 1918 he and Lavergne met the liberal politicians Struve and Astrov to discuss the developments on the Volga and ask whether General Alekseev might now be able to move from his redoubt beyond the Don to the lower reaches of the Volga. At the second meeting, on 21 July 1918, an emissary from Alekseev promised to try to capture Tsaritsyn, and Lockhart promised to try to get Struve to Archangel, to strengthen liberal representation in any new government formed; the British clearly hoped that he might head the new administration. At both meetings Lockhart handed over considerable sums of money.[55]

What particularly pleased Lockhart when he reported to London on 25 July 1918 was that the 'Centre [URR] has come to complete agreement with Savinkov's League' and were jointly seeking to contact the Czechoslovaks; as part of the broader preparations for the landing General Boldyrev had moved to Vologda, while Savinkov had gone to rendezvous with Lebedev in Kazan. Meanwhile those of Savinkov's partisans who had escaped from Yaroslavl were being regrouped under General Lavergne's orders: some would cut the Archangel railway as the Allies landed, to prevent the Bolsheviks reinforcing the local detachments, while the rest, some 3–5,000 men would be regrouped in both Vyatka and Kazan.[56]

As to plans for the insurrection in Archangel, these also depended on co-operation between the URR and the National Centre. Chaikovskii arrived in Archangel in disguise on approximately 24 July 1918, and at his first meeting with Chaplin, he made clear that he was acting in accordance with the URR programme; his government would include both liberals and SRs. Chaplin, whose main contact with the Archangel opposition was N.A. Startsev, a local liberal politician and a member of the National Centre, immediately proposed that Startsev should be included in Chaikovskii's government; Chaikovskii stressed the abilities of his associates Maslov and Dedusenko, and also of another colleague Likhach, also a veteran of the SR military commission during the preparations for the opening of the Constituent Assembly and later a leader of the Petrograd Assembly of Factory Delegates. There was no sense at this stage of any tension between these two sides.

Throughout July 1918 Chaplin had become increasingly nervous and more and more convinced that the Bolshevik authorities knew of his plans. He began to make urgent appeals to Poole to land at once, but, despite these requests, Poole would not bring forward the date of the landing.[57] The situation only changed at the end of the month with the evacuation of the Allied ambassadors from Vologda. Abandoning Vologda had first been considered by the diplomatic corps on 10 July 1918 when, after the assassination of the German ambassador Mirbach, the Soviet Foreign Affairs Commissar Chicherin had invited the Allied ambassadors to move to Moscow, ostensibly for their safe-keeping; fearing a trap, the ambassadors had refused. A week later, on 17 July 1918, a messenger from General Poole suggested the ambassadors should move to Archangel since he planned to land early in August. Then, when on 23 July 1918 Chicherin repeated his request in more threatening tones, the ambassadors left Vologda on 25 July and arrived in Archangel on Friday the 27th.[58]

They held immediate talks with Chaplin, and stressed to him that the insurrection would lead to the establishment of a new democratic government, excluding reactionaries as well as Bolsheviks; at the same time they accepted Chaplin's view that immediate action was essential. On 29 July 1918 they sailed to Kandalachka, a small port on the western shore of the White Sea, linked to Murmansk by the Petrograd–Murmansk railway line and occupied by the British since Poole's arrival. From there they immediately telephoned Poole, urging him to land whatever troops he had at once, even if it was only 1–2,000. Poole hesitated, but the ambassadors insisted that an insurrection would break out at once; Poole still refused, but ultimately Lindley succeeded in persuading him to promise to act on 31 July 1918. As Poole himself recorded, he had planned to start on 3 August 1918, but:

> I received information from Mr Lindley . . . that the state in Archangel
> was so desperate that our friends there had decided that it was impossible
> to delay any longer and that they had arranged for a revolution against the
> government to start on the 31st and that unless we could arrive very
> shortly after the outbreak that it would certainly be suppressed. As I was
> most anxious to take advantage of any internal disturbances, I decided . . .
> that we would start the same night.

Poole's decision was made all the easier since the anticipated French
reinforcements had arrived in Murmansk on 26 July 1918.[59]

Poole's landing and Chaplin's insurrection enabled the URR leader
Chaikovskii to assume power on 2 August 1918. He noted at the time
that 'in a few days time our troops and Allied troops will be moving
up to Vologda and Vyatka . . . A new Eastern Front will be established'. Lockhart had written a fortnight earlier that Poole still hoped
to link up with the Czechoslovaks, and Lindley noted on the eve of
the insurrection in Archangel, on 31 July 1918, that 'there is a
reasonable prospect of the Czechoslovaks joining hands with Alekseev
on the Volga and ourselves at Vyatka'. It was not to be.[60]

On 2 August 1918 Poole's advance up the Archangel–Vologda
railway and river Dvina began, but despite great hopes of action by
Green patriotic socialists, any such activities were poorly co-ordinated.
The force advancing up the railway was stopped by stiff resistance on
11 August 1918, despite the hopes that the partisan remnants of
Savinkov's Yaroslavl units might attack the Bolsheviks to the rear. The
advance up the Dvina fared slightly better, but was hampered by
leaking boats; although Kotlas was reached, the Allied forces failed to
establish a bridgehead with the Kotlas–Vyatka railway, and failed to
link up with the URR group led by Sorokin waiting for instructions
on what to do in the rear to help the advancing British boats.[61]

Despite these setbacks, as late as 15 August 1918 Poole was still
optimistic that Vologda could be reached. He was much cheered by
the receipt of fresh instructions on 10 August 1918 making clear that
the Czechoslovaks were now co-operating with the Allies after all and
he should establish communications with them. On 7 August 1918 the
French had appointed General Maurice Janin to head the
Czechoslovak Army and his instructions clearly stated he was to try
and establish links with the Allied bases on the White Sea by taking
Vyatka and ascending the Dvina. Unfortunately Poole's desperate
telegram to the Czechoslovaks, urging them 'to take Perm and Vyatka
and effect a junction with the Allies at Vologda as soon as possible'
had no effect; on 22 August 1918 he abandoned his advance when it
became clear that he would not reach Vologda before winter.[62]

On the Kazan front there was a similar swing from boundless optimism to pessimism, but what caused the pessimism here was not the success of the Bolsheviks in resisting their enemy's advance, but the first symptoms of disunity within the anti-Bolshevik front. In accordance with the Allies' plan, Lebedev's assault on Kazan began on 7 August 1918 and the town was occupied on the 8th. With Allied forces at Archangel and Kazan Lebedev was determined thereafter to push on up the Volga before the Red Army had time to regroup; he hoped to be in Moscow within two months. To Lebedev's surprise and dismay, no sooner had Kazan been taken, than the main body of his troops was withdrawn; instead of rushing on to Vologda, Vyatsk and the Allies, his political masters told him they needed the troops to consolidate their position in Samara. Indeed, it had taken the intervention of Bordes, and the high-handedness of Lebedev himself, who ignored a last minute attempt by the People's Army General Staff to cancel the assault, to get SR politicians in Samara to agree to the attack on Kazan in the first place.[63]

Travelling with Lebedev to Kazan was one of Savinkov's closest lieutenants A. Dikgof Derental. He recalled the despairing cry of a captain in the French military mission, exasperated at the inability of the politicians who surrounded him to appreciate the strategic importance of Kazan: 'My God, my God, why do your fellow countrymen talk so much!'.[64] This tension between Lebedev, a leading member of the URR, and his SR superiors was symptomatic of an unanticipated problem; the Czechoslovak mutiny had not only wrecked the Allies' great enterprise, but had brought into the anti-Bolshevik struggle SRs who were not party to the URR agreement with the Allies, and did not share the political vision on which it was based.

## NOTES

1.  As early as 29 December 1917 British military officers were proposing a plan of this kind to London, see Public Records Office, FO371.3319.15; it was also the crux of the scheme outlined to Lockhart on 10 May 1918 by 'representatives of two large organizations of the old army', see Milner Papers, 364.287.
2.  Milner Papers, 372.179 and 365.40.
3.  Entitled 'Proposals for Allied Enterprise for Russia (assuming French concurrence)', the map coloured the area from Vologda to Archangel red and designated it 'the main effort to organise the Czechoslovaks'. Arrows

pointing westward from Ufa and Chelyabinsk towards Vologda showed clearly the direction of troop movements, see Milner Papers, 365.67.

4. Public Records Office, WO32.5643.24a.
5. J. Kalvoda, *The Genesis of Czechoslovakia* (Columbia 1986), p. 325; V.M. Fic, *The Bolsheviks and the Czechoslovak Legion* (Delhi 1978), p. 231.
6. Fic, *Bolsheviks*, p. 187 et seq.; A. Verge, *Avec les Tchecoslovaques* (Paris 1926), pp. 107, 111.
7. The Marinovka incident is in Fic, *Bolsheviks*, p. 279; this summary follows Fic closely.
8. Milner Papers, 365.40.
9. B.V. Savinkov, *Borba s Bolshevikami* (Warsaw 1920), pp. 3–25; *Delo Borisa Savinkova* (Moscow 1924), p. 11; Kalvoda, *Genesis*, pp. 244–8.
10. ' "Soyuz zashchity rodiny i svobody" i Yaroslavskii myatezh 1918g.' *Proletarskaya revolyutsiya* no. 10 (1923), pp. 203–8; G. Hill, *Go Spy the Land* (London 1932), p. 196. For Savinkov's links with the army, see V.I. Gurko, 'Iz Petrograda cherez Moskvy, Parizh i London v Odessu' *Arkhiv Russkoi Revolyutsii* (Berlin 1924), p. 11.
11. 'Soyuz zashchity rodiny i svobody', p. 203; *Delo Savinkova*, p. 38.
12. For the National Centre, see ' "Natsional'nyi tsentr" v Moskve v 1918' *Na chuzhoi storone* Berlin/Prague no. 8 (1924); Gurko, 'Iz Petrograda', p. 12; B. Kazanovich, 'Poezdka iz Dobrovol'cheskoi armii v "Krasnuyu Moskvu" ' *Arkhiv Russkoi Revolyutsii* Berlin (1922), vol. 7, p. 191.
13. S.P. Melgunov, *N.V. Chaikovskii v gody grazhdanskoi voiny* (Paris 1929), p. 49; L.A. Krol, *Za tri goda* (Vladivostok 1921), p. 13; S. Nikolaev, 'Vozniknovenie i organizatsiya Komucha' *Volya Rossii* Prague (1928), vols 8–9, p. 238.
14. Melgunov, *Chaikovskii*, pp. 50–8; 'Natsional'nyi tsentr', p. 135; V. Myakotin, 'Iz nedalekogo proshlogo' *Na chuzhoi storone* Berlin/Prague no. 2 (1923), p. 180; V.G. Boldyrev, *Direktoriya, Kolchak, Interventy* (Novonikolaevsk 1925), p. 24.
15. Myakotin, 'Iz nedalekogo', p. 191; *Delo Savinkova*, p. 37. The clash of personalities between Savinkov and Boldyrev is noted in Kazanovich, 'Poezdka', p. 195.
16. 'Natsional'nyi tsentr', pp. 135–6; Myakotin, 'Iz nedalekogo proshlogo' pp. 180, 189; P. Sorokin, *Leaves from a Russian Diary* (London 1924), p. 141.
17. For the SR Council, see M. Jansen, *A Show Trial under Lenin* (The Hague 1982), p. 2; for the Kadets, see W.G. Rosenberg, *Liberals in the Russian Revolution* (Princeton 1974), p. 295; for the soviet meeting J. Bunyan and H.H. Fisher, *The Bolshevik Revolution: Documents and Materials* (Stanford 1961), pp. 122–4.
18. The inter-group conference is mentioned by J. Noulens, *Mon Ambassade en Russie Soviétique, 1917–19* (Paris 1933), vol. 2, p. 114. However, the Milner Papers give more details: 359.108 et seq. gives details of the resolution passed and the conditions on which Allied help would be sought, as reported by Kerensky to Lloyd George on 24 June. Lockhart reported on 16 May, at the time this conference was being planned, that Kerensky had contacted him and wanted to visit London, see 364.290.

19. Noulens *Ambassade* vol. 2, p. 107; Myakotin, 'Iz nedalekogo', p. 180; Milner Papers, 359.108. In a letter to Chaikovskii, Kerensky made clear he had travelled to Europe as a URR emissary, see Melgunov, *Chaikovskii*, p. 55.

20. Myakotin, 'Iz nedalekogo', p. 191.

21. The meeting is described in Gurko, 'Iz Petrograda', p. 13 and referred to obliquely in 'Natsional'nyi tsentr' p. 132 and directly in Kazanovich, 'Poezdka', p. 193.

22. Krol, *Za tri goda*, p. 130. Complaints about Allied favouritism towards the URR rather than the National Centre can be seen in Kazanovich, 'Poezdka', p. 199.

23. 'Iz arkhiva V.I. Lebedeva: ot Petrograda do Kazani' *Volya Rossii* nos 8–9 Prague (1928), p. 63; S.N. Gorodetskii, 'Obrazovanie severnoi oblasti' *Beloe Delo* no. 3 Berlin (1927), p. 7.

24. Myakotin, 'Iz nedalekogo', p. 194; Melgunov, *Chaikovskii*, pp. 70–3.

25. G.E. Chaplin, 'Dva perevorota na Severe' *Beloe delo* no. 4 Berlin (1928), p. 15 et seq.

26. Melgunov, *Chaikovskii*, p. 70; Sorokin, *Leaves*, p. 149 et seq.

27. Sorokin, *Leaves*, p. 153; Chaplin, 'Dva perevorota', p. 17; M. Kettle, *The Road to Intervention* (London 1988), p. 257. For Maclaren, see Wiseman Papers, 20 March 1918.

28. M.J. Carley *Revolution and Intervention: the French Government and the Russian Civil War* (Montreal 1983), pp. 63–5.

29. I. Nesterov, 'Pered vystupleniyem na Volge' *Volya Rossii* nos 10–11, p. 96; I. Brushvit, 'Kak podgotovlyalos' volzhskoe vystuplenie' *Volya Rossii* nos 10–11, p. 93.

30. P.D. Klimushkin, 'Pered volzhskim vosstaniem' *Volya Rossii* nos 8–9 Prague (1928), pp. 222–5. These events are summarized in English in S. Berk, 'The democratic counter-revolution: *Komuch* and the civil war on the Volga' *Canadian-American Slavic Studies* vol. 7 (1973), pp. 443–59. The fullest version is State Archive of the Russian Federation (GARF) 749.1.4.16.

31. Klimushkin, 'Pered volzhskim', p. 229; Brushvit, 'Kak podgotovlyalos'', p. 94; GARF 667.1.17.24.

32. J.F.N. Bradley, *La Légion Tchécoslovaque en Russie 1914–20* (Paris 1965), p. 88; J.F.N. Bradley, *Allied Intervention in Russia* (London 1968), p. 99; L.M. Spirin, *Klassy i partii v grazhdanskoi voine v Rossii, 1917–20* (Moscow 1968), p. 233; S. Cecek, 'Ot Penza do Urala' *Volya Rossii* nos 8–9 Prague (1928), p. 262.

33. 'Iz arkhiva V.I. Lebedeva: ot Petrograda do Kazani' *Volya Rossii* nos 8–9 (Prgaue 1928), pp. 52, 68, 96; V.I. Lebedev, *Russian Democracy and its Struggle against the Bolshevist Tyranny* (New York 1919), pp. 12, 20.

34. Vergé, *Avec les Tchécoslovaques*, pp. 116–21.

35. Kalvoda, *Genesis*, pp. 354, 357, 368; Cecek, 'Ot Penza', p. 264. For Lockhart, see Milner Papers, 365.133.

36. Public Records Office WO32.5703 Poole's report; R.H.B. Lockhart, *Memoirs of a British Agent* (London 1946), p. 285; Milner Papers, 366.203, 365.82–5.

37. Public Records Office WO32 5643.26a
38. Public Records Office FO371.3319.270
39. Milner Papers, 365.95, 365.103, 365.109, 366.239.
40. LLoyd George Papers, House of Lords Record Office, F.60.2.36; Milner Papers, 366.310.
41. Savinkov talks about the impact of the arrests on his organization in his *Borba*, p. 31. Otherwise, see G. Gopper, 'Belogvardeiskie organizatsii i vosstaniya vnutri Sovetskoi Respubliki', in S.A. Alekseev (ed.), *Revolyutsiya i grazhdanskaya voina v opisaniyakh Belogvardeitsev* (Moscow 1926), pp. 308–14. Details of the surrender are given in U. Germanis, 'Some observations on the Yaroslavl revolt of July 1918' *Journal of Baltic Studies* vol. 4 (1973), p. 241.
42. A. Dikgof-Derental 'Iz perevernutykh stranits' *Na chuzhoi storone* no. 2 (1923), p. 57.
43. Boldyrev, *Direktoriya*, p. 25; Kazanovich, 'Poezdka', p. 195; Germanis, 'Some observations', p. 239; *Delo Savinkova*, p. 14; Savinkov, *Borba*, p. 43.
44. Milner Papers, 365.140, 365.156.
45. *Delo Savinkova*, p. 38; Gopper, cited in Germanis, 'Some observations', p. 238; Noulens, *Ambassade* vol. 2, p. 107.
46. The reference to intervention by 25 June is problematic: the text is 25 January, clearly a typing error; but whether the true date is June or July is possibly open to debate, see Milner Papers 365.48–50. Lockhart's requests for information are in Milner Papers, 365.73, 365.82, 365.85. Lockhart was closely involved in Savinkov's work with the National Centre and URR. Balfour's instruction 'to have nothing to do with Savinkov's plans' – see R. Ullman, *Anglo-Soviet Relations, 1917–21: Intervention and the War* (Princeton 1961), p. 190 – was either an instruction to keep a diplomatic distance from the details of the plotting, or an order Lockhart simply ignored. When he returned to London, however, he felt the need to distance himself from the whole affair and in his report rather disingenuously stressed 'French misinformation' as the cause of the Yaroslavl disaster; see Milner Papers, 365.346.
47. Wiseman Papers, 7 July 1918.
48. Milner Papers, 365.147.
49. L. Hafner, 'The assassination of Count Mirbach and the "July Uprising" of the Left SRs in Moscow, 1918' *Russian Review* vol. 50 (1991), p. 325; M. Philips-Price, *My Reminiscences of the Russian Revolution* (London 1921), p. 314.
50. Hafner, 'Assassination', p. 337; Spirin, *Klassy*, p. 187; V. Vladimirova, 'Levye esery 1917–1918gg.' *Proletarskaya revolyutsiya* no. 4 (1927), p. 120; 'Likvidatsiya levoeserovskogo myatezha v Moskve v 1918g.' *Krasnyi Arkhiv* (1940), p. 106.
51. 'Iz arkhiva' p. 68; Hafner, 'Assassination', p. 341; Spirin, *Klassy*, p. 194; S. Nikolaev, 'Narodnaya armiya v Simbirske' *Volya Rossii* nos 10–11 Prague (1928), pp. 114–16.

52. Vladimirova, 'Levye esery', p. 130; D.L. Golinkov, *Krushenie antisovetskogo podpolya v SSSR* (Moscow 1975), p. 165.
53. Bradley, *Allied Intervention*, p. 100; Bradley, *La Légion*, p. 88.
54. 'Iz arkhiva', pp. 127–33.
55. For developments in Archangel, see Melgunov, *Chaikovskii*, p. 73; for Lockhart, see Milner Papers, 365.145; 365.156, 365.182.
56. Milner Papers, 365.171, 366.340.
57. Melgunov, *Chaikovskii*, p. 73; Chaplin, *Dva perevorota*, pp. 16–19.
58. Bunyan and Fisher, *Documents*, p. 136; Noulens, *Ambassade* vol. 2, p. 58.
59. Public Records Office WO32.5703 Poole's report; see also Noulens, *Ambassade* vol. 2, p. 167.
60. For Chaikovskii's comment, see Melgunov, *Chaikovskii*, p. 77; for Lockhart, see Milner Papers, 365.181.
61. Milner Papers, 366.340, 366.346, and 366.371; Sorokin, *Leaves*, p. 154.
62. Milner Papers, 366.109, 366.346; Lloyd George Papers, 50.3.16.
63. Lebedev, *Russian Democracy*, pp. 24, 27, 36; 'Iz arkhiva', pp. 133, 176; I. Maiskii, *Demokraticheskaya Kontrrevolyutsiya* (Moscow 1923), p. 27.
64. Dikgof-Derental, 'Iz perevernutykh', p. 65.

# CHAPTER SEVEN

# Disunity in the Green Camp

At the start of August 1918 it looked as if the Green side in Russia's Red versus Green civil war had overcome the military problems caused by the mutiny of the Czechoslovak Legion and the premature Yaroslavl uprising. The Czechoslovaks were not in Archangel, but they were fighting on the Allied side, supporting the SRs' People's Army in its march north up the Volga river; and the URR forces had landed in Archangel and were marching south towards Vologda. It seemed as if a giant pincer movement might lead to a rendezvous at Vologda or Vyatka, thus securing a new Eastern Front. By the middle of August 1918 the People's Army and the Czechoslovak Legion had not advanced beyond Kazan, and the URR forces and their British and French supporters had not broken out of Archangel. There was to be no giant pincer movement. Of course, there were military reasons for this failure, but there were also political ones: in August 1918 political divisions within the Green camp helped stall the military advance.

These divisions were felt most acutely in Samara. The tensions felt between the URR People's Army commander Lebedev, as he planned his advance from Kazan, and his SR political masters in Samara were only part of a broader problem facing the whole of the territory liberated in the course of the Czechoslovak mutiny. For by mutinying in the way they did the Czechoslovaks involved in the anti-Bolshevik struggle groups both to the left and right of the URR whose attitude was not always as favourable to the Allies as they might have hoped. At the core of the problem lay the long-standing disunity within the SR Party. Those on the right of the party were always ready to co-operate with the Popular Socialists and the left-leaning Kadets; the bulk of the party eschewed all alliances and was loyal only to its own party programme.

The URR had put at the head of its agenda re-opening the Eastern Front with the help of the Allies; the decision of the Eighth SR Party Conference in Moscow in May 1918 had been rather different. The SRs, unlike the URR, had drawn a clear distinction between the international war against Germany and the civil war with the Bolsheviks; while they were prepared to co-operate with the Allies in the war with Germany, the SRs' prime concern was the domestic civil war and they were determined not to involve the Allies in this.[1] The struggle with the Bolsheviks was their affair, as was what they saw as the equally important domestic issue, the continuing struggle against counter-revolutionary White forces of the 'Kornilovite reaction'. Lebedev at Kazan and the SRs in Samara were following different agendas.

## KOMUCH AND ITS RIVALS

By the end of June 1918 the SRs had established a power base in Samara. Implementing the policy agreed by deputies to the March 1918 first Inter-group Conference of Constituent Assembly Deputies, that everything should be done to make the assembly quorate and resume its work, they set about establishing a Committee of the Constituent Assembly (Komuch) comprising any member of the Constituent Assembly who could reach Samara, with the exception of Bolsheviks and Left SRs who were excluded on principle for having supported the dissolution of the assembly in January 1918. Initially there were just five deputies, all involved in the Czechoslovak action in liberating Samara: Klimushkin, Brushvit and Fortunatov, who were deputies for Samara; they had been joined on the eve of the insurrection by V.K. Volskii, deputy for Tver and a member of the SR Central Committee, and I.P. Nesterov, deputy for Minsk. In those first days after 8 June 1918, Komuch stood quite alone and a few dozen Bolsheviks could have overthrown them; it was a full week before people really began to rally to the cause, but by the end of July 1918 some fifty to sixty deputies had arrived, and by mid-August 1918 Komuch had elected a fourteen-member governing administration known as the Council of Departmental Directors (CDD), which included several people who were not deputies to the Constituent Assembly but were considered experts in their field.

The most prominent of these was I.V. Maiskii, the Menshevik and future Soviet ambassador to Great Britain, who was Departmental Director for Labour; other leading figures were Klimushkin,

Departmental Director for Internal Affairs; V.N. Filipovskii, Departmental Director for Trade and Industry; V.I. Almazov, Departmental Director for Produce and Supply; N.A. Galkin, Departmental Director for War; Nesterov, Departmental Director for Railways; and M.A. Vedenyapin, Departmental Director for Foreign Affairs. The chairman of the CDD was E.F. Rogovskii, who was also Departmental Director for State Security. As Komuch grew, it established its own presidium, with Volskii as president, Brushvit and Gendelman as vice-presidents and S.N. Nikolaev as secretary; the presidium was empowered to implement Komuch decisions and to call its meetings and arrange its agenda and activities. This arrangement meant that the lines separating the CDD and Komuch itself were sometimes confused and the precise constitutional relationship was never defined. Even after the CDD had been established, the old habit of letting rank and file deputies attend the CDD, and even take part in the voting, died hard.[2]

The Komuch administration was aggressively socialist – its egalitarian ethos included paying its departmental directors 400 roubles per month, the same as drivers and only twice the salary of cleaners. It was determined to turn the clock back to before October 1917, but no further. Thus it continued to fly the red flag, it talked of forming a federal democratic republic, and its slogan was 'all power to the people'. All bath-houses, cinemas, and hotels remained under local authority control, and the leather monopoly was retained. It wanted to undo the excesses of the Bolsheviks' socialist experiment, while retaining the social gains of February 1917. Thus on 12 June 1918 the banks were denationalized; on 6 July 1918 Kerensky's government's land committees were restored; on 9 July 1918 a commission of thirty (thirteen workers, thirteen employers and four arbitrators from the city council) began the task of denationalizing industry; and factory committees were to operate according to the legislation of 23 April 1917. On the other hand, on 7 July 1918 lockouts were made illegal and all soviet laws on labour protection endorsed; on 24 July 1918 trade union rights were guaranteed; and after the Bolshevik-controlled soviet had been dissolved a new soviet was elected in August 1918, although its political powers had been transferred to the restored local government councils. At the end of August 1918 Maiskii introduced the same law on the eight-hour day once shelved by Kerensky's government.[3]

This policy inevitably led to contradictions. On 15 July 1918 Komuch's Finance Committee was the scene of a bitter row over the future of the denationalized commercial banks: the former owners wanted compensation for their losses under Bolshevik rule, but the egalitarian instincts of the SRs were enraged at the amount demanded and the dubious way in which they felt it had been calculated. Yet, having antagonized local capitalists in this way, on the same day Komuch antagonized the workers by overruling the suggestion that striking workers should receive 25 per cent of their pay. On 21 July 1918 Komuch felt the need to issue a programmatic declaration, signed by the leader of the SR group of deputies to the Constituent Assembly V. Ya Gurevich as well as the Komuch leaders, designed to clear up any doubts about its socialist credentials. The declaration conceded that those working for the restoration of soviet power had had some success in questioning the regime's social policy, and made clear that peasants would not lose their land in any revision of the land reform, and that workers would never again be victims of capital. It added, however, that workers were expected to do a fair day's work for a fair day's pay, and could be legally sacked if they did not show sufficient commitment.[4] The declaration was only a partial success in calming popular concerns. It did not prevent the re-elected soviet becoming an arena for criticism; roughly half its members were Bolsheviks, thinly disguised as 'internationalists', and on 30 August 1918 it passed a resolution proposed by them critical of the Komuch administration.

Komuch had far less trouble retaining the support of the peasantry. The Bolshevik policy of grain requisitioning had inevitably alienated the peasants; in its place Komuch established a free trade in grain and thereby retained peasant support to the end. Komuch's grain policy was similar to that of Kerensky's government. Komuch retained the right to fix the price of grain, but contracted out rights to food procurement to private and co-operative organizations; distribution was the task of the regional councils and their so-called 'provisions assemblies'. This policy soon led to a thriving market and ample supplies; those people arriving in Samara from Moscow were always struck by the low prices and ample supplies.[5] The only element of Komuch's agrarian policy which caused some peasants concern was the way in which an attempt to regulate land seizures was implemented in some parts of the territory.

In an attempt to secure the harvest and end what it felt had become 'anarchic land seizures', Komuch decreed on 22 July 1918 that winter sown land should not be subject to seizure and redivision but temporarily retained by either the existing owner or the local food supply authorities. While this did not contradict Komuch's constantly repeated refrain that the land reform was irreversible, it did prompt some land-owners to try and seize back their land by force, incidents that the Bolsheviks were always willing to exploit in their propaganda.[6] What eventually turned some peasants against Komuch was not its agrarian policy but its policy of conscription to the People's Army, an army charged with the ambiguous remit not only of defending Samara and its free trade in grain from the Bolsheviks but also of resuming the First World War by opening a new Eastern Front; for peasants who welcomed the end of the war, and with a harvest to bring in, the decision to introduce conscription seemed questionable. Yet, even in Samara's last days, when rationing had been introduced and deserters were being threatened with execution, the SR leader Chernov could persuade the Samara provincial congress of peasants to give Komuch a vote of confidence.[7]

The SRs in Samara took their slogan of power to the people seriously by establishing a never-ending series of committees. Thus to oversee the economy Komuch established a 'special meeting on defence', comprising representatives from trade and industry, the local authorities, the war department, the trades unions, the co-operatives, and the Samara Council of the National Economy (established by the Bolsheviks and retained by the SRs). Its main concerns were worthy enough, combating speculation and combating unemployment by creating public works, but its administration was unwieldy. On 20 August 1918 it established a special unit for supplying the army. This unit had enormous powers: it could override any previous orders, and any claims by the former factory owners; but even this unit was overseen by the duly elected representatives of all those groups represented on the special meeting on defence, with additional representation from the trades unions. Decisions were frequently postponed since agreement among such disparate groups was impossible. To its critics, Komuch was 'committee-mad'.[8]

Where the SRs' love of committees led to most problems was in the People's Army. Formally established on 8 June 1918, the People's Army at first had a General Staff comprising Galkin, Fortunatov and Bogolyubov plus the Czechoslovak commander Colonel Cecek. Initially relying on 5–6,000 volunteers, it soon resorted to conscription and eventually mobilized some 50,000 men; however, the volunteers remained the core of those 10,000 soldiers considered to be capable of holding their own under fire, while 40 per cent of the total were never properly armed.[9] The People's Army's defining characteristic was its democratic structure: it instituted eight ranks distinguished by plain coloured epaulettes and paid officers only 250 roubles per month, little more than the basic workers' wage. Officers also had to contend with a regular diet of lectures from the cultural educational recruitment section of the SR Party and the 'hidden commissars', or Komuch representatives, who exercised the same powers granted to Kerensky's commissars in the period prior to October 1917. Galkin and his senior commander Lebedev were constantly in dispute with Komuch over the related questions of which institution, Komuch or the General Staff, made senior military appointments, and whether or not to turn the hidden commissars of the cultural educational recruitment section into a formalized system of Komuch commissars modelled on the Bolshevik political commissars in the Red Army. Komuch decided against a formalized system, but by retaining the informal and costly activities of the cultural educational recruitment section succeeded in alienating many of the more conservative officers without ever really controlling them.[10]

Komuch, as the re-creation of Kerensky's political system which had apparently brought Russia to its knees in the autumn of 1917, was not to the liking of those more conservative politicians who came to the fore in Siberia as the mutinous Czechoslovak Legion fought its way eastward. Here power fell into the hands of former SRs, so disenchanted with the 'committee madness' of their fellows that they had swung dramatically to the political right since the autumn of 1917 and considered a return to the policies of Kerensky as a recipe for chaos and disaster. Yet ironically what brought these former SR politicians to power in Siberia was their pre-October association with the SR Party.

Siberia had long been an area of strong popular support for the SRs. After the Constituent Assembly was dissolved on 5 January 1918, the SR-dominated Siberian Regional Assembly met in Tomsk on 7 January 1918 and announced plans for the formation of a Siberian government. These deliberations were interrupted on 26 January 1918 when the Bolsheviks dispersed the regional assembly, but during the night of 25–26 January 1918 some twenty regional assembly deputies representing the major party groups met in secret under the presidency of the SR P. Ya Derber and appointed an underground Siberian government. These circumstances meant that many of those elected to the government were chosen in their absence and by reputation alone: two of those chosen in particular had by the winter of 1918 only the most tenuous links with the SR Party they had once served; I.A. Mikhailov was at one time Director of the Economic Council of the Provisional Government and as such an SR, but his experience in economic policy-making had pushed his views far to the right, and P.V. Vologodskii was a former SR member of the 1907 Tsarist Duma.

Control of the extensive Siberian co-operative movement enabled the SRs to retain a considerable organizational network in the region throughout the spring and early summer of 1918; doctrinaire persecution of the co-operatives by the area's ruling Bolsheviks served to strengthen rather than weaken the SRs' position since the Bolshevik attempt to turn all credit co-operatives into branches of a nationalized bank and put all co-operative shops under the control of the local councils of the national economy sparked off widespread anger. Thus the underground Siberian government retained a shadowy influence throughout the first half of 1918, even after it had divided its authority with six ministers basing themselves in Omsk and a further seven, led by Derber, moving to the Far East. To exercise some sort of democratic control over the 'ministers' in the underground Siberian government, the Siberian Regional Assembly divided itself into west Siberian and east Siberian 'commissariats'.

During March and April 1918 the SRs of the west Siberian commissariat, based in Novonikolaevsk, began to co-operate with various officers' organizations like those of A.N. Grishin-Almazov and 'organization 13' headed by P.P. Ivanov-Rinov with a view to the military overthrow of the Bolsheviks. In April they contacted the British consul in Vladivostok to see if he would help arm the troops being formed by the underground Siberian government, but, in line with the then British policy of supporting the Bolsheviks, he turned the proposal down. By May 1918, however, these organizations were strong enough to hold a congress of underground military groups in Novonikolaevsk and declare that some 7,000 men were under arms, being fed at the expense of the local co-operatives. Thus when in mid-May 1918 the Bolsheviks broke with the Allies and at the end of the month the Czechoslovak mutiny began, the Czechoslovak forces based in Chelyabinsk and the anti-Bolshevik forces gathered in Novonikolaevsk united. As the Czechoslovaks took control of the Trans-Siberian railway, so the underground Siberian government in Omsk reasserted its authority. But as the Siberian government was reformed, it came to the notice of the SRs for the first time that its Siberian government was dominated by people whose views were now far to the right of the SR Party.[11]

On 30 June 1918 the SR-controlled west Siberian commissariat endorsed the proposal that the six members of its underground Siberian government then on Czechoslovak controlled territory – P.V. Vologodskii, V.M. Krutovskii, G.B. Patushinskii, I.A. Mikhailov, I.I. Serebrennikov and B.M Shatilov – should formally establish a Siberian government; the SRs then looked on in disbelief as that Siberian government dissolved the soviets and the land committees, restored private ownership and private trade, and declared martial law on the railways, such was its determination to remove all traces of 'Bolshevik' socialist experimentation. The Siberian government argued that its real authority lay not with the SR-controlled Siberian Regional Assembly which had spawned the underground government back in January 1918, but in its own insurrection, the fact that it had 'carried out the coup against the Bolsheviks and was unanimously supported by all sections of the population and public organizations'. The reality of the times, the Siberian government stressed, meant it had to act 'in a sovereign manner, dependent on no other source of authority'; it certainly should not be responsible to the Siberian Regional Assembly. To ensure this desire for unfettered self-legitimacy was not sullied by the claim of Komuch to be governing the whole of non-Bolshevik Russia in the name of the Constituent Assembly, on 4 July 1918 the Siberian government declared Siberia, with its western border tantalisingly undefined, independent until the formation some time in the future of an All-Russian government.[12]

## THE URR AND THE CHELYABINSK TALKS

It was into this burgeoning dog-fight between the SRs in Samara and the former SRs in Siberia that a URR delegation arrived early in July 1918, trying to persuade both sides to support the programme agreed between the URR and the Allies in their absence. The SRs who had established Komuch in Samara and the former SRs who had established the Siberian government in Omsk had not been in Moscow when the URR was founded and knew nothing of its detailed plans drawn up with the support of the Allies. Even the Komuch Departmental Director for Foreign Affairs Vedenyapin, who had arrived in Samara sometime after the founding group had staged its successful insurrection, knew nothing about the URR until 8 July 1918. While the SR Central Committee knew of the existence of the URR, and that many of its leading right-wingers were members, the party as a whole did nothing to encourage its members to join.[13] The big issue which divided Komuch and the URR was the question of the future of the Constituent Assembly. To the URR the assembly dispersed in January 1918, by the very fact of being dispersed, had lost all authority: even if reformed, it would lack authority since it would inevitably operate without the Left SRs and Bolsheviks, who made up a considerable proportion of its membership, and would be forced to operate without representatives from the Ukraine and Baltic provinces; a clean slate was needed. When in the first week in June 1918 the URR received news of the Czechoslovak mutiny, a high level URR delegation of Argunov (SR), Pavlov (Popular Socialist) and Krol (Kadet) was assembled and sent east to investigate, leaving Moscow in the last week of June and arriving in Samara between 8–10 July 1918. What the delegation found in Samara was not to its liking. Vesting supreme authority in the haphazard collection of SR deputies who had arrived in Samara was far from the creation of an All-Russian government which all parties would respect. While Komuch representatives talked of the need for a coalition government, and did in August include the Menshevik Maiskii in their administration, the fact was that, with the exclusion of the Bolsheviks and Left SRs, a reconvened Constituent Assembly would be made up almost exclusively of SRs; to talk of a coalition government controlled by an assembly made up entirely of SRs was a nonsense.[14]

The URR delegation arrived in Samara shortly after the Siberian government in Omsk had announced its independence. On 11 July 1918 one of its members, Krol, a Constituent Assembly deputy himself, attended a session of Komuch and with the fifteen or so others present heard the French liaison officer Major Guinet ask what Komuch's attitude was to the Siberian government recently formed in Omsk, since its programme seemed acceptable to the Allies. Clearly the Allies were looking to co-ordinate common action between Samara and Omsk, but the omens did not look good. Most of the Komuch members present were hostile to the Omsk government, insisting that it challenged the position of Komuch as the voice of the Constituent Assembly, the representative body of all Russians. Krol, however, intervened for the URR and made a speech developing what was to become the key to future URR policy; the task of the moment was not to assert the authority of any one government over any other government but to unite these local anti-Bolshevik governments into one All-Russian government. This was music to Guinet's ears and the URR delegation set off with Guinet for Chelyabinsk where talks between Komuch and the Siberian government were planned. They arrived in Chelyabinsk on 13 July 1918.

Allied pressure had persuaded the Siberian government that, despite its declaration of independence, it had to hold talks with Komuch. In Chelyabinsk the Siberian War Minister Grishin-Almazov and the Finance Minister Mikhailov were delighted to find that they would not be talking to the Samara-based Komuch administration alone, but to a URR delegation as well; they soon developed a rapport with Krol and his colleagues. The atmosphere worsened dramatically when the Komuch delegation arrived. Before any formal talks began, one of the Komuch delegation Brushvit sent a note to 'Comrade' Grishin-Almazov reminding him of SR Party policy in view of the latter's one-time party membership; Almazov responded that he was not a 'comrade' but the Minister of War. To the bewilderment of Allied representatives, the Komuch train and Siberian government train were soon stationed in neighbouring sidings but communicating only by diplomatic notes, with the URR group acting as an unwanted go-between; the Komuch delegation was particularly hostile to the URR group, since all three members of the group were deputies to the Constituent Assembly but all three had refused to join Komuch. A way out of this extraordinary impasse was only found on 15 July 1918 when Major Guinet suggested that a photograph should be taken of the two government delegations and the URR group: as the photographer took charge, Guinet and a Czechoslovak representative Bogdan Pavlu publicly proposed a formal joint session at 3 p.m.; even so Komuch at first seemed quite ready to spurn even a public invitation to talks, and were only persuaded to do so after further private pleadings from the URR and the Allies.[15]

When the formal talks began on 15 July 1918, there was no meeting of minds. The full Siberian delegation comprised Grishin-Almazov, Mikhailov, and M.P. Golovachev, Deputy Minister of Foreign Affairs; the Komuch delegation was Brushvit, Vedenyapin, and Galkin. Mikhailov, Finance Minister in the Omsk government took the lead for the Siberian side, insisting that they had been delegated simply to explore how practical day-to-day tasks could be co-ordinated between the two governments; the question of how an All-Russian government should be formed was beyond their powers. Brushvit, who had been elected to preside over the session, proposed that even though the talks represented not negotiations but simply an exchange of information, they nevertheless should discuss Komuch's project for how a central government authority could be established. That project was this:

1. that any central government authority recognize the Constituent Assembly;
2. until this assembled, its committee (Komuch) would be made up of all its deputies, except Bolsheviks and Left SRs;
3. all basic laws (constitutions etc.) should be taken out of the

government's sphere of interest and delayed until the assembly met;

4.  the government's immediate tasks were to convene the Constituent Assembly, democratize the country and establish an army;

5.  to achieve these aims Komuch would form a coalition-based central executive, acting on behalf of the central government which would exercise all state functions;

6.  routine legislation would be in the hands of Komuch, but the war, finance and foreign policy would be the exclusive concern of central government. Komuch would receive these powers when its membership reached thirty.

Since this merely restated the Komuch position there was little chance of agreement.[16]

Clear as to the legitimacy of its own delegation, Komuch was keen to clarify what the mandates were of those present; it objected especially to the idea of the URR attending since they seemed to have no constitutional authority. The URR did not, therefore, attend the talks on 15 July 1918, but after Guinet's and Pavlu's intervention Komuch allowed the URR delegation to attend subsequent sessions and thereafter progress was quickly made. It was resolved to establish a commission, on which Argunov would serve for the URR, whose purpose would be to summon a so-called state conference which would decide how best to establish a new central government for all of liberated Russia. In some ways this was a big concession by Komuch, since the very fact that other groups would be involved undermined its claim that the existing Constituent Assembly was the only source of governmental authority; but the agreement also made clear that this new central government would have to be sanctioned by Komuch, since it represented the Constituent Assembly. The commission was instructed to organize the state conference in three weeks time in Chelyabinsk to be attended by all members of the Constituent Assembly; delegations of the central committees of the major political parties and the URR; and representatives of governments formed in the liberated territories. In reality, however, this planned Chelyabinsk State Conference was not held until 23 August 1918, a delay occasioned by the fact that, rather than the planned conference resulting in improved relations between Komuch and Siberia, relations worsened dramatically as both sides jockeyed for advantage in the run up to its opening.[17]

# CUSTOMS WAR, POLITICKING AND PARANOIA

Immediately after leaving the July 1918 talks in Chelyabinsk, the Siberian government decided to clarify the western borders over which it claimed authority. On 18 July 1918 it asserted that Chelyabinsk, Zlatoust and Troitsk districts, claimed by Komuch, actually fell under its administration. Komuch issued an immediate protest and sent Brushvit to Siberia for talks, but before he arrived the situation deteriorated even further. On 26 July 1918 the Siberian government established a customs border between the two territories, and Komuch could only protest once again that the Siberian government had no jurisdiction outside the administrative borders of Siberia.[18] This 'customs war' had developed around the fate of a large quantity of supplies destined for transportation to central Russia but still within the confines of Siberia when the Bolsheviks were overthrown. Komuch assumed that, as the new All-Russian government, the supplies were now destined for the new All-Russian capital Samara; the Siberian government, however, decided to keep them, first refusing to allow the trains to travel further west than Chelyabinsk and then distributing the supplies throughout Siberia. Komuch responded by refusing to deliver oil and manufactured goods to Siberia; the Siberians refused to pay Komuch for postal distribution; and as the atmosphere worsened the customs barrier was established.[19]

As recrimination followed recrimination, the SRs became increasingly intransigent. On 5 August 1918 the SR Party held a congress for the whole Komuch area; this resolved that only the Constituent Assembly deputies had the power to form a new central government, a view endorsed by the party's Central Committee and the Volga Regional Committee. Then, as part of the war of words surrounding preparations for the Chelyabinsk State Conference, Komuch's Departmental Director for Foreign Affairs Vedenyapin gave the French a summary of the Komuch views to be presented at Chelyabinsk:

> Above all Komuch considers Russia to be a united whole which, on the basis of a democratic republic, must restore internal order with a state administration that guarantees the rights of national and regional self-rule and ends the shameful Brest peace by forming an army to drive the enemy from Russia. Komuch considers itself to be a democratic body, empowered by national elections, which will unite and organise the country. All regional governments without exception are considered to be regional rather than national and provisional. The state sovereignty of all these governments is denied by Komuch, as it denies the state sovereignty

of Krasnov, Skoropadskii and other traitors to Russia; therefore Komuch considers Russia must now be united not on the basis of a union of statelets, but only on the basis of uniting all that is strong in a united Russia – a scattering of new statelets will leave Great Russia torn to shreds. Such shreds are not recognised by Komuch, which considers the Constituent Assembly alone as the united body around which state power can be built.

The statement went on to denounce reactionaries of all kinds as 'traitors as harmful as the Bolsheviks', insisting that only democrats were really committed to fighting German militarism. It concluded by expressing its willingness to talk to other regional governments and even form a central government authority, but one 'responsible to the Constituent Assembly until its re-election'. This was not only a repeat of the stance taken on 15 July 1918, but an escalation of the attack on the Siberian government; putting it on a par with the pro-German governments of Skoropadskii and Krasnov was a doctrinaire exaggeration which the Siberian government could hardly be expected to appreciate.[20] Not surprisingly, perhaps, when Brushvit arrived for talks in Omsk on 9 August 1918 he was not received. Feelings were running so high in Samara that when it came to deciding who should be sent to Chelyabinsk, a vociferous minority argued that there was no point in sending any delegation to the talks since agreement with the Siberian government would be impossible.[21]

That might well have been the majority view of the Komuch deputies if the Chelyabinsk State Conference was to be confined to bi-lateral talks between Komuch and the Siberian government. However other groups were to be represented in Chelyabinsk and some of those invited to attend could play a useful role in weakening the Siberian government from within. Among the groups to be invited were the deputies from Siberia to the Constituent Assembly, and those same deputies were also to be involved in the work of the Siberian Regional Assembly. The Siberian Regional Assembly was the Achilles' heel of the Siberian government, enabling the Samara SRs to take their battle into the enemy camp; for the struggle between the Siberian government and the Siberian Regional Assembly in the second half of August became the main element in the political life of the region.

The Siberian government was nominally responsible to the Siberian Regional Assembly on which the SRs had a clear majority. In the first week of its existence, between 30 June and 6 July 1918, the Siberian government debated at length its relationship with the assembly. The main point at issue was the proposal that the assembly elected back in

January 1918 was not representative of all shades of political opinion, since property-owners had not been allowed to take part in its election. The Siberian government therefore argued that the regional assembly should not be allowed to meet until it was fully representative and property-owners adequately represented; when this caused the most unreformed SR member of the government, Shatilov, to walk out in protest, it was agreed to compromise by summoning the regional assembly in its existing form but asking it immediately to legislate for adequate representation from the property-owning bourgeoisie.

Having agreed that the Siberian Regional Assembly still had a role to play, the Siberian government had no choice but to come to terms with it. A delegation of Siberian government ministers travelled from Omsk to the regional assembly's base in Tomsk for talks with the elders of the assembly prior to the planned opening on 15 August 1918; they were presented with a series of demands they found unacceptable. The regional assembly was willing to concede the point about representation from the property-owners, but determined to get its way on two other issues: it should be represented at the Chelyabinsk State Conference, and its authority increased by co-opting to it the Siberian deputies to the Constituent Assembly. During the talks between Vologodskii, Prime Minister of the Siberian government, and the elders of the regional assembly, it was quickly agreed that the Constituent Assembly deputies from Siberia could join the Siberian Regional Assembly, but on the question of the Chelyabinsk State Conference Vologodskii tried to stand firm. In prior discussions the elders had agreed to drop any suggestion that the assembly be represented in Chelyabinsk, but this issue suddenly reappeared on the agenda. Vologodskii insisted that there could not be two delegations, one from the assembly and one from the government; as a compromise it was eventually agreed that an assembly delegation could attend simply to 'welcome' the opening of the conference.[22]

This was a two-fold victory for the SRs. The Siberian members of the Constituent Assembly would be able to attend both the Siberian Regional Assembly and the Chelyabinsk State Conference, and a Siberian Regional Assembly delegation would be able to attend the Chelyabinsk State Conference if not fully participate in it. SR deputies to these two assemblies could launch a two-pronged assault on the Siberian government. No wonder the message sent from Tomsk to Komuch in Samara was the cheery news that 'all was well'. On 20 August 1918, however, the SRs overplayed their hand. In a further resolution to the regional assembly in Tomsk, they suggested that not only should the regional assembly delegation to the Chelyabinsk State Conference make a speech of welcome, but read out a resolution; this went well beyond the agreement with the Siberian government, which promptly suspended the assembly's sitting until 10 September 1918.[23]

For the Allies the situation was infuriating. As relations between Komuch in Samara and the Siberian government in Omsk steadily worsened, little fighting was being done on the supposed new Eastern Front. In July and August 1918 even enthusiastic supporters of the Siberian government in Omsk recognized it only had a 'paper army': it was only in early September 1918 that its forces took the decision to mobilize fully and advance to the Urals; in the summer its commanders refused point blank to fight on the Volga.[24] The Allies had to rely on the People's Army which had its own rather different priorities. Vologda and Vyatka were the Allies' goal, but the capture of Kazan, so crucial to Allied strategy, was not a priority of the Komuch administration in Samara, so absorbed had it become in its struggle with the 'reactionary' Siberian government in Omsk. Relations between Komuch and the Allies were therefore strained.

In the middle of July 1918 Departmental Director for Foreign Affairs Vedenyapin received what he described as a 'rude telegram' from the French liaison officer Major Guinet, and although when Kazan was captured the leading SR Brushvit could report on 9 August 1918 that Guinet had informed him that the sympathy of the French mission was with Komuch, the reality was that there was much mutual distrust.[25] As far as Komuch was concerned, far too many resources were wasted in trying first to take and then to hold Kazan; when the French agent Colonel Bordes had flown from newly liberated Kazan to talk to Komuch in Samara, he had upset them by suggesting that the red flag should no longer be flown. During the mid-July 1918 talks in Chelyabinsk, a paranoid Vedenyapin interpreted French talk about moving the centre of gravity of the struggle from the Volga to the Urals as a deliberate attempt to weaken Komuch, rather than recognize the real motive of concentrating Allied forces in the Vyatka area; Komuch had rejected the idea. Vedenyapin was instinctively hostile to the Allies. He was convinced they were imperialists trying to undermine a state which tolerated the red flag, soviets, land socialization and a regulated economy. On 3 August 1918 Komuch issued a decree concerning co-operation with the Allies which implied, by tone if nothing else, that, whatever the Allies might have said to the contrary, in reality they intended to make territorial claims on Russia, something Komuch considered unacceptable. The decree repeated the SR view that Allied forces were in Russia only to fight the Germans and should not be used against the Bolsheviks unless explicitly invited by Komuch or the full Constituent Assembly.[26]


## THE URR, THE EKATERINBURG GOVERNMENT, AND THE ALLIES

Not surprisingly, therefore, the Allies decided to cultivate their good relations with the URR, rather than with Komuch or the Siberian government, and adopted a strategy which both favoured the URR and concentrated on the need to make progress towards the capture of Vyatka. After desperate fighting, during which Tsar Nicholas II and the whole of his family were executed on 16 July 1918, the Czechoslovak Legion captured Ekaterinburg on 25 July 1918 and established their army headquarters there. Ekaterinburg, from where a thrust towards Perm and Vyatka could most easily be developed, was the home town of one of the leading URR members L.A. Krol. At the insistence of the Allies – he was specifically approached by the French liaison officer Major Guinet on 25 July 1918 as the Czechoslovak Legion marched in – Krol established a Urals government based in Ekaterinburg, separate from both the Komuch administration in Samara and the Siberian government in Omsk. This Allied sponsored URR government would be used to broker an agreement between Komuch and the Siberian government, and focus attention on the Allies' needs. Krol set to work at once; by 1 August 1918 the talks were well ahead and the government formed in under a week. Soon other key URR figures like Argunov, Pavlov and Breshko-Breshkovskaya had passed through Chelyabinsk on their way to take up residence in Ekaterinburg.[27]

The Allies' clear preference for this new Urals government had an immediate effect on both the Siberian government in Omsk and the Komuch administration in Samara. The URR government in Ekaterinburg found itself wooed by delegations from both Omsk and Samara: War Minister Grishin-Almazov, joined later by Finance Minister Mikhailov, arrived from Omsk on 10 August 1918, and the next day an SR delegation including Bogolyubov arrived from Samara. Krol's concerns about the All-Russian pretensions of Komuch were of long-standing and his sympathies were clearly at first with the Siberian government in Omsk. The attitude of the Komuch delegation from

Samara hardly improved things: it criticized Krol's introduction of martial law and his refusal to introduce factory committees for industry. In fact, the Komuch delegation of SRs spent much of its time in Ekaterinburg talking to the Czechoslovak command, who were also unhappy with the sudden 'French' interest in a Urals government and had expressed the hope that 'the adventure might be liquidated'. Komuch decided to use the same sort of tactics against Krol's URR government in Ekaterinburg as were being used against the Siberian government in Omsk: rather than engaging talks, the best thing to do was to try and mobilize the local working population against Krol's administration. On 14 August 1918 Bogolyubov simply issued a protest to the Allied representatives in Ekaterinburg and the Czechoslovak National Council that the question of the formation of a Urals government was one of principle and should not have been taken before the Chelyabinsk State Conference.[28]

The attitude of the Siberian government in Omsk was quite different. Realizing that Allied support for the Urals government was an overt snub to the All-Russian pretensions of the Komuch administration in Samara, they were immediately conciliatory and had no qualms about recognizing Krol's administration as an autonomous government, insisting only, but crucially, that its military power should be limited and put under the control of Omsk. It was also agreed that the Siberian government in Omsk would have overall control of the Trans-Siberian railway, allowing Ekaterinburg joint control over its Urals section, with no tariffs between the Urals government in Ekaterinburg and the Siberian government in Omsk. As part of the agreement, finalized on 19 August 1918, the Siberian government in Omsk recognized the Ekaterinburg government's right to attend the Chelyabinsk State Conference. With the Ekaterinburg issue resolved in its favour, the Siberian government in Omsk could afford to be magnanimous concerning its customs war with the Komuch administration in Samara, thus improving its standing with the Allies still further. On 20 August 1918 the Siberian government in Omsk reaffirmed in a long telegram to Samara that it considered itself sovereign, and that in the absence of a national government, all regional governments should operate on federal lines, while co-operating together in trying to reconstruct a national government. It was then at pains to point out that the establishment of a customs barrier and other financial disagreements between the two administrations resulted from a misunderstanding; no barrier existed, it had simply been a question of temporary taxes imposed to resolve temporary financial problems experienced by the government.[29]

As the delegations gathered for the Chelyabinsk State Conference on 23 August 1918, the URR and the Allies began to reap the rewards of their hard work; it was in most ways their show. The proceedings were dominated by Avksentiev, the former president of the Preparliament and a founder member of the URR, who constantly stressed that he was acting as a member of the URR not the SR Party, and whose arrival, with that of the other URR activist Argunov, gave hope to the Siberian government that not everything would go Komuch's way. In his first press interview Avksentiev made clear that he thought it preposterous that those members of the Constituent Assembly gathered in Samara, numbering about fifty, could claim to represent the nation; a coalition government, he said, which was what the country needed, could never realistically be seen to be dependent on a group of deputies from just one political party. Avksentiev also made clear that there were, in his view, no possible parallels to be drawn between the Siberian government in Omsk and the actions of Skoropadskii in the German-occupied Ukraine.[30]

The URR's dominance of the Chelyabinsk State Conference proceedings was clear to all. It was opened by Argunov on behalf of the Organisation Bureau, and Breshko-Breshkovskaya was elected honorary chairwoman. The elected presidium comprised: president Avksentiev (URR), vice-presidents Rogovskii (Komuch) and Mikhailov (Siberia); secretaries Murashev (URR) and Moiseenko (URR). Krol had been joined by fellow Kadet and URR member V.N. Pepelyaev. But the most important new arrival was General Boldyrev: he had reached Samara early in August 1918, but had turned down the invitation of the Komuch president V.K. Volskii to take up the post of Komuch's Departmental Director for War; in turning down the post he stressed that his mission on behalf of the URR was to form a united government and he would therefore continue his journey to the Chelyabinsk State Conference.

There was only one minor hiccough in this URR triumph. In order to work out the details of a future agreement, the conference resolved to establish an agreement commission comprising representatives from all the relevant delegations. Arguing that the URR Urals government in Ekaterinburg had not existed at the time of the mid-July meeting between Komuch and the Siberian government, Volskii, the leader of the Komuch delegation, prevented the Urals government having a seat on the agreement commission. However, in a compromise arrangement the Urals government leader Krol won a place as the URR representative on the agreement commission and so could defend what he called 'this first born of the

URR'.[31] Thereafter, in spite of the original expectations of many of the participants, the Chelyabinsk State Conference passed peacefully, never even having to resort to a vote. With complete unanimity it was agreed to allow all groups who wanted to attend a more representative state conference, originally scheduled for 1 September 1918. Typical of that spirit of compromise was Avksentiev's proposal that this conference should be held in Ufa, a town in Komuch territory but far enough away from Samara for the Siberian government to feel it was not being forced to come cap in hand to its political rival.[32]

This willingness to compromise was prompted in part by a partial reconciliation between Krol and Komuch. In the days immediately preceding the opening of the Chelyabinsk State Conference the Siberian government had started trying to enforce conscription in territory claimed by the Urals government. The Ekaterinburg government protested, and talks were called to resolve the matter, talks which soon broke down. For Krol conscription went beyond the scope of his original agreement to allow the Siberian government authority in military matters, which he had interpreted as simply meaning Ekaterinburg troops would be put under Siberian command. Thus, although Krol travelled to Chelyabinsk with Mikhailov, the Finance Minister in the Siberian government, and on the surface their relations seemed good, in fact Krol felt he had been deceived by Mikhailov as to the real degree of autonomy he had achieved for his government. On arrival in Chelyabinsk Krol was determined to try and mend fences with Komuch by exploiting his personal friendship with the SR Central Committee member Zenzinov, using him as a channel through which to stress to Komuch that, far from being an appendage of the Siberian government in Omsk, the URR Urals government in Ekaterinburg was acting as an honest broker.[33]

However, the willingness of all sides to compromise at the Chelyabinsk State Conference was also due to Allied pressure. With the successful landing in Archangel and the capture of Kazan constantly in their minds, the Allies wanted all squabbling put on one side. As Maiskii, the Menshevik Departmental Director for Labour in the Komuch administration, arrived in Chelyabinsk, the Czechoslovak representative Bogdan Pavlu told him that in his view both the army and the central government administration were being formed too slowly: the Czechoslovaks, he reminded Maiskii, had agreed to help the Russians onto their feet and stay for perhaps two or three months; instead they were doing all the fighting. If things did not improve radically, he warned, the Czechoslovaks might have to review their position. Immediately after the Chelyabinsk State Conference the

Czechoslovaks tried to use their influence to introduce a common economic policy between the Samara, Omsk and Ekaterinburg governments when they asked Komuch on 30 August 1918 to come into line with a policy already agreed between Omsk and Ekaterinburg.[34]

## THE ARCHANGEL GOVERNMENT AND THE WHITE DANGER

It was not only on the Kazan front that political in-fighting behind the Green lines was weakening the military position, on the Archangel front too there were political problems; but in the north the threat came not from a dispute between SRs, the URR and former SRs, but the resurgence of White counter-revolutionary officers. In Archangel, as in Samara, the new government tried to turn the clock back to September 1917 and the days of Kerensky, only to be reminded that in August 1917 the White Kornilovite generals had preferred to move against Kerensky's government rather than act against the Bolsheviks in co-operation with it.

The administration established by Chaikovskii, at its first meeting at 12.00 a.m. on 2 August 1918, was like that in Ekaterinburg, a child of the URR. Its key members were Chaikovskii himself, who was also Departmental Director for Foreign Affairs; his old associates of Petrograd and Vologda, Maslov, Departmental Director for Defence, Dedusenko, Departmental Director for Trade and Industry, and Likhach, Departmental Director for Labour; plus Departmental Director for Justice A.I. Gukovskii, Departmental Director for Finance G.A. Martyushin and Departmental Director for the Interior P. Yu Zubov. All Chaikovskii's colleagues were SRs and deputies to the Constituent Assembly, except for Zubov who was a Kadet and formerly deputy mayor of Vologda. Chaplin, organizer of the insurrection, was appointed Commander of the Armed Forces. Since the URR insisted that all members of the government had to be members of the Constituent Assembly, or at least some elected representative body where this was impossible, Chaplin's local contact, the liberal Startsev, did not become a departmental director but was appointed provincial commissar.[35]

The government's daily *The Regeneration of the North* echoed both the theme of the URR and its political outlook; it retained on its masthead the SRs' twin legends 'workers of all countries unite' and 'through struggle you will obtain justice'. As on the Volga, until the formation of an All-Russian government, the ministers called themselves departmental directors, rather than ministers, and their government was called the Supreme Directorate. True to their inspiration, that they were returning to the glorious heritage of the February 1917 Revolution, the pre-October 1917 committees for overseeing the railways were restored and the Bolshevik committees closed down. In its proclamation 'To the Workers' of 7 August 1918, the government made clear that, if Bolshevism had been overthrown, the clock had only been turned back to the summer of 1917: thus, while recognizing the importance of reviving private trade and industry, the government asserted this would be overseen by 'broad state control with the participation of workers' representatives'; 'only with the most energetic support of the workers and their class organizations' could the Department of Labour do its job. Later, on 13 August, the government made clear that only the Bolshevik decree on workers' control had been suspended, all other labour legislation remained in force and 'state regulation of economic life' would continue.[36]

Unexpectedly, given the close relationship between the Allies and the URR, the first problems faced by Chaikovskii's administration came from General Poole. The URR quickly found that there was a gap between the theory of co-operating with the Allies and the reality of that co-operation. Ever conscious of the small number of troops at his disposal, and the fact that the bulk of them had already left Archangel in a dramatic dash towards Vologda and Vyatka, Poole was obsessed with what he saw as the security problem in Archangel; with so few reliable troops, a Bolshevik counter-insurrection might succeed at any moment. The first sign of this tension on security matters between the URR administration and the British military came on 4 August 1918 when Poole's adjutant sent a letter to the directorate asking for the red flag flying over a government building to be taken down. The following day Poole repeated the order direct to Chaikovskii, reminding him that Archangel and its province were under martial law and he saw the issue of the flag as a military rather than a political issue.[37]

The directorate, however, was working to a very different agenda. The very first topic to be discussed by the new government at its first full session on 4 August 1918 was not the requirements of martial law but what it saw as the urgent need to re-establish the system of civilian justice; it ordered the reappointment of magistrates and the restoration of the Archangel district court. Concern for the rule of law soon became a cause of tension both within the government and between the government and the British military. On 5 August 1918 the Departmental Directors of Justice and Labour, Gukovskii and Likhach, clashed over the proposed 'temporary decree on assemblies', which required all public meetings to give 24 hours notice to the authorities and gave the government power to close such meetings down if they threatened 'social peace'. Likhach argued that this temporary decree had not gone through proper cabinet discussion and should not be issued; as it turned out this row was unnecessary, the decree was not draconian enough for Poole who refused to publish it.[38]

The row about security continued the next day when Likhach, whose experience with the Petrograd Assembly of Factory Delegates made him the obvious choice for the labour portfolio, protested at the arrests of workers, restrictions on the trades unions, and in particular, the closure of the arbitration chamber; he also raised the issue of whether or not the soviet should be allowed to operate, as a class, rather than a political body. The Departmental Director for the Interior Zubov responded that the conciliation chamber would be reopened, but, as Chaikovskii made clear, the question of the soviet would have to be raised with the Allied ambassadors when they arrived before any final decision was taken.[39] But before then the security row with Poole reached a climax.

On 7 August 1918 Poole informed Chaikovskii he was appointing Colonel Donop, the French military attaché, to the post of Military Governor of Archangel: this was sensible, he explained, since an Allied officer needed to be responsible for those military measures necessary both to defend Archangel and keep order within it; Chaikovskii was instructed to appoint a subordinate Russian officer to work with Donop and inform all concerned. When Chaikovskii reported this to his directorate on 8 August 1918 he made clear that Poole had acted without consulting him and in ignorance of Russian law, which did not recognize a military governor of this type since the Russian military governor had long-established civilian as well as military powers. In protest at Poole's action the directorate resolved to break off all relations with Poole until the matter was clarified.[40]

Poole was exasperated. His attitude to the directorate was clearly summed up in a report he sent back to London at the end of September 1918:

> The government which had assumed control about two hours before our arrival here was hopeless to a degree. It was composed entirely of Left Social Revolutionaries who in politics and ideas are not far removed from Bolsheviks . . . Their immediate needs of urgent necessities for [the]

town and occupied district they absolutely neglected ... [and were] totally incapable of understanding the necessity for any military precautions being taken for the safety of the port. Any action of this kind they considered as repressive and as undue interference with the liberties of the people.[41]

The Allied ambassadors arrived in Archangel in the middle of this blazing row and at once held long talks with Chaikovskii on 10 August 1918. The British consul Francis Lindley came down firmly on Chaikovskii's side and defended the position of the URR; Poole's proposal was withdrawn. In a long telegram to London dated 12 August 1918 Lindley outlined his fears concerning Poole. While he thought that tension between the civilian and military 'will probably disappear should our movement succeed in embracing a large area', he was nevertheless worried that Poole had behaved as if 'he was in conquered territory'. He went on:

> He considered having declared martial law he was completely free to deal with any question which might arise and make any regulation he chose without consulting anyone. I trust I have convinced him this is a radically wrong point of view and that while it is necessary to avoid the fatal weakness of Kerensky's government, it is still more vital to avoid the mistakes made by the Germans in the Ukraine. Without active good will of the inhabitants our movement is doomed to ignominious failure.

Lindley went on to point to a far more worrying aspect of the affair. In his talks with Poole on 11 August 1918 it had emerged that many Russian officers were dissatisfied with Chaikovskii and proposed overthrowing him. Lindley expressed himself forcibly:

> I pointed out to General Poole the folly of allowing a lot of Russian officers to turn out the government just set up whose members had been working for months in our cause whose programme suited us, whose leader was in touch with Moscow Centre and who by being members of the Constituent [Assembly] had some legal claim to authority. The only object of turning them out was to place some openly monarchical party in power which in my opinion would at present ruin us completely.

Poole promised to talk to the officers and make clear that both the British military and British civilian authorities supported Chaikovskii's administration, but he clearly did not share Lindley's view that 'it would be difficult to find a man more suitable for head of the Provisional Northern Government' than Chaikovskii, nor Lindley's view that the other departmental directors 'have indubitable following among the peasantry whom they have been most successful in gaining over'.[42]

Even after the intervention by the ambassadors, tension continued between Poole and Chaikovskii. Some of this was rather silly: Chaikovskii objected to orders from Poole bearing the words 'I forbid'; and he also protested that Poole had requisitioned all the biggest and best houses in town. Other issues were more serious: when *Regeneration of the North* published an article on 14 August talking about the 'colonial policy of the Allies', Poole sent a military officer to the paper's offices to make a protest and promptly requisitioned the available newsprint to support the launch of a right-wing paper. Earlier, however, the head of British military intelligence Captain Thornhill had complained that newsprint, destined for a right-wing paper at Poole's specific request, had been appropriated by the Archangel civil authorities.[43]

The question of public meetings also dragged on. On 18 August 1918 it was agreed that legislation should ensure that granting permission for these should primarily be a civilian rather than a military concern. However, on 19 August 1918 the government was persuaded to agree to transfer from the police to the military authorities the question of granting permission for such meetings within the city boundaries, and on 22 August 1918 it finally agreed to an amendment making it clear that in all areas of military operations, the military command had to give its consent to all public meetings. Yet none of this fully resolved the issue, since on 23 August 1918 Likhach was again protesting at the arbitrary arrest of sixteen workers by Captain Thornhill. A similar security row developed over the question of summary courts.[44]

Poole had first requested on 12 August 1918 that civilian summary courts and military courts should be established; the government delayed discussion until 15 August 1918 and then simply took note of the request, with Chaikovskii reporting to his directorate the same day on the 'cases of interference by the British command in the internal affairs of the region'. The following day the directorate explained its inactivity on the issue by referring to the delay on Poole's side in clarifying certain points of the proposed legislation, although the real reason for the delay was a split within the directorate itself over the issue of the death penalty. On 22 August 1918 the Departmental Director for Justice Gukovskii told his colleagues that he could not accept a law which gave military courts the power to condemn to death; his colleagues disagreed, the cabinet split and as the vote was taken and the death penalty endorsed, Gukovskii announced his resignation. Chaikovskii refused to accept the resignation, but the split meant Poole's law was only finally agreed on 30 August 1918. In the meantime Poole had lost all patience with the scruples of philosophe politicians and sent an angry letter to Chaikovskii demanding to know why, after more than a week, his orders had not been carried out.[45]

## CHAIKOVSKII AND THE ARCHANGEL MILITARY

However, the main source of tension in Archangel was not thi constant and unexpected bickering between the Allies and the URR Poole and Chaikovskii, but a specifically Russian issue; the rif opening up between the directorate and its army. In the first few day of Chaikovskii's administration Departmental Director for Defence Maslov and the Russian Army Commander Chaplin collaborated quite well. British policy was to ignore the Russian Army as a fighting force and subsume it within 'Slavo-British Allied Legions' staffed by Britisl officers; even these would be used for auxiliary rather than active service.[46] When this idea was first discussed on 4 August 1918 at directorate meeting attended by Chaplin, Deputy Departmenta Director for Defence General N.I. Zvegintsev and Startsev, they suggested it might be possible to achieve something less demeaning i the Allies were approached in the right way; Maslov undertook to draw up proposals. The directorate was determined that Russian troop formations should be put under a Russian commander and, meeting on 5 August 1918, an order to this effect was passed; front-line troops would be subject to the Supreme Allied Command, but through the hierarchy of a Russian high command Poole initially welcomed Maslov's plans.[47]

Thereafter, however, Maslov's relations with Chaplin were characterized by antagonism rather than co-operation, a dispute in which Poole clearly came down in favour of Chaplin. Maslov, who was not lacking in military experience and who at the time of the SR walk-out form the Second Congress of Soviets had been an active member of the CSRM's military commission during the Junker rising in November 1917, became almost a departmental director without a job; his active involvement with SR politics only made the situation worse. On 13 August 1918 Poole asked the directorate to explain reports he had received that Maslov intended to give a talk entitled 'The aim of Allied interference in Russian affairs'. Increasingly the directorate found itself operating through, and being dependent on Maslov's deputy Zvegintsev rather than Maslov himself. By 16 August 1918 it was Zvegintsev who was reporting on the need to introduce conscription and Zvegintsev who was using his good offices with Poole to try to persuade the British both to pay for their use of the railway network and to supply the railway workers with food. From 17 August 1918 on it was decided to invite both Chaplin and Zvegintsev to the Tuesday, Thursday and Saturday cabinet meetings to ensure joint discussion of military affairs. At their insistence, it was agreed a military treaty should be signed between the government and the Allies; something implemented on 19 August 1918.[48]

It was Maslov's determination to reassert his authority over the army that provoked Archangel's White officers to action. On 23 August 1918, the date of the opening of the Chelyabinsk State Conference, Maslov brought a paper to the directorate which sought to end what he saw as the harmful competition that had arisen between his department and Chaplin's staff: the staff had grown from a body concerned primarily with operational matters, to a body that had taken over economic and supply issues, the correct concern of the department for defence; the solution was to merge the two organizations into an expanded war department. Discussion of this contentious issue was shelved until 25 August 1918 when it was debated in Chaplin's presence and the decision taken to go ahead. Then the issue of the new powers for the war department and the routine wrangling with Poole about security matters became intertwined. Likhach had already protested to the directorate on 23 August 1918 about the arbitrary arrest of sixteen workers by Captain Thornhill. On 29 August 1918 Chaikovskii got the whole directorate to endorse a letter of protest to Poole about these arrests; this simply provoked the Allied command into publishing a series of decrees on public order without consulting the directorate. Chaikovskii sought the intervention of the ambassadors, but on this occasion they were far from sympathetic. After a bruising session with the US ambassador David Francis, who had bluntly informed him that Poole would not have had to issue any of his decrees if Chaikovskii had got a grip on the security issue earlier, Chaikovskii arrived at the directorate meeting of the 30th late and angry.[49]

Poole's decrees had been issued through the offices of the Archangel commandant. On 31 August 1918 Maslov announced that the commandant had been sacked and ordered Chaplin to implement this decision at once, thus intervening directly in a purely military appointment. This put the rivalry between Maslov and Chaplin into sharp focus, as did Maslov's co-ordinated decision to take the first step in revamping the war department by establishing a war economy committee. Then, on 3 September 1918, with Maslov's enthusiastic support, the directorate revived the notion of establishing a military governor: the job, they suggested, should be offered not to a French officer but to Dedusenko, Chaikovskii's closest confidant. Dedusenko was asked to approach the Allied ambassadors forthwith and discuss with them the thorny question of the boundaries between military and civilian administration in view of the Allies' declared position that they would not interfere in Russian affairs.[50]

The proposal for a military governor would have gone some way to satisfying Poole's concerns, while the delimitation of military and civilian authority was something diplomats of the calibre of Lindley, Noulens and Francis could have resolved in no time. However, a military governor in the person of a current member of the directorate, an SR and a close associate not only of Chaikovskii but of Maslov as well – against the background of the newly strengthened war department's determination to interfere in military appointments – none of this was what was needed in the eyes of White officers, who saw in it the revival of military commissars and the traditional SR obsession with politicizing the army. Clashes between Chaplin and Maslov increased in number and intensity, and on 5 September 1918 Chaplin acted. He and his fellow officers staged a coup, arrested the directorate and imprisoned them in the monastery on Solovetskii Island in the White Sea. It was left to the Allies' diplomats to try and sort things out.[51]

The British consul Lindley was horrified at Chaplin's coup. He had been worried about the growing antagonism between Chaplin and Maslov, but his solution was a minor cabinet reshuffle – Maslov and Likhach were his targets as a later report made clear – not a coup. As he told London, he had rather been hoping that it might be possible to remove from the government some of the departmental directors 'not whole-heartedly pro-ally'; the coup attempt had strengthened rather than weakened the position of these men.[52] Lindley first learned that something was afoot on the evening of the 5th when the French ambassador Noulens warned him that Chaplin intended to act; Lindley had in turn informed Poole, who ordered Chaplin to abandon his plans. In retrospect, Poole should perhaps have acted more forcefully: other British officers sympathized more or less openly with Chaplin; in particular Thornhill, described by Chaplin as his personal friend and 'the scourge of the local reds', did nothing to prevent the directorate's arrest even though his intelligence headquarters were opposite the directorate building. Lindley certainly believed that the language of General Poole's officers 'no doubt led Captain Chaplin to believe [the coup] would be winked at'.[53]

On the other hand Lindley believed that since the government had 'taken quite unnecessary measures which could not fail to irritate the military authorities' simply reinstating the existing ministers might not be the best way forward. He was therefore prepared to negotiate when talks were held with Chaplin on 6–7 September 1918. The ambassadors demanded Chaplin restore a democratic government; Chaplin, realizing he would get no support from Poole, agreed to a new government being formed without Likhach, Maslov and Dedusenko; while Chaplin and his fellow plotters would not be accused of treason but allowed quietly to resign their posts.[54] However, this was not acceptable to Chaikovskii. He would accept the departure of Likhach and Maslov, but not Dedusenko. So, instead of accepting the compromise the ambassadors had reached with Chaplin, Chaikovskii issued a public statement on 9 September 1918 making clear that all members of the government would stay in office. Then, when the directorate resumed its activities on 12 September 1918, Chaikovskii dissolved all its departments, including the war department, appointed a Russian Colonel, V.A. Durov, Military Governor, and resigned.[55]

This at first sight rather strange decision was motivated by two things: first, Chaikovskii had agreed to head a government on the understanding that rapid progress would be made towards Vologda, the Czechoslovaks and liberation; but none of this had happened. Second, even if Chaikovskii had gone on to head an All-Russian government covering the territory from Archangel in the north to Samara in the south, he would have considered his position as being only temporary until some sort of constitutional body had been set up; the news reaching Archangel by the middle of September 1918 suggested that at that very moment moves were underway in Ufa to establish an All-Russian government linked to an All-Russian representative body. Chaikovskii's resignation was in favour of these All-Russian institutions. In future, he believed, power should be exercised in Archangel through a governor, ultimately to be appointed by the All-Russian government but in the first instance to be appointed by Chaikovskii himself.[56] At first Chaikovskii seemed intent on leaving Archangel and joining the All-Russian government which he believed had been formed in Ufa, but Lindley persuaded him to stay on as its Archangel representative. The younger members of the dissolved directorate, however, were determined to try and reach Ufa; Maslov, Likhach and Dedusenko left Archangel on 21 September 1918.[57]

Chaikovskii's decision to resign on 12 September 1918 was fully in line with URR policy. He had established a URR government which was supposed to evolve into an All-Russian government but had failed to do so because of the vicissitudes of war; it was logical that he should abandon the attempt in favour of that being made by his URR colleagues at the Chelyabinsk State Conference when they resolved to call a further Ufa State Conference. His experience of power, however, was a bad omen for the URR in Siberia. If the URR had at first considered the greatest hindrance to unity came from the more doctrinaire SRs in the Komuch administration who were prepared to compare the Siberian government in Omsk to that of pro-German reactionaries like Skoropadskii and Krasnov, the experience of Archangel showed the impatience of White officers with any regime which looked back only to the summer of 1917; just as Kornilov moved against Kerensky, so Chaplin moved against Chaikovskii. The URR would face the same problems of a revenge-seeking military after the Ufa State Conference; but in Siberia there would be no compromise-seeking diplomats of the stature of Lindley to ensure that Allied policy was actually carried out.

## NOTES

1. M. Jansen, *A Show Trial under Lenin,* (The Hague 1982) p. 2.
2. For the founding of Komuch, see S. Nikolaev, 'Vozniknovenie o organizatsiya Komucha' *Volya Rossii* (Prague 1928) vols 8–9, p. 241, and I. Maiskii, *Demokraticheskaya Kontrrevolyutsiya* (Moscow 1923), pp.49, 56–8; for its insecurity during the early days, see state Archive of the Russian Federation (GARF) 749.1.4.17–19.
3. For the salaries, see GARF 749.1.28.7; otherwise Maiskii, *Demokraticheskaya,* pp.60, 74, 85, 89, 91. A summary of some of these points appears in S. Berk, 'The democratic counter-revolution: *Komuch* and the civil war on the Volga' *Canadian-American Slavic Studies* vol. 7 (1973).
4. GARF 749.1.3.4, 749.1.28.5, and 749.1.28.10.
5. For the grain procurement policy, see O. Figes, *Peasant Russia and Civil War: the Volga Countryside in Revolution, 1917–21* (Oxford 1989), p.170. I find it hard to accept Figes's view that the abundance of goods in Samara was largely the result of a good harvest than the policies of Komuch; the problem with the supply situation in Russia has always been to persuade peasants to part with their grain rather than an absolute shortage of grain. His point that the Bolsheviks introduced a more relaxed grain policy on retaking Samara, suggests that they had been forced to recognize the popularity of such a policy with the peasantry. On a related point, Figes's

assertion on p.168 that the Komuch administration was weak in the countryside seems hard to square with the massive scale of their agitation and propaganda department.

6. Again, I find myself in disagreement with Figes. Although the incidents of land-owners using force to drive poor peasants off land that had recently been allocated to them did occur, just how typical they were is open to doubt. Writing in order to ingratiate himself with the Bolshevik authorities, Maiskii's account of 1922 has to be considered with great caution, and the frequent repetition of such incidents in Soviet sources does not prove that the incidents were widespread, simply that they help propagate the Soviet myth that the Komuch regime was counter-revolutionary because it favoured the rich 'kulak' peasant at the expense of the, allegedly pro-Bolshevik, poor peasant. The Bolsheviks themselves were always thinking of ways 'model farms' could be saved from those dividing up the land in order to ensure grain supplies.

7. Nikolaev, 'Vozniknovenie', p. 243; Maiskii, *Demokraticheskaya*, pp. 128, 135. Although I disagree with Figes's assessment of the popularity of Komuch's agrarian policy, he is probably right to suggest that the Komuch administration had great difficulty persuading peasants that its policy towards the war with Germany was correct. Whether this unwillingness to fight reflected a deeper hostility to Komuch I doubt – as will be shown below, some peasants did volunteer and the volunteer brigades were eventually very successful. Most peasants wanted peace, welcomed Komuch's agrarian policy, and felt that volunteers could go and fight the Germans.

8. GARF 749.1.27.5, 749.1.27.9, 749.1.27.15.

9. Maiskii, *Demokraticheskaya*, pp. 55, 162; V.G. Boldyrev, *Direktoriya, Kolchak, Interventy* (Novonikolaevsk 1925), p. 32.

10. For People's Army wages, see V.L. Utgofa, 'Ufimskoe Gosudarstvennoe Soveshchanie 1918' *Byloe* no. 16 (Petrograd 1921), p. 17, but note Maiskii, *Demokraticheskaya*, p. 149 talks of extra payments to the families of serving soldiers. For tension over military appointments and the role of commissars, see Maiskii, *Demokraticheskaya*, pp. 153–60. For the 'hidden commissars', see Nikolaev, 'Vozniknovenie', p. 242 and K.V. Sakharov, *Belaya Sibir'* (Munich 1923), p. 11. The records of the cultural educational recruitment section form one of the biggest collections in the archives of Komuch, see GARF 671.

11. This summary is taken from S.P. Melgunov, *Tragediya Admirala Kolchaka* Part 1 (Belgrade 1930), pp. 62–72. For the contacts with the British consul, see GARF R–1005.1a.348.67.

12. G.K. Gins, *Sibir', Soyuzniki i Kolchak* vol. 1 (Peking 1921), pp. 95, 105, 142. An edited version of this appeared as 'Organizatsiya beloi vlasti v Sibiri', in S.A. Alekseev (ed.), *Revolyutsiya i grazhdanskaya voina v opisaniyakh Belogvardeitsev* vol. 3, p. 380 et seq; the quoted passage is p. 388.

13. For the attitude of the SRs, see L.A. Krol, *Za tri goda* (Vladivostok 1921), p. 29; for the Samara SRs, see GARF R–1005.1.348.202.

14. Krol, *Za tri goda*, pp. 12, 50.
15. Krol, *Za tri goda*, pp. 60–5; for the Allied pressure on the Siberian government, see Utgofa, 'Ufimskoe', p. 20.
16. GARF 749.1.41.1; for the composition of the delegations, see Gins, *Sibir'* vol. 1, p. 133.
17. For the establishment of the commission, see Krol, *Za tri goda*, p. 66; for the sanction of Komuch, see GARF 667.1.27.22; see also Maiskii, *Demokraticheskaya*, p. 202.
18. For the Siberian government, see Gins, *Sibir'* vol. 1, p. 142; for Komuch see GARF 749.1.2.1, 667.1.27.1v.
19. Gins, *Sibir'*, p. 147; Boldyrev, *Direktoriya*, p. 30 n. 17.
20. GARF 667.1.27.1b; for the SR congress, see Melgunov, *Tragediya* part 1, p. 95.
21. For Brushvit, see GARF 667.1.32.3; for the views in Samara, see 670.1.1.9.
22. Gins, *Sibir'* vol. 1, pp. 122, 151 et seq.
23. For the attitude of Komuch, see GARF 667.1.19.23; for the suspension of the Duma, see Gins, *Sibir'* vol. 1, p. 178.
24. Gins, *Sibir'* vol 1, p. 131; Boldyrev, *Direktoriya*, p. 30.
25. For the 'rude' telegram, see GARF 667.1.27.1b; for Guinet on Komuch, see 667.1.32.3.
26. For Vedenyapin, see GARF R–1005.1a.346.206; for the Komuch decree, see Maiskii, *Demokraticheskaya*, p. 76. Boldyrev, although a member of the URR, also felt too much effort was being made to take Kazan; but as a close ally of Chaikovskii, he may well have had his eyes focused on Vologda and Perm, see *Direktoriya*, p. 32.
27. Krol, *Za tri goda*, pp. 71–8. These arrivals were noted sadly by Komuch, see GARF 667.1.33.5.
28. For the URR, see Krol, *Za tri goda*, pp. 71, 76; for the SRs, see GARF 667.1.19.66, 667.1.33.3.
29. For the URR's right to attend the Chelyabinsk conference, see Krol, *Za tri goda*, p. 78; otherwise, Gins, *Sibir'* vol. 1, pp. 134, 148.
30. For Avksentiev on the URR, see Maiskii, *Demokraticheskaya*, p. 208; for his press interview, see Gins, *Sibir'* vol. 1, p. 183.
31. For Boldyrev's arrival, see his *Direktoriya*, p. 28; otherwise Krol, *Za tri goda*, pp. 80–4.
32. For the absence of any votes, see Gins, *Sibir'* vol. 1, p. 184; for the date of 1 September and the proposal of Ufa, see Maiskii, *Demokraticheskaya*, pp. 206–8.
33. Krol, *Za tri goda*, p. 82.
34. For Pavlu and Maiskii, see the latter's *Demokraticheskaya*, p. 172; for the economic plan, see GARF 677.1.7.7.
35. For the importance of membership of the Constituent Assembly see G.E. Chaplin, 'Dva perevorota na severe' *Beloe delo* no. 4 (Berlin 1928), p. 25; otherwise GARF 17.1.1.1.
36. GARF 16.1.1.8, 16.1.1.11, 16.1.1.20, 16.1.1.34.
37. I. Mints (ed.), *Interventsiya na severe v dokumentakh* (Moscow 1933), p. 17.

38. GARF 16.1.1.2, 16.1.1.56.
39. GARF 16.1.1.11.
40. For the instruction to Chaikovskii, see Mints, *Interventsiya*, p. 18; for Chaikovskii's response, see GARF 16.1.1.22.
41. Public Records Office WO32.57903 Poole's report.
42. For Chaikovskii's talks with the ambassadors on 10 August, see L.I. Strakhovsky, *Intervention at Archangel: the Story of Allied Intervention and Russian Counter-revolution in North Russia, 1918–20* (Princeton 1944), p. 39; Lindley's telegrams of 12 August 1918 are in Public Records Office FO 371.3319.423, 371.3339.81.
43. Public Records Office FO371.3339.110; Mints, *Interventsiya*, p. 19.
44. GARF 16.1.1.52–8.
45. For Poole, see Mints, *Interventsiya*, p. 29, otherwise GARF 16.1.1.39, 16.1.1.49, 16.1.1.57, 16.1.1.69.
46. For the plans to exclude the Slavo–British Allied Legions from active service, see Public Records Office WO32.5673 Report of General H. Needham.
47. GARF 16.1.1.6, 16.1.1.11; Mints reproduces part of this discussion in *Interventsiya*, p. 26.
48. For Maslov's role in the CSRM, see G. Semenov, *Voennaya i boevaya rabota Partii Sotsialistov–Revolyutsionerov za 1917–18* (Moscow 1922), p. 11; otherwise GARF 16.1.1.34, 16.1.1.46, 16.1.1.51–3.
49. GARF 16.1.1.58, 16.1.1.61, 16.1.1.67, 16.1.1.69.
50. GARF 16.1.1.70, 16.1.1.76. In his book Strakhovsky was able to link Chaplin's attempted coup to the commandant's dismissal (*Intervention* p. 49), but until the Russian archives were opened the details of the proposals for a new war department and a military governor were unknown.
51. Chaplin, 'Dva perevorota', p. 27.
52. For the idea of a reshuffle, see Public Records Office FO371.3339.178; for the impact of the coup on Maslov and Likhach's position, see 371.3339.122.
53. Lindley's relations with Poole are in Public Records Office FO371.3339.129 and 3319.440; for Thornhill, see Chaplin, 'Dva perevorota', p. 23; for the intelligence building, see Strakhovsky, *Intervention*, p. 51. Noulens (*Mon Ambassade en Russie Soviétique, 1917–19* (Paris 1933) vol. 2, p. 200) also suspected British officers of sympathizing with Chaplin.
54. For Lindley, see Public Records Office FO371.3319.440; for Chaplin, see Chaplin, 'Dva perevorota', pp. 29–30.
55. For Chaikovskii and Dedusenko, see Public Records Office FO371.3339.131b; for the public statement, see FO371.3339.140; for the dissolution of the directorate, see GARF 16.1.1.79, 16.1.1.93. These developments are summarized in Strakhovsky, *Intervention*, pp. 63–70.
56. Public Records Office FO371.3339.143; FO371.3339.183.
57. For Chaikovskii's plans to leave Archangel, see Noulens, *Ambassade* vol. 2, p. 221; for Lindley, see Public Records Office FO371.3339.165; for

those going to Ufa, see 3339.175 and 3339.188. Chaikovskii delayed making the resignation of his administration public because no firm news had come from Ufa about the formation of an All-Russian government. On 24 September he received a report from Omsk suggesting there was still a question mark over whether a stable government had been formed or not, and so on 27 September he reluctantly agreed to form a modified cabinet, see 3339.188–200. The formation of Chaikovskii's second administration is summarized in Strakhovsky, *Intervention*, p. 76 et seq.

# CHAPTER EIGHT

# Green Directory, White Counter-revolution

As the British consul Francis Lindley and his fellow Allied ambassadors were sorting out the crisis in Archangel caused by Chaplin's attempted White coup, delegates were gathering for the second, more representative, Ufa State Conference, which would resolve the question of what sort of government should be established in liberated Russia. The URR programme was clear on this: a 'directory' should be formed from three or more representative politicians who would head an interim administration until a new Constituent Assembly could be elected. After much debate, the Ufa State Conference resolved the differences within the Green camp between SRs, the URR and former SRs, and by mid-September 1918 a directory had duly been formed. But in less than two months it was to share the fate of Chaikovskii's Archangel directorate, despite showing greater willingness than Chaikovskii had ever done to make concessions to the military.

On 18 November 1918 the directory was overthrown by Admiral Kolchak, that veteran of some of the very earliest attempts at counter-revolution in the summer of 1917. This White coup was by no means inevitable. Although the divisions within the Green patriotic socialist camp did not go away, the directory was able to keep them in check. Furthermore, although the directory made a rather inept start and was militarily on the retreat in October 1918, something which forced it to concede much to the Siberian government in Omsk as it moved ever eastward, by early November 1918 the directory had reasserted its political authority, and some of its military forces at least seemed poised to resume the attack. Contrary to the verdict of its Bolshevik and White critics, the directory was overthrown not because it was on the point of collapse, but because it was on the point of success.

## THE UFA STATE CONFERENCE

The Ufa State Conference was a triumph for the URR. It lasted the best part of two weeks and resulted in all participants agreeing on 23 September 1918 to the formation of a five-member directory comprising the former president of the Preparliament Avksentiev (URR), General Boldyrev (URR), the leading SR Zenzinov (Komuch), a Siberian Kadet V.A. Vinogradov (who took the place originally intended for the Moscow Kadet N.I. Astrov) and Vologodskii (the former SR Prime Minister of the Siberian government). Had circumstances permitted it, the membership of the directory would have shown the URR's predominance even more clearly since Chaikovskii would have occupied the place taken by Zenzinov. The conference opened on 8 September 1918, however since the Siberian government delegation had not yet arrived, this was a purely formal session with Avksentiev making a speech of welcome to the 200 delegates representing not only such obvious organizations as Komuch, the Urals government and eventually the Siberian government, but also the cossack government of Orenburg, the cossack government of Uralsk, the Siberian cossack voisko, the Irkutsk cossack voisko, the Semirechenskii cossack voisko, the Yeniseisk cossack voisko, the Astrakhan cossack voisko, the Bashkir government, the Alash-Ordy government, the Turkestan government, the Tyurko-Tatar government and, bizarrely, the Estonian government. There were also representatives from the SR Party, the Menshevik Party, the Popular Socialist Party, the Kadet Party, the Unity Mensheviks, the URR and the various town and regional councils of Siberia, the Urals and the Volga. As to the political affiliation of those present, although over 100 delegates were members of the SR Party, many were simultaneously members of the URR; thus the URR could claim to represent the majority of delegates, and, since it had been agreed in Chelyabinsk that all votes had to be unanimous, it was in a good position to lay the basis for any consensus.[1]

On 10 September 1918 a second conference session was held which agreed to establish a Council of Elders: this was to be composed of representatives from all the groups present who would act much as the agreement commission had acted in Chelyabinsk; but since the Siberian delegation had still not arrived the membership of the council could not be finalized. The Siberian delegation finally arrived on 12 September 1918 and the proceedings proper got under way with a speech from the Czechoslovak leader Bogdan Pavlu: he made clear that for the Czechoslovaks a turning point had been reached; either the Russian politicians established an All-Russian government by agreement, preferably giving some recognition to the Constituent Assembly although precise details did not concern them, or they would resume their broken journey to France. Each delegation was then allowed to make an opening statement, and the first to speak was the Komuch president and member of the SR Central Committee V.K. Volskii; to the surprise of many he gave the first hint of a possible compromise agreement.[2]

Although Volskii spoke at great length about the democratic credentials of the Constituent Assembly, he reminded those present that since the Constituent Assembly was sovereign, it was quite capable of reacting to new circumstances and even of reducing its own powers. He went on: 'for a whole series of reasons, we think that the Constituent Assembly will come to the conclusion without much difficulty that a new Constituent Assembly needs to be elected'. Until those elections, however, the only body capable of sanctioning the government formed in Ufa was a Congress of Deputies to the Constituent Assembly; once this principle had been accepted, the details of how the congress and the government should relate to one another could easily be agreed, since the government would be responsible to the congress 'only in the most general form'.[3] By suggesting that the existing Constituent Assembly might call early elections to a new Constituent Assembly, and that current Constituent Assembly deputies would only exercise their right to control the government in the vaguest possible way, Volskii was abandoning the aggressive tone that had once seen the SRs compare the Siberian government in Omsk to that of Skoropadskii.

Volskii's willingness to open the way towards a compromise stemmed from the three-way split within the SR delegation to the conference. The left argued simply that, since the SRs had won the November 1917 Constituent Assembly elections, power was theirs; on the right Zenzinov favoured compromise as a point of principle; Volskii stood in the centre, trying to balance the extremes, and he came down for compromise for two reasons. First, there were the military realities at the front. The SRs' willingness to compromise partly reflected their shrinking power base as the Bolsheviks counter-attacked. Kazan fell to the Bolsheviks on 8 September 1918, and on 16 September 1918 Komuch decided, after consultations with Volskii, that the State Bank should be evacuated to Ufa; by 18 September 1918 Komuch had taken the difficult decision to shoot deserters, and on 19 September 1918 the evacuation of Samara itself began.[4] However, there was a second pressure for compromise besides the military situation, for even without the weakening military position, Volskii would have found it difficult to enforce the left-wing line. Before leaving Samara, the Komuch delegation had debated the question of whether those attending had been mandated by the party to follow a particular policy. The question of whether party members in parliament or government were bound by party policy had been a running sore among SRs since February 1917; many party members had bitter memories of right-wingers like Kerensky ignoring party policy once in office. Yet on 29 August 1918 the Komuch presidium resolved that, since those attending the Ufa State Conference would do so as members of the sovereign Constituent Assembly and not as members of Komuch or the SR Party, they could not be instructed how to vote by the SR Party or any other body; any other decision would violate the principle of parliamentary immunity. Thus Volskii had to recognize that, whatever way his centre group went, the right would join the URR in working for compromise.[5]

What strengthened the URR still further were parallel divisions within the liberal Kadet camp. When V.N. Pepelyaev had arrived at the Chelyabinsk State Conference from Moscow to represent the Kadets, he informed Krol that the Kadet Central Committee had finally decided that a dictatorship was the only way forward for Russia. In Chelyabinsk, Pepelayev had spoken for the Kadets, and Krol had been free to ignore the Central Committee message concerning a dictatorship and speak on behalf of the URR. In Ufa, Pepelyaev staged a diplomatic illness and left Krol to put the views of the Kadet Party. This put Krol in a dilemma since as a leading member of the URR he was opposed to dictatorship, but in a neat squaring of the circle, Krol informed the delegates that the Kadet Party wanted a dictatorship, but since no suitable candidates stood ready to take up the post, it would be prepared to accept a directory, but a directory which was not subject to any control by a pseudo-constitutional body like Komuch.[6]

The one gap in the URR programme concerned precisely this question: whether, in the time between a directory being formed and a new Constituent Assembly being summoned, the government had to be responsible to any semi-constitutional body. General Boldyrev stated that the URR did not believe that the future government's power should be limited by some 'parallel controlling apparatus'; power should belong to a directory which should appoint an All-Russian executive cabinet comprised of people known for their abilities who would cover the main functions of state – war, foreign affairs, finance, railways, supply, state inspection and control. The

URR-run Urals government, however, suggested that the directory should be responsible to some sort of interim constitutional body until elections to a new Constituent Assembly had been organized; indeed the Ufa State Conference itself could perform that function.[7]

The Siberian delegation when it arrived had little of substance to add to the Ufa talks. It too favoured a directory, but like General Boldyrev and the liberal Krol, one responsible to a future elected body rather than the existing Constituent Assembly or any interim body. Its main concern was to stress that the directory should be small, no more than five, and that all powers other than those concerning the key ministries of war, foreign affairs, post and telegraph, railways and finance, should be devolved to autonomous regional governments; this would mean retaining an autonomous government for Siberia as well as for the other regions.[8]

The conference session on 12 September 1918 ended by finalizing the composition of the Council of Elders which had 21 members, including General Boldyrev, Zenzinov and Krol, with a presidium of Avksentiev, Rogovskii, Moiseenko, P.V. Murashev (of the Urals government) and I.I. Serebrennikov (of the Siberian government). This council was where the real work was done as an acceptable compromise was hammered out at meetings of delegations and meetings between delegations held in corridors or hotel bedrooms, with the Allies frequently being brought in to arbitrate. Inevitably there was an atmosphere of gossip, intrigue and even threat; but the key figures in the backstairs negotiations, Rogovskii, chairman of the Komuch Council of Departmental Directors (CDD), and Gurevich, leader of the SR group of deputies to the Constituent Assembly, did have a clear basis on which they could work. As Komuch president Volskii had intimated in his opening speech, the first concession made during sessions of the Council of Elders came from the Komuch side when Zenzinov suggested that, although the ultimate aim remained to reconvene the Constituent Assembly of January 1918, in the immediate future the government could be responsible to a different body. This was close to the view of some of those in the URR: a pre-existing body, like the state conference itself, could be used to supervise the government, perhaps expanding its composition to include all Constituent Assembly members. The question of whether this expanded state conference would exercise day-to-day control over the government, or would only be recalled after several months, could be left until later.

When discussion began in the Council of Elders on this topic, the SRs again made another concession. They were lukewarm about diluting their sovereign assembly by creating an expanded state conference – it smacked of the little-lamented Preparliament. In the immediate future, they proposed, the directory and All-Russian government need not be responsible to any constitutional body, on condition only that they were allowed one last chance to reconvene a quorate session of the Constituent Assembly by January 1919. Since the Constituent Assembly numbered some 500 deputies without the Bolsheviks and Left SRs, the figure of 250 was quickly seized on as a quorum. This suggestion could have alienated the Siberian delegation, who were determined that the 1918 Constituent Assembly should dissolve itself to allow the directory once formed to organize elections to a new assembly; and so a recess was called while the Siberian government in Omsk was contacted. Meanwhile the SRs reassured delegates that the 1918 Constituent Assembly need not meet for long, simply implementing essential measures for the defence of the liberated territory, then 'in the quickest time' new elections would be organized, and, having called these elections, all power would be transferred to the directory and All-Russian government until the new assembly met. Although they were still insisting on reconvening the 1918 Constituent Assembly, the SRs were increasingly doing so simply as a matter of constitutional propriety alone: the government could ignore the assembly until it was quorate, and after the briefest of sessions, ignore it thereafter until a new Constituent Assembly was elected.

By 18 September 1918 agreement had been reached. The Siberian delegation was still adamant that the directory and All-Russian government should not be responsible to the Constituent Assembly, but were prepared to accept a transparent sleight of hand: if the quorate Constituent Assembly gathered by 1 January 1919 the assembly would by definition be sovereign, not the directory and All-Russian government; thus the directory and All-Russian government established in Ufa would not be under the Constituent Assembly's control but would have ceased to exist. Since reconvening the Constituent Assembly as a quorate body meant bringing from Soviet Russia to liberated territory a further 170 deputies to add to the 90 already there – something virtually impossible – the Siberian delegation was prepared to recognize that this fudge was simply a device to save SR *amour propre*. Not surprisingly many SRs were unhappy with the compromise, but did not protest; they insisted only that a congress of all the Constituent Assembly deputies present in Ufa should be held to endorse the agreement.[9]

Carried away with this triumph, on 19 September 1918 the

Council of Elders began to discuss the relationship between the directory and All-Russian government and the existing regional governments. This proved more difficult than delegates had anticipated, since it was here, in the practical details rather than the constitutional formalities, that the Siberian government from Omsk dug in its heels. It had already made clear that it felt the directory and All-Russian government's power should be limited to All-Russian issues, allowing the regions the greatest possible autonomy; the Siberian government was determined to protect its local prerogatives and it took several interventions from the Allies before the bitter rows of 21 September 1918 gave way to the agreement of the 23rd.[10] In the final analysis, this issue was never satisfactorily resolved, since at the suggestion of the URR leader Krol, although the principle of the regional governments surrendering authority to the directory and All-Russian government was agreed, the precise details of the future relationship between the All-Russian and regional governments was to be left to the 'wisdom' of both sides.[11]

The other area where the Siberian delegation dug in its heels was the personal composition of the directory. As the conference moved on to discuss the question of personnel, the Siberian delegation was reinforced by the arrival of the Deputy Minister of Internal Affairs and the War Minister. They had been expressly instructed that no SRs should be allowed onto the directory, but soon compromised and accepted that Avksentiev represented the URR rather than the SR Party.[12] The original composition of the directory – Chaikovskii, Avksentiev, Boldyrev, Astrov and Vologodskii – met their wishes, but as it became clear that not all those appointed could take up their seats, the Siberian delegation found itself outflanked. It gained from the inability of the Moscow-based Kadet Astrov to take up his seat, since it meant the local Siberian Kadet Vinogradov became a member; however, since Chaikovskii was also unable to reach Ufa from Archangel they had to accept the man elected as his deputy, Zenzinov, a member of the SR Central Committee. Zenzinov's appointment brought the directory's composition closer to that proposed by the SRs, i.e. Timofeev (an SR), Zenzinov, Vologodskii, General Boldyrev and Astrov. For the Siberian delegation, Zenzinov's appointment deprived the directory of much of its moral authority. Nevertheless, the Ufa accord had been reached.[13]

## THE UNSUCCESSFUL WHITE COUP IN SIBERIA

The URR was so successful at the Ufa State Conference not only because of the willingness of the SRs to make crucial concessions, but also because of the state of crisis into which the Siberian government had descended in Omsk. The Siberian government delayed so long in sending its delegation to Ufa, and was so passive once it had arrived until the very last moment, because in the aftermath of the Chelyabinsk State Conference it was torn apart by dissension, originating from a speech made in Chelyabinsk by the Minister of War Grishin-Almazov. He had insulted the Allies by stating 'that the Russians have less need of the Allies than the Allies have of the Russians',[14] and then in private talks with the Czechoslovak leader Bogdan Pavlu suggested that if the Czechoslovaks did not like it in Russia they could go home.[15] On 4 September 1918 the Siberian government decided to sack Grishin-Almazov for these tactless remarks and replace him with General Ivanov-Rinov; this move brought to a head the ever-simmering tension between the SR and the former SR members of the government.

For the former SRs in the Siberian government Grishin-Almazov's retention in the government, whatever he might have told the Allies, was an essential point of principle. For, at the end of the Chelyabinsk State Conference in August 1918, an SR delegation had asked to see the Siberian Prime Minister Vologodskii and told him that the SRs did not want either the Minister of Finance in the Siberian government Mikhailov or the War Minister Grishin-Almazov to form part of the Siberian government's delegation to the Ufa State Conference. This attempt by the SRs to dictate who should, and who should not, be a member of this delegation so incensed the former SRs that they saw it as essential that these ministers should be members of the delegation to Ufa. To them the call for Grishin-Almazov's dismissal for insulting the Allies was a pretext, part of an SR plot to prevent him attending the Ufa State Conference, and not genuine outrage at his comments, a view reinforced by the fact that at the first government meeting after the Chelyabinsk State Conference, the one loyal SR minister in the Siberian government Shatilov threatened to resign if the government did not accept his views on the question of who should be in the Ufa delegation. Despite these threats and counter-threats Grishin-Almazov was sacked as Minister of War.

In moving against Grishin-Almazov the Siberian government acted against the advice of its administrative council. The administrative council had been set up on 24 August 1918 in recognition of the fact that, with only six government members and the likelihood of a powerful delegation being absent in Ufa for much of September 1918, the government was overstretched. The administrative council comprised ten junior ministers, met in almost continual session, and was soon running the government in all but name; its undisputed leader was the former SR Finance Minister in the Siberian government Mikhailov and the administrative council rapidly became his power base. Mikhailov was incensed at the dismissal of Grishin-Almazov, and for several days would not speak to his cabinet colleague the Justice Minister Patushinskii, whom he held responsible for the dismissal. All government activity was paralysed as ministers met and lobbied in private and rumours circulated first that Mikhailov had resigned, then that Patushinskii and Shatilov had resigned. In the end it was Patushinksii who resigned, issuing a statement in which he condemned the role played by the administrative council and its interference in government. He would, he said, make a report to the Siberian Regional Assembly.[16]

In the aftermath of the Grishin-Almazov affair and the resignation of Patushinskii, the powers of the administrative council were greatly increased. It was agreed that the government would take no further decisions of such importance without first consulting the administrative council, and on 7 September 1918 – the day before the opening of the Ufa State Conference – the ministers agreed that the administrative council could act in the government's name when a majority of ministers were away from Omsk; this included the right to dissolve or summon the Siberian Regional Assembly. The question of the assembly's future was again of crucial importance since its session in July had only been prorogued and it was due to reconvene on 10 September 1918. Not only did Patushinskii intend to denounce the Siberian government when the regional assembly met, but the whole situation in Siberia had been transformed on 31 August 1918 when the Czechoslovak Legion succeeded in liberating the Trans-Siberian Railway all the way to Vladivostok and reuniting Siberia with the Far East; now deputies from all over Siberia could attend the Siberian Regional Assembly session, and contact could be re-established between the Siberian government in Omsk and those ministers elected to the underground Siberian government back in January 1918 but stranded in the Far East. As the Ufa State Conference opened, the Prime Minister of the Siberian government Vologodskii set off by train for the Far East to secure recognition from the former leader of the underground government P. Ya Derber.[17]

The Siberian Regional Assembly was opened on 10 September

1918 by its chairman I.A. Yakushev and immediately launched a campaign to bring the Siberian government under democratic control. It demanded that Patushinskii should be reinstated as Minister of Justice; it demanded that the SR A.E. Novoselov, who had just returned from the Far East and had in January 1918 been Minister of the Interior in the underground Siberian government, should be given a post in the Siberian government; it established a permanent quorum of deputies to be based in Omsk and empowered to supervise the work of the Siberian government; and finally it sent a delegation to the Far East to contact other Far Eastern members of the underground government in order to win them to the assembly's side. As the Siberian Prime Minister Vologodskii travelled east, he ordered the arrest of the regional assembly's delegation to the Far East as it reached Irkutsk; he then dissolved the Siberian Regional Assembly, determined that his talks with the remaining members of the underground government should not be complicated by this unwanted intervention.

Enraged, the Siberian Regional Assembly refused to dissolve and decided on 18 September 1918 to send a delegation comprising its chairman Yakushev, the loyal SR minister Shatilov and the former underground minister Novoselov to Omsk to protest. This delegation held talks on the 19th with V.M. Krutovskii, who was standing in for Vologodskii as Prime Minister of the Siberian government, and on 20 September 1918 all four confronted Mikhailov. The support of Krutovskii was crucial: at that moment there were three Siberian government ministers in Omsk, Krutovskii, Shatilov and Mikhailov. So, at what was ostensibly a routine cabinet meeting, Krutovskii and Shatilov raised three issues: first, the need to change the regulations governing the powers of the administrative council; second, the need to change the composition of the government's delegation to the Ufa State Conference; and third, the demand that the former minister in the underground government Novoselov be recognized as a full member of the government. Mikhailov, realizing he would be out-voted by two votes to one, left the meeting in haste to prevent it being declared quorate. But the regional assembly delegation did not give up. On 21 September 1918 Krutovskii, as Acting Prime Minister, and Yakushev, as regional assembly chairman, jointly contacted Vologodskii in Vladivostok and exchanged angry telegrams: Vologodskii insisted he had suspended, not dissolved the assembly and had done so because it had strayed well beyond the agenda agreed in advance; Yakushev stressed that the assembly would insist on Novoselov being given a ministerial post.

Later on 21 September 1918, just as it seemed the SRs' campaign was going to succeed and the Siberian regional government would be brought under democratic control and prised out of the control of Mikhailov's administrative council, White officers in Omsk staged a coup of sorts. Krutovskii, Shatilov, Yakushev and Novoselov were arrested by Colonel Volkov of the Siberian department of state security on the grounds that they were attempting to overthrow the legitimate government; the following day Novoselov was summarily shot. Although the official statement issued at the time insisted that Mikhailov knew nothing of the action by the White officers, his involvement in some capacity was certain since the morning after the arrests, on 22 September 1918, the administrative council accepted letters of resignation from both Krutovskii and Shatilov; even though these had been dictated at gun-point. The same meeting endorsed the suspension of the Siberian Regional Assembly. The announcement on 23 September 1918 that the administrative council of the Siberian government had established a commission to investigate the arrests and murder, and that Colonel Volkov had been arrested, did little to counteract the widely held view that the administrative council had encouraged the White officers to act. That, certainly, was how the local Czechoslovak military authorities interpreted events. On 24 September 1918 the Czechoslovak military command arrested the acting Siberian Minister of the Interior Gratsianov and issued an order for the arrest of Mikhailov; Mikhailov, however, was able to give his pursuers the slip.[18]

## THE RULE OF THE DIRECTORY

Thus at the very moment the directory was founded in Ufa, the Siberian government was in disarray; to prevent its democratization, to prevent SRs and SR supporters challenging the power of the administrative council and bringing the Siberian government into line with the URR sponsored Ufa State Conference, White officers had been prepared to take up arms. The first crisis the directory faced, therefore, was what to do about Novoselov's brutal murder and the attempted coup in Siberia. It was presented with a golden opportunity to assert its authority, and it flunked it. As the directory held its first sitting in Ufa on 24 September 1918 it heard a report from the Czechoslovak military authorities that the chief suspect in the affair and instigator of the plot seemed to be Mikhailov. Yet the directory's response was cautious: its leader General Boldyrev clarified that the

Siberian Regional Assembly had been suspended, not dissolved, and announced that the pre-crisis composition of the Siberian government would be restored and that those ministers who had resigned at gun-point would be reinstated; finally Argunov for the URR would be sent to Omsk to investigate the criminal aspects of the case. In Ufa, where the spirit of compromise still reigned, this might have seemed a statesmanlike solution, but to the SRs it was betrayal. It meant an end to their campaign to bring the Siberian government under democratic control: the suspension of the Siberian Regional Assembly had been confirmed and the demands for the reinstatement of Patushinskii and a government post for Novoselov had been ignored. The Czechoslovaks too were appalled. They had wanted firm action and offered the directory armed units should it resolve to clear things up by force. Although the directory agonized throughout the night of 24–25 September 1918, it turned down the Czechoslovak offer and in Omsk the arrested Gratsianov was released from custody.[19]

This was an enormous blunder by the directory, for it meant that in their first action they threw away the initiative; it would be fully six weeks before they succeeded in regaining it. The directory took no action against the murderous activities associated with Mikhailov, the leader of the administrative council, yet as an All-Russian government without an administrative apparatus of its own it would soon itself be dependent on that very same administrative council. The military situation at the front meant that Samara was too dangerous a home for the directory, but should it go to Ekaterinburg or Omsk – in both cities efficient government apparatuses existed? The URR leader Krol tried to persuade the directory to base itself in Ekaterinburg, warning both Avksentiev and Boldyrev of Mikhailov's true nature: but having first resolved to go to Ekaterinburg, then to Omsk, then to Ekaterinburg, the directory finally stopped dithering and resolved on 6 October 1918 to base itself in Omsk, fearing that this was the only city the Siberian army was actually willing to defend. They would, as Avksentiev told Krol, 'visit the wolf in its den'.[20]

Few omens in Omsk were good. True the military situation improved somewhat: on 13 October Boldyrev 1918 received an agent sent from Archangel by Poole, and plans were drawn up to advance to Ekaterinburg and launch an attack on Vyatka, linking to Poole's advance on Kotlas; but all other developments were bad. The directory was housed in a small two-storey house on the outskirts of town and had to request permission from the Minister of Communications in the Siberian government each time it wanted to use the telegraph network. On grounds of security, the SR press found itself systematically suppressed, thus on 11 October *Delo Sibiri* was closed down, as was its replacement *Delo naroda* a week later.[21] Mikhailov's clear purpose in treating the directory in this way was to make the administrative council's co-operation with the directory dependent on the directorate accepting the same sort of arrangement with the administrative council that the Siberian government had been reluctantly forced to accept; the directory, like the Siberian government, Mikhailov hoped, could be reduced to a talking shop while the administrative council ran the show. Thus when talks between the directory and the administrative council began on 13 October 1918, both sides knew where they stood, but the cards were stacked heavily in favour of the administrative council. Avksentiev was determined that the directory should not be dependent on the administrative council, but ultimately there was little he could do to prevent it. Zenzinov shared his apprehension noting the hostile attitude of Mikhailov and his clear intention of 'turning us into a decoration', but neither could prevent an agreement being reached which gave substantial powers to the administrative council, based around the pretence that the Siberian government and the administrative council were separate entities and the administrative council a neutral civil service rather than a political power broker.

It was not difficult to agree that, until the Siberian government Prime Minister and directory member Vologodskii returned from the Far East, precise details could not be agreed as to how much autonomy the Siberian government should retain in its new guise as a Siberian regional government working under the directory. In the meantime, the directory could use the administrative council's administrative apparatus; but in return, Mikhailov exacted a heavy price. Just as had been the case for the Siberian government since the War Minister Grishin-Almazov's dismissal, all directory decisions would have to be agreed with the administrative council. In particular, when the directory came to appoint its executive ministries all ministerial appointments would have to be discussed jointly by the administrative council and the directory. To gain an administrative apparatus, the directory was being asked to lose the right to appoint the ministers it chose. In essence the administrative council, which Zenzinov considered had become a toy in the hands of White officers – as the September coup attempt had shown – had the right of veto when it came to forming new All-Russian ministries.[22]

For SRs like Komuch member Brushvit, who was in Omsk at the time, as well as for URR activists like Krol, also in Omsk, this agreement betrayed the Ufa accord. The directory was not standing above all regional governments, as had been agreed, but 'trading' with them; it was not truly sovereign. The directory preferred to see things in a different light. Avksentiev was optimistic and based that optimism on the activities of General Boldyrev: he was working hard, becoming popular among the troops, strengthening his position, uniting the army – in a month's time, Avksentiev felt, White officers would no longer be strong enough to stage a coup against the directory, and in a month's time the Allies would recognize the directory; it would then be strong enough to assimilate the administrative council, strengthening it with sympathetic ministers brought in from Samara. The only alternative to this was force, and Avksentiev insisted: 'I will not have on my conscience unleashing a civil war in the anti–Bolshevik camp', a view shared fully by fellow directory member Zenzinov. So when Vologodskii returned from the Far East on 18 October 1918 the directory settled down to negotiate with the administrative council over the composition of its executive ministries.[23]

This process took two weeks. Most ministerial appointments were uncontroversial. The directory had wanted to appoint the former Komuch Departmental Director for Labour, Maiskii, Minister of Labour, but he had turned down the post even before it became apparent that the administrative council might object. The possibly contentious appointment of Minister of War proved quite uncontentious. Admiral Kolchak arrived in Omsk on 13 October 1918, having arrived in Vladivostok a month earlier: he seemed the obvious man for the job since he was a nationally known figure and as a recent arrival could stand above the Samara–Omsk politicking; after his first meeting with General Boldyrev on 14 October 1918 he was offered the job on the 16th, with the formal appointment being made on the 22nd. Vologodskii was keen that Savinkov should be made Minister of Foreign Affairs, but made no fuss when Boldyrev quashed the idea after representations from Avksentiev, and no doubt his personal objections as well. It was only the proposal that Rogovskii should be Minister of the Interior in charge of state security which caused controversy.[24]

As well as being chairman of the Komuch Council of Departmental Directors (CDD) Rogovskii had been Komuch Departmental Director for State Security and had a brigade of some 200 loyal troops at his disposal. White officers in Omsk were obsessed with the possible threat this armed force might pose to their power and independence. To such officers the appointment of Rogovskii as 'police minister' had almost mythical significance. As General K.V. Sakharov recalled:

It was certain that if Rogovskii formed his police force, his SR Party police force, then in fact all power in the country would again fall into the hands of that ill-fated party. Nobody would agree to that.[25]

Mikhailov's administrative council shared the view, common among conservative opinion in Omsk, that, if made Minister of the Interior, Rogovskii would arrive with his special armed guards from Samara and stage an SR coup. Kolchak, sucked into the general mood, made it clear he would not work with Rogovskii.[26]

The row was furious, for the administrative council counter-attacked by proposing that Mikhailov should be appointed Minister of Finance, the post he held in the Siberian government. On 27 October 1918 Avksentiev threatened to resign. The following day the directory tried to make a concession: it would agree to drop Rogovskii if the administrative council dropped Mikhailov; but the administrative council would not back down. The Czechoslovaks then intervened, insisting that Mikhailov be excluded from the list. On 29 October 1918 Zenzinov joined Avksentiev when he again threatened to resign, but after seeking the views of URR and SR advisors like Krol, Yakushev, Pavlov, Argunov, and Rogovskii himself, they decided to back down.[27] In the end the directory made a further concession. Mikhailov was appointed Minister of Finance, and Rogovskii was made Deputy Minister of the Interior, but in charge of state security and head of the police, with the right both to take part in ministerial meetings and to report directly to the directory. In a chilling reminder of the sort of police work Rogovskii might become involved in, on 26 October 1918 Moiseenko, the one-time head of the SR military commission and a founder member of the URR, was murdered by a gang of officers.[28]

However, once the ministers had been appointed, the administrative council lost the initiative it had held ever since the directory's fateful decision after the Ufa State Conference to come to Omsk despite the murder of Novoselov. Thereafter the directory stopped making concessions and began to assert its authority. On 2 November 1918 the Urals government surrendered power to the directory and transformed itself into a purely regional government; on 4 November 1918 the Siberian government did the same; and on 5 November 1918 the new executive ministers met for the first time. Their composition reflected the work put in by the administrative council: Vologodskii was made Prime Minister and nine of the fourteen ministers had served in the Siberian government at some level; but there were still all the junior government posts to fill, and the directory, as Avksentiev had hinted in October, was determined to redress the balance at this stage. Thus on 4 November 1918 the right-wing SR and Constituent Assembly deputy Oganskii – in December 1917 a member of the SR commission to welcome the Constituent Assembly – was offered the post of Deputy Minister of Agriculture.[29] On 8 November 1918 the final point of conflict between the directory and the administrative council was removed when it was agreed that the Siberian Regional Assembly would be allowed to reconvene for a final one-day session and then dissolve itself. On 10 November 1918 Avksentiev went to Tomsk and persuaded the regional assembly to do just that.

With its constitutional position finally clear, the directory really could begin to assert itself. Avksentiev was determined to handle foreign affairs as a directory matter; the Minister of Foreign Affairs he appointed had no executive powers. Vinogradov was equally determined that when the executive ministers met together they did not do so as a cabinet, but simply as a council appointed by the directory to act as advisors and executors. Thus the directory insisted that it had the power to legislate in its own right, and no laws needed to go through any Council of Ministers. A press law was quickly passed without discussion in the Council of Ministers, and the directory began to appoint its own departmental directors on all matters concerning legislation. As had been anticipated by the directory, this soon paralysed the cabinet ambitions of the Council of Ministers.[30] The directory, then, was beginning to recover the initiative when on 5 November 1918 Vologodskii raised at one of its meetings the question of the so-called Chernov Charter.

## THE DIRECTORY AND THE FUTURE OF KOMUCH

At the height of the row over the appointments of Rogovskii and Mikhailov, the Omsk branch of the Kadet Party, dominated by White officers, organized a public meeting on 29 October 1918 at which it was suggested that Avksentiev and Zenzinov were insisting on Rogovskii's nomination because they were being put under pressure by the SR Party. The nomination had been dictated to them by the SR Party Central Committee, and in this way the SRs were seeking first to control the directory and through it the executive ministries. The allegation was supported by telegrams, at the time being routinely intercepted by the administrative council's security apparatus. Central to these allegations was the document which became known as the Chernov Charter.[31]

The SR leader Chernov had arrived in Samara on 19 September 1918, but although he was given a salary of 2,500 roubles, ten times the Samara minimum, there was little in practice for him to do. He made a stirring speech to the Samara Peasant Union Congress, held from 15–23 September 1918, and no doubt was involved in the decision to grant the union 100,000 roubles for its propaganda work, and the decision of 27 September 1918 to allocate the government's agitation and cultural education department 500,000 roubles, but the tide was turning against Komuch. The Komuch Council of Departmental Directors (CDD) returned to Samara from the Ufa State Conference on 29 September 1918, but by 1 October 1918 the decision had been taken to abandon the city, and by the 6th the Bolsheviks were back in control and Komuch had retreated back to Ufa. All these upheavals meant that it was the second week in October before the CDD began to address the question of its future relationship with the directory and the All-Russian ministries once formed.[32]

Komuch was at first conciliation itself. On 13 October 1918 the CDD informed Zenzinov that its affairs had more or less been wound up: it no longer considered itself a national government, and would transform itself into a regional government for what remained of the Volga territory under the terms of the Ufa accord as soon as details were finalized. In the meantime a four-member team had been appointed to administer All-Russian concerns in the locality – Filipovskii, Vedenyapin, Nesterov and Klimushkin. These tasks were essentially two-fold, but expensive: the four-member team faced pay demands from the railway workers and the army, and would need to settle these in the name of the directory. When Zenzinov made light of these difficulties and pointed out that it was now the responsibility of the administrative council to sort out these problems, Vedenyapin snapped that his team wanted to resign these residual responsibilities as soon as possible, but since local workers and soldiers were approaching them, not the administrative council, with pay demands they had to respond.[33]

The SRs' willingness to accept the Ufa accord and wind up the affairs of the CDD changed dramatically after the Congress of Constituent Assembly Deputies had met for the first time since the Ufa State Conference. The congress had endorsed the decisions made in Ufa and had been recognized as a 'permanently functioning state legal institution' charged with reconvening the Constituent Assembly with a quorum of 250 by 1 January 1919.[34] But as its members, including Chernov and Gendelman, began to arrive in Ufa on 14 October 1918 they had more on their minds than how to assemble the Constituent Assembly. Those on the left of the SR Party had already protested at the Ufa accord: some had refused to sign it, one had even returned to Bolshevik territory in protest; in fact nearly half the SRs who had taken part in the Ufa State Conference had reservations about the accord. At the congress of deputies on 14 October, discussion centred on the protocols of the meetings of the Council of Elders held during the Ufa State Conference: many deputies were clearly unaware of the crucial concession made on this occasion, especially the notion that the only real task the existing Constituent Assembly had to perform was to dissolve itself and call fresh elections. Deputies also queried the validity of the Central Committee's vote to accept the accord, since only seven members had taken part and a telephone call from Chernov urging members not to sign had been ignored. Thus deputies were already in angry mood when the details of the agreement reached in Omsk between the directory and the administrative council began to emerge, an agreement which breached the spirit of the Ufa accord since it gave the administrative council a say in the appointment of executive ministers.

Meeting contemporaneously with the congress, the SR Party took a series of decisions hostile to the directory. A quorate Central Committee meeting of nine (the Central Committee had twenty members, but only eight were needed for a quorum) voted six against two with one abstention to reject the Ufa accord and return to the long-held SR view that a 'democratic third force' was needed to fight on two fronts, against both the Bolsheviks, the reactionaries of the left, and the White reactionaries of the right. The work of the party's delegation to the Ufa State Conference was criticized, and it was decided that, while the directory could not be opposed, the party would bypass it since its primary concern was not the directory but working to reconvene the Constituent Assembly. Joint membership of the party and the URR was also banned at this meeting.[35] All this anger was suffused in the Chernov Charter resolution adopted on 22 October 1918, which seemed to cast the White reactionary right as the main enemy. It stated:

> In anticipating the possibility of political crises, which might be brought on by the dreamers of counter-revolution, all the party's strength at the present time must be mobilized, trained in military affairs and armed so that it is ready at any moment to withstand the blows of counter-revolutionaries organizing civil war in the rear of the anti-Bolshevik front.

The work of arming the party's forces, of closing ranks, of all-round
political education and purely military mobilization, must be the main task
of the Central Committee; this, it is hoped, will give it new points of
influence along side its current, purely state influence.[36]

Clearly talk of extending party influence into military affairs and of
putting the party on a military footing in the event of armed clashes
with counter-revolutionaries would not go down well in Omsk. But
those directory members associated with the SR Party, Avksentiev and
Zenzinov, thought they could distance themselves from the Chernov
Charter. Despite the allegations of White propaganda – like that heard
in Omsk on 29 October 1918 about the charter being binding on all
SR Party members, and in particular on Zenzinov since he was an
elected member of the Central Committee – the SR Central
Committee had announced at the Ufa State Conference that it
opposed the notion of exercising political control over those of its
members who joined the directory; the Kadet Party and the Popular
Socialist Party made similar statements at the same time. Indeed, all
those joining the directory offered to leave their parties to underline
this independence, but the Council of Elders at the Ufa State
Conference decided that this was not necessary.[37]

When the Chernov Charter was shown to Zenzinov by the head of
the telegraph agency in Omsk, he decided to ignore it and instructed
the agency not to publish it under any circumstances, a decision
endorsed by Avksentiev. On 24 October 1918 Zenzinov informed the
Central Committee in Ufa that while the content of the Chernov
Charter did not bother him too much, its timing was most
unfortunate 'complicating the situation and strengthening the other
side; all the more so since we are concluding an agreement where we
are standing up for what is accepted and essential for everyone'. The
charter, he argued, reflected a misunderstanding of developments in
Omsk. He went on:

> We are standing firm on the personal make-up of the executive ministries
> and I hope we will get an agreement on conditions which are acceptable
> to us. Do not forget that, because of the collapse of the Volga front we
> have to talk about agreements when we should be concerned simply with
> implementing our decisions; the balance of real forces is apparent at every
> step.[38]

Right-wing SRs immediately sought to challenge the charter. Meeting
in Ekaterinburg on or slightly before 4 November 1918 the SR group
of deputies to the Constituent Assembly heard Oganskii, just
nominated Deputy Minister of Agriculture, and a dozen other

right-wing deputies protest at the Chernov Charter. When it came to the vote, the group split into three: Komuch president Volskii and Chernov for the left supported the charter and won the support of 22 of the 45 deputies present; Gendelman and a centre group accounted for a further ten; while the right also comprised ten, and three deputies abstained. The left alone did not have a majority, but unlike at the Ufa State Conference where the centre of the party had tended to support the right, events since had pushed the centre nearer the left. A compromise resolution was cobbled together by the left and centre, which conceded only that it had been tactless to publish the Chernov Charter resolution; Oganskii therefore informed Avksentiev that as a consequence the group of SR deputies to the Constituent Assembly was likely to split, for the right was determined to publish its protest. Avksentiev endorsed the idea of a public split: 'we have learned nothing and, it seems, are again capable of wrecking, or at least damaging the situation', he concluded.[39]

However, if Avksentiev and Zenzinov thought they could handle the impact of the Chernov Charter by ignoring it and using their allies in the SR Party to discredit it, they were mistaken. By early November 1918 versions of its contents were being reproduced by various White groups and a version of it was eventually published in the press. Thus when on 5 November 1918 Vologodskii raised the matter in the directory there was an angry scene. Zenzinov and Avksentiev stressed how little they had had to do with it; they had only seen the extracts provided for them by the head of the telegraph agency, they said. General Boldyrev was incensed by the charter and called for the arrest of the SR Central Committee; Vologodskii asked Zenzinov directly if, as a member of the SR Central Committee until joining the directory, he had been consulted on the matter. Once tempers had cooled a little, Zenzinov, Avksentiev and Vinogradov persuaded their fellow directory members Vologodskii and Boldyrev that the SR Central Committee could only be arrested if proper legal channels were followed, and a proper judicial enquiry established. This was duly done, and the executive Minister of Justice was instructed to undertake the matter. A few days later he informed Zenzinov that the whole thing had 'blown over' and there would be no arrests. That might indeed have been the case if the charter had been the only incident of SR action against the directory.[40]

A week after having said it would resign, the Komuch Council of Departmental Directors (CDD) in Ufa changed its mind. After the adoption of the Chernov Charter on 22 October 1918, the CDD informed Zenzinov on the 24th that it had decided not to liquidate itself. Its situation was in many ways desperate – a strike by railway workers and river boat crews was imminent since October's pay had not been received, the Czechoslovak troops were demoralized and uncertain why they were fighting since news of Czechoslovak independence had been received – but a response to these problems had been found; the SR Party was forming volunteer units into so-called Constituent Assembly battalions, and these would become the core of a new armed force. To help establish these, and associated Russo-Czech volunteer brigades, a special war sub-department of the Komuch CDD's agitation and cultural education department was set up on 1 November 1918 and General Notbek appointed to head it.[41]

In line with the winding up of the Urals and Siberian governments, on 3 November 1918 General Boldyrev informed the Komuch CDD that its dissolution was imminent; but rather than accept this, the Komuch CDD decided to resist, after holding talks with Czechoslovak representatives and the Congress of Constituent Assembly Deputies, which had by then moved to Ekaterinburg. The Komuch CDD pointed out that the manner in which the executive ministries had been formed – in other words the role played in this by the administrative council – meant that, far from being dissolved, the Siberian government, the parent of the administrative council, had actually been retained in a disguised form. Why, it asked, should it resign when in recent days it had done so much to restore the front: the Constituent Assembly battalions, the Russo–Czech volunteers, and other units organized by General Kappel, Fortunatov and Colonel Makhin had done much to raise morale. Work in forming more of these units and expanding them was already underway on a broad front, yet all this good work could be threatened by the news that the Komuch CDD had been dissolved. The directory would have to annul its decision, the Komuch CDD insisted and informed the directory that it intended to seek the support of the Czechoslovak National Council to this end. At all costs the public announcement of dissolution had to be delayed.[42]

On 5 November 1918, the very day the Chernov Charter was discussed in the directory, Komuch's Departmental Director for Foreign Affairs Vedenyapin contacted Zenzinov and in a forceful telegram spelt out once again the case for not dissolving the Komuch CDD, and reminding Zenzinov that the SR Central Committee had called every party member to arms. The party's volunteers, he went on, were by then not only holding the front but advancing back towards Samara; if the Komuch CDD were dissolved these forces would abandon the front, so an exception had to be made and the

Komuch CDD spared from dissolution. Zenzinov was taken aback: the Komuch CDD had known for three weeks that it would be dissolved, he said; their demand was quite impossible, since, as a *quid pro quo*, the Siberian government would be restored, which would destroy all the directory's work. By 7 November 1918 the Komuch CDD was only slightly more amenable. It demanded to know the precise terms on which the Urals and Siberian governments had been dissolved, so that it could consider the full implications of taking such a step.[43]

When on 10 November 1918 the directory summonsed the Komuch CDD to Chelyabinsk to meet the so-called liquidation commission charged with winding up its affairs, the Komuch CDD decided not to attend and informed the Congress of Constituent Assembly Deputies of this decision asking them to endorse it. On 12 November 1918 the Komuch CDD was again protesting to Zenzinov that the Ufa accord had been broken by the directory coming to what was essentially a bilateral arrangement with the Siberian government. It therefore put down the terms to be met before it would agree to dissolve: these amounted to a public statement by the new ministers that they would stick by the Ufa accord and surrender their mandate to the Constituent Assembly when quorate, at the same time granting immunity from arrest for all Constituent Assembly deputies. Ignoring this ultimatum, Zenzinov informed the Komuch CDD that the liquidation commission was about to leave Chelyabinsk for Ufa and would soon be with them. He urged them not to rock the boat, especially since he believed the Allies were on the point of recognizing the directory. The Komuch CDD made no substantive response, but curtly reminded Zenzinov that its volunteer divisions were now advancing and had recently captured a Bolshevik regiment; the Czechoslovaks could report that the front in Ekaterinburg was also firm.[44]

But behind this war of words, some sort of compromise stance was beginning to emerge. The directory could object to the tenor of the Komuch CDD's ultimatum, but its content, that the Ufa accord be implemented, was easy for it to accept since all its actions were governed by the accord. Equally, by 15 November 1918, when the Komuch CDD was considering its negotiating stance for the arrival of the liquidation commission, it too was beginning to show more flexibility. It informed the Congress of Constituent Assembly Deputies that it planned to put forward a scheme which just might find favour with the directory. The idea was to give a wide degree of autonomy to the Ufa region, putting it under the authority of a chief plenipotentiary. The plenipotentiary, to be appointed by the directory from a list of three names, would appoint a number of assistants, all deputies to the Constituent Assembly, to take charge of departments such as internal affairs, production, education, state property, and work within Bolshevik-controlled zones.

This was a greater degree of autonomy than that proposed for other regions, but it would be under the overall control of the directory and it could possibly be justified with reference to the unique conditions operating so near the front. In any event, it was clearly part of a bargaining strategy which would enable the Komuch CDD to dissolve itself formally, while retaining its distinctive commitment to the Constituent Assembly; there were also clear parallels with Chaikovskii's proposal in Archangel for a military governor responsible to the directory in the northern battle zone. Was there the basis here for a compromise? White officers clearly did not like what they heard, for the telegraph between the Komuch CDD in Ufa and the Congress of Constituent Assembly Deputies in Ekaterinburg was suddenly cut as this negotiating stance was being discussed.[45]

While Zenzinov was busy trying to persuade the SRs to wind up the Komuch CDD, General Boldyrev was determined to put an end to the volunteer units; having struggled to establish a unified command at the Ministry of War it was unacceptable to have to cope with armed units controlled by the agitation department of the Komuch CDD. On 6 November 1918 Boldyrev ordered the Komuch CDD to stop forming volunteer battalions and to dissolve those already formed.[46] There was no satisfactory response. Indeed on 8 November 1918 the Congress of Constituent Assembly Deputies endorsed the decision to establish worker-peasant volunteer brigades and Russo-Czech battalions; it also sung the praises of the volunteers fighting in Izhevsk and the Kama valley who, isolated from the rest of Komuch territory since their initial insurrection in early August 1918, were staging a dramatic, if doomed, counter-offensive. It was equally clear that the Czechoslovaks were turning a blind eye to this clear challenge to General Boldyrev's authority.[47] On 15 November 1918 Boldyrev set off on a tour of the front, determined to put a stop to all political-cultural educational work in the army, including the illegal formation of volunteer units. He had Avksentiev's agreement summarily to execute anyone found responsible for founding party-based military units within the army.[48]

## THE WHITES OVERTHROW THE GREEN DIRECTORY

Among White officer circles in Omsk vague plans to overthrow the directory had been under discussion since its arrival in the city. From mid-October 1918 General Boldyrev was being warned about coup attempts, and he was well aware of the 'thirst for dictatorship' developing among the officer corps.[49] Such talk had been particularly current during the row about Rogovskii, Mikhailov and the composition of the All-Russian ministries; on 27 October 1918, at one point in this long running dispute, Vinogradov had, momentarily, resigned from the directory and suggested to General Boldyrev that all the other members of the directory should resign as well so that he, Boldyrev, could take over as dictator. The same day Boldyrev noted in his diary that Admiral Kolchak and the conservative politicians gathering in Omsk were increasingly of the view that the directory should be slimmed down to one; the following day he noted that in such officers' discussions it was increasingly Kolchak rather than himself who was cast in the role of dictator.[50]

Once the All-Russian ministries had been formed at the beginning of November, however, such speculation was quelled for a while, although some officers toured the front finding widespread support for the idea of a dictatorship among the fellow officers they canvassed. The favoured candidate for dictator, Kolchak, travelled to Ekaterinburg on 9 November 1918 to attend a ceremony to present medals to members of the Czechoslovak Legion. In private Kolchak spoke in the most disparaging terms of the Czechoslovak soldiers, believing that the sooner they left Russia the better, and perhaps he said as much to General Boldyrev when their trains crossed on 16 November 1918 as Kolchak returned to Omsk and Boldyrev set off for the front. Certainly a British officer with Kolchak, Colonel John Ward, gained the impression that the two men had quarrelled about something, and on his return on 17 November 1918 Kolchak informed the All-Russian ministers that he intended to resign as Minister of War.[51] With General Boldyrev out of the way, and Kolchak's relations with him soured, serious plotting began.

During 17 November 1918, several officers approached Kolchak and urged him to act against the directory; Kolchak was non-committal, but his supporters decided to act. During the night of 17–18 November, as they were holding talks with Dedusenko, Maslov and Likhach, victims themselves of the thirst for dictatorship among White officers in Archangel, Avksentiev and Zenzinov were arrested by the Omsk officer corps, along with Argunov and Rogovskii. On 18 November 1918 the executive ministers met and Vinogradov proposed, as he had done once before, the establishment of a dictatorship; in the subsequent voting one minister (presumably Vinogradov) voted for General Boldyrev, the rest for Admiral Kolchak. Vologodskii and Vinogradov, the surviving members of the directory, resigned their posts, but Vologodskii, the former Prime Minister in the Siberian government, was persuaded to accept a new job within Kolchak's administration.[52]

Hearing of the coup on 18 November 1918, General Boldyrev ordered Admiral Kolchak to surrender power, and toyed with the idea of getting Czechoslovak support for a counter-move. However, he had no desire to seek the support of Chernov and the SRs, whom he was in the process of trying to discipline, and on 20 November 1918 rejected an SR plea to issue a call to arms. A dignified resignation then seemed the only honourable course.[53] As to the SRs, the Komuch CDD announced from Ufa on 18 November 1918 that it had assumed power in all the territory that had once belonged to Komuch and that it was seeking to hold talks with the Czechoslovaks: it also asked the Congress of Constituent Assembly Deputies to convene in full session in Ekaterinburg. Meanwhile the Congress of Constituent Assembly Deputies had already established a committee headed by Chernov, and including Volskii and Brushvit, which called on citizens to obey its instructions in the defence of democracy.[54]

Both General Boldyrev and the SRs had instinctively looked to the Czechoslovaks for support. Their representative in Ufa contacted the Czechoslovak headquarters in Ekaterinburg on 18 November 1918 seeking instructions, but clearly expecting the National Council to condemn the coup firmly. Krol too expected the Czechoslovaks to act to restore Boldyrev and the directory; but the Czechoslovaks did not respond.[55] Back on 2 November 1918 General J. Syrovy, the new Czechoslovak Commander-in-Chief, had informed his French superior General Janin that both divisions of the Czechoslovak Legion were so demoralized they needed to be 'taken out of line, rested and purged of agitators'. By 6 November 1918 Boldyrev could claim that it was Russian troops alone who held the Siberian front. The armistice with Germany at the end of the First World War on 11 November 1918 only reinforced the Czechoslovak demand to leave Russia.[56] When the coup occurred, Syrovy was called on by his superiors to order the Czechoslovaks not to become involved, supporting neither Boldyrev nor Kolchak. When the Czechoslovak National Council issued a statement on 21 November 1918 it was an appeal of despair and protest, not a call to arms; it merely regretted that the coup had meant that troops needed at the front were active in the rear, and that a government based on law had been destroyed so soon after it had begun to operate. On 23 November 1918 the Komuch CDD issued a bitter protest at this weak response by the Czechoslovak National Council and sent a copy to Masaryk himself.[57]

The coup was the work of headstrong and embittered young officers, for whom, like for Chaplin in Archangel, the directory was repeating all the old mistakes of Kerensky. The leader of the coup was Colonel Volkov, the same Colonel Volkov involved in the attempted coup in Omsk in September 1918. As antagonistic to the SRs as to the Bolsheviks, men of this type felt left-wing politicians were interfering in everything, just as had happened to the army under Kerensky. The official gloss on the coup made this clear. The plotters' motivation was considered fully justified: links had been discovered between the arrested members of the directory and political activists engaged in anti-state activity by propagandizing in the army for the formation of purely party-based armed groups. These links were established by the refusal of those concerned to act against the Chernov Charter – far from leaving the party or protesting in any way, Zenzinov had continued to report to the SR Central Committee on the work of the directory.[58]

However, the real position of the directory was rather different. The plotters made their move when the directory was taking determined action against both left and right. One element of the SRs' alleged interference in military affairs was their success in disciplining monarchist White officers. On 13 November 1918 a certain cossack officer, Ataman Krasilnikov, had publicly sung 'God Save the Tsar' at a banquet given for Allied representatives; this was not the first occasion on which this had happened and Zenzinov succeeded in persuading the directory to order his arrest. Krasilnikov became Volkov's co-conspirator in the 18 November coup.[59] By acting as he did Krasilnikov not only avoided arrest, but brought down the directory at the very moment it was discovering a new authority. It had established the All-Russian ministries; it had begun to assert its powers over the administrative council; it showed no signs of giving in to the Komuch CDD in Ufa and appeared to be about to coax them towards agreeing a satisfactory compromise; far from being dictated to by the SR Party, Avksentiev and Zenzinov were prepared to see a split among the congress of Constituent Assembly deputies publicly to discredit the Chernov Charter; Boldyrev had gone to the front with powers to execute on the spot all concerned with volunteer party-based units; and finally, as Zenzinov had tried to make clear in his bitter exchanges with the Komuch CDD, the directory was on the point of being recognized by the Allies.

The British Cabinet decided to recognize the directory on 14 November 1918, and on the 16th the British consul in Siberia was informed of the fact, and told that the only likely condition to be put on recognition was that the directory should 'deal firmly' with Chernov. This news reached Omsk from the Russian representative in London, K.D. Nabokov, whose facility for coded communication with Russia had just been restored by the British as a sign of growing confidence in the directory, and who was already in communication with Avksentiev.[60] The directory was overthrown not because it was inherently weak, but because it was in danger of succeeding. Much as its opponents had feared when they started the brouhaha about the Chernov Charter, the Green patriotic socialists were getting a grip on the directory, and via that were seeking to control the All-Russian ministries and outmanoeuvre the administrative council.

Unlike in Archangel, where the Allies took prompt action against the White plotters, in Omsk the Allies just looked on. This was because in the Allies' original plan for intervention in Russia Siberia was to be a sideshow. Diplomats of the calibre of Lindley and Noulens had all been moved to Archangel; quite who was responsible for the political side of developments in Siberia was a constant concern of the British government at cabinet meetings throughout September 1918. Apart from the Czechoslovaks, the only Allied representation of any weight in the region was the military mission under the command of General Knox, in 1917 the British military attaché in Petrograd; but this was a military rather than a political mission, which had arrived in Siberia at the same time as Admiral Kolchak and was charged with encouraging all forces sympathetic to the Allies to advance on Perm and Vyatka. Knox's personal views were well-known. As General Boldyrev noted in his diary after their first meeting on 21 October 1918: 'Knox hated socialists, and considered that a firm military dictatorship was quite enough to deal with a bunch of rebels'. This meeting took place during the row concerning Rogovskii, Mikhailov and the composition of the All-Russian ministries, and Knox 'threatened to get together a band of soldiers and overthrow us if we did not reach an agreement with the Siberians; he was, he said jokingly, a Siberian'. Knox was also known to consider Avksentiev as 'no better than Kerensky', and had told Boldyrev that in Britain Chernov would have been shot for issuing the Chernov Charter. However, this was simply ill-humoured rhetoric. Before leaving Omsk for Vladivostok ten days before the coup occurred, Knox reported to London: 'Kolchak is being urged by right elements to effect a coup d'état. I told him that any attempt of this sort would at present be fatal.'[61]

During and immediately after the coup, Colonel J.F. Nielsen, left in charge by Knox, became carried away with excitement and enthusiastically endorsed what Kolchak's supporters planned and achieved; but this was the exuberance of an officer who had been with Kornilov at the time of his unsuccessful coup attempt in August 1917.[62] Kolchak's coup was a Russian affair, a move by White officers to hijack the Allies' carefully laid plans for intervention in support of Russian democracy. The wheel had turned full circle since Kornilov's failed coup fourteen months earlier, only this time there was no pretence that the plotters were working with the directory in order to strengthen it. Back in August 1917, Savinkov had proposed a democratic government combined with firm military discipline, only to find this did not accord with the true motives of Kornilov's backers. In autumn 1918 it was General Boldyrev, not Admiral Kolchak, who had restored discipline in the army; the directory was a democratic regime with a disciplined army, but it was still overthrown by White officers of the reactionary right. Just as when Kornilov's true intentions were revealed in the casual asides of his adjutant Zavoiko to the liberal politician V.N. Lvov, so Kolchak's coup was a straightforward attempt at counter-revolution, turning the clock back to the ambitions of the first counter-revolutionary conspirators of April 1917.

## NOTES

1. The fullest accounts of the Ufa State Conference are I. Maiskii, *Demokraticheskaya Kontrrevolyutsiya* (Moscow 1923), p. 215 et seq; V.G. Boldyrev, *Direktoriya Kolchak, Interventy* (Novonikolaevsk 1925), p. 35 et seq.; and L.A. Krol, *Za tri goda* (Vladivostok 1921), p. 95 et seq. See also V.L. Utgofa, 'Ufimskoe Gosudarstvennoe Soveshchanie 1918' *Byloe* no. 16 (Petrograd 1921), p. 38; G.K. Gins, *Sibir' Soyuzniki i Kolchak* (Peking 1921) vol. 1, p. 204 et seq; and V.M. Zenzinov, *Iz zhizni revolyutsionera* (Paris 1919), p. 110.

2. For the council of elders, see Krol, *Za tri goda*, p. 96; for the Czechoslovaks, see Maiskii, *Demokraticheskaya*, p. 232 and K.V. Sakharov, *Belaya Sibir'* (Munich 1923), p. 14.

3. State Archive of the Russian Federation (GARF) 144.1.30.3, 144.1.30.7.

4. Utgofa, 'Ufimskoe', pp. 28–30; Krol, *Za tri goda*, p. 130. For the

evacuation of the bank and executions, see GARF 670.1.1.65 and 670.1.1.67.

GARF 670.1.1.30.

Krol, *Za tri goda*, pp. 80, 100.

Krol, *Za tri goda*, p. 100; GARF 670.1.37.4.

Gins, *Sibir'* vol. 1, p. 205.

Maiskii, *Demokraticheskaya*, p. 219; Krol, *Za tri goda*, pp. 102–22; Utgofa, 'Ufimskoe', p. 30. For the atmosphere of 'threat', see Boldyrev, *Direktoriya*, p. 45.

Krol, *Za tri goda*, pp. 125, 130.

Krol, *Za tri goda*, p. 122; Gins, *Sibir'* vol. 1, p. 242.

Maiskii, *Demokraticheskaya*, p. 243; Gins, *Sibir'* vol. 1, p. 227.

For the SR proposal, see GARF 667.1.17.25. For unease about Zenzinov, see Krol, *Za tri goda*, p. 130; Boldyrev, *Direktoriya*, p. 48; and V.M. Zenzinov (ed.), *Gosudarstvennyi perevorot Admirala Kolchaka v Omske 18 noyabrya 1918 goda: Sbornik Dokumentov* (Paris 1919), p. 21.

Gins, *Sibir'* vol. 1, p. 195.

Krol, *Za tri goda*, p. 86.

Gins, *Sibir'* vol. 1, pp. 185, 197, 201.

For the right to dissolve the assembly, see S.P. Melgunov, *Tragediya Admirala Kolchaka* (Belgrade 1930) Part 1, p. 174; for the Siberian railway, see A. Vergé, *Avec les Tchécoslovaques* (Paris 1926), p. 140; otherwise Gins, *Sibir'* vol. 1, pp. 198, 207.

Gins, *Sibir'* vol. 1, pp. 212, 219–22, 235.

Krol, *Za tri goda,* p. 136; Maiskii, *Demokraticheskaya*, p. 255. For the Czechoslovaks, see Boldyrev, *Direktoriya*, p. 49.

Krol, *Za tri goda*, p. 140; Boldyrev, *Direktoriya*, p. 63.

For the military plans, see Boldyrev, *Direktoriya*, pp. 61, 73; for the situation of the directory, see Maiskii, *Demokraticheskaya*, p. 304; for the SR press, see Melgunov, *Tragediya* Part 2, p. 69.

Gins, *Sibir'* vol. 1, pp. 263–6; Boldyrev, *Direktoriya*, p. 70; Krol, *Za tri goda*, p. 147.

For Brushvit, see Krol, *Za tri goda*, p. 145; for Avksentiev and Zenzinov, see Maiskii, *Demokraticheskaya*, pp. 310, 312.

For Maiskii, see his *Demokraticheskaya*, p. 314; for Kolchak and Savinkov, see Boldyrev, *Direktoriya*, pp. 72, 81–3.

Sakharov, *Belaya Sibir'*, p. 17.

Gins, *Sibir'* vol. 1, pp. 276, 306.

For Avksentiev's first threat to resign, see Boldyrev, *Direktoriya*, p. 86; for th Czechoslovaks, see Melgunov, *Tragediya* Part 2, p. 53; otherwise, Krol, *Za tri goda* p. 151.

Maiskii, *Demokraticheskaya*, pp. 307, 315; V.M. Zenzinov (ed.), *Gosudarstvennyi perevorot Admirala Kolchaka v Omske 18 noyabrya 1918 goda: Sbornik Dokumentov* (Paris 1919), p. 19.

For the Urals government, see Krol, *Za tri goda*, p. 155; for the government, see Gins, *Sibir'* vol. 1, p. 282; for Oganskii, see Zenzinov, *Perevorot*, p. 68.

30. For the assembly, see Boldyrev, *Direktoriya*, p. 95; for the directory, see Gins, *Sibir'* vol. 1, p. 288.
31. Krol, *Za tri goda,* p. 151.
32. Maiskii, *Demokraticheskaya*, pp. 66, 264. For Chernov's salary, see GARF 670.1.1.78; for other financial matters, see 670.1.1.81 and 670.1.2.48.
33. GARF 144.1.22.1–3.
34. Maiskii, *Demokraticheskaya*, p. 238; GARF 144.1.22.3.
35. M. Jansen, *A Show Trial under Lenin* (The Hague 1982), pp. 4, 100; S.P. Melgunov, *N.V. Chaikovskii v gody grazhdanskoi v iny* (Paris 1929), p. 155.
36. Krol, *Za tri goda*, p. 156.
37. Zenzinov, *Perevorot,* pp. 171, 187.
38. GARF 144.1.22.7. For the decision not to publish, see Zensinov, *Perevorot*, p. 191.
39. Zenzinov, *Perevorot*, pp. 68–9, 192.
40. Zenzinov, *Perevorot,* pp. 191–2.
41. For Notbek's appointment, see GARF 670.1.1.95; otherwise 144.1.22.6–9.
42. GARF 144.1.22.9–11.
43. GARF 144.1.22.12, 144.1.22.17.
44. GARF 144.1.22.19–23.
45. GARF 144.1.22.24.
46. GARF 144.1.22.16.
47. Melgunov, *Tragediya* Part 2, pp. 29–30; Melgunov, *Chaikovskii*, p. 156. For Izhevsk, see S.M. Berk, 'The "Class Tragedy" of Izhevsk: working class opposition to Bolshevism in 1918' *Russian History* vol. 2, no. 2 (1975), pp. 176–90.
48. Zenzinov, *Perevorot*, pp. 189, 192.
49. Krol, *Za tri goda*, p. 146; Boldyrev, *Direktoriya*, p. 59.
50. Boldyrev, *Direktoriya*, p. 86.
51. P. Fleming, *The Fate of Admiral Kolchak* (London 1963), pp. 104–9.
52. The coup is discussed in exhaustive detail in Melgunov, *Tragediya* Part 2, and is described in Fleming, *Kolchak* p. 108; Maiskii, *Demokraticheskaya* p. 322; Gins, *Sibir'* vol. 1, p. 306 et seq. The official justification for the coup is in Zenzinov, *Perevorot*, p. 19 et seq.
53. Zenzinov, *Perevorot*, p. 9; Melgunov, *Tragediya* Part 2, pp. 159–63.
54. GARF 144.1.22.26, 144.1.22.32; Gins, *Sibir'* vol. 2, p. 12.
55. GARF 144.1.22.27; Krol, *Za tri goda*, p. 158.
56. Fleming, *Kolchak*, p. 100; Gins, *Sibir'* vol. 1, p. 296.
57. For Syrovy, see Melgunov, *Tragediya* Part 2, p. 160 and GARF 144.1.22.37; for the statement, see Zenzinov, *Perevorot*, p. 73; for the protest, see 144.1.20.1–4.
58. Zenzinov, *Perevorot*, pp. 19, 37.
59. V.M. Zenzinov, *Iz zhizni revolyutsionera* (Paris 1919), p. 115; Melgunov, *Tragediya* Part 2, p. 90.
60. M. Kettle, *Churchill and the Archangel Fiasco* (London 1992), pp. 8–13.
61. Fleming, *Kolchak*, p. 113. For Knox's comments to Boldyrev, see the latter's *Direktoriya*, pp. 79, 83, 93.

62. For Nielsen and Kornilov, see Sakharov, *Belaya Sibir'*, p. 18. In his study Kettle (*Archangel* p. 13) paints a picture of Nielsen being in close touch with plotters like Sakharov, something confirmed by Sakharov (p. 18), but suggests his influence was limited to giving the mistaken advice that the Allies would welcome a coup.

# Conclusion

By staging the coup in Omsk on 18 November 1918, the White generals hijacked the civil war, turning it from a war between Bolsheviks and patriotic socialists, a Red versus Green civil war, into a war between Whites and Reds. By their action, by turning the first civil war into a second civil war, the White generals guaranteed the Bolshevik victory; whether the patriotic socialists could have won their first civil war was left unknown, for they had suffered military reverses, but not a military defeat. But after the White versus Red civil war was over, after seven million deaths, the Russian population was in no state to see a resumption of the Red versus Green struggle in 1921. The Russian Civil War did much to form the nature of the Bolshevik regime; but it was in the Red versus Green civil war that the Bolsheviks' nature was first revealed. When peace returned to Russia, the Bolsheviks put the victors of the Constituent Assembly elections on trial; seventy years later, when they put their own record to the electorate for the first time, the Bolsheviks were no more successful than they had been in 1918.

## FROM TERROR TO DEFENCE OF THE NATION

When news of Kolchak's coup reached Archangel, Lindley responded with typical far-sightedness. He informed Balfour:

> The coup d'état of Kolchak seems to me as unfortunate as it could well be. I do not believe that any dictator relying for support on the officers and upper classes only, has any chance of success. He will only serve to

alienate the mass of the population from the cause of order and throw the waverers into the arms of the Bolsheviks . . . We have got to choose between supporting the old officers and upper classes, who, thoroughly discredited under the old regime, have learned nothing and dream of a return to the old order, and supporting people who are unpractical and difficult to work with but who have a real following in the country and wish to see a new order arise out of the present chaos.[1]

Realistically there was no more chance of Kolchak succeeding in his mission than there had been of Kornilov succeeding in his. Those standing behind them were the same industrial interest groups that had bandied around the names of both Kornilov and Kolchak as possible saviours of Russia in the conspiracies of spring 1917. They had no chance of success, and they did indeed 'throw waverers into the arms of the Bolsheviks'.

This was all the more remarkable because in August and September 1918 the Bolshevik regime had never been more isolated; with the loss of Kazan, it clung to power sandwiched between the democratic forces on the Volga and the Germans in the Ukraine, sustaining itself by a trade treaty with Germany which reduced Russia to a state of 'slavery' and the ruthless application of terror. While the economic terms of the treaty were indeed humiliating – Russia had to supply Germany with one quarter of all Baku's oil production and pay six billion marks in alleged compensation for nationalizations and other losses[2] – the treaty enabled Lenin to win the first round of the civil war on the Volga. The battles for Kazan, lost by the Bolsheviks at the start of August but retaken at the start of September, were crucial in this regard. Had the People's Army been able to retain control of Kazan the whole future of the war would have been different.

Three days after the fall of Kazan, the Russo–German trade agreement was initialled on 10 August 1918. Although the treaty would not be signed until 27 August 1918, Lenin at once began a massive reorientation of his army on the correct assumption that the Germans had taken his bait. Troops were pulled away from the defensive screens established in the spring to check a German advance and sent to the Volga; between 25 July and 18 August 1918 30,000 men were moved to the Eastern Army Group to confront the People's Army. By 28 August 1918 the fighting on the Volga reached a crucial turning point. General Kappel's People's Army made a dramatic move to outflank the Red Army and seize the Romanov bridge across the Volga at Sviyazhk, some twenty miles west of Kazan. The manoeuvre failed, the Red Army advanced and Kazan was recaptured. Lenin's reliance on the Germans had worked; if Field Marshal Haig saved

Lenin in the early summer of 1918, when British troops stemmed the German advance in France and dissuaded the Kaiser from overthrowing the Bolshevik regime, then in the late summer the Kaiser saved Lenin by agreeing to the August 1918 trade treaty.[3]

Whether Lenin had won a definitive victory against the democratic forces was by no means certain. The capture of Kazan in September and then Samara in October certainly put the People's Army on the defensive, but as the SRs constantly stressed during the last days of the directory, after an initial rout, volunteer units were staging a successful counter-offensive by the first fortnight in November 1918. On 5 November 1918 an offensive aimed at recapturing Samara was begun, and on 12 November 1918 the SR administration in Ufa could boast that a whole Bolshevik regiment had been taken prisoner. The successful recapture of Samara was expected with some confidence.[4]

The other prop on which the survival of Lenin's isolated regime had depended in the autumn of 1918 was terror. Official statistics put the number of those shot by the Bolsheviks in the second half of 1918 at 4,500, but that figure included only those who underwent some sort of trial; summary executions after incidents like the Yaroslavl insurrection gave a total, admittedly calculated by hostile commentators, of over 50,000 executions. Martov put the number of those executed by the end of October at 10,000. Whatever the precise figures, Lenin and his regime had no qualms about admitting that their regime depended in the autumn of 1918 on the judicious use of 'red terror'.[5]

That terror also affected the Allies. Captain Cromie had been killed in Petrograd when the Bolsheviks raided the British Embassy on 3 September 1918, and Lockhart had been arrested and held virtual hostage, along with the whole of what remained of the British community in Russia. They were released only when Germany's defeat in the First World War was certain. The end of that war removed the reason for Allied intervention; after 11 November 1918 there was no need for a new Eastern Front on the Volga. What motivated continued intervention was Lenin's use of terror. When on 13 November 1918 the British government debated whether or not to continue its efforts in Russia, its decision to do so was to be accompanied with the publication of all the details Lockhart had gathered about the true nature of the Bolsheviks' bloody regime: Balfour pointed out that 'the people they had treated worst were people whom we should regard in this country as "blood-red socialists" '. Such was the nature of the civil war within democracy.[6]

Kolchak's coup put an end to the Bolsheviks' isolation and brought many patriotic socialists into an unhappy alliance with Lenin, just as

Lindley had predicted it would. Lenin was no less committed to the doctrinaire socialist experiment on which he had embarked and which had led to his isolation than he had been in November 1917 when he expelled the conciliatory Bolsheviks, in January 1918 when he dissolved the Constituent Assembly, or in May 1918 when he decided on an alliance with German imperialism; but after Kolchak's coup he was able to wrap that experiment up in the twin flags of progress and nationalism. The Allies, although inspired by Balfour's moral outrage at the evils of Bolshevism, took an essentially pragmatic stance of supporting any anti-Bolshevik government that might emerge; this dragged them down the road not only of half-hearted support for Kolchak but support for the generals on the Don who, with the end of the First World War, the defeat of Turkey and the German evacuation of the Ukraine, could suddenly be reached with ease through the Black Sea.

Kolchak's coup destroyed the URR: it had looked to the Allies to support democracy, and the Allied willingness, no matter how half-hearted, to continue to aid Kolchak and the other civil war generals after the coup simply removed the organization's *raison d'être*; some members swallowed hard and joined Kolchak, others quietly emigrated. As an organization it simply evaporated, leaving no records other than the memoirs of a few activists – and yet it had so nearly succeeded in forming a patriotic socialist government for Russia. The URR's fellow socialists, the SRs and Mensheviks, had always been suspicious of Allied motives, and with the defeat of Germany on 11 November 1918 could see little justification for continued Allied involvement, and none at all after the 18 November 1918 coup.

In October and November 1918, as the First World War came to an end, the Mensheviks began to issue statements critical of the continuing foreign intervention, banning further armed struggle against the Bolsheviks and recognizing the July 1918 Soviet Constitution; reconvening the Constituent Assembly was relegated to a long-term aim. As early as October 1918 British agents were picking up rumours of secret talks between the Bolsheviks and the SR and Mensheviks about the formation of a coalition government. Kolchak's coup accelerated this process. The first three months of 1919 saw 'something like pluralism' develop in the political life of Moscow, and the key development in this regard was the willingness of the more left-wing SRs to sink their differences with the Bolsheviks in a joint struggle against reaction.[7]

On 5 December 1918, as the Red Army approached Ufa, the remnants of the Komuch (CDD), the remnants of the Congress of

Constituent Assembly Deputies, and those members of the SR Central Committee then in Ufa, met and resolved to end the armed struggle with the Bolsheviks. This was in line with the decision reached on 8 December 1918 by the Moscow Bureau of the Central Committee that the struggle on two fronts now meant temporarily suspending the armed struggle against the Bolsheviks. Thus when Ufa fell Volskii, the former president of Komuch, and Central Committee member K.S. Burevoi stayed in the city and took the lead in opening talks with the Bolsheviks on 10 January 1919 which culminated in a public call by the Congress for the People's Army to stop fighting the Red Army and turn its weapons instead on Kolchak.[8]

The Ufa delegation then came to Moscow for further talks, conducted on the soviet side by Kamenev, that long-term protagonist of the idea of a socialist coalition. The talks were in Ufa's eyes talks held not between the Bolshevik and SR parties, but between the Constituent Assembly and the Soviet; the Ufa delegation's demand was a coalition socialist government, responsible to the Constituent Assembly, but in line with their earlier stance in the directory negotiations, a new Constituent Assembly would be elected at once. As the talks continued into February 1919, Volskii appeared willing to concede that the reconvening of the Constituent Assembly was no longer essential, a stance for which he was censured by an SR conference in Moscow on 6 February 1919; but even this conference hinted that a reform of the Soviet constitution to give peasants equal voting rights with workers might be the basis of a compromise. On 20 February 1919 Kamenev announced that the ban on the SR Party participating in the soviets had been lifted, a ban imposed on 14 June 1918 after the insurrection on the Volga had begun. Political pluralism within the Soviet constitution seemed to be back on the agenda with the reappearance of both the Menshevik and SR press.[9]

Political pluralism was not Lenin's style, especially since defeat at the hands of Kolchak had seriously weakened the SRs' negotiating stance; once the order for the People's Army to lay down its arms had been obeyed, the SRs had played their only card and, as during the Railway Workers' Union talks and the fighting on Pulkovo Heights in October 1917, Lenin could safely ignore any political agreement once the military position was clear. Freedom for the SR and Menshevik press lasted for only a few weeks as the Bolsheviks reasserted their dictatorship, and only one faction of the SR Party signed a formal agreement with the Bolsheviks.

Nevertheless, the Mensheviks and SRs loyally sank their differences with the Bolsheviks until victory had been achieved and Admiral

Kolchak, General Denikin and General Yudenich defeated. Then, with the strike wave in Petrograd in February 1921, the insurrection in Kronstadt in March 1921, and the peasant war in Tambov from August 1920 to June 1921, the Red versus Green civil war burst into flames again. Of these incidents the most serious was Tambov, since it was inspired by SR policies, organized by SRs and former SRs, and forced on Lenin the New Economic Policy based on concessions to the peasantry. For these concessions to be purely economic and not political, it was essential to ensure that the SR Party was destroyed. And so in 1922 a show trial of the surviving SR leaders was staged which involved such prominent participants in the events of 1918 as Gendelman, Gots, Likhach, Vedenyapin, Dedusenko, Perkhurov and Verkhovskii.[10] This was the last, brutal act of the Red versus Green civil war which had started in June 1918 with the insurrection in Samara, but had been smouldering since Lenin's seizure of power in October 1917; it finally buried the hope that legitimacy might be restored to the regime by a return to political pluralism within the soviets.

## UNPRACTICAL PEOPLE

The Russian Civil War was an unnecessary war. It was a war brought about by Lenin when he wrecked the Railway Workers' Union talks on 4 November 1917, but held in check by the political crisis brought about by the Treaty of Brest-Litovsk. That crisis led Lenin to amend his strategy, but not his vision. His vision was a muddled version of Marx's writings on the Paris Commune, his strategy at first a European-wide revolutionary insurrection to turn the First World War into an international civil war. He did not abandon his vision, but realized that in the absence of an international civil war he would have to impose his views through a civil war in Russia, and could do so by relying on the greed of the German imperialists. The German alliance enabled him to win the difficult civil war with Russian patriotic socialists; he could manage the easy civil war with the White generals without any assistance.

But once this unnecessary civil war had started, why did the regime established by the patriotic socialists collapse so ignominiously, especially since by the autumn of 1918 the Bolsheviks had so little popular support and the SRs appeared to have retained the support of the peasantry? The British consul Lindley talked in his letter to

Foreign Minister Balfour of the difficulty of working with 'unpractical people' like the leaders of the URR; the failure of Russian patriotic socialists to overthrow the Bolshevik dictatorship could well have such a simple explanation. There were, of course, other reasons, but if what was meant by unpracticability was an absence of the sort of political ruthlessness shown by their opponents on both left and right, then Lindley's judgement had more than a grain of truth in it.

At one level the URR leaders were very practical people. They nearly succeeded in turning a disaster into a triumph. The URR would certainly have succeeded if the Allies' 'great enterprise' had all gone according to plan. If the Czechoslovaks had started moving towards Archangel on 22 May 1918 they would have arrived in position spread out along the track from Archangel to Vologda well before General Poole's full complement arrived on 23 June 1918; Savinkov's insurrection would then have been a success in the first week of July, and Chaikovskii would have found himself at the head of a URR administration commanding a new Eastern Front extending from Archangel to Kazan. When none of these things happened, the URR set about retrieving a near impossible situation.

Their greatest triumph was to win round the SRs to the idea of a directory. The mutiny of the Czechoslovak Legion was responsible for involving the SRs in the 'great enterprise', by agreeing to help the insurgents in Samara. This chance act opened up divisions between the URR and the SRs about the future role of the Constituent Assembly, divisions which severely weakened the anti-Bolshevik front; at the very moment Kazan fell to the insurgent People's Army, antagonism between the Samara, Urals and Siberian governments was at its height and the so-called customs war in full swing. Yet these antagonisms were overcome: the directory, despite all the disagreements, was formed; and although the Vologda plan might have to be abandoned, the Vyatka route towards a new British, Czechoslovak and People's Army rendezvous remained viable. The 'unpractical' politicians had actually achieved quite a lot by the autumn of 1918.

Where their lack of practicality was evident, however, was in military matters. Both in Archangel and Omsk the army interpreted the actions of the URR administrations as interference in military affairs, and used this to justify their unconstitutional activities. And yet not even in Samara was it official policy to establish political commissars in the army. For all the complaints from officers about 'hidden commissars', and the activities of cultural education units, the army was left to itself as a point of principle, since the politicization of the army was widely seen as one of the causes for the Provisional

Government's collapse. On the eve of Admiral Kolchak's coup, General Boldyrev was en route to destroy once and for all the idea of volunteer party militias. In retrospect this was a profound error of judgement, he should have been using the same vigour to enforce the sort of political commissar system operated by the Bolsheviks; an army committed to the Constituent Assembly would have been less willing to act against the directory.

During the Volga campaign of August–September 1918 the Red Army took a much more determined approach to the politicization of the army and forged a command structure that would ultimately lead it to victory. The old army leaders were finally removed from office, the Supreme War Council wound up and the political commissar system used to determined effect. But it was not simply a question of organization. Trotsky showed in his command of the Red Army all the ruthlessness seen since the moment the Bolsheviks seized power. The battle at the Romanov bridge, the key to the recapture of Kazan, was closely fought and during it a Red Army unit deserted; Trotsky's response was to shoot one man in ten, killing twenty in all.[11] This was the sort of determined use of terror of which he had boasted back on 29 November 1917 when he had told the Soviet Executive:

> You wax indignant at the naked terror which we are applying against our class enemies, but let me tell you that in one month's time at the most it will assume more frightful forms, modelled on the terror of the great French revolutionaries. Not the fortress but the guillotine will await our enemies . . .[12]

The unpractical people of the URR could not so easily resort to terror, indeed in Archangel the question of restoring the death penalty had almost brought the directorate down. At the lowest point in the life of the Omsk directory, when it was forced into a humiliating deal with the administrative council of the Siberian government, Avksentiev stressed: 'I will not have on my conscience unleashing a civil war in the anti-Bolshevik camp'. Lenin was less troubled by his conscience; little had changed since he had written back on 30 August 1917: 'we must speak about [taking power] as little as possible in agitation (remembering very well that even tomorrow events may put us in power and then we will not let it go)'.[13] An excess of conscience was perhaps that element of 'unpracticality' that Lindley found so infuriating in the Russian patriotic socialists with whom he worked.

## NOTES

1. Lloyd George Papers, F/29/1/27.
2. R. Debo, *Revolution and Survival* (Liverpool 1979), pp. 349–51.
3. E. Mawdsley, *The Russian Civil War* (London 1987), p. 66; B. Pearce, *How Haig saved Lenin* (Basingstoke 1987), p. 69.
4. State Archive of the Russian Federation (GARF) 144.1.22.12, 144.1.22.21, 144.1.22.23.
5. S.P. Melgunov, *Krasnyi terror v Rossii* (New York 1979), p. 45. For Martov, see V. Brovkin, *The Mensheviks After October* (Cornell 1987), p. 282.
6. War Cabinet 502.
7. V.N. Brovkin, *Behind the Front Lines of the Civil War* (Princeton 1994) pp. 25, 31; for the rumours reaching British agents, see P. Dukes, *Red Dusk and the Morrow* (New York 1922), p. 67.
8. Brovkin, *Behind*, p. 41; L.M. Spirin, *Klassy i partii v grazhdanskoi voine v Rossii, 1917–20* (Moscow 1968), p. 297; M. Jansen, *A Show Trial under Lenin* (The Hague 1982), p. 5.
9. Jansen, *Show Trial*, pp. 6–8, 31; Brovkin, *Behind*, pp. 25, 39, 42–5.
10. Jansen, *Show Trial*, pp. 53, 77.
11. Mawdsley, *Civil War*, pp. 67, 69.
12. J.L.H. Keep (ed.), *The Debate on Soviet Power: the Minutes of VTsIK, Second Convocation* (Oxford 1979), p. 177.
13. For Avksentiev, see I. Maiskii, *Demokraticheskaya Kontrrevolyutsiya* (Moscow 1923), p. 310; for Lenin, see *Collected Works* (Moscow 1960) vol. 25, p. 263.

# Glossary

*administrative council*
Name given to the council of junior ministers within the Siberian government headed by I.A. Mikhailov, which by mid-September 1918 appeared to have usurped many of the powers of the Siberian government itself, a development which led to a murderous political crisis described in Chapter 8. When the directory moved to Omsk, the seat of the Siberian government, in October 1918 Mikhailov tried to tie it also firmly to the coat tails of the administrative council, but only with limited success.

*Assembly of Petrograd Factory Delegates*
Established by Mensheviks and SRs in the spring of 1918 as a rival to the Petrograd Soviet. M.A. Likhach was a prominent SR involved in it.

*CDD* (Council of Departmental Directors)
The name given by Komuch to its governing administration.

*Chelyabinsk State Conference*
Events at the Chelyabinsk State Conference on 23 August 1918, culminating in the summoning of the Ufa State Conference, are described in Chapter 7. At Chelyabinsk the Allies and the URR took the initiative in calling a representative assembly for all anti-Bolshevik Russia at which an All-Russian government would be formed.

*Committees of Poor Peasants*
Established by Lenin in May 1918 to weaken the Left SRs' hold on the peasantry. By allowing delegates from these committees to attend the Fifth Congress of Soviets in July 1918, the Bolsheviks were able to achieve a majority at the congress; but the legality of this was contested by the Left SRs.

## Constituent Assembly

Russia's first fully democratic elected assembly in which all men and women could vote. The elections began on 12 November 1917, and within days it was clear that the Socialist Revolutionaries had won. Summoned on 5 January 1918, it was dissolved by Lenin after a session lasting only a day. (Details on these events are given in Chapter 3.) Deputies elected to the assembly held two subsequent meetings in March and May 1918; and the Committee of the Constituent Assembly was established by some deputies in Samara in June 1918. Whether the 1918 Constituent Assembly should be reconvened in non-Bolshevik Russia, or a new assembly elected, became a point of contention between some SRs and supporters of the URR.

## CSRM (Committee for the Salvation of the Revolution and the Motherland)

Established by those SRs and Mensheviks who walked out of the Second Congress of Soviets on 25 October 1917 in protest at the Bolshevik seizure of power. Some of its members wanted to overthrow the Bolsheviks by force and became involved in the military action started at the 'Junker' officers' academy on 29 October 1917; most favoured a negotiated settlement and were prepared to attend the Railway Workers' Union talks.

## Czechoslovak Legion

Attempts at recruiting Czechoslovak prisoners of war to special units within the Russian Army had begun even under the Tsar. By the autumn of 1917 these had been transformed into a volunteer legion, based near Kiev, and organized entirely separately from the Russian Army under the leadership of the Czechoslovak National Council and Thomas Masaryk; it thus escaped the soldiers' committee structure which by the autumn of 1917 had sapped the fighting capacity of the Russian Army. It played a central role in the Red versus Green civil war: it was wooed by Somerset Maugham in his mission to Russia in autumn 1917; it fought the Germans in February 1918 when fighting momentarily resumed; and in late May 1918 it mutinied when ordered to move north to Archangel, fearing a trap by Trotsky but actually wrecking a carefully planned operation dreamt up in London. Until Czechoslovak independence was announced as the First World War ended, the legion was the centrepiece of Allied support to the Green People's Army.

## Democratic Conference

Established by the Soviet Executive, it met from 14–22 September 1917 in the immediate aftermath of the Kornilov conspiracy. After much, at times contradictory debate it agreed to Kerensky's proposal that a Preparliament should be summoned and a Third Coalition Government formed.

*directorate*
The name given to Chaikovskii's governing administration in Archangel during the months of August and September 1918.

*directory*
The name given to the All-Russian government established by the Ufa State Conference on 23 September 1918. It ruled non-Bolshevik Russia until its overthrow by Admiral Kolchak on 18 November 1918. The formation of a directory was part of the programme of the URR from its foundation in April 1918.

*Kadet Party*
Russia's major liberal party, led by P.N. Milyukov. Although individuals from the party were involved in General Kornilov's conspiracy in autumn 1917, most kept their distance from what was seen as a doomed enterprise. However, the party's public stance during the crisis meant that in the popular imagination it was associated with counter-revolution. After the October 1917 seizure of power by the Bolsheviks and the party's poor showing in the Constituent Assembly elections, the party moved its activities first to the Don, where they were associated with General M.V. Alekseev's Volunteer Army and its attempt to overthrow the Bolsheviks by force. After the defeat of this venture, the party became divided into pro-Allied and pro-German factions, with the pro-German faction moving to the Ukraine. Pro-Ally Kadets were associated in the spring of 1918 first with the National Centre, and then with the URR. The keenest supporters of the URR were Central Committee members N.I. Astrov and L.A. Krol, whose activities in Samara and Ekaterinburg are described in some detail in this book.

*Komuch* (the Committee of the Constituent Assembly)
Established by SR members of the Constituent Assembly in Samara in mid-June 1918, its organizers hoped that it would become a rallying point for all assembly deputies. As things turned out many deputies were unwilling to associate themselves with what appeared to be a venture supported only by the SR Central Committee and preferred to join up with the URR, which brought together right-wing SRs, Popular Socialists and some left-leaning liberals. The administration established by Komuch became the regional government for the Volga over the summer of 1918 and established there a goverment based on

the socialist principles of the SR Party; whether that government should continue to administer the area after the formation of the directory in September 1918 became a central issue in November 1918 in the final days before Kolchak's coup.

## Left SRs

A party established by SRs disenchanted by the performance of their party members in Kerensky's governments. Always keen to distance themselves from Lenin, they supported those Bolsheviks who wanted to see the formation of a coalition socialist government, and joined the Bolsheviks in forming such an administration in December 1917. They left this government when Lenin signed the Brest-Litovsk Treaty with the Germans, and thereafter opposed the Bolshevik government and worked for a revolutionary war to be declared on Germany; in retaliation Lenin established 'committees of poor peasants' to weaken the hold of the Left SRs on the peasantry. In early July 1918 during the Fifth Congress of Soviets the Left SRs tried to force a German attack by issuing a declaration of war and assassinating the German ambassador.

## Mensheviks

The moderate wing of the Russian Social Democratic Labour Party, from which Lenin's followers had split away to form the Bolsheviks. By 1917 the party was split three ways, with some on the left opposed to participation in government and hostile to the war; some agnostic on the war and in favour of participating in government; and the *Unity* group led by the founder of Russian marxism G.V. Plekhanov, vociferously pro-war. Although the party Central Committee opposed armed action against the Bolsheviks in the summer of 1918, I.M. Maiskii, a member of the Central Committee, ignored this injunction and became a leading member of the Komuch CDD.

## Moscow State Conference

Organized by Kerensky from 12–15 August 1917 to give support to his Second Coalition Government, the conference allowed representation from Russia's propertied classes and was the occasion for much back-stage intrigue by those involved in General Kornilov's conspiracy.

## MRC (Military Revolutionary Committee)

The committee established by the Petrograd Soviet in October 1917 to supervise troop movements, and used by Lenin to implement the seizure of power. See Chapter 2.

*National Centre*
The role played by this liberal organization opposed to the Bolsheviks is discussed in Chapter 6. Perhaps its leading member was N.I. Astrov, but its effectiveness was severely weakened by a split between pro-German and pro-Allied liberals.

*People's Army*
The name given to the army established by Komuch in June 1918.

*Popular Socialist Party*
Founded in 1907 as a breakaway from the SRs, the party was opposed to the use of terror and favoured concentrating on small scale improvements in the peasants' lot, particularly through the development of co-operatives. Its most prominent leader was N.V. Chaikovskii.

*Preparliament*
A representative body established by Kerensky in order to give his Third Coalition Government of September and October 1917 some sort of legitimacy. Its sessions opened on 7 October 1917 and delegates from all sections of society were represented on it, with the purpose of providing some sort of constitutional check on Kerensky's government until a properly elected Constituent Assembly could be summoned. At its final session a vote of no confidence in Kerensky's government was passed. The Preparliament went into oblivion with Lenin's successful seizure of power on 25 October 1917. The president of the Preparliament was N.D. Avksentiev, later a member of the directory and a leading supporter of the URR.

*Rada*
The name given to the Ukrainian government.

*Railway Workers' Union*
The talks organized by the Railway Workers' Union aimed at establishing a coalition socialist government in autumn 1917 are detailed in Chapter 2.

*Revolutionary Convention*
A term given to the idea, mooted by the Bolshevik–Left SR coalition government in December 1917, that the Constituent Assembly and Congress of Soviets could merge into a completely new representative body.

*Siberian government*
Although an underground Siberian government had existed from January to July 1918, it was the Czechoslovak Legion's mutiny which

enabled those members of the underground government resident in Omsk to announce the formation of a Siberian government in the first days of July 1918. Composed of both former SRs and SRs, its relations with Komuch and the Urals government are described in Chapter 7.

*Siberian Regional Assembly*
Established in Siberia in January 1918, the assembly was closed by the Bolsheviks but revived when the Czechoslovak Legion and People's Army established an anti-Bolshevik government. The assembly met in July 1918 and September 1918 in Tomsk, and on both occasions sought to bring the Siberian government under greater democratic control.

*Society for Economic Rehabilitation of Russia*
A counter-revolutionary organization established by the industrialists A.I. Putilov and A.I. Vyshnegradskii in April 1917, which was closely linked to General Kornilov.

*SRs* (Party of Socialist Revolutionaries)
Founded in 1901, the party continued the ideals of the Russian populists of the 1870s and worked to establish a vision of socialism based on rural and urban co-operatives; until the abdication of the Tsar in 1917, the party was also committed to the use of terror. In 1917 a strong right-wing group emerged within the party, which produced its own newspaper and strongly supported SRs joining the government. Other SRs were less committed to participation in government, particulary after the resignation of the party leader V.M. Chernov as a minister. By October 1917 a strong group within the party was so disenchanted with the behaviour of SR government ministers that they split away to form the Left SR party.

The party continued to be racked by division after the Bolshevik seizure of power, but in the period leading up to the dissolution of the Constituent Assembly in January 1918 the divisions between the party's Central Committee and the more right-wing assembly deputies were kept in check. Once fighting had begun in the Red versus Green civil war in June 1918, tensions re-emerged. Many right-wing assembly deputies associated themselves with the URR and distanced themselves from the Central Committee, something which caused particular controversy in October and November 1918, the period of the directory.

*Ufa State Conference*
Events at the Ufa State Conference from 8–23 September 1918,

culminating in the establishment of the directory, are described in Chapter 8. The agreement reached there was known as the Ufa accord.

*Urals government*
Established by the Allies and the URR at the start of August 1918, its chief figure was L.A. Krol. Its relations with Komuch and the Siberian government are described in Chapter 7.

*URR* (Union for the Regeneration of Russia)
By far the most important anti-Bolshevik organization, this was set up in April 1918 by right-wing SR deputies to the Constituent Assembly, Popular Socialists and left-leaning Kadets. It proposed close co-operation with the Allies and the formation of a directory, to govern anti-Bolshevik areas of Russia until elections could be held to a new Constituent Assembly. (More details are given in Chapter 6). Its pro-Allied policy meant it was favoured by the British, who helped the establishment of the government in Archangel. It was also involved with the Allies in establishing the Urals government, before finally succeeding in bringing all local governments together in the directory in September 1918 at the Ufa State Conference. N.V. Chaikovskii and N.D. Avksentiev were perhaps its most prominent members, but all those involved in the Archangel directorate and the Ufa directory were prominent members of the URR.

# Bibliography

(1) UNPUBLISHED DOCUMENTS

State Archive of the Russian Federation, Moscow (GARF)
    fond 5498 opis 1 (the Vikzhel talks)
    fonds 144, 667, 670, 671, 749 (Komuch)
    fond R-1005 (the SR trial)
    fond 16 (the Archangel government)
Public Records Office, London
    FO371
    CAB 24 GT series
    WO32
Lord Milner papers, the Bodleian Library, Oxford
Lloyd George papers, the House of Lords Record Office, London
The William Wiseman papers, Yale University Library


(2) PUBLISHED DOCUMENTS

M.S. Bernshtam (ed.), *Nezavisimoe rabochee dvizhenie v 1918 godu* (Paris 1981).
*Bolsheviks and the October Revolution: Central Committee Minutes of the RSDLP(b)* (London 1974).
R.P. Browder and A.F. Kerensky, *The Russian Provisional Government 1917: Documents* (Stanford 1961).
J. Bunyan and H.H. Fisher, *The Bolshevik Revolution: Documents and Materials* (Stanford 1961).
*Delo Borisa Savinkova* (Moscow 1924).

M. Gorky, *Untimely Thoughts* (New York 1968).

*Izvestiya TsK KPSS* (1989) no. 3.

*Izvestiya TsK KPSS* (1989) no. 4.

M. Jensen, *The SR Party after October 1917: Documents from the PSR Archives* (Amsterdam 1989).

.L.H. Keep (ed.), *The Debate on Soviet Power: the Minutes of VTsIK, Second Convocation* (Oxford 1979).

G.D. Kostomarov and R.I. Golubeva (eds), *Organizatsiya Krasnoi Armii: Sbornik dokumentov i materialov* (Moscow 1943).

V.I. Lenin, *Collected Works* (Moscow 1960).

. Mints, (ed.), *Interventsiya na severe v dokumentakh* (Moscow 1933).

K.A. Popov (ed.), *Dopros Kolchaka* (Leningrad 1923).

War Cabinet Minutes (Public Records Office microfilm).

K. Young (ed.), *The Diaries of Sir Robert Bruce Lockhart* vol. 1, (London 1973).

V.M. Zenzinov (ed.), *Gosudarstvennyi perevorot Admirala Kolchaka v Omske 18 noyabrya 1918 goda: Sbornik Dokumentov* (Paris 1919).

## (3) MEMOIRS

V.G. Boldyrev, *Direktoriya, Kolchak, Interventy* (Novonikolaevsk 1925).

I. Brushvit, 'Kak podgotovlyalos' volzhskoe vystuplenie' *Volya Rossii* nos 10–11.

G. Buchanan, *My Mission to Russia and Other Diplomatic Memories* (London 1923).

S. Cecek, 'Ot Penza do Urala' *Volya Rossii* nos 8–9 (Prague 1928).

G.E. Chaplin, 'Dva perevorota na Severe' *Beloe delo* no.4 (Berlin 1928).

V.M. Chernov, *Pered burey* (New York 1953).

A. Choulgine, *L'Ukraine contre Moscou* (Paris 1935).

A.I. Denikin, *The Russian Turmoil* (London 1920).

A.I. Denikin, *Ocherki russkoi smuty* (Paris 1921) vol. I.

A. Dikgof-Derental, 'Iz perevernutykh stranits' *Na chuzhoi storone* no. 2 (1923).

P. Dukes, *Red Dusk and the Morrow* (New York 1922).

G.K. Gins, *Sibir', Soyuzniki i Kolchak* vol. 1 (Peking 1921).

G. Gopper, 'Belogvardeiskie organizatsii i vosstaniya vnutri Sovetskoi Respubliki', in S.A. Alekseev (ed.), *Revolyutsiya i grazhdanskaya voina v opisaniyakh Belogvardeitsev* (Moscow 1926).

V.I. Gurko, 'Iz Petrograda cherez Moskvy, Parizh i London v Odessu' *Arkhiv Russkoi Revolyutsii* (Berlin 1924).

G. Hill, *Go Spy the Land* (London 1932).

'Iz arkhiva V I Lebedeva: ot Petrograda do Kazani' *Volya Rossii* nos 8–9 (Prague 1928).

B. Kazanovich, 'Poezdka iz Dobrovol'cheskoi armii v "Krasnuyu Moskvu" ' *Arkhiv Russkoi Revolyutsii* vol. 7 (Berlin 1922).

P.D. Klimushkin, 'Pered volzhskim vosstaniem' *Volya Rossii* nos 8–9 (Prague 1928).

L.A. Krol, *Za tri goda* (Vladivostok 1921).

A. Knox, *With the Russian Army, 1914–17* (London 1921).

V.I. Lebedev, *Russian Democracy and its Struggle against the Bolshevist Tyranny* (New York 1919).

R.H.B. Lockhart, *Memoirs of a British Agent* (London 1946).

A.S. Lukomskii, *Vospominaniya* vol. 1 (Berlin 1922).

I. Maiskii, *Demokraticheskaya Kontrrevolyutsiya* (Moscow 1923).

T.G. Masaryk, *The Making of a State* (New York 1969).

W.S. Maugham, *A Writer's Notebook* (London 1949).

V.D. Medlin and S.L. Parsons (eds), *V.D. Nabokov and the Russian Provisional Government* (Yale 1976).

P.N. Milyukov, *The Russian Revolution* (Gulf Breeze 1984).

V. Myakotin, 'Iz nedalekogo proshlogo' *Na chuzhoi storone* no. 2 (Berlin/Prague 1923).

' "Natsional'nyi tsentr" v Moskve v 1918' *Na chuzhoi storone* no. 8 (Berlin/Prague 1924).

I. Nesterov, 'Pered vystupleniyem na Volge' *Volya Rossii* nos 10–11.

H. Niessel, *Le Triomphe des Bolcheviques et la Paix de Brest Litovsk* (Paris 1940).

S. Nikolaev, 'Vozniknovenie o organizatsiya Komucha' *Volya Rossii* nos 8–9 (Prague 1928).

S. Nikolaev, 'Narodnaya armiya v Simbirske' *Volya Rossii* nos 10–11 (Prague 1928).

J. Noulens, *Mon Ambassade en Russie Soviétique, 1917–19* (Paris 1933).

B. Pares, *My Russian Memoirs* (London 1931).

M. Philips-Price, *My Reminiscences of the Russian Revolution* (London 1921).

F.I. Rodichev, *Vospominaniya i ocherki o russkoi liberalizme* (Newtonville 1982).

J. Sadoul, *Notes sur la Révolution Bolchevique* (Paris 1920).

K.V. Sakharov, *Belaya Sibir'* (Munich 1923).

B.V. Savinkov, *Borba s Bolshevikami* (Warsaw 1920).

G. Semenov, *Voennaya i boevaya rabota Partii Sotsialistov-Revolyutsionerov za 1917–18* (Moscow 1922).

S.I. Shidlovskii, *Vospominaniya* (Berlin 1923).

P. Sorokin, *Leaves from a Russian Diary* (London 1924).

A. Suvorin, *Pokhod Kornilova* (Rostov on Don 1918).

A. Tarasov-Rodionov, *February 1917* (Westport CT 1973).

A. Tyrkova-Williams, *From Liberty to Brest Litovsk* (London 1919).

V.L. Utgofa, 'Ufimskoe Gosudarstvennoe Soveshchanie 1918' *Byloe* no. 16 (Petrograd 1921).

A. Vergé, *Avec les Tchécoslovaques* (Paris 1926).

A.I. Verkhovskii, *Na trudnom perevale* (Moscow 1959).

A.I. Verkhovskii, *Rossiya na Golgofe* (Petrograd 1918).

Z.A. Vertsinskii, *God Revolyutsii* (Tallin 1929).

E. Voska, *Spy and Counter-spy* (London 1941).

V.M. Zenzinov, *Iz zhizni revolyutsionera* (Paris 1919).


## (4) BOOKS

R. Abraham, *Alexander Kerensky* (Columbia 1987).

W. Blunt, *Lady Muriel* (London 1962).

E. Bosh, *God borby: borba za vlast' na Ukraine s aprelya 1917g. do nemetskoi okkupatsii* (Moscow 1928).

J.F.N. Bradley, *La Légion Tchécoslovaque en Russie 1914–20* (Paris 1965).

J.F.N. Bradley, *Allied Intervention in Russia* (London 1968).

G.A. Brinkley, *The Volunteer Army and Allied Intervention in Southern Russia* (Notre Dame 1966).

V. Brovkin, *The Mensheviks After October* (Cornell 1987).

V.N. Brovkin, *Behind the Front Lines of the Civil War* (Princeton 1994).

M.J. Carley, *Revolution and Intervention: the French Government and the Russian Civil War* (Montreal 1983).

R.V. Daniels, *The Conscience of the Revolution* (Harvard 1960).

R. Debo, *Revolution and Survival* (Liverpool 1979).

N.G. Dumova, *Kadetskaya kontrrevolyutsiya i ee razgrom* (Moscow 1982).

J. Erikson, 'The origins of the Red Army', in R. Pipes (ed.), *Revolutionary Russia* (Harvard 1968).

O. Fedyshyn, *Germany's Drive to the East and the Ukrainian Revolution* (New Brunswick 1971).

V.M. Fic, *Revolutionary War for Independence and the Russian Question* (Delhi 1977).

V.M. Fic, *The Bolsheviks and the Czechoslovak Legion* (Delhi 1978).

P. Fleming, *The Fate of Admiral Kolchak* (London 1963).

W.B. Fowler, *British–American Relations 1917–18: the Role of Sir William Wiseman* (Princeton 1969).

D.L. Golinkov, *Krakh vrazheskogo podpolya* (Moscow 1971).

D.L. Golinkov, *Krushenie antisovetskogo podpolya v SSSR* (Moscow 1975).

N.N. Golovin, *Rossiiskaya Kontr-revolyutsiya v 1917–18gg.* (Talinn 1937) Part 1, Book 2.

K. Gusev, *Krakh partii levykh eserov* (Leningrad 1963).

N. Ya Ivanov, *Kontrrevolyutsiya v Rossii v 1917g. i ee razgrom* (Moscow 1977).

M. Jansen, *A Show Trial under Lenin* (The Hague 1982).

J. Kalvoda, *The Genesis of Czechoslovakia* (Columbia 1986).

G. Katkov, *The Kornilov Affair* (London 1980).

M. Kettle, *The Road to Intervention* (London 1988).

M. Kettle, *The Allies and the Russian Collapse* (London 1989).

M. Kettle, *Churchill and the Archangel Fiasco* (London 1992).

V.V. Komin, *Istoriya pomeshchikh, burzhuaznykh i melko-burzhuaznykh partii v Rossii* (Kalinin 1970).

R.I. Kowalski, *The Bolshevik Party in Conflict* (Basingstoke 1991).

V. Ya Laverychev, *Po tu storonu barrikad* (Moscow 1967).

L. Lande, 'The Mensheviks in 1917', in L. Haimson (ed.), *The Mensheviks: from the Revolution of 1917 to the Second World War* (Chicago 1974).

M. McAuley, *Bread and Justice: State and Society in Petrograd, 1917–22* (Oxford 1992).

E.I. Martynov, *Kornilov: popytka voennogo perevorota* (Moscow 1927).

E. Mawdsley, *The Russian Civil War* (London 1987).

S.P. Melgunov, *The Bolshevik Seizure of Power* (Oxford 1972).

S.P. Melgunov, *N.V. Chaikovskii v gody grazhdanskoi voiny* (Paris 1929).

S.P. Melgunov, *Tragediya Admirala Kolchaka* Part 1 (Belgrade 1930).

S.P. Melgunov, *Krasnyi terror v Rossii* (New York 1979).

T. Morgan, *Somerset Maugham* (London 1986).

B. Pearce, *How Haig Saved Lenin* (Basingstoke 1987).

A Rabinowitch, *The Bolsheviks Come to Power* (New York 1978).

O.H. Radkey, *The Sickle under the Hammer* (Columbia 1963).

O.H. Radkey, *Russia Goes to the Polls* (Cornell 1990).

J. Reshetar, 'The Communist Party of the Ukraine and its role in the Ukrainian Revolution' in T. Hunczak (ed.), *The Ukraine, 1917–21: a Study in Revolution* (Harvard 1977).

W.G. Rosenberg, *Liberals in the Russian Revolution* (Princeton 1974).

L. Schapiro, *1917: the Russian Revolution and the Origins of Present-Day Communism* (London 1984).

T.A. Sivokhina, *Krakh melkoburzhuaznoi oppozitsii* (Moscow 1973).

L.M. Spirin, *Klassy i partii v grazhdanskoi voine v Rossii, 1917–20* (Moscow 1968).

L.I. Strakhovsky, *Intervention at Archangel: the Story of Allied Intervention and Russian Counter-revolution in North Russia, 1918–20* (Princeton 1944).

G.R. Swain, *The Bolshevik Seizure of Power*, computer assisted learning package, the HiDES Project, University of Southampton, 1994.

A. Tanyaev, *Ocherki dvizheniya zheleznodorozhnikov v revolyutsii 1917g.* (Moscow 1925).

V. Vladimirova, *Kontr-Revolyutsiya v 1917* (Moscow 1924).

V. Vladimirova, *God sluzhby sotsialistov kapitalistam* (Moscow 1927).

P. Vompe, *Dni oktyabr'skoi revolyutsii i zheleznodorozhnikov* (Moscow 1924).

R. Ullman, *Anglo-Soviet Relations, 1917–21: Intervention and the War* (Princeton 1961).

B.M. Unterberger, *The United States, Revolutionary Russia and the Rise of Czechoslovakia* (University of North Carolina Press 1989).

A.K. Wildman, *The End of the Russian Imperial Army* (Princeton 1980) vol. 2.

O.N. Znamenskii, *Vserossiiskoe uchreditel'noe sobranie* (Moscow 1976).

## (5) JOURNAL ARTICLES

V.P. Agapeev, 'Korpus generala Dovbor-Musnitskogo' *Beloe Delo* no. 4 (Berlin 1928).

'Aprel'skie dni 1917 g. v Petrograde' *Krasnyi arkhiv* vol. 33 (1929).

H. Asher, 'The Kornilov Affair; a reinterpretation' *Russian Review* vol. 29 (1970).

S. Berk, 'The democratic counter-revolution: *Komuch* and the civil war on the Volga' *Canadian-American Slavic Studies* vol. 7 (1973).

S. Berk, 'The "Class Tragedy" of Izhevsk: working class opposition to Bolshevism in 1918' *Russian History* vol. 2, no. 2 (1975).

J.F.N. Bradley, 'T.G. Masaryk et la revolution russe' *Etudes Slaves et Est-Europeenes* vol. IX (1964).

R.F. Christian, 'Alexis Aladin: Trudovik leader in the first Russian Duma: materials for a biography' *Oxford Slavonic Papers* vol. 21 (1988).

N.G. Dumova, 'Maloizvestnye materialy po istorii Kornilovshchiny' *Voprosy istorii* no. 11 (1968).

U. Germanis, 'Some observations on the Yaroslavl Revolt of July 1918' *Journal of Baltic Studies* vol. 4 (1973).

S.N. Gorodetskii, 'Obrazovanie severnoi oblasti' *Beloe Delo* no. 3 (Berlin 1927).

L. Hafner, 'The assassination of Count Mirbach and the "July Uprising" of the Left SRs in Moscow, 1918' *Russian Review* vol. 50 (1991).

V.L. Israelyan, 'Neopravdivshiisya prognoz Grafa Mirbacha' *Novaya i noveishaya istoriya* no. 6 (1967).

D. Jones, 'Documents on British relations with Russia, 1917–18' *Canadian-American Slavic Studies* vol. 7, no. 2 (1973).

V.K. Koblyakov, 'Bor'ba sovetskogo gosudarstva za sokhranenie mira s Germaniei v period deistviya Brestskogo dogovora' *Istoriya SSSR* no. 4 (1958).

V. Ya Laverychev, 'Russkie monopolisty i zagovor Kornilova' *Voprosy istorii* no. 4 (1964).

V. Ya Laverychev, 'Vserossiiskii Soyuz Torgovli i Promyshlennosti' *Istoricheskii Zhurnal* no. 70 (1961).

'Likvidatsiya levoeserovskogo myatezha v Moskve v 1918g.' *Krasnyi Arkhiv* (1940).

L.G. Murashev, ' "Odnorodno-sotsialisticheskoe" pravitel'stvo v anti-sovetskikh planakh men'shevikov v dni oktyabrskogo vooruzhennogo vosstaniya v Petrograde' *Uchennye zapiski kafedr obshchestvennykh nauk vuzov Leningrada: Istoriya KPSS* (Leningrad 1990).

S. Naida, 'Pochemu den' sovetskoi armii prazdnuetsya 23 fevralya' *Voenno-istoricheskii zhurnal* no. 5 (1964).

D.V. Oznobishin, 'Burzhyaznaya diktatura v poiskakh parlamentskogo prikritiya' *Istoricheskie zapiski* 93.

B. Pearce, 'Lenin versus Trotsky' *Sbornik* 13 (1987).

W.G. Rosenberg, 'Russian labour and Bolshevik power after October' *Slavic Review* (1985).

N.F. Slavin, 'Krizis vlasti v sentyabre 1917g. i obrazovanie Vremennogo Soveta Republiki (Predparlament)' *Istoricheskie zapiski* 56.

' "Soyuz zashchity rodiny i svobody" i Yaroslavskii myatezh 1918g.' *Proletarskaya revolyutsiya* no. 10 (1923).

'Soyuz zemel'nykh sobstvennikov v 1917 godu' *Krasnyi arkhiv* (1927).

G.R. Swain, 'Before the fighting started' *Revolutionary Russia* vol. 4 (1991).

S.P. Turin, 'Ot"ezd P.A.Kropotkina iz Anglii v Rossii' *Na chuzhoi storone* no. 4 (Berlin/Prague 1924).

F.I. Vidyasov, 'Kontrrevolyutsionnye zamysli inostrannykh imperialistov i Kornilovshchina' *Voprosy istorii* no. 5 (1965).

V. Vladimirova, 'Levye esery 1917–1918gg.' *Proletarskaya revolyutsiya* no. 4 (1927).

J.D. White, 'The Kornilov Affair: a study in counter-revolution' *Soviet Studies* vol. 20 (1968).

*Maps*

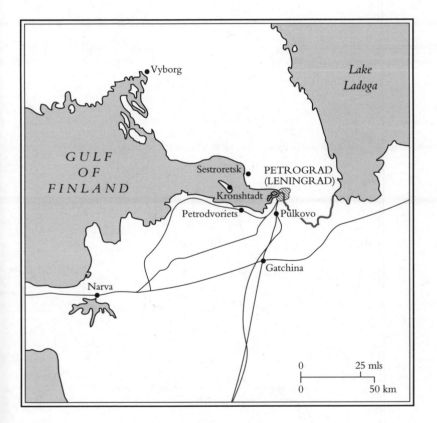

Map 1  Pulkovo and Gatchina with connecting rail links

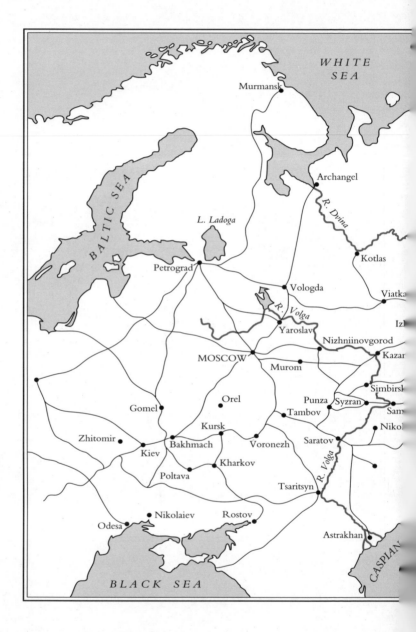

Map 2  Russia's Railway network in 1918

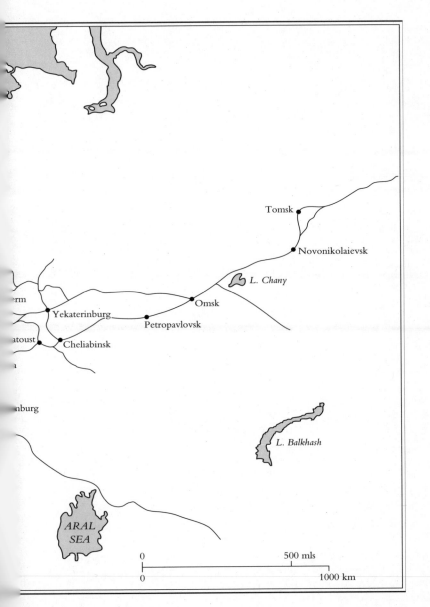

Tomsk

Novonikolaievsk

*L. Chany*

rm

Yekaterinburg

Omsk

Petropavlovsk

atoust

Cheliabinsk

nburg

*L. Balkhash*

*ARAL
SEA*

0                              500 mls

0                              1000 km

# Index